A HISTORY OF TORT LAW 1900–1950

Many of the defining features of the modern law of tort can be traced to the first half of the twentieth century, but, until now, developments in that period have never received a dedicated historical examination. This book examines both common law and statutory innovations, paying special attention to underlying assumptions about the operation of society, the function of tort law and the roles of those involved in legal changes. It recovers the legal and social contexts in which some landmark decisions were given (and which put those decisions in a very different light) and draws attention to significant and suggestive cases that have fallen into neglect. It also explores the theoretical debates of the period about the nature of tort law, and reveals the fascinating patterns of influence and power at work behind statutory initiatives to reform the law.

PAUL MITCHELL is Professor of Laws at University College London, where his main research interests are the law of tort, contract and unjust enrichment.

CAMBRIDGE STUDIES IN ENGLISH LEGAL HISTORY

Edited by
J. H. Baker
Fellow of St Catharine's College, Cambridge

Recent series titles include

A History of Tort Law 1900–1950
Paul Mitchell

Sir Edward Coke and the Reformation of the Laws
Religion, Politics and Jurisprudence, 1578–1616
David Chan Smith

Medieval English Conveyances
John M. Kaye

Marriage Law and Practices in the Long Eighteenth Century
A Reassessment
Rebecca Probert

The Rise and Fall of the English Ecclesiastical Courts, 1500–1860
R. B. Outhwaite

Law Courts and Lawyers in the City of London, 1300–1550
Penny Tucker

Legal Foundations of Tribunals in Nineteenth-Century England
Chantal Stebbings

Pettyfoggers and Vipers of the Commonwealth
The 'Lower Branch' of the Legal Profession in Early Modern England
C. W. Brooks

Roman Canon Law in Reformation England
R. H. Helmholz
Sir Henry Maine

A Study in Victorian Jurisprudence
R. C. J. Cocks

Sir William Scott, Lord Stowell
Judge of the High Court of Admiralty, 1798–1828
Henry J. Bourguignon

The Early History of the Law of Bills and Notes
A Study of the Origins of Anglo-American Commercial Law
James Steven Rogers

The Law of Treason in England in the Later Middle Ages
J. G. Bellamy

William Sheppard, Cromwell's Law Reformer
Nancy L. Matthews

A HISTORY OF TORT LAW 1900–1950

PAUL MITCHELL

Professor of Laws, University College London

CAMBRIDGE
UNIVERSITY PRESS

CAMBRIDGE
UNIVERSITY PRESS

University Printing House, Cambridge CB2 8BS, United Kingdom

Cambridge University Press is part of the University of Cambridge.

It furthers the University's mission by disseminating knowledge in the pursuit of education, learning and research at the highest international levels of excellence.

www.cambridge.org
Information on this title: www.cambridge.org/9780521768610

First published 2015

A catalogue record for this publication is available from the British Library

Library of Congress Cataloguing in Publication data
Mitchell, Paul, 1972– author.
A history of tort law 1900–1950 / Paul Mitchell, Professor of Laws, UCL.
pages cm – (Cambridge studies in English legal history)
Includes bibliographical references and index.
ISBN 978-0-521-76861-0 (hardback)
1. Torts–England–History–20th century I. Title.
KD1949.M58 2014
346.420309'041–dc23
2014032050

ISBN 978-0-521-76861-0 Hardback

for Susan, Ben and Amelia

CONTENTS

ACKNOWLEDGEMENTS

Several institutions and individuals have helped me in writing this book. King's College London and University College London both provided periods of sabbatical leave, and the Leverhulme Trust awarded a Research Fellowship. I would like to be able to say that the periods of leave (merely) transformed the project, but the truth is starker – it could not have been attempted without them. The Law Faculty Library at the University of Cambridge, and especially the Librarian, Lesley Dingle, the Archive Centre at King's College Cambridge and the University of Warwick were extremely helpful with manuscript sources. Some of the material was presented at conferences and research seminars, and I would particularly like to acknowledge the helpful comments of members of the Oxford Private Law Discussion Group, the UCL Private Law Group and the Staff Seminar at the City University of Hong Kong. I have benefited from insightful comments on draft chapters made by Eric Barendt, Susan Chan, Maria Lee and Charles Mitchell. Shida Galletti worked as a research assistant on the manuscripts of Kurt Lipstein and Harold Gutteridge, which are produced as appendices, and I remain especially grateful for her help with Lipstein's Italian sources.

TABLE OF STATUTES AND STATUTORY INSTRUMENTS

TABLE OF CASES

1

Introduction

I

Any title containing dates immediately raises questions: Why start *there*? Why stop *then*? When the answer is not immediately obvious – the start and end of a monarch's reign, say, or a war – there may be little consolation in the reader's discovering that the contents of such books almost always break their titles' implicit promises to confine themselves to events between certain dates. So it might be as well to come clean right at the very start, and admit that nothing special or symbolic happened in either 1900 or 1950 that will serve as the beginning and end points of this book. Indeed, in a discipline like law where so much turns on interpreting what has happened in the past, a pedantically strict attitude to start dates is always likely to create more problems than it solves. As readers may have guessed from the suspiciously round numbers in the title, this is a book about the history of tort law that focuses on the first half of the twentieth century, but has no hesitation in straying slightly outside the period where the subject matter calls for it.

The focus on the first half of the twentieth century has been inspired by two interrelated factors. The first is that the period includes several defining moments in the history of tort law, moments where structures were established or directions set. Such moments, naturally, have not gone unremarked by writers on contemporary tort law, but they have received little historical attention because, quite simply, English legal history scholarship has tended to run out by the end of the nineteenth century. Indeed, not the least important of the many reasons for which the recent *Oxford History of the Laws of England* volumes stand out is that they venture into the last century, by taking the story up to the outbreak of the First World War.[1] This relative neglect forms the second reason for

[1] W. Cornish *et al.*, *The Oxford History of the Laws of England*, Volumes XI, XII and XIII (Oxford University Press, 2010).

this book's focus on the early twentieth century, for otherwise there is the danger of losing sight of the true significance of the period, falling as it does between traditional historical coverage and the primary focus of contemporary writers.[2]

It might, perhaps, be suggested that articles, textbooks and other forms of legal scholarship on current law provide an adequate account of what is worth remembering about the period, and it is worth pausing for a moment to address this potential objection to a work concerned with relatively recent legal history. We might begin by reflecting that periodical literature written with its eye on current controversies is unlikely to provide a balanced historical account: it may *use* history, but does not aspire to *be* history. Indeed, there is no obligation on writers about contemporary law to provide any historical account, and those who do might be suspected of wanting the past to control the present if they give too much weight to historical factors. Textbook writers might, at first glance, appear to be in a different position: for them, we might feel, historical exposition need not form part of an argument; it can have a legitimate part to play in giving a sense of historical sweep. Of course, even if we should take this argument at face value (and I would contest it), the history to be gathered from contemporary textbooks would be incomplete. It would be both self-indulgent and eccentric to favour the hard-pressed student reader with a detailed account of the defence of common employment (abolished 1948),[3] for example, or the torts of seduction and enticement (abolished 1970).[4] These topics, by contrast, have leading roles to play in this book. But even for topics where a historical introduction is relevant, and appropriate, such an introduction is serving a purpose that cannot help but control an author's choices: it is explaining how we got to where we are today, and the temptation is to slide into what Herbert Butterfield famously called 'The Whig interpretation of history', that is, an interpretation that identifies an inevitable progression towards current, enlightened values as history unfolds.[5] The common law's commitments to the doctrine of precedent, and to the declaratory theory of law, encourage

[2] S. Collini, 'Introduction' in C. Snow, *The Two Cultures* (Cambridge University Press, 1993) at ix encapsulates the point, when he describes C. P. Snow's 1959 lecture on the two cultures as beginning to 'fall into a murky limbo, no longer accurately recalled as part of living contemporary culture but not yet beginning to benefit from patient historical reconstruction'.

[3] Law Reform (Personal Injuries) Act 1948 s. 1.

[4] Law Reform (Miscellaneous Provisions) Act 1970 s. 5.

[5] H. Butterfield, *The Whig Interpretation of History* (London, G. Bell and Sons, 1931).

writers of all kinds (including judges) to be complicit in such Whiggish interpretations. The historian's standpoint relieves him or her of the need to explain the past in terms of the present, and replaces it with an obligation to deal patiently and sensitively with legal developments in their own time and social context. Such a historical approach may well lead to the identification of certain events as important, despite them having been forgotten (for whatever reason) by later lawyers; more intriguingly, it may also lead to the construction of rival significances where events remain in legal consciousness, but for reasons that have changed over time. To take the simplest example, what the judges hearing a case, and the commentators writing about it immediately afterwards, thought it had decided may be wildly different from what the case has come to stand for. The point about these rival significances is not that the original interpretation is 'right' and the later one 'wrong' (or vice versa). The point is to register the change.

II

These general arguments for twentieth-century legal history justify the genre, but do not mandate that the work must take a particular form. One possibility would be to treat legal ideas in their own organising categories, which would generate a series of chapters with titles like 'Negligence', 'Defamation', 'Damages for Personal Injury', and so on. As readers may already have noticed, that strategy has not been pursued here. Instead, the book is divided into two parts. The first part (the longest) examines how tort ideas developed in particular contexts, beginning with an exploration of different writers' attempts to define and structure their subject. The focus then moves to tort's responsiveness to dramatic social upheaval, in the form of wartime conditions, before considering how tort rules applied to women and children during the first half of the twentieth century. Part I concludes with three chapters on particular kinds of activities where tort developments were especially notable: the media (that is, newspapers and radio broadcasting), driving and (manual) work. In each of the chapters in Part I, apart from the very first one, the material is very deliberately drawn from across the tort spectrum, in order to set alongside each other rules and ideas that would traditionally not be found in close proximity. The aim in doing so is to develop a picture of how tort saw the world: what assumptions were being made about the roles of those to whom its doctrines were applied, and what contribution did tort conceive of itself as making to social life?

Part II focuses on the creation and activities of the Law Revision Committee. Its scope is, therefore, narrower than Part I, but its subject matter is no less significant, for the Law Revision Committee was the first state body to be created that had ongoing responsibility for the reform of private law. The Committee was particularly active in torts, producing reports on the rule that a tort claim died with the claimant, a husband's liability for his wife's torts, joint tortfeasance and contributory negligence. Its recommendations on each of these topics were all translated into legislation. How the Committee created its reports, and how its recommendations progressed into statutes, is a fascinating story in itself, but it also casts light on larger questions, such as co-operation between civil servants, judges and academics, and the relationship between tort and politics in one specific historical milieu.

The aims of the book have informed both its methodology and coverage. It is a book that is especially concerned with assumptions, attitudes and self-understandings, which are rarely made explicit, and may even be unconscious. They can, however, be revealed by paying very close attention to the linguistic features of the texts, and the following pages are, therefore, much concerned with questions about choice of language, tone and register. The texts to which particular attention is paid are those judgments, law review articles, law reform reports, letters and passages from textbooks that cast the most light on the ideas, assumptions and attitudes animating developments in the area concerned. The coverage of tort doctrines does not aim to be comprehensive. Rather, the emphasis has been deliberately given to themes and materials that have traditionally received little or no historical treatment.

There is one case, in particular, whose failure to feature may raise eyebrows: *Donoghue* v. *Stevenson*[6] seems an obvious, perhaps even *the* obvious candidate for a starring role in a treatment of tort history in the first half of the twentieth century. But it turns out that *Donoghue* v. *Stevenson* is a peculiar, and compelling, example of a case that has come to stand for something very different to what it was originally thought to represent. Today, of course, it is known for Lord Atkin's articulation of the neighbour principle as the unifying explanation for when duties of care are owed in negligence. That foundational status, however, was only acquired after the principle had been taken up by judges in the 1960s and 1970s.[7] In

6 [1932] AC 562.

7 On the reception of *Donoghue* v. *Stevenson*, see D. Ibbetson, *A Historical Introduction to the Law of Obligations* (Oxford University Press, 1999) 190–5. On the broader significance

the 1930s the response was less enthusiastic. Commentators appreciated that Lord Atkin's speech was significant, but tended to see it, in the context of the case as a whole, as playing out an ongoing and unresolved conflict about the structure of negligence liability.[8] They, at least, regarded it as potentially significant. For judges, by contrast, *Donoghue* v. *Stevenson* was initially seen as a valuable decision on manufacturers' duties to the ultimate consumers of their products. To the extent that they regarded it as containing a 'principle', that principle was articulated in strikingly narrow terms, as being confined to the supply of products where there was no opportunity to detect that the product was defective.[9] Attempts to draw a more ambitious message from the case, which would have resulted in the recognition of duties of care in a broader range of situations, were unsuccessful.[10] The case's iconic status was all in the future.

III

It is, I hope, now becoming clear what this book is about. But it may also be helpful to conclude this introduction by explaining *whom* it is about. The English law of tort was – and continues to be – formed from judicial decisions, academic writings and legislation. The headings of the first two categories indicate their personnel. Those judges who contributed to the development of tort law began their judicial careers in the High Court.[11] They were predominantly drawn from the ranks of successful barristers, in a process where open competition was conspicuous by its absence. Promotion to the appellate courts, where there was far greater potential to develop the law, was similarly veiled, being in the prime minister's gift. There were some notable exceptions, where high judicial office was

of the case, see generally J. Thomson (ed.), *The Juridical Review: Donoghue v. Stevenson: The Paisley Papers* (Edinburgh, W. Green, 2013).

8 W. Stallybrass, 'Landon v. Winfield: An Intervention' (1932) 10 *Bell Yard* 18, 20–1; W. Stallybrass, *The Law of Torts: A Treatise on the English Civil Law of Liability for Civil Injuries by Sir John Salmond*, 8th edn (London, Sweet & Maxwell, 1934) x–xi: 'a decision which may prove to have raised at least as many problems as it has settled'. Strikingly, the House of Lords' decision that Stallybrass identified as 'epoch-making' was *Lochgelly Iron and Coal Co* v. *M'Mullan* [1934] AC 1 (see page viii of the Preface to the eighth edition of *Salmond*). The *Lochgelly* case is discussed in Chapter 8.

9 *Dransfield* v. *British Insulated Cables Ltd* [1937] 4 All ER 382, 386–7.

10 E.g. *Searle* v. *Wallbank* [1947] AC 341, discussed in Chapter 7.

11 Judicial appointments between 1850 and 2000 are explained in P. Mitchell, 'The impact of institutions and professions on fault liability in England' in P. Mitchell (ed.), *The Impact of Institutions and Professions on Legal Development* (Cambridge University Press, 2012) 14, 15–17.

conferred on politicians, perhaps as an expression of gratitude for their loyalty, or as compensation for disappointed political expectations. But the judges were a body with an overwhelmingly homogeneous profile of professional formation and, consequentially, age. Harold Laski calculated the average age of new appointees to the High Court between 1832 and 1906 as 53, and there was no change in the system in the following half-century.[12] Appellate judges were, on average, older – there was no statutory retirement age[13] – and this has led Brian Simpson to describe the English judiciary as 'gerontocratic'.[14] While this was literally true, it would be both unkind and unfair to the judges concerned to allow it to be implied that their performances were affected my mental frailty. There were, of course, disputes between appellate judges about how the law should develop, and some of the legal analyses produced on these occasions were more compelling than others. But there is no sign, in the materials examined in this book, of judicial careers outliving mental competence. One final, and perhaps rather obvious point should be made: all the judges whose work is discussed in this book were men. This was, perhaps, inevitable since the first woman to be called to the Bar was Ivy Williams, in 1922, and most judges had something like thirty years' experience at the Bar before their appointment to the bench.[15] More strikingly, women appeared as counsel in significant tort cases with extreme rarity: a woman barrister's name comes as a surprise, almost a shock, when reading the law reports of this era.

Some judges' names, on the other hand, become deeply familiar. It is not possible to get very far into this book without becoming immersed in the work of Lord Wright, Scrutton LJ and McCardie J, for instance. Part of the explanation for the prominence of particular names is a mere function of numbers: there were only three divisions of the Court of Appeal (consisting of three judges each), and nine Lords of Appeal in Ordinary to hear House of Lords cases, during the period.[16] As a matter of raw probability, the same names could be expected to turn up reasonably frequently. But

[12] H. Laski, 'The Technique of Judicial Appointment' in *Studies in Law and Politics* (London, George Allen & Unwin, 1932) 163, 172.

[13] A statutory retirement age was introduced in Judicial Pensions Act 1959 s. 2.

[14] A. W. B. Simpson, 'The Common Law and Legal Theory' in *Legal Theory and Legal History: Essays on the Common Law* (London and Ronceverte: Hambledon Press, 1987) 359, 377.

[15] H. Fox, 'Williams, Ivy' in *Oxford Dictionary of National Biography* (online edition).

[16] Lord Justice Cohen, 'Jurisdiction, Practice and Procedure of the Court of Appeal' (1951–1953) 11 *CLJ* 3, 5; Lord Morton, 'Address' (1949) 32 *Yearbook of the Canadian Bar Association* 107, 114.

this can be only part of the explanation for the peculiar prominence of particular judges. The other part of the explanation must surely involve a more qualitative assessment of how individual judges interpreted their judicial roles.[17] Differences in judicial attitudes to fundamental questions, such as the constraints of precedent, or the need for the common law to reflect social changes, were particularly likely to come to the surface, and to be played out, in certain kinds of tort cases: the sheer range and diversity of tort principles gave them the potential to intersect with an extraordinarily wide variety of social questions. Understanding how, exactly, different judges responded to the challenges raised by such intersections is central to this book's theme.

If the number of appellate judges was small, the number of academic writers contributing to the development of tort was yet smaller. Over the course of the period, the number of teachers had increased, but, as L. C. B. Gower pointed out in 1950 in a devastating critique, legal education remained unimaginative and unambitious.[18] Gower was particularly scathing about the absence of theory and the prominence of learning by rote. He does not seem to have been overstating the position – even a student as intellectually curious as the future distinguished solicitor and poet Roy Fuller found nothing memorable about the lectures he attended while qualifying as a solicitor.[19] A nice illustration of the intellectual tepidity of even the more reputable university law schools is provided by the foundation of the *Cambridge Law Journal* in the 1920s. The idea was first put forward by H. A. Hollond, a Cambridge don who had been much impressed by the *Harvard Law Review* on a visit to the United States.[20] But, as A. L. Goodhart later recalled, the prospects for the *Cambridge Law Journal* were initially 'extremely dim', since it was thought that the *Law Quarterly Review* satisfied any English demand for scholarly publishing on law.[21] Early issues of the *Cambridge Law Journal* might have seemed to confirm that pessimism, containing, as they did, elements of an in-house magazine for the Cambridge Law Faculty. Gower was urging law

17 See Mitchell, 'The impact of institutions and professions on fault liability in England', 25–7 (dealing with a slightly later period).

18 L. Gower, 'English Legal Training' (1950) 13 *MLR* 137.

19 R. Fuller, *Souvenirs* (London, London Magazine Editions, 1980) 143. The only memorable incident seems to have occurred when the lecturer was provoked by seeing a copy of D. H. Lawrence's *Nettles* on Fuller's desk.

20 H. Hollond, 'Arthur Lehman Goodhart' (1964) *CLJ* 1; H. Hollond, 'The Origin of the Law Journal: Introductory Note' (1972B) *CLJ* 3.

21 A. Goodhart, 'The Origin of the Journal' (1972B) *CLJ* 4, 5. See also A. Goodhart, 'Henry Arthur Hollond: 1884 to 1974' (1975) 34 *CLJ* 1.

academics to be altogether more outward-looking, to be open to theory, and to take a more energetic attitude to law reform. His readers may well not have appreciated it, for he paid little attention to legal literature, but, in tort at least, there were works that already lived up to these demands, whose writers would have endorsed Gower's position.

The doyen of tort scholars was a man who would not have welcomed being described as an academic, and who had an unsatisfactory relationship with legal education.[22] Frederick Pollock managed to occupy a unique position, which placed him outside both the practising and academic sections of the legal profession but which, paradoxically, also allowed him, and his writings, to exercise a profound influence over the profession as a whole.[23] The influence of his successors was more limited – partly because they were competing with Pollock, or among themselves – but the importance of their work should not be underestimated. Two writers particularly stand out in this group: P. H. Winfield, and Wolfgang Friedmann. Winfield took his degree and spent his entire academic career in Cambridge, eventually becoming the first Rouse Ball Professor of English Law.[24] In addition to an extraordinary array of articles and essays on tort topics, both contemporary and historical, he produced major books on the subject. *The Province of the Law of Tort* was based on a course of lectures delivered as the Tagore Professor at the University of Calcutta, and advanced a distinctive thesis about the foundations and scope of tortious liability.[25] *A Text-Book of the Law of Tort* was, at first glance, a more conventional work, but it too put forward some important arguments about liability in general, as well as illuminating more specific developments.[26]

Wolfgang Friedmann's career contrasted with Winfield's in almost every way. A German refugee from Nazi persecution, Friedmann arrived in London in the 1930s and found work teaching at University College. He was involved in the establishment of the *Modern Law Review*, and contributed a provocative article on 'Modern Trends in the Law of Torts' to its inaugural volume.[27] His work on tort was more sporadic than Winfield's,

22 N. Duxbury, *Frederick Pollock and the English Juristic Tradition* (Oxford University Press, 2004) 41–64.

23 N. Duxbury, *Jurists and Judges* (Oxford, Hart Publishing, 2001) 85–7; Duxbury, *Frederick Pollock*, chapter 5.

24 S. Bailey, 'Winfield, Sir Percy Henry' in *Oxford Dictionary of National Biography* (online edition).

25 P. Winfield, *The Province of the Law of Tort* (Cambridge University Press, 1931).

26 P. Winfield, *A Text-Book of the Law of Tort* (London, Sweet & Maxwell, 1937).

27 W. Friedmann, 'Modern Trends in the Law of Torts' (1937) 1 *MLR* 39.

and his academic career positively nomadic by comparison: he would leave London in the late 1940s for a chair in Melbourne, and, while in Australia, worked on *Law and Social Change in Contemporary Britain*, which featured an important critique of tort law.[28] From Melbourne he would soon move on to Toronto and, finally, to Columbia University in New York; in his later years, his interests turned more towards international law.[29] The contrast with Winfield was not confined to differences in career path. Winfield was very much writing within the common law tradition – he had a deep respect for, and intellectual interest in, the historical development of common law concepts, and tended to argue for legal changes that would reflect, or at least be consistent with, that development. Friedmann was not averse to historical arguments, but he evinced no affinity with the common law past; he tended to be more alert to, and impatient with, what he saw as tort's failure to reflect social relations. Between them, the two authors offered compelling criticisms from very different standpoints.

Judges and academics formed two mutually exclusive communities. Gower depicted an unhappy, unequal relationship – 'nothing is more nauseating than the patronising air of mock humility usually affected by one of his Majesty's judges when addressing an academic gathering'[30] – which got the editor of the *Modern Law Review* (where the piece was published) in trouble with the Law Lords.[31] Gower's claims were not universally true – as Neil Duxbury has shown, both Pollock and A. L. Goodhart exercised a genuine influence across a range of judicial developments.[32] Furthermore, the creation of law reform committees, in particular the Law Revision Committee and the Committee on Defamation (chaired by Lord Porter), provided the opportunity for certain, carefully selected, judges and academics to work together, and there is no evidence of hostility or resentment in their dealings. Indeed, a close examination of the workings of these committees reveals a surprisingly pervasive academic influence. Conversely, it also turns out that members of

[28] W. Friedmann, *Law and Social Change in Contemporary Britain* (London, Stevens and Sons, 1951).

[29] J. Bell, 'Wolfgang Friedmann (1907–1972), with an Excursus on Gustav Radbruch (1878–1949)' in J. Beatson and R. Zimmermann (eds.), *Jurists Uprooted* (Oxford University Press, 2004) 517. Friedmann's contribution to Australian tort law is sensitively analysed in M. Lunney, 'Legal Émigrés and the Development of Australian Tort Law' (2012) 36 *Melbourne University Law Review* 494.

[30] Gower, 'English Legal Training', 198.

[31] L. Gower, 'Looking Back' (1978) 14 *JSPTL* ns 155.

[32] Duxbury, *Jurists and Judges*, 85–96.

both Houses of Parliament had a purely procedural function in statutory reforms in the 1930s and 1940s; they were (generally) content to accept the substantive choices made elsewhere. Who made those choices and how they arrived at them lies at the heart of this book's analysis of those reforms.

PART I

2

Definition and theory

> There is no doubt that the law of tort has been well taught and understood with tolerable ease for a long time, though no two teachers or writers of text-books are agreed as to its exact contents.
>
> P. H. Winfield

I

This chapter examines controversies about the definition of tort law. Such controversies were not new in 1900, nor – of course – have they entirely disappeared from the contemporary scene. To some extent, therefore, the format of early twentieth-century discussions will seem very familiar. But familiarity of format should not be mistaken for identity of substance: the particular issues in relation to which controversies arose, and the terms in which the debate was conducted, demonstrate historically specific concerns. Furthermore, the protagonists may have disagreed about virtually everything else, but they did at least agree that more was at stake in this controversy than mere meanings of words. For all of them the choice of definition was inextricably linked to fundamental questions about the law's nature, purpose and development – both historical and future. Finally, where the debates were carried out, and the *personae* adopted by their authors, are highly suggestive about the role and influence of academic lawyers in the early twentieth century.

II

The emergence of the collection of causes of action that we classify as 'torts' was both lengthy and involved.[1] Remedies for personal injury date back to the Anglo-Saxons; the medieval royal courts heard actions for trespass;

[1] D. Ibbetson, *A Historical Introduction to the Law of Obligations* (Oxford University Press, 1999).

and defamation started life in the ecclesiastical courts. From the fourteenth century onwards the action on the case played a central role in expanding the circumstances in which damages for what we would now call 'torts' were awarded. Throughout the process of development and expansion, however, there had been no pressing need to generalise about the circumstances in which liability arose. The primary question for any claimant was whether the claim satisfied the requirements of a particular action and, if it did, to ensure that the claim was correctly expressed. Classification was by form of action. Of course, substantive questions often arose about the scope of certain forms of action, but these did not entail questions about the scope of tort law as a conceptual category, for the simple reason that there *was* no conceptual category of 'tort'.

During the course of the nineteenth century law reform initiatives led to the abolition of a strict insistence on the use of forms of action. Set words were no longer to be required. There were also intimations of the conceptual categories that are familiar to us today – particularly in the County Courts Act 1867 requirement to distinguish between actions in contract and actions in tort, and in the appearance of treatises, such as Addison's 1860 work on tort.[2] However, it would be a mistake to assume that the procedural structure of the forms of action was seamlessly replaced by substantive categories. On the contrary, the removal of the forms of action created a vacuum, and presented an opportunity. How that opportunity should be exploited was an important question in the early twentieth-century controversies about the definition of tort law.

The abolition of the forms of action thus provided the immediate, practical impetus for debates about the definition and theory of the law of tort. Two further factors shaped how the debates would be approached. The first was a growing interest in scientific study of law. Such interest had, for instance, inspired the foundation of the *Law Quarterly Review* in 1885, and prized rationality and analysis.[3] The expansion of law as a university subject also lent greater legitimacy and prominence to general questions about the nature of the subject. The second factor was empire. English tort law in 1900 did not apply to England alone; indeed, the 1920s marked the highest point of the British empire's geographical area.[4] The

[2] C. Addison, *Wrongs and their Remedies: Being a Treatise on the Law of Torts* (London, V. and R. Stevens and Sons, 1860).

[3] A. W. B. Simpson, 'The Salmond Lecture' (2007) 38 *Victoria University of Wellington Law Review* 669, 670ff.

[4] J. Brown and W. Louis (eds.), *The Oxford History of the British Empire: Volume IV: The Twentieth Century* (Oxford University Press, 2001) particularly the map at 4.

result of both of these factors was that a parochial or purely historical explanation – along the lines of 'We've always done things like this here' – would not have wide appeal. What was needed – or, at least, what seemed to be sought – was nothing less than a proof of the universal validity of English tort law.

III

The first attempt to provide such proof came in Frederick Pollock's treatise on tort. On the opening page of the first edition of his book to be published in the twentieth century, he presented tort law as a necessary consequence of community:

> All members of a civilized [*sic*] commonwealth are under a general duty towards their neighbours to do them no hurt without lawful cause or excuse. The precise extent of the duty, as well as the nature and extent of the recognised exceptions, varies according to the nature of the case. But this does not affect the generality of the principle.[5]

After making a comparison with the principles of contract, he explained that:

> In fact the principle was enunciated long ago by Ulpian in his familiar statement of the commandments of the law, preserved in the introductory chapter of Justinian's Institutes: 'Iuris praecepta sunt haec: honeste vivere, alterum non laedere, suum cuique tribuere'.[6]

These precepts, Pollock continued, contained 'a broad summary of a lawful man's duties which is founded on the permanent elements in human affairs, and is therefore still true and useful'. After a brief exposition of the three headings, Pollock made a link to a different source: 'As the English Church catechism has adapted Ulpian's words, it belongs to my duty towards my neighbour "To hurt nobody, by word nor deed: To be true and just in all my dealing".' A footnote came close to acknowledging the tendentious nature of the attribution to Ulpian: 'Goodrich, Bishop of Ely, by whom this was probably framed, was a learned civilian, and no other origin has been suggested.'[7] 'Probably' rather gives the game away here, but the appeal to universality could not have been clearer.

In a move that would be followed by other writers on the subject, Pollock then descended into how tort was to be distinguished from

[5] F. Pollock, *The Law of Torts*, 6th edn (London, Stevens and Sons, 1901) 1.
[6] *Ibid.*, 1–2. [7] *Ibid.*, 2.

crime (actionable as a civil wrong) and contract (duties owed generally), although the awkward reality of concurrent liabilities in contract and tort was relegated to a footnote.[8] 'We shall not find laid down in our authorities any such broad principles as above indicated', he continued airily, 'nor is there anything surprising in this.'[9] An explanation of the historical development of the forms of action followed, before Pollock returned to his discussion of the current law of tort, and proposed a threefold classification into personal wrongs, wrongs to possession and property, and 'wrongs to person, estate and property generally'.[10] This classification in terms of the consequences of the tort could also be justified, he suggested, in terms of the relationship to moral fault. In personal wrongs, such as assault, battery and defamation, 'there is deliberate injury, or there is something like the self-seeking indulgence of passion, in contempt of other men's rights and dignity, which the Greeks call ὕβρις'. Doubting readers were referred to 'Homer or the Psalter at random'.[11] In wrongs to property such as trespass to land, no moral fault was required. The third group – which included nuisance and negligence – had some relationship, but not a systematic one, with morality. Pollock was uneasy about the continuing inclusion of the property torts, and toyed with excluding them; ultimately he decided that they could remain, but only because they could usually be justified in moral terms: 'A man can but seldom go by pure unwitting misadventure beyond the limits of his own dominion.'[12]

The logical conclusion of this analysis arrived in the next chapter, in a passage headed 'General duty not do harm in modern law':

> we can be no longer satisfied in the region of tort with a mere enumeration of actionable injuries. The whole modern law of negligence, with its many developments, enforces the duty of fellow-citizens to observe in varying circumstances an appropriate measure of prudence to avoid causing harm to one another … If there exists, then, a positive duty to avoid harm, much more must there exist the negative duty of not doing wilful harm, subject, as all general duties must be subject, to the necessary exceptions. The three main heads of duty with which the law of torts is concerned – namely, to abstain from wilful injury, to respect the property of others, and to use due diligence to avoid causing harm to others – are all alike of a comprehensive nature.[13]

The most striking thing about Pollock's analysis was its sense of freedom. As he openly acknowledged, there was no authoritative support

[8] *Ibid.*, 3, n. (c). [9] *Ibid.*, 3–4. [10] *Ibid.*, 7–8.
[11] *Ibid.*, 9. [12] *Ibid.*, 16. [13] *Ibid.*, 22.

for his exposition. History, in the shape of the forms of action, could be thrown aside, and the existing remedies moulded into a structure based either on the interest interfered with, or on a hybrid classico-Christian scheme of morality. Although he presented a choice, Pollock seems to have been more attracted by the moral approach, as the terms of his decision to retain property torts in his book showed. This was a highly ambitious, and potentially tendentious approach, and it is quite revealing that Pollock had only felt confident enough to advance such broad claims in the fifth edition of 1897, when, as he put it, 'Now that ten years have passed since the first issue of this work, it seems both safe and desirable to state the leading conceptions of the subject in a more direct and simple form. The first chapter has therefore been recast in accordance with this view.'[14] 'Safe' was an interesting adjective to use here, for in one obvious sense the 'safe' way to explain tort was in terms of the categories defined by the forms of action; what Pollock meant, of course, was that the work was now firmly enough established, and trusted by its readers, that he could risk a little experimentation without damaging the book's reputation for legal accuracy.

IV

Other writers preferred to avoid the risks and dangers that were inevitable in Pollock's decision to throw away the safety net of the forms of action. For them, essentially, the forms of action might have been abolished, but the torts they had shaped remained fixed legal artefacts, and required neither justification nor rearrangement. Thus, for instance, Sir John Miles drew readers' attention to the continuation of separate torts in his introduction to the *Digest of Civil Law*,[15] prompting a disappointed review from Pollock.[16] Sir John Salmond began his textbook with what would become the most famous exposition of this approach, saying:

> Does the law of torts consist of a fundamental general principle that it is wrongful to cause harm to other persons in the absence of some specific ground of justification or excuse, or does it consist of a number of specific rules prohibiting certain kinds of harmful activity, and leaving all the residue outside the sphere of legal responsibility? It is submitted that the second of these alternatives is that which has been accepted by

[14] F. Pollock, *The Law of Torts*, 5th edn (London, Stevens and Sons, 1897) ix ('Advertisement to the Fifth Edition').

[15] E. Jenks and J. C. Miles, *A Digest of English Civil Law* (London, Butterworth, 1910).

[16] F. Pollock, 'Review of J. C. Miles, A Digest of English Civil Law' (1910) 26 *LQR* 420, 421.

> our law ... Whether I am prosecuted for an alleged offence, or sued for an alleged tort, it is for my adversary to prove that the case falls within some specific established rule of liability, and not for me to defend myself by proving that it is within some specific and established rule of justification or excuse.[17]

In an important footnote, Salmond acknowledged that Pollock took a different view. He continued:

> His view that all harm is actionable unless it falls within some specific and recognised ground of justification or excuse is one which I should gladly accept as affording a comprehensive and logical basis for the law of torts; but it seems hard to reconcile it with the actual contents of our legal system. It is difficult to see that English law contains any reasoned and exhaustive list of the grounds of exemption from liability. The only adequate answer to many claims for damages is the mere *ipse dixit* of the law that no such cause of action is recognised.[18]

In other words, the difference between Pollock and Salmond could be explained partly by their different ambitions in writing books with identical titles. Pollock wanted to fill the vacuum left by the forms of action with a rational, morally coherent exposition of principle; Salmond's stated aim was to provide a work of 'practical utility',[19] for use by lawyers and students. Salmond's experience as a legal practitioner may have made him disinclined to suggest that the basic framework of tort law was up for grabs, whilst Pollock's peculiar position as neither academic nor practitioner may – on this occasion, at least – have freed him from conventional restraints.[20] We should also note a certain paradox. Pollock, as an Englishman writing in London, on the periphery of the Inns of Court, could have been forgiven for saying that tort was as it was because 'that's how we've always done things here'. Salmond, in Wellington, might have been expected to be driven to formulating a broader justification, especially given his earlier essay on tort theory,[21] and an article on precedents

[17] J. Salmond, *The Law of Torts*, 2nd edn (London, Stevens and Haynes, 1910) 8–9 (not in first edition).

[18] *Ibid.*, 9 n. 7.

[19] J. Salmond, *The Law of Torts* (London, Stevens and Haynes, 1907), Preface at v. The Preface to the first edition was reprinted in the second edition (London, Stevens and Haynes, 1910) at vii.

[20] For the biographical backgrounds see A. Frame, *Salmond; Southern Jurist* (Wellington, Victoria University Press, 1995) and N. Duxbury, *Frederick Pollock and the English Juristic Tradition* (Oxford University Press, 2004) respectively.

[21] J. Salmond, 'The Principles of Civil Liability' in *Essays in Jurisprudence and Legal Theory* (London, Stevens & Haynes, 1891) 123.

that highlighted judicial creativity and the source of legal principles in 'natural justice, practical expediency and common sense'.[22] But it was Salmond who took the conservative, Anglocentric approach, and Pollock who sought something broader. As Salmond's subsequent editor, himself of German origin, observed, the book was notably lacking in its coverage of valuable material from other jurisdictions, particularly the United States.[23] Indeed, it is fortunate that Salmond signed off the preface to the first edition 'Wellington, New Zealand', as it would have been otherwise impossible to tell whether the book had been written in Northamptonshire or North Island. Salmond's ambivalent sense of place could also be seen elsewhere in his work. When, in an essay published in the *Law Quarterly Review*, he referred to the fashion 'on this side of the Channel', he did not mean the Cook Strait.[24] Perhaps most tellingly, in the preface to his *Essays in Jurisprudence and Legal History* the reason for confiding that 'These essays have been written at the ends of the earth' was not to explain their particular perspective, but to ask for 'their defects [to] be charitably attributed ... to the obvious difficulties attending historical research in regions so remote'.[25] The geography had nothing positive to offer. Whatever the reasons underlying this attitude – and Salmond does not go into them – being at a distance from London had not prevented him from, and perhaps even encouraged him in, adopting a limited definition of tort.

V

Pollock and Salmond's contrasting views of tort mirrored their opposing attitudes to history. For Pollock the history of tort was fatally tainted by its submersion in the forms of action; for Salmond the forms of action defined the wrongs for which liability arose. But an emphasis on history did not automatically commit one to a conservative account of tort law. Percy Winfield, to whose work we now turn, showed how a sympathetic reading of tort history could be combined with an ambitious definition of the subject.

[22] J. Salmond, 'The Theory of Judicial Precedents' (1900) 16 *LQR* 376, 389.

[23] W. Stallybrass, *Salmond on the Law of Torts*, 7th edn (London, Sweet & Maxwell, 1928) x. On Stallybrass see H. Hanbury, 'Stallybrass [formerly Sonnenschein], William Teulon Swan' in *Oxford Dictionary of National Biography* (online edition).

[24] J. Salmond, 'The Law of Nature' (1895) 11 *LQR* 121, 122.

[25] J. Salmond, *Essays in Jurisprudence and Legal History* (London, Stevens & Haynes, 1891) iv.

From the very beginning of his academic career Winfield had undertaken research in both current law and legal history. As he made clear in his inaugural lecture as Rouse Ball Professor of English Law in Cambridge, he did not regard these interests as separate. Rather, they should inform and reinforce each other. Thus, 'the highest type of research into legal history is that which has in view law reform, either consciously or unconsciously'.[26] Similarly, textbooks were needed 'that attack … the law in really scientific fashion … The ideal pattern for them would be a statement of what the law has been, what it is now, and what it ought to be.'[27]

A year before his inaugural lecture, Winfield had made the first of several significant contributions to the debate about the definition of tort law in an article published in the *Columbia Law Review*.[28] Without coming down in favour of Pollock or Salmond, he subjected the premiss that there was 'a definite number of torts outside which liability in tort does not exist' to historical critique. The argument progressed in two stages. First, he demonstrated that mere novelty had never been a conclusive objection to judicial recognition of a new remedy, emphasising the importance of new forms of action on the case. He then turned his focus to torts, drawing attention to the increase in specific torts, and the central role of the action on the case. 'It is in action upon the case in one form or another – frequently none whatever – that the development of the law of torts outside trespass must be sought', he explained. But the search would not be easy, since this form of action was 'extremely elastic', and 'It was more difficult for jurists to state this branch of the law scientifically than for judges to make the law itself'.[29] He had made a similar point in more colourful language in an article on negligence – 'The action on the case has been the life-blood of the English law of torts, but it is calculated to make any professor of jurisprudence desperate.'[30] Winfield was careful to make clear that the action on the case did not permit unlimited expansion – there were constraints such as public policy, the role of Parliament and the influence of other legal areas – but what he was emphatic about was that the courts had the ability 'to manufacture new torts'.[31]

[26] P. Winfield, 'Law Reform' (1928) 44 *LQR* 289, 299.

[27] *Ibid.*, 295–6.

[28] P. Winfield, 'The Foundation of Liability in Tort' (1927) 27 *Columbia Law Review* 1.

[29] *Ibid.*, 5.

[30] P. Winfield, 'The History of Negligence in the Law of Torts' (1926) 42 *LQR* 184, 197.

[31] Winfield, 'The Foundation of Liability in Tort', 11.

Winfield's article marked out a position that was distinct from both Pollock and Salmond. Where Pollock's historical analysis was designed to set aside the restrictions of the forms of action, Winfield's approach underlined the potential for the action on the case to generate change. And where Salmond's position committed him to specific, established rules of liability, Winfield saw the law – in historical perspective – as capable of constant development.

The fullest statement of Winfield's position came in his lectures as Tagore Professor, delivered in 1930 at the University of Calcutta, and published in 1931.[32] Right at the start of the first lecture, entitled 'The Definition of Tort', he confronted the question: why define? There were two kinds of reasons, theoretical and practical. The chief theoretical reason was that it would make teaching more 'scientific'. The practical reasons centred around being able to distinguish tort from contract, quasi-contract and other heads of liability, which might be subject to different procedural rules, remedies, limitation periods, and so on. In defining the province of tort law Winfield made it clear that it would be necessary to engage with the growing United States literature on the topic, and he also alerted his audience to two obstacles: first, the 'dead hand of history',[33] and second, the need to define the boundaries of other, as yet ill-defined areas. Quasi-contract was particularly problematic. 'At present', he commented, '[quasi-contract] is regarded here as territory which is more useful for the deportation of undesirable ideas than for colonization.'[34] Where 'here' was is a difficult question. And what the audience made of his quip about colonisation, which seemed to be a kind of back-handed compliment – one wouldn't want to colonise a territory full of undesirables, after all – we can only guess.

In his next lecture Winfield presented a general historical outline of the development of tort, giving appropriate weight to actions on the case. He also drew students' attention to work by Finch in the early seventeenth century, which had defined tort as a personal action for damages,[35] and to Blackstone's definition of torts as personal actions 'whereby a man claims a satisfaction in damages for some injury done to his person or property'.[36] Blackstone, however, marked an end of general analysis, for, in Winfield's words, 'legal education had perished in the Inns of Court and was scarcely reborn in the Universities'.[37]

[32] P. Winfield, *The Province of the Law of Tort* (Cambridge University Press, 1931).

[33] *Ibid.*, 6. [34] *Ibid.*, 7. [35] *Ibid.*, 22.

[36] *Ibid.*, 25. [37] *Ibid.*, 30.

The third lecture, 'Tort Defined', set out Winfield's own test:

> Tortious liability arises from the breach of a duty primarily fixed by the law: such duty is towards persons generally and its breach is redressible by an action for unliquidated damages.[38]

He then moved on to address the issue that had divided Pollock and Salmond, namely, are all injuries to another torts, unless there is some justification recognised by law? Or does the law consist of a definite number of torts, outside of which no liability exists?

Winfield firmly committed himself to the former view. 'The greatest difficulty in the way of those who support the second, or "inexpansibility", theory is the development of the law of torts itself', he explained,[39] and proceeded to illustrate the point with recent examples such as the emergence of conspiracy as a tort[40] and the recognition of invasion of privacy as a tort 'well known in India in Gujerat and the North-West Provinces'.[41] The lecture concluded with a short discussion of the French Civil Code Article 1382, and the German BGB Article 826, both of which contained general prohibitions against wrongdoing.

The next six lectures concerned themselves with the boundaries of other legal categories, but Chapters X and XII returned to the definition of tort. Chapter X, headed 'Tort and Quasi-Delict', began by drawing attention to the variety of terminological uses of quasi-delict in Roman and Scots law, but the real focus of the chapter made good Winfield's promise to address American literature. His central concern was the argument advanced by Nathan Isaacs that a wrongful state of mind was needed for tort liability; it followed from Isaacs' premiss that a category of 'quasi-delict' would be needed for situations, such as vicarious liability, where the defendant's state of mind was irrelevant.[42] Winfield's response was a mixture of slightly banal pragmatism and history. In his view, the proposed distinction was unnecessary, because textbooks on tort would still have to deal with strict liability, 'though the Workmen's Compensation Acts could – indeed must be – omitted'.[43] 'More importantly', he continued, there was no historical basis for insisting on fault as part of a definition of tort. Winfield returned to this theme at the conclusion of his final lecture, reiterating the point about history and also highlighting the

[38] *Ibid.*, 32. [39] *Ibid.*, 34.

[40] *Sorrell* v. *Smith* [1925] AC 700.

[41] Winfield, *The Province of the Law of Tort*, 34.

[42] N. Isaacs, 'Quasi-Delict in Anglo-American Law' (1921–1922) 31 *Yale Law Journal* 571.

[43] Winfield, *The Province of the Law of Tort*, 216.

analytical difficulties in allocating particular torts to one category or the other if its principles involved elements of fault.[44]

Winfield devoted the remainder of his final lecture to explaining why he was rejecting other definitions of tort. Two points deserve attention. First, he acknowledged that the idea of a duty owed 'to persons generally' might prove problematic, for instance in an action for breach of statutory duty owed to the inhabitants of a small town. He also explained that it would not be an improvement to regard tortious duties as owed to the world at large (or 'in rem', to use the rather confusing terminology he preferred), because tortious duties could arise where the duty was owed to a particular person, for instance, a carrier's duty to carry goods on request.[45] Second, Winfield dissociated himself from the statement of Pollock that torts were, by definition, wrongs dealt with by the common law courts before the passing of the Judicature Acts. This reference to the common law courts did not add to the clarity of the definition, 'however necessary it may be to explain the historical anomalies which still appear in the fabric'.[46]

Winfield's *The Province* was a distinctive and important contribution, which shared the scientific, rationalising ambitions of Pollock, but came to its own conclusions. Thus, the general underlying principle of tort liability was reached by historical analysis rather than by appeals to the nature of communal life, Roman law or the Church catechism. Indeed, Winfield's account of the relationship between tort and morality was far more muted than Pollock's – thus, crucially, Winfield saw no inherent difficulty in the inclusion of strict liability as part of tort law, nor did he feel that he had to apologise for strict liability in trespass to land. On the other hand, the role of history in the arguments used in *The Province* was less steady than in Winfield's own earlier work. The lectures are framed by emphatic assertions about 'the dead hand of history' and the importance of 'cut[ting]' 'the net' of nineteenth-century procedural restrictions,[47] but Winfield's key argument in favour of a general principle of tort liability was based on historical analysis, and his rejection of fault as a definitional requirement was also historically based. As we shall see in the next section, reviewers of the book picked up on, but did not confine themselves to, these issues.

[44] *Ibid.*, 244. Winfield gives the compelling example of *Rylands* v. *Fletcher*, where liability was strict, but defences such as act of a stranger were effectively fault-based.

[45] Winfield, *The Province of the Law of Tort*, 238.

[46] *Ibid.*, 236–7. [47] *Ibid.*, 6 and 240.

VI

Pollock's review of *The Province* began with the counter-suggestible observation that 'English readers are not concerned to wonder whether the contents, even if the tougher parts were omitted in delivery, were not too strong meat for an audience of Indian law students who had barely heard of the old forms of action'.[48] He himself had found it 'rather hard reading', and he went on carefully to position himself as an authoritative outsider in the debate:

> As between members of an active teaching Faculty, such as Prof. Winfield and his colleagues, [assuming detailed knowledge] is justifiable, and may be laudable for the saving of time. The profession at large, including those who have endeavoured to teach law in their time but are no longer teachers may be allowed a little grumble.[49]

Here we might note that Pollock managed to portray himself also as an outsider in 'the profession at large' because of his teaching past. His main objection was the 'dialectic zeal' of Winfield's discussions of definitional points. Questions of definition were better left to draftsmen of statutes, Pollock felt; and, in paying such attention to definitions, Winfield had allowed himself to be distracted from the bigger picture. In particular, argued Pollock, he had failed to seize the opportunity to alert his audience to the support for a general principle of tort law that could be found in Ulpian and the Church catechism.

Leaving aside the fact that Pollock was hardly in a position to question others' shortcomings as lecturers,[50] and assuming for the moment that a helping of Latin would have helped the students, Pollock's comments raise an important point. In *The Province* Winfield was adopting the same position as Pollock on the existence of an underlying general principle of tort liability, but he omitted Pollock's sources. Was this – as Pollock thought – an unfortunate oversight? Winfield never responded to Pollock's review, but it seems inherently implausible to impute carelessness or confusion on a fundamental issue to such a meticulous scholar. The more plausible explanation, surely, is that the omission was deliberate, and may well have been prompted by the location and audience of the lectures.

[48] F. P[ollock], '*Review of Winfield, The Province of the Law of Tort*' (1931) 47 *LQR* 588.

[49] *Ibid.*, 588.

[50] Duxbury, *Frederick Pollock and the English Juristic Tradition*, 41–64, particularly the damning assessment of F. H. Lawson quoted at 53.

The key to the explanation may lie in Winfield's allusion, in his illustrations of tort's ability to develop, to the tort of invasion of privacy 'well known in India in Gujerat and the North-West Provinces'.[51] In *The Province* itself no further information is given, but in an article on privacy published in 1931 (the same year as the publication of *The Province*), he described the right of privacy that arose under Indian customary law, to safeguard the seclusion of *parda-nashin* women, and applied only in the North West Provinces.[52] This right, he commented approvingly, showed 'the pliability of Indian law'.[53] Such approval was entirely consistent with the broader approach he had taken in his inaugural lecture as Rouse Ball Professor, where he had observed that 'Law, in the main, has discharged its function, if it corresponds with reasonable accuracy to the existing needs of the community'.[54] He added that law should not seek to be more moral, or more religious, than those to whom it applied. Whilst he did not make it explicit, the obvious corollary of his position was that law should not seek to impose a *different* morality or a *different* religion on those who were governed by it. Had he told his Calcutta lecture audience that the foundations of the law of tort should be sought in Ulpian and the Church catechism, he would surely have both alienated them from the subject and misrepresented his own views about the importance of law reflecting the needs of its community.

Edward Jenks' review, entitled 'The Province of Tort in English Law', made no allusion to the Indian context, but engaged in more detailed analysis than Pollock's review.[55] He picked up on the difficulties with the 'persons generally' formula and, more significantly, pointed out that Winfield's definition was rather unsatisfying, in that it gave no flavour of what a tort actually was.[56] Jenks drew a revealing contrast with contract, where a satisfyingly substantial definition in terms of promises for consideration was available. The difference, Jenks explained, was the generalising of contractual liability in actions on the case for assumpsit; tort had experienced no similar generalising force, and the result was an array of wrongs shaped by the forms of action. In his view, that was still the most accurate depiction of tort law. Pollock's and Winfield's general prin-

[51] Winfield, *The Province of the Law of Tort*, 34.
[52] P. Winfield, 'Privacy' (1931) 47 *LQR* 23, 29–31.
[53] *Ibid.*, 30. [54] Winfield, 'Law Reform', 290.
[55] E. Jenks, 'The Province of Tort in English Law' (1932) 14 *Journal of Comparative Legislation and International Law* 4 207.
[56] *Ibid.*, 209.

ciple shifted too uneasily between 'an ideal to be striven for' and 'an actual statement of the existing law' to be convincing.[57]

VII

The most detailed response to *The Province* was to come from P. A. Landon in fourteen closely argued pages in *Bell Yard*, the journal of the Law Society's School of Law.[58] Landon acknowledged that Winfield had produced an 'original and important contribution to English legal literature',[59] but he took issue with both its methodology and its content. A 'traditional lawyer', he said, would define tort as being 'exactly co-terminous with the sphere of the old writs of trespass, case and detinue'.[60] Winfield's definition was 'a very different affair. It breathes jurisprudence at us.'[61] Landon made it clear what had gone wrong: Winfield had been reading American books that encouraged bad habits – 'We must not try to force our grossly unscientific system into a Procrustean bed of juristic categories. That is what they are doing in America.'[62]

Given his starting point, it was hardly surprising to find that Landon disagreed with Winfield's identification of a general principle of tort liability, but his way of dealing with Winfield's examples of new torts was quite revealing. In relation to Winfield's tentative identification of a distinct tort of conspiracy he commented that no caution was needed, since 'the profession as a whole has now accepted [Lord Dunedin's] judgment in *Sorrell* v. *Smith*'.[63] His comment on the existence of a tort of invasion of privacy, which Winfield had identified in Indian law, was equally dispositive: 'Nor, we think, is there any doubt that our law rejects any such tort as "invasion of privacy"; Tolley's counsel did not dare argue that there was such a thing.'[64]

Landon concluded with an approval of Winfield's chapter on quasi-delict, where he made two significant points. First, he said that Winfield should not have assumed that a leading case on intention in battery was correct, since 'we find that, at the Bar, Beven's view that the decision was

[57] *Ibid.*, 210.

[58] P. A. Landon, 'The Province of the Law of Tort' (1931) 8 *Bell Yard* 19.

[59] *Ibid.*, 19. [60] *Ibid.*, 20. [61] *Ibid.*, 20.

[62] *Ibid.*, 21. [63] *Ibid.*, 25.

[64] *Ibid.*, 25. The allusion is to *Tolley* v. *JS Fry & Sons Ltd* [1930] 1 KB 467 (CA); [1931] AC 333, a case where the facts potentially raised issues about the claimant's right (if any) to control his own image, but where a remedy was found in defamation.

wholly erroneous, is generally accepted'.[65] Second, Landon took issue with Winfield's omission of workmen's compensation:

> it is obvious that everyone intending to practise in common law cases must know this branch of the law thoroughly, and it is so intimately bound up with the question of the employer's liability to his employee that it is most fittingly set out, as Stephen continues to set it out, as part of the law of tort.[66]

In the context of Landon's article as a whole, this point about workmen's compensation was relatively minor, but its significance should not be overlooked. Plainly a claim under the workmen's compensation legislation did not qualify as a tort under Landon's own test, yet Landon was insisting that it should be included in books on tort. In other words, accounts of tort law should not be confined to explaining torts. Landon's reasoning was also significant: future practitioners needed to understand both regimes, and workmen's compensation was 'intimately bound up with' employer's liability. The former point was a minor variation on Landon's theme of the centrality of legal practice, but the latter was more suggestive, because it implied an unsettling question. It was all very well to go to the trouble of marking off the 'provinces' of tort, contract, property, and so on, but a far more pressing question for thinkers on tort was how to respond to a large-scale no-fault compensation scheme, which had been introduced as a result of perceived shortcomings in tort liability.[67] The question that the existence of workmen's compensation implied was not so much 'what is the analytical territory of tort?' as 'what is tort's social function; and is it carrying out that function?'

Landon's critique had its ridiculous aspects, and he was deservedly mocked by Winfield and Stallybrass for his programmatic anti-Americanism and pretensions to speak for the entire legal profession.[68] But his more moderate arguments deserved to be taken seriously, because they implied a fundamentally different approach to what tort was, and how it functioned, to the approach taken by Winfield. For Landon, Winfield was in the wrong place (university), talking to the wrong people (students) and reading the wrong books (American), which led to wrong-headedly scientific ambitions for tort law. In Landon's world, the place to find out

[65] Landon, 'The Province of the Law of Tort', 30. The case in question was *Stanley* v. *Powell* [1891] 1 QB 86.

[66] Landon, 'The Province of the Law of Tort', 31.

[67] See further Chapter 8.

[68] P. Winfield, 'The Province of the Law of Tort: A Reply' (1932) 9 *Bell Yard* 32; W. Stallybrass, 'Landon v. Winfield: An Intervention' (1932) 10 *Bell Yard* 18.

about tort (and not just tort) was London, and the books to read were the classic practitioner works – like Bullen and Leake on pleadings – or traditional introductory books such as Stephen's *Commentaries*. The emphasis was on the common law tradition, and the best evidence of its current state was the informed judgments of its practitioners. On this view of the world, a barrister's professional (and, in all likelihood, strategic) decision about which arguments to advance in a case took on compelling authority for the state of the law. The contrast with Winfield's underlying assumptions could hardly have been starker: Landon's was a law of tort that was defined by tradition, and which was only fully accessible to the London insiders who participated in that tradition.

In their responses to Landon, both Winfield and Stallybrass highlighted the constraining role of history in his account. Landon had underestimated the importance of the abolition of the forms of action, they argued, and had made no allowance for legal change. Stallybrass pointed out that there was a resemblance between the debate between Winfield and Landon and the division of the House of Lords in the (then) very recent decision in *Donoghue* v. *Stevenson*.[69] Lords Atkin and Macmillan, he suggested, might have read Winfield's book.[70] But interestingly neither writer dealt with Landon's point about workmen's compensation. Only Winfield mentioned the matter, and whilst he agreed with Landon that a practitioner needed a 'thorough' knowledge of workmen's compensation, 'can you expect a [practitioner] to get his thorough knowledge from a text-book on the general law of tort? May one remind Mr Landon that in about ten years there were 1,200 decisions in appellate courts *alone* on these Acts?'[71]

We might feel that Winfield was making rather too much of the point about 'thorough' knowledge here. After all, an adequate summary of the system – for textbook purposes – need not give a blow-by-blow account of every decided case.[72] But the exchange also highlighted the limitations imposed by the terms of the debate. Landon's position that workmen's compensation should be included in books on tort was at its most compelling when seen in terms of theory, and broader questions about the function of tort law. It was not so much a point about the contents

[69] [1932] AC 562. [70] Stallybrass, 'Landon v. Winfield', 22.

[71] Winfield, 'The Province of the Law of Tort: A Reply', 38.

[72] Stallybrass incorporated a two-page summary of the workmen's compensation scheme in the next edition of *Salmond*: W. Stallybrass, *The Law of Torts: A Treatise on the English Law of Liability for Civil Injuries*, 8th edn (London, Sweet & Maxwell, 1934) xii and 117–19.

page of a book as a point about the conceptual relationship between tort and workmen's compensation. But Landon had set his stall out against such academic speculation, and, to be consistent, had to put the point in pragmatic, practitioner-oriented terms. Winfield met it in even more pragmatic terms, with an argument about the physical limitations of publishing. The conceptual issue had disappeared. On his argument, the only thing that kept workmen's compensation out of the tort books was the binding holding them together.[73]

VIII

Whilst Winfield's position on the definition of tort would remain stable, other works underwent significant changes. The editorship of Salmond's textbook was taken over by W. T. Stallybrass, who took a view similar, but not precisely identical, to Winfield's. Stallybrass' position was that the law was moving towards Winfield's position, but had not quite yet reached it – and an 'Excursus' added to the first edition under Stallybrass' editorship drew attention to the new editor's view. By an almost fairy-tale coincidence, the editorship of Pollock was taken over at around the same time by P. A. Landon, thereby perpetuating the opposition of views, but reversing the treatises in which they were expressed. By the time Winfield came to publish the first edition of his textbook in 1937, the names of the editors might have changed, but the issues were the same.

Much of Winfield's first chapter reproduced the ideas from *The Province*, and the definition of tort he relied on was in identical terms to the earlier work. When he came to discuss the arguments for a general theory of tort, however, it was clear that his thinking had moved on. Edward Jenks, in reviewing *The Province*, had argued that, whilst there was no general principle of liability, the courts retained the ability to recognise new torts, provided that those new torts were 'substantially similar' to torts already recognised.[74] In his *Text-Book* Winfield took up this point, arguing that Jenks was describing the *mode* in which new torts emerged, but not the principle that explained '*why* they were born'.[75] '[I]f we look at what the Judges did, and not merely at what they said', he continued:

[73] Cf. T. Weir, *An Introduction to Tort Law*, 2nd edn (Oxford, Clarendon Press, 2006) ix: 'Tort is what is in the tort books, and the only thing holding it together is their binding.'

[74] Jenks, 'The Province of Tort in English Law', 210.

[75] P. Winfield, *A Text-Book of the Law of Tort* (London, Sweet & Maxwell, 1937) 20.

> we might reasonably infer that they were acting on the idea that all unjustifiable harm is tortious. The idea was usually subconscious, and though, as we have seen, some distinguished Judges have given voice to it, others perhaps would not have admitted to it.[76]

It was also important, he added, to remember that only unjustifiable harm called forth new torts. There was a parallel with medicine, which, whilst creating remedies for the alleviation or cure of human ills, drew the line at procuring abortions or accelerating death.[77]

Winfield's exposition prompted two responses. Glanville Williams undertook a careful, closely argued analysis of the cases and concluded that there was insufficient authority to support Winfield's claim for a general principle of tortious liability.[78] He left unexplored the 'extra-legal' reasons that produced advances in tort law.[79] Winfield's former colleague A. L. Goodhart took a more confrontational approach, treating the argument about subconscious development with patronising sarcasm:

> This attempt to prove the existence of a fundamental principle of law by analysing the subconscious thoughts of the Judges is undoubtedly an interesting experiment, but it falls somewhat short of conclusive evidence … they seem to have succeeded pretty thoroughly in suppressing their subconscious.[80]

The truth was, Goodhart argued, that the courts created new torts by gradually extending old ones, not by using a general principle of liability. His parting shot was that 'It will be interesting to see what happens when the coming generation of lawyers, who have been so ably taught by Professor Winfield, first advance this theory in Court'.[81] The insinuation was, of course, that Winfield's students would be embarrassed and humiliated if they advanced his theories in court. Any teacher would be dismayed by such an accusation of self-indulgence verging on betrayal, and Winfield acted promptly. In the second edition of his book he deleted the discussion of Jenks, all references to the subconscious, and the analogy with medicine. In its place he introduced a passage that made clear that he had taken Goodhart's criticisms to heart:

> I had taken the view that the [general principle] theory is nearer the truth, but on further consideration I prefer to modify it as follows. From a

[76] *Ibid.*, 20–1. [77] *Ibid.*, 21.

[78] G. Williams, 'The Foundation of Tortious Liability' (1939–1941) 7 *CLJ* 111.

[79] *Ibid.*, 131.

[80] A. Goodhart, 'The Foundation of Tortious Liability' (1938–1939) 2 *MLR* 1, 7.

[81] *Ibid.*, 11.

> narrow practical point of view, the [specific torts] theory will suffice, but from a broader outlook, the [general principle theory] is valid. If we concentrate attention on the law of tort at this moment (which is what most practitioners do), entirely excluding the development of the law, past and future, then it corresponds to the [specific torts] theory. If we take the wider view that the law of tort has grown for centuries and is still growing, then the [general principle] theory seems to be at the back of it.[82]

Winfield ventured to reintroduce a reference to courts creating new torts 'unconsciously' in the third edition of 1946; but it was only in a footnote.[83] The medicine analogy never reappeared in any form.

Looking back on the changes that Winfield made to his textbook in the wake of Goodhart's criticism, it is difficult to avoid a sense of regret. Goodhart's position insisted on taking judicial language at face value; Winfield's allowed for the possibility that the language of the judgment did not tell the whole story, and this was surely the more convincing approach. Indeed, the common law's commitment to precedent meant that it was almost inevitable that judicial innovations in tort would emphasise continuity rather than change. There were also political incentives to package change as continuity, which later extra-curial writing by judges would acknowledge.[84] Winfield's approach also opened up the possibility that judicial changes might occur despite a judge's conscious commitment to making no legal innovation. What exactly Winfield had in mind is impossible to know, because his development of the idea was cut short. One possibility is that changes in society – as experienced or observed by the judge as a member of that society – became an unarticulated part of the judicial reasoning process. At all events, Winfield's sense that there might be a complex relationship between a judge's written reasons and that judge's decision-making process was supported by contemporary and later work in judicial studies.[85]

Goodhart's point about students using Winfield's theories in court also seems to have been misplaced. It rested on the assumption that a statement about (tort) law was only valuable or worthwhile if a barrister could repeat it to a judge without criticism. I hope that readers of a book on

82 P. Winfield, *A Text-Book of the Law of Tort*, 2nd edn (London, Sweet & Maxwell, 1943) 20.

83 P. Winfield, *A Text-Book of the Law of Tort*, 3rd edn (London, Sweet & Maxwell, 1946) 15.

84 Lord Radcliffe, *The Law and its Compass* (London, Faber, 1961) 39.

85 E.g. the American legal realist school, on which see N. Duxbury, *Patterns of American Jurisprudence* (Oxford University Press, 1997) chapters 1 and 2, and W. Twining, *Karl Llewellyn and the Realist Movement*, 2nd edn (Cambridge University Press, 2012).

legal history will be easily persuaded to question that assumption. But, even granting the premiss a temporary validity, its application to the disagreement with Winfield was peculiarly unconvincing. For Winfield's whole point was that judicial language did not tell the complete story. If a Winfield student had advanced the general theory of liability to a court, and had been told 'No, that's wrong', the judge's response would have told us nothing about the subconscious motivations that Winfield argued lay behind legal development.

Winfield's retreat from the general principle of liability in the second edition of his *Text-Book* led him to abandon the analogy between tort and medicine. As with his decision to excise the suggestion about subconscious legal development, in retrospect this seems a pity. For although he had had the aspiration to produce a 'scientific' exposition in a textbook for at least ten years,[86] the specific analogy between tort and the applied science of medicine was both original and illuminating. As Winfield pointed out, medicine constantly strove to create new remedies for human ills, but there were some conditions that were off limits for moral and/or conventional reasons. In tort, the courts' similar role was to identify 'in the interests of the community' comparable situations where the law should or should not go. This view explicitly attributed to the courts the role – we might even say the mission – of developing the law in response to perceived social needs. It also, implicitly, attributed to tort law a function in respect of social ills that was the counterpart of medicine's function for physical ills. This was the most ambitious claim that Winfield would ever make about the function of tort: unfortunately, only those reading the first edition were exposed to it.

In one respect, however, Goodhart's criticism did prompt improvement, because it led Winfield to develop the sophisticated position – evident in the second edition – on the importance of history in the debate. Essentially Winfield came to the conclusion that there were two ways of looking at it. The first, the historical view, emphasised the elasticity and ability of the law to expand; the second, focussing on the present and adopting the perspective of a practitioner, acknowledged that the dominant impression of tort was as a list of specific wrongs. As an academic and legal historian, he retained his preference for the former view;[87] but now, at least, there should be no danger of future practitioners embarrassing themselves in court on his account.

[86] Winfield, 'Law Reform', 295.

[87] Winfield, *A Text-Book of the Law of Tort*, 2nd edn, 20.

IX

The controversies about the definition and structure of tort in the first half of the twentieth century should lead us to reflect on several important, broader themes.

First, we might be struck by the consistently reiterated ambition to produce a scientific, rational account of tort law. There is a sense that (tort) law needed the *discipline* of the sciences in at least two senses: it needed to smarten up its act, and to ally itself with a respectable stalwart of academic endeavour. Broader changes in academic culture – in particular, the prominence of research – created an environment in which the aspiration to be scientific was natural, but the growing recognition that history could no longer be relied upon as an adequate legal explanation *in itself* was surely the main catalyst. For whatever the arguments might have been for conceiving of tort in terms of the forms of action in the early nineteenth century, by the late nineteenth century such arguments were starting to look dangerously antiquarian. There was also a practical incentive to explain tort in contemporary terms, since English law was being applied across the empire. Whilst it might have been just about possible, in England, to sit back and regard tort law as part of the unfolding pageant of English legal history, its application overseas invited – even demanded – a broader and more universal explanation.

Writers on tort appreciated and responded to these factors in their own ways. Pollock's textbook, which from its first edition included his draft code of tortious obligations for India, came to invoke sources and values from outside English law – most notably Ulpian and the Church catechism – to explain the law's moral role. His introduction of the general principle of liability for damage caused without justification gave effect to that moral role, and stood the traditional way of looking at tort on its head. Rather than a series of specific wrongs, tort in Pollock's version was a sea of liability for damage punctuated by exceptions. Salmond felt unable to subscribe to Pollock's worldview, preferring the traditional approach. Winfield, delivering his major contribution on the issue to an Indian lecture audience, took a position that was distinctively his own, although closer to Pollock than to Salmond. Winfield agreed with the general principle view, but he preferred not to rely on Pollock's classico-Christian sources. Winfield's work was also distinctive in its formulation of an analytical definition of tort law, and both this, and the title of his book, clearly hinted at the influence of the analytical jurisprudence of John Austin, author of *The Province of Jurisprudence Determined.*

The trouble with Winfield's analytical definition was that it was neither a thing of beauty, nor was it suggestive about the function or development of tort law. It suffered from the same ahistorical sterility that made Austin's own work unappealing. The general principle approach, by contrast, was more engaging. Indeed, such was the volume of counter-argument that Winfield may have come to think it was a bit *too* engaging. Some of those counter-arguments were formidable, and undoubtedly established that, as a matter of authority, the evidence for the general principle was less than compelling. It was also pointed out that the general principle was formulated in such vague terms as to be practically useless: it could not be used to predict how an English court would decide a new case.[88]

Looking back at these critiques of the general principle, there is a strong sense that the parties were at cross-purposes. The root of the problem lay in Pollock's (and Winfield's) use of the word 'principle'. The more conventional use of the word, at least in its legal context, denotes a general proposition that governs the outcome of a particular case. Thus, the principle that I owe a duty of care not to cause physical injury to those whom I ought to foresee will suffer damage can be applied to a particular factual situation to determine whether I owe a duty of care. The 'principle' that tortious liability is imposed for unjustifiable harm is – in conventional terms – a failure. It begs too many questions. But the point is that it should not be approached as a legal principle in the conventional sense: it is more like a statement of aim, purpose or function that justifies future legal development. Winfield's later experiments with an analogy between tort and medicine suggest that this was how he understood the 'general principle'.

As is now clear, I hope, writers in the first half of the twentieth century were engaged in a lively debate about not just the definition of tort law, but also its structure, purpose and justification. One might even call it legal theory. Indeed, jurisprudentially inclined readers may have noticed that the title of this chapter is half a quotation from H. L. A. Hart's 'Definition and Theory in Jurisprudence', the lecture given in 1954 to inaugurate his tenure of the Chair of Jurisprudence in Oxford. The allusion to Hart is not intended to imply that the writers discussed in this chapter anticipated Hart, nor that Hart was influenced by – or, even, interested in – their work. The point is rather to draw attention to the fact that such rich and searching investigations were being undertaken at a time when legal theory – on one view – was in the doldrums, in need of rescue.[89]

[88] See particularly Goodhart, 'The Foundation of Tortious Liability', 3.

[89] N. Duxbury, 'English Jurisprudence between Austin and Hart' (2005) 91 *Virginia Law Review* 1.

I suspect, however, that all the writers discussed in this chapter would have rejected (and perhaps resented) the label 'theoretical', regarding it as the antonym of 'useful'. Salmond was very clear that he wanted his work to be useful to practitioners and students. Pollock's attitude was similar. For instance, he made it clear that he retained the draft of the Indian tort code in later editions of his textbook on the grounds of its usefulness to the profession.[90] He was also careful to distance himself from teachers of law when reviewing Winfield's *The Province*. We might expect professional university academics to be more warmly inclined towards pure theory, but even in his most obviously theoretical work Winfield justified his investigations in pragmatic, practical terms.[91] The quotation used as the epigraph to this chapter typifies that defensive tone, and betrays a readiness to concede that the topic could be seen as inconsequential bickering between textbook writers. His textbook was almost apologetic on the subject, prefacing a discussion of the nature of tort liability with the explanation that 'a student is entitled to know what the author of a book is talking about'.[92] Sixteen closely argued pages later, we may feel that he had been too quick to anticipate customer complaints, but that the material was valuable on its own terms.

The emphasis on practicality and pragmatism did not stop at the authors' presentation of their own roles, but extended to the terms of their debates and their criteria of assessment. Thus, the theoretical implications and challenges of workmen's compensation for tort law were discussed not on their own terms, but in terms of what a book on tort law should contain. That, it turn, collapsed into an argument about how much could fit into a book.[93] Claims about the underlying structure of liability were attacked for their failure to predict the result in concrete cases.[94] Perhaps most tellingly, a writer might pretend to be a practitioner-insider, or might base a critique on what a practitioner might make of the work.[95] In other words, the debate about the nature and function of tort law was being obscured

[90] F. Pollock, *The Law of Torts*, 10th edn (London, Stevens and Sons, 1916) viii: 'I am assured on excellent Indian authority that magistrates and practitioners outside the Presidency have not ceased to find [the draft Code] useful as a compendious manual of principles.'

[91] Winfield, *The Province of the Law of Tort*, 1–2.

[92] Winfield, *A Text-Book of the Law of Tort*, 6.

[93] Landon, 'The Province of the Law of Tort', 31. Winfield, 'The Province of the Law of Tort: A Reply', 38.

[94] Goodhart, 'The Foundation of Tortious Liability', 3.

[95] Landon, 'The Province of the Law of Tort'. Winfield's reply ('The Province of the Law of Tort: A Reply') was careful to characterise Landon as a teacher (35) in Oxford (37, 38).

and distorted by the protagonists' own conceptions of their roles as legal writers, and their guesses about the demands of legal practice.

But despite the pressure towards an imagined legal practice, the work discussed in this chapter did manage to articulate competing accounts of the underlying structure and purposes of tort law. At the heart of the debate was the question whether, and if so, how, tort was responsive to its social context and the changing needs of the community it served. In the next chapter we shall investigate how tort responded to one of the most abrupt and radical social changes imaginable: war.

3

War

If hard cases make bad law, emergencies may make worse. Either the emergency is not allowed to disturb the permanent and immutable principles or else it smashes its way through them.

Cecil Carr

What legal problems does total war raise for the average man?

Thomas Lund and Eardley McDougall

I

Britain's involvement in two World Wars in the first half of the twentieth century precipitated dramatic political, social and cultural changes. Legal changes, such as they were, tended to be more subtle. Victorious states have no immediate need of new legal systems or constitutional arrangements in the aftermath of war, although wartime conditions may compel clarification of the legal basis of their activities.[1] Indeed, the legal system may seem to be an expression of the values that, with the benefit of hindsight, led to victory. When it comes to private law, the changes prompted by war tend to be marginal. The obvious examples would be refinements of the doctrine of frustration in the law of contract, or the principles governing the consequences of frustration in unjust enrichment. We do not expect tort to be affected, since civil wrongs go on with or without national war.

As this chapter shows, however, wartime conditions have had an important influence on tort liability that has been both diverse and complex. At one end of the spectrum is the invocation of 'permanent and immutable principles', as Cecil Carr described them in the passage used as an epigraph to this chapter.[2] On the surface this might seem to be an

[1] *Attorney-General* v. *De Keyser's Royal Hotel Limited* [1920] AC 508.

[2] C. Carr, 'Crisis Legislation in Britain' (1940) 40 *Columbia Law Review* 1309, 1309.

example of non-influence. But Carr is surely right to regard it as a choice on the part of the decision-maker not to 'allow' the wartime context to change the law. The alternative hypothesis – that the decision-maker was somehow ignorant of the context, or dismissed it out of hand, requires an assumption that the English judiciary was remote from society to an implausibly extreme extent. At the other end of the spectrum of influence is the tort development that, prompted by wartime conditions, 'smashes its way through' the existing principles. As we shall see, cases of motorists smashing into unlit air-raid shelters eventually fell into that category. In between these two extremes are two further situations. The first is where existing principles of liability are expanded so as to apply to novel wartime problems; the second is where the underlying bases of principles are clarified or elaborated as a result of wartime incidents. In both of these situations, the tort response to war is more subtle than in either of the extreme cases, but it is very revealing nonetheless. In particular, the immediate, pressing and national nature of the emergency seemed to prompt courts denying the claims of sympathetic claimants to formulate elaborate justifications for doing so. As a result the law developed – not in the sense that certain kinds of cases would now be decided differently, but in the sense that the underlying principles were now better articulated.

Having drawn on Cecil Carr's comments to explain the theme of this chapter, I should make clear at the outset that I would not apply Carr's assessment of crisis legislation to the common law. What the courts did was not worse than bad. Indeed, it was often characterised by careful, nuanced judgments about whether, and to what extent, emergency conditions should be allowed to influence tort liability.

II

Wartime decisions on defamation illustrate the range of careful judicial responses to emergency conditions. One group of cases concerns statements made in connection with judicial proceedings. By the start of the twentieth century it was well established that no liability in defamation arose where a person made a statement in the course of legal proceedings, whether as party, representative, judge or witness.[3] The House of Lords had extended the protection to preliminary statements by a decision in

[3] P. Mitchell, *The Making of the Modern Law of Defamation* (Oxford, Hart Publishing, 2005) chapter 10.

1905.[4] It was also clear that this protection was not confined to courts of law strictly defined; it was also available to participants in proceedings such as disciplinary tribunals. The Military Service Act 1916 created a new type of tribunal that was responsible for issuing certificates of exemption from military service. In *Copartnership Farms* v. *Harvey-Smith*[5] the question arose whether statements made in the course of such a tribunal's proceedings, by one of its members, were protected by absolute privilege. The answer turned on whether the tribunal operated 'in a manner similar to a court of justice'.[6]

Sankey J held that it did so operate. In coming to this conclusion he examined the tribunal's constitution, functions and procedure. So far as its constitution was concerned, the judge emphasised that the fact that the tribunal was appointed by a local authority did not automatically prevent it from being analogous to a court. Its decision-making functions resembled those of a court, as did the provision for a penalty for making false statements to the tribunal. Finally, its procedures were not sufficiently different to those of a court to make the analogy fail. Thus, the chairman's casting vote in the event of the tribunal being evenly split was a little troubling, but 'It would be extremely inconvenient if a tribunal sitting with twelve members should be equally divided with a necessity for a rehearing of the case at a time of national emergency'.[7] Similarly, the tribunal's power to hear 'such witnesses as they think fit' could be contrasted with the rules of evidence in mainstream courts, but ultimately this showed merely that the tribunal had greater powers than a court, not that it was essentially different from a court.

Whilst the *Copartnership Farms* case established absolute privilege for statements made by a member of the tribunal in the course of proceedings, the Court of Appeal's slightly later decision in *Gerhold* v. *Baker*[8] showed the limits of the courts' generosity. Here the claimant had applied for exemption from military service on the basis that he was producing food at his farm in Essex. A representative of the tribunal adjudicating on the claim wrote to the defendant, requesting assistance. The defendant, who was a member of the War Agricultural Committee for Essex and the representative of the Board of Agriculture at the tribunal, gave a disparaging assessment of the claimant's agricultural abilities. The Court of Appeal cursorily rejected the defendant's attempt to claim absolute privilege, holding that the only possible defence was qualified privilege (which,

[4] *Watson* v. *M'Ewen* [1905] AC 480. [5] [1918] 2 KB 405.
[6] [1918] 2 KB 405, 408. [7] [1918] 2 KB 405, 413. [8] [1918] WN 368.

unlike absolute privilege, was lost on proof of the defendant's malice). On the facts, they held, there was no evidence of malice, so the defence succeeded.

The final case to consider in relation to wartime tribunals is *Szalatnay-Stacho* v. *Fink*,[9] which concerned a letter written to the Military Office of the President of Czechoslovakia by the General Prosecutor of the Czechoslovak Military Court of Appeal. The letter drew attention to information received from soldiers, whose statements were enclosed, about acts of disloyalty and criminality by the claimant, who was at that time the Czechoslovakian government's Acting Minister in Cairo. The Court of Appeal rejected the attempt to claim absolute privilege for two reasons. First, since Czechoslovakia was under German occupation when the letter was sent, there were no Czech courts before which a trial of the claimant could take place. It was, therefore, impossible to regard the sending of the letter as a preliminary step in criminal proceedings. Second, the defendant was merely forwarding a dossier for investigation by the relevant authorities, which was too remote from any future legal proceedings to count as a step in those proceedings. As in *Gerhold* v. *Baker*, the Court of Appeal held that the appropriate defence was qualified privilege, the defendant here having a moral duty to pass on evidence about disloyalty by a government servant. There was no evidence of malice, so the claim failed.

These three cases demonstrate both the strengths and limitations of the courts' response to wartime conditions. Existing legal tests were capable of being applied to the new wartime tribunals but, significantly, the principles were not being used obstructively. Thus, the chairman's casting vote in the event of a tie was completely uncharacteristic of judicial decision-making, but that feature of the tribunal's power was seen in the context of the need for swift resolutions in a national emergency. On the other hand the courts were clearly wary – perhaps, in *Gerhold* v. *Baker*, too wary – of recognising situations of absolute privilege. This was surprising in the light of the House of Lords' recognition of absolute privilege for preliminary steps in litigation a few years earlier, and it is possible that the courts were concerned that the wartime context should not furnish a pretext for abuses of power by officials. The preference for qualified privilege, taking account of a defendant's malice, would offer a way to monitor such potential abuse. It is also difficult to avoid the feeling that the Court of Appeal's decision in the *Szalatnay-Stacho* case was excessively literal-

[9] [1947] KB 1.

minded. After all, it was hardly the defendant's fault that Czechoslovakia was under enemy occupation, and that there would, as a consequence, be a delay in bringing on criminal trials. The fact that there was no immediate criminal trial pending might have been thought less important than the need to review the evidence that might be relied on once criminal trials could resume. Perhaps here the wartime conditions should have been allowed a greater influence.

Two further defamation cases show traditional principles being applied to war-related situations. The first, *Winstanley* v. *Bampton*,[10] concerned a claim by a captain in the Army in respect of a letter written by the defendant, a captain in the Royal Navy, to the claimant's commanding officer. The letter criticised the claimant for being in arrears with rent owed to the defendant under the tenancy of a house. The claimant alleged that the letter imputed 'conduct unbecoming to an officer and a gentleman', and the military theme continued in the particulars of defence.[11] The defendant was seeking to rely on qualified privilege, which requires that the defendant have either a duty or interest in publishing the words and that the recipient should also have a corresponding duty or interest in receiving them. The obvious objection to such a defence on these facts was that the claimant's relationship with his landlord was none of his employer's business,[12] but the defendant submitted that things were different in the services. Lord Caldecote CJ agreed:

> The evidence of naval and military officers, who have had wide experience, satisfied me that a commanding officer in His Majesty's forces has an interest in seeing that officers, especially junior officers, serving under him do not incur debts which they are unable or unwilling to discharge, and I, therefore, think that the plaintiff's commanding officer had a common, or, as it is sometimes called, a corresponding, interest with that of the defendant in the payment of the plaintiff's debt.[13]

This is a revealing passage. The seniority and number of officers attending to give evidence hints that the military authorities regarded this as an important point. After all, it is not difficult to imagine that there were other demands on the time of military officers in February 1943. The Lord Chief Justice was clearly impressed by their evidence, and effectively

[10] [1943] KB 319; [1943] 1 All ER 661.
[11] [1943] KB 319, 320.
[12] See *Speake* v. *Hughes* [1904] 1 KB 138, where it seems to have been assumed that qualified privilege was unarguable on similar facts concerning a barman.
[13] [1943] KB 319, 322.

deferred to their view; there is no sense here that the existence of the privilege was a question of law that the judge should decide. On the contrary, the law should march in step with the military code of honour.

The text of the official report of the judgment in *Winstanley* v. *Bampton* ends on this satisfactorily triumphant note, but the attentive reader will spot that in fact the defence failed, and damages were awarded. The *All England Reports* provide a more complete account. As that report explains, the defendant had subsequently written to the letting agent of his house, expressing anxiety about whether the local shopkeeper might also be owed money by the claimant. In fact this 'aspersion' was completely unfounded and, in Viscount Caldecote CJ's view, it showed that the defendant 'had worked himself up into a state of indignation' and abused the privileged occasion.[14]

The two reports suggest contrasting impressions of the case: the Lord Chief Justice gives in the official report, and takes away in the *All England*. There are also very different senses of military discipline: the official report's emphasis on a code of honour and high standards is rather undermined by the *All England* revelations of pettiness and spite. Perhaps most importantly, given their readership, the two reports give subtly different impressions of what the law was. The official report suggests a defence of qualified privilege with firm foundations; the *All England* version, by contrast, suggests a defence vulnerable to judicial readiness to conjure up proof of malice from very little. These differences between the two reports raise questions about the official reporter's editorial decisions. Certainly the explanation cannot be reasons of space: the material on malice in the *All England* reports only occupies a page. Nor was the material lacking in intrinsic interest for lawyers, since it showed a court using extrinsic evidence to make a finding about the defendant's state of mind; the processes behind such a finding were typically unreportable because such decisions were usually made by juries. The most obvious explanation is that the reporter felt that he had covered the main point of the case. That was, on balance, highly debatable: it reflected a contested value-judgment about the court's reasoning on malice.

All of the cases examined in this section thus far have involved courts acknowledging and – to some extent – responding to wartime and military situations. The final case to be considered here is different. Its wartime factual basis was impossible to ignore, but it was decided by the application of a very traditional common law principle. To use, again, the

[14] [1943] 1 All ER 661, 664.

expression of Cecil Carr quoted in the epigraph to this chapter, the emergency was 'not allowed to disturb the permanent and immutable principles'. The case was *Knuppfer* v. *London Express Newspapers Ltd*, in which the defendant had published an article alleging that the 'Young Russian Party' was assisting Hitler.[15] The Party apparently had branches all over the world, and about 2,000 members; the claim was brought by the party's leader in Britain, where there were twenty-four members. He succeeded before Stable J, who awarded £3,500 damages, but lost in the Court of Appeal and House of Lords. Both appellate courts based their decisions on the principle that a member of a class could not generally sue for defamation of that class. For an individual to have a successful claim, they held, it was necessary to show that the particular individual was referred to in the defamatory language. That did not require reference by name, but a reference to a broad class could not be read as a reference to every single one of its members. It followed that the defamatory allegation about the Young Russian Party could not be taken to refer to all, or even the most prominent, of its members.

No political leader can want to be remembered for his failure as a libel litigant, but that was to be Mr Knuppfer's fate; today no one except law students and libel lawyers would recognise his name. The case he lost has come to epitomise the principle governing libel of a class and, as inevitably happens with landmark cases over time, has become detached from its context and stripped of its nuances. A careful reconstruction of the context and restoration of the nuances, however, reveals a more interesting picture. If we first examine the case in the terms that the appellate courts set out – as being about reference to the claimant – the position is more subtle than it first appears. The judges emphasised that the fundamental principle was, in Lord Atkin's words, whether 'the defamatory words must be understood to be published of and concerning the plaintiff'.[16] This suggested that the focus of the court's attention would be on responses by readers; but the evidence from four witnesses who said that they had understood the words as referring to the claimant was given no weight. As Lord Atkin went on to explain, the relevant response was that of a rather more discriminating reader:

> The reason why a libel published of a large or indeterminate number of persons described by some general name generally fails to be actionable is the difficulty of establishing that the plaintiff was, in fact, included in

[15] [1943] KB 80; [1944] AC 116.
[16] [1944] AC 116, 121.

> the defamatory statement, for the habit of making unfounded generalizations is ingrained in ill-educated or vulgar minds, or the words are occasionally intended to be a facetious exaggeration.[17]

In other words, reasonable readers would often discount generalisations, at least if those generalisations were uttered by people with ill-educated or vulgar minds, or were evidently intended to be facetious. A carefully considered assertion, however, would be different. Lord Porter, with whom Lord Atkin expressly concurred, gave the following example: 'I can imagine it being said that each member of a body, however large, was defamed where the libel consisted in the assertion that no one of the members of a community was elected as a member unless he had committed a murder.'[18] On a close reading of the judicial analysis, therefore, *Knuppfer*'s case rests on an unsteadiness about whose interpretation of the defamatory language is to be determinative – the answer seems to be not an actual reader, but an idealised, discriminating reader. The case also stands for a narrower proposition than is often assumed: only those generalisations that appear to emanate from ill-educated or vulgar minds, or are facetious exaggerations, fall outside the scope of the tort. As we shall see in Chapter 6, the connection between ill-educated vulgarity and newspapers was not only made by Lord Atkin, or confined to the judiciary.

When placed in a broader context, the decision in *Knuppfer* takes on an air of artificiality. As David Riesman had pointed out in the *Columbia Law Review* in 1942, the law's insistence on a dispassionate, discriminating reader in circumstances such as *Knuppfer* was 'much too rationalistic'.[19] The reality, as Riesman forcefully explained, was that contemporary political rhetoric traded in generalisations that were effective precisely because of their sweeping, apparently revelatory power. Riesman's work also drew attention to political parties' readiness to exploit the law of defamation in order to gain public attention, make money and give policies an appearance of legitimacy.[20] These issues must surely have been in the background in *Knuppfer*'s case. Indeed, the courts may have been relieved that they could take refuge in legal arguments about the meaning of words, rather than becoming embroiled in political wrangling.

[17] [1944] AC 116, 122. [18] [1944] AC 116, 124.

[19] D. Riesman, 'Democracy and Defamation: Control of Group Libel' (1942) 42 *Columbia Law Review* 727, 770.

[20] See also D. Riesman, 'Democracy and Defamation: Fair Game and Fair Comment I' (1942) 42 *Columbia Law Review* 1085, and 'Democracy and Defamation: Fair Game and Fair Comment II' (1942) 42 *Columbia Law Review* 1282. Riesman's later work in sociology focussed on groups.

III

Wartime conditions do not lead to an inevitable increase in the number, or severity, of defamatory publications. The position is very different for personal injuries, to which we now turn. Mass casualties are inevitable, and it might be expected that one consequence of this would be a lessening in judicial enthusiasm to award damages. That, at any rate, seems to have been Lord Hoffmann's understanding. In *White* v. *Chief Constable of South Yorkshire*[21] he commented that the House of Lords' 1942 decision in *Bourhill* v. *Young*,[22] which denied liability to a woman suffering psychiatric injury following a road accident, was based on 'a robust wartime view of the ability of the ordinary person to suffer horror and bereavement without ill effect'.[23] The point was, apparently, about distributive justice – a topic to which he returned later in his speech in that case: the argument for recognising liability for a new kind of damage was less compelling when made in a world where devastating personal injuries were being suffered daily.

This is, of course, a powerful point, but its force depends on what the law does about those war injuries. Clearly there was nothing to be gained by suing the enemy in negligence. But that did not exhaust the possibilities. Service personnel were eligible for war pensions, although the requirement that the injury be caused by war service could present analytical difficulties.[24] The treatment of civilians changed dramatically between the First and Second World Wars. The 4,500 people killed or wounded on British soil by German bombs in the First World War received no government compensation.[25] They also failed to make out any claim over money paid to the British government under the terms of the Treaty of Versailles as war reparations.[26] In the Second World War the position was very different. Civilians injured by enemy action were entitled to compensation under a scheme created by the Personal Injuries (Emergency Provisions) Act 1939. Section 3 of the Act abolished parallel claims for workmen's compensation, negligence, nuisance and breach of statutory duty. As Morris Finer, writing in the *Modern Law Review*, put it, 'the Scheme raises a national responsibility for civilian injury in war time, which responsibility should

[21] [1999] 2 AC 455. [22] [1943] AC 92. [23] [1999] 2 AC 455, 501.

[24] *W* v. *Minister of Pensions* [1946] 2 All ER 501.

[25] M. Finer, 'The Personal Injuries (Civilians) Scheme, 1941' (1941–1942) 5 *MLR* 224.

[26] *Civilian War Claimants Association, Limited* v. *The King* [1932] AC 14.

be discharged by speedy administrative action, and not be subjected to the dangers, delays and uncertainties of litigation'.[27]

Judges generally took a broad approach to interpreting the scheme. Thus, only 'physical' injuries were eligible for compensation,[28] but the courts were sympathetic to sufferers from post-traumatic stress disorder. In *ex parte Haines*[29] a fireman who suffered 'nervous debility' after attending at the scene of a heavy bombing raid had been denied compensation on the basis that he had suffered no trauma. Tucker J held that trauma was not necessary: 'a man may suffer serious physical harm or injury, for example, from strain, exposure or shock, without any trauma.'[30] The Court of Session went further, characterising a claimant's psychiatric illness as physical injury to the nerves.[31]

The dominant approach to causation was similarly broad. A quartet of decisions by Denning J established that the chain of causation between enemy act and civilian injury was not broken by the acts of curious children (or adults); injuries suffered in taking cover from enemy attack were included in the scheme; and, perhaps most importantly, so long as the enemy action was *a cause* of the damage, the presence of other contributory causes was irrelevant.[32] This latter point had been the subject of doubt, with the Court of Appeal taking a narrower view.[33] Denning J, however, claimed that, although the House of Lords had not expressly said so, its decision in *Adams* v. *Naylor*[34] was inconsistent with the Court of Appeal's narrower interpretation of causation under the compensation scheme.[35] Denning's view was accepted,[36] and the upshot was that the compensation scheme extended to a wide range of personal injuries.

There were, of course, some limits, and these are particularly important for us since they mark the point at which claimants must rely on tort law, or some other basis of liability such as workmen's compensation. One important limit concerned causation. Multiple interventions between enemy action and civilian injury could break the chain of causation, as

27 Finer, 'The Personal Injuries (Civilians) Scheme, 1941', 231.

28 Personal Injuries (Emergency Provisions) Act 1939 s. 8.

29 [1945] 1 KB 183.

30 [1945] 1 KB 183, 188.

31 *Carlin* v. *Donaldson Atlantic Line, Limited* 1943 SC 172.

32 *Minister of Pensions* v. *Ffrench* [1946] 1 KB 260; *Minister of Pensions* v. *Chennell* [1947] 1 KB 250; *Minister of Pensions* v. *Williams* [1947] 1 KB 875; *Evans* v. *Minister of Pensions* [1948] 1 KB 1.

33 *Greenfield* v. *London and North Eastern Railway Company* [1945] 1 KB 89.

34 [1946] AC 543.

35 *Minister of Pensions* v. *Chennell* [1947] 1 KB 250, 256–7.

36 *Howgate* v. *Bagnall* [1951] 1 KB 265.

it did in *Smith* v. *Davey Paxman (Colchester) Ltd*.[37] There, a small metal object had been found by a boy at the site of a crashed German aircraft. The boy took it to the defendant's engineering works, where it was passed around and inspected by the engineers. One toolmaker decided to investigate further, by sawing the object apart. The resulting explosion killed him and injured the nearby claimant, a fellow employee. The Court of Appeal held that the chain of causation was broken. It was also possible for lapse of time and inactivity to break the chain, as in *Pope* v. *St Helen's Theatre Limited*,[38] where the impact of a bomb falling near to the defendant's cinema had disturbed plaster on the ceiling and – five years later – the plaster fell on the claimant cinema-goer. Finally, there were limitations inherent in the statutory language defining the acts that triggered compensation:

> physical injuries –
> (a) caused by –
> (i) the discharge of any missile ... or
> (ii) the use of any weapon, explosive or other noxious thing; or
> (iii) the doing of any other injurious act;
>
> either by the enemy or in combating the enemy or in repelling an imagined attack by the enemy.[39]

For our purposes, perhaps the most significant limitation derived from this section established that injuries caused by the blackout were not covered by the scheme. The blackout was not a 'weapon', nor were the measures taken pursuant to it 'injurious' acts, since they were neither 'intended to cause injury, nor is their natural and probable consequence to cause injury'.[40] Nevertheless, as we shall see, a large number of people were killed or injured during the blackout; for them, the law of tort offered the only compensation.

IV

Blackout regulations prohibited street lighting and prescribed a very low level of vehicle lighting.[41] The road traffic accidents that inevitably ensued raised legal issues about the standard of care, contributory negligence and, most controversially, the duty to take positive steps to avoid damage. The standard of care was relatively easily adapted. As one Scottish court

37 [1943] 1 All ER 286. 38 [1947] 1 KB 30.
39 Personal Injuries (Emergency Provisions) Act 1939, s. 8(1)(a).
40 *Minister of Pensions* v. *Ffrench* [1946] 1 KB 260.
41 Lighting (Restrictions) Order 1939 (St R & O 1939, no. 1098).

put it, 'blackout conditions involve a new factor in the performance of the duty to take reasonable care' by requiring 'a higher standard of vigilance'.[42] Another Scottish court was even prepared to contemplate that reasonable care required a driver to be able to stop within the limits of his vision; in blackout conditions that rule would impose a significant obligation on motorists.[43]

However, the burden was not all on motorists. The leading English Court of Appeal case, *Franklin* v. *Bristol Tramways and Carriage Company, Limited*,[44] recognised that pedestrians had 'a new duty of bearing in mind the difficulty which the driver of an oncoming vehicle must have in seeing a person or vehicle bearing no light'.[45] Glanville Williams regarded the case as establishing 'no new principle',[46] and that was true, but it was acknowledged elsewhere that *Franklin*'s case rebalanced the onus of responsibility between driver and pedestrian. Scottish judges commented on the 'the higher standard' and 'very high degree of duty' required of pedestrians towards motorists.[47] Pedestrians were also expected to be alert to obstructions on the pavement.[48] Cyclists' obligations underwent a similar reassessment, but with less stringent results. The English Court of Appeal went out of its way to retain a test of fault that was fact-sensitive, rejecting in the process the proposition that contributory negligence could be equated with the inability to stop within the cyclist's range of vision.[49] Scottish judges were prepared to go further, and to emphasise a cyclist's failure to carry prescribed lighting, so that 'drivers generally were entitled to expect that cyclists travelling … on roads frequented by motor traffic would obey the law by carrying the prescribed lights, and were entitled to rely upon their so doing'.[50] The Scots approach hinted at a relationship between statutory regulation and tort duties that was not pursued by the English courts in relation to

[42] *M'Geown* v. *Greenock Motor Services Company* 1943 SC 33, 42 (Lord Wark).

[43] *Griffiths* v. *W Alexander & Sons Limited* 1941 SLT 66. Cf *Morris* v. *Luton Corporation* [1946] 1 KB 114.

[44] [1941] 1 KB 255. [45] [1941] 1 KB 255, 256.

[46] G. Williams, 'Negligence and Contributory Negligence – Collision during Blackout' (1941–1942) 5 *MLR* 71.

[47] *M'Geown* v. *Greenock Motor Services Company* 1943 SC 33, 37 (Lord Justice-Clerk Cooper) and 43 (Lord Jamieson).

[48] *Jelley* v. *Ilford Borough Council* [1941] 2 All ER 468.

[49] *Morris* v. *Luton Corporation* [1946] 1 KB 114. The issue of contributory negligence seems not to have been raised in *Fox* v. *Newcastle-Upon-Tyne Corporation* [1941] 2 KB 120.

[50] *Connachan* v. *Scottish Motor Traction Company, Limited* 1946 SC 428, 435 (Lord Justice-Clerk Cooper).

cyclists, but which became central to questions about local authorities' duties to light obstructions.

V

The earliest case to address a local authority's responsibilities in respect of dangerous obstructions was *Morrison* v. *Lord Mayor &c of Sheffield*.[51] There the defendant, exercising statutory powers, had planted trees in streets; the trees had been surrounded with guards made from iron posts. To deter children from climbing on the guards, the posts ended in spikes, which were bent down. In 1916 the chief constable of Sheffield, acting under the Defence of the Realm regulations, ordered that street lamps be extinguished after a certain hour. The unfortunate claimant was walking along a Sheffield street at 9 p.m., after the lights had been extinguished, and collided with a spiked guard. The jury found that the guard was dangerous in the circumstances, and the defendant ought to have neutralised it. The defendants appealed, arguing that having erected the guard when it was safe to do so, it owed no duty to take positive steps after the lighting order was imposed. The Court of Appeal disagreed: the obligation to take reasonable care 'continues as long as the trees and guards are maintained in the public highway'.[52] Pickford LJ was careful to point out that he appreciated the potential consequences of the decision:

> It is said that our decision will involve a hardship on local authorities and will impose on them an obligation to guard or to paint every post and kerb, but in truth it only imposes an obligation to take reasonable care that what they have put in the roadway shall not become a nuisance and a danger under altered conditions.[53]

Morrison's case took up only seven pages of the law reports, of which the judgments occupied four. But the clarity and brevity came at a price. The court had recognised an exception to the general rule that there was no duty to take positive steps, but there was no analysis of why this situation was special. There was also an eerie lack of authority to support the assertions about continuing duties. Nor was it clear what role the lighting restrictions had to play in the analysis of tortious duties. It was possible to infer – from the lack of discussion of the regulations – that the Court of Appeal regarded them as irrelevant, but some analysis of the issue would surely have been helpful, and it was unconvincing to exclude

[51] [1917] 2 KB 866. [52] [1917] 2 KB 866, 870 (Viscount Reading CJ).
[53] [1917] 2 KB 866, 872.

them altogether. At the very least, it is difficult to imagine that the court was envisaging a tortious duty that conflicted with those regulations.

In one respect, however, the Court of Appeal in *Morrison* did make clear how its analysis fitted into the wider picture, because it was careful to distinguish a recent House of Lords decision in *Great Central Railway Company* v. *Hewlett*.[54] That case had not involved the liability of a local authority, but it did concern a collision occurring during lighting restrictions between a user of the highway and an obstruction in his path. The obstruction was a wooden post, the presence and precise position of which was expressly permitted by a special Act of Parliament. The claimant's claim failed, and two grounds for this result could be identified in the speeches. First, although a person exercising a statutory power owed a duty not to injure others by doing so negligently, that principle only held true for positive, overt acts. Here the defendant's exercise of statutory power had been purely passive. Second, the specific, precise terms of the special Act were to be contrasted with broader powers. Parliament could be taken to permit the specific state of affairs identified in the special Act; but when a defendant had choices about how to exercise powers conferred, Parliament could not be presumed to have authorised carelessness. This second ground was the basis on which the Court of Appeal in *Morrison* felt able to distinguish *Hewlett*, but it is not clear that, as a matter of authority, it was entitled to do so, as the point about the specific nature of the statutory authority in *Hewlett*'s case had been made only by Lord Sumner.[55] The two other Law Lords hearing the case had based their decision on the absence of a positive act of negligence.[56] If this was the true basis of the decision in *Hewlett*'s case, it was rather more difficult to distinguish it from *Morrison*, as later judges would find.

The scope of the *Morrison* principle was clarified in *Sheppard* v. *Mayor, Aldermen and Burgesses of the Borough of Glossop*,[57] where the Court of Appeal emphasised that Sheffield Corporation had failed to light fences that it had previously erected. There was no duty to light where the local authority had not created the obstruction. Scrutton LJ also took the opportunity to reaffirm that *Hewlett*'s case turned on express statutory authorisation of the obstacle.[58] It therefore seemed that the principle from *Morrison* v. *Lord Mayor &c of Sheffield* was coming to dominate. But two

[54] [1916] 2 AC 511. [55] [1916] 2 AC 511, 523–4.

[56] [1916] 2 AC 511, 519–20 (Lord Parker), 525 (Lord Wrenbury: 'it is impossible to be negligent in not doing anything').

[57] [1921] 3 KB 132. [58] [1921] 3 KB 132, 148.

other developments highlighted that the law was not yet settled. In *Baldock* v. *Westminster City Council*[59] the claimant's taxi had been damaged in a collision with an unlit street refuge. The refuge, like other refuges in the borough, had previously been lit, but on the night of the accident the light had gone out. The question for the Court of Appeal was whether the jury's verdict for the claimant at the trial was against the evidence, and whilst Scrutton LJ was content to point out the factual similarity to *Morrison*'s case, Bankes LJ, with whom Warrington LJ agreed, felt that an explanation of the basis of the defendant's duty was needed. The duty was, he said, 'self-imposed':

> If a local authority consistently lights all the shelters in its streets, it does publicly indicate to the persons who are in the habit of traversing those streets that the shelters are still lighted, and if it comes to the knowledge of the local authority that the lights which they so provide are untrustworthy or erratic, and are sometimes out and sometimes on, the local authority, as it seems to me, are providing something which is in the nature of a trap to the travelling public, because the public are allowed to believe that the shelters are lighted, and to the knowledge of the local authority they are sometimes lighted and sometimes not.[60]

A different, but equally significant concern was highlighted by *Carpenter* v. *Finsbury Borough Council*.[61] There the claimant's husband had been killed when, driving his van down a street at night when lighting restrictions were in force, he had collided with a low arch. Shearman J held the authority liable for negligently failing to provide adequate lighting, in breach of its statutory duty.

Both cases hinted at the difficulties that lay in the background of *Morrison* v. *Lord Mayor &c of Sheffield*. Bankes LJ's (over-)elaborate attempt in *Baldock* v. *Westminster City Council* to conjure up a representation that street refuges would always be lit was vulnerable to at least three powerful objections. First, it was simply implausible: why would lighting a street refuge today necessarily imply a promise to do so tomorrow? Second, the rationale of the rule led to capricious results: a claimant visiting the borough for the first time, or simply unaware of the past practice of illuminating refuges, could not claim to have been misled by that past practice; he would therefore be unable to claim. Third, the rule invited a cynical response from local authorities: if you turn off all the lights, no one can complain that they expected the lights to be on. Why, then, did

[59] [1918–19] All ER Rep 430. [60] [1918–19] All ER Rep 430, 432.
[61] [1920] 2 KB 195.

Bankes LJ choose to advance this analysis based on representations, when the less complicated approach from *Morrison*'s case was to hand? The answer, surely, is that Bankes LJ's approach, contrived as it was, at least based liability on a positive act of misrepresentation. The contrived artificiality of the analysis was a price he was willing to pay to avoid imposing liability for a careless omission.

The reasoning in *Carpenter* was far less elaborate than that of Bankes LJ in *Baldock*'s case, but its breezy imposition of liability for negligent breach of statutory duty was disconcerting. In *Morrison*, it may be recalled, statutory duties and powers played no part in the analysis. The explanation for the contrast may, in part, be geographical: London metropolitan authorities were under a duty to provide street lighting, whereas other authorities merely had the power to do so.[62] There was, therefore, no question of liability for breach of statutory duty in *Morrison*'s case. But the larger question, which neither court addressed, was how questions of duty, and breach of duty, could be compatible with obedience to regulatory lighting restrictions.

VI

The litigation generated by First World War lighting restrictions had established that liability was owed by local authorities to highway users, although the analytical basis for such liability was hardly compelling, and there were some loose ends. When lighting restrictions became necessary again, in September 1939, and the inevitable accidents and litigation followed, the courts were called on to review their earlier efforts. As we shall see, the five years of case law culminating in *Fisher* v. *Ruislip-Northwood Urban District Council*[63] were an extraordinarily volatile period, in which previously certain positions unravelled, and liability was consistently denied; but then the Court of Appeal overruled three of its own recent decisions, and recognised a duty by a new route.

The first case in the process of reassessment arose within a couple of hours of lighting restrictions being imposed, when the taxi in which P. A. Wodehouse was travelling collided with an unilluminated street refuge. The claimant sued the taxi-driver in negligence and the local authority for both negligence and breach of its statutory duty under the Metropolis

[62] The point is made particularly emphatically in *Sheppard* v. *Mayor, Aldermen and Burgesses of the Borough of Glossop* [1921] 3 KB 132, 144 (Scrutton LJ).

[63] [1945] 1 KB 584.

Management Act 1855, s. 130, which imposed the duty to see that the streets were 'well and sufficiently lighted'.[64] Cassels J found in the claimant's favour, rejecting the argument that the lighting restrictions regulations implicitly repealed the statutory duty. In the judge's view the lighting restrictions had modified, rather than eliminated, the duty to provide lighting. It followed that the local authority could not be criticised for failing to light the street lamps – that was prohibited by paragraph 1 of the Lighting (Restrictions) Order 1939 – but that it should have provided lighting on obstructions, as permitted by paragraph 4 of the Order. The local authority appealed.

Before the appeal was heard, the Court of Appeal decided *Greenwood* v. *Central Service Company Limited*,[65] which raised the identical issue of breach of statutory duty. It ruled that the Lighting (Restrictions) Order's prohibition on street lighting temporarily repealed the 1855 statutory duty to light; and that the Order's provisions on lighting obstructions were permissive, rather than mandatory. As the Court of Appeal acknowledged, it followed that the decision in *Wodehouse* v. *Levy* on breach of statutory duty was incorrect, although the case was not necessarily wrongly decided: a decision in the claimant's favour, said Mackinnon LJ and Luxmoore LJ, might still be supported on the ground of negligence.[66]

Just over a month later the appeal in *Wodehouse* v. *Levy* was heard.[67] It turned out that Mackinnon LJ and Luxmoore LJ had been too sanguine about the strength of the negligence claim: the same two judges now rejected it. Mackinnon LJ took the view that this result flowed from the fact that the statutory duty to light under the Metropolis Management Act had been temporarily repealed: 'if there is any obligation to light [the obstruction]', he said, 'that … must be discovered from some statute'.[68] The common law options, in his view, were excluded by *Hewlett*'s case. Luxmoore LJ placed *Hewlett*'s case at the centre of his analysis – indeed, he explained away the Court of Appeal's earlier readiness to contemplate a duty in negligence by its having overlooked the importance of that case.[69] He also explained that the 'self-imposed duty' set out by Bankes LJ in *Baldock* v. *Westminster City Council* could not be applied since here, the incident having taken place on the very first night of the blackout, there had been no past practice of lighting obstructions by which highway users could have been misled.[70]

[64] *Wodehouse* v. *Levy* [1940] 2 KB 298. [65] [1940] 2 KB 447.
[66] [1940] 2 KB 447, 462 (Luxmoore LJ), 464 (Mackinnon LJ).
[67] [1940] 2 KB 561. [68] [1940] 2 KB 561, 564. [69] [1940] 2 KB 561, 567.
[70] [1940] 2 KB 561, 568.

Only three months had passed between Cassels J's decision in *Wodehouse* v. *Levy* and its reversal by the Court of Appeal. In that short period the Court of Appeal had demolished its own previous position that a duty to take positive steps was owed by local authorities to road users. But the manner in which it had done so – with the two leading judges changing their minds in the space of a month – hardly inspired confidence. And whilst the earlier position had had its analytical weaknesses (see section V), the new approach was scarcely an improvement. Its most obvious defect was that it took no account of – indeed, did not even *mention* – *Morrison* v. *Lord Mayor, &c of Sheffield*,[71] which was the cornerstone of the view that there was a duty of care in negligence. The failure to deal with *Morrison*'s case also meant that there was no engagement with how that case had interpreted *Great Central Railway Company* v. *Hewlett*.[72] Indeed, there is no sense at all that there was controversy about what *Hewlett*'s case had decided. There was at least more of an attempt in the earliest Second World War cases to explore the relationship between the lighting regulations and tortious duties, but the diametrically opposed views of Cassels J and Mackinnon LJ seem merely to mark out contrasting positions rather than identifying any broader underlying principle. Behind these different positions were very different, but unarticulated, assumptions about the role of tortious obligations in situations already covered by regulations.

The Court of Appeal's decision in *Wodehouse* v. *Levy* settled the question of a local authority's duty to light obstructions, at least for the moment. But lighting was not the only way in which potential blackout injuries could be avoided; painting the obstruction white could work just as well in some circumstances. In *Lyus* v. *Stepney Borough Council*,[73] decided three weeks after the Court of Appeal's decision in *Wodehouse*, the claimant had found himself in such a situation, having walked into a sandbin on the pavement. The sandbin had been placed on the pavement in 1936, pursuant to statutory powers. There was no dispute that, under ordinary lighting conditions, its presence was perfectly legitimate. The question was whether the local council had an obligation to take positive steps to prevent the bin being a danger during the blackout. Humphreys J concluded that it both owed such a duty and had breached it. The duty analysis was based on the principle that an authority must exercise its statutory powers with reasonable care, a principle supported by selective

71 [1917] 2 KB 866. 72 [1916] 2 AC 511.

73 [1940] 2 KB 662; [1941] 1 KB 134.

quotation from *Hewlett*'s case.[74] *Morrison* v. *Lord Mayor &c of Sheffield* was cited, and the decision in *Wodehouse* distinguished, as being concerned with an obligation to *light*, not to *paint*.[75]

The Court of Appeal, in a judgment delivered by Luxmoore LJ, allowed the defendant's appeal.[76] It described Humphreys J as having 'refused to follow'[77] *Wodehouse*, and criticised his use of *Hewlett*'s case. The key point about *Hewlett*'s case, it said, was that no liability arose from failing to act when the initial placement of an obstruction was legitimate. Here the council's alleged negligence, in leaving the unmarked sandbin on the pavement, had not been involved in 'any active operation'.[78] *Morrison*'s case could only be explained as a situation where placing spiked railings at eye-level was, in itself, illegitimate from the start.[79] The court would also have overturned the finding of breach of duty on the ground that it was not reasonable to expect the council to have painted a sandbin in a side street within fifteen days of lighting restrictions being imposed. It is interesting to note that Humphreys J had been absolutely certain that a jury would have regarded fifteen days as 'ample time' to apply 'a great splash of whitewash'.[80]

After the decision in *Lyus* v. *Stepney Borough Council* a local authority's potential liability for blackout injuries was very limited. It could not be made liable for failing to provide lights; nor did it owe a duty of care to mark things that had become dangerous obstacles in the blackout. This position was the exact opposite of what it had been five months earlier. At that point the leading case was *Morrison* v. *Lord Mayor &c of Sheffield*, but the later developments had either overlooked or marginalised that decision. There was, however, still the potential for liability in two situations. The first was where an authority's past practice of lighting obstructions gave rise to a 'self-imposed duty' to continue lighting them. The second was where the authority's own active operation, combined with the blackout, caused the accident. The Court of Appeal's emphasis on the absence of active operation in *Lyus*'s case seemed to indicate that this category of duty was well established.

But Mackinnon LJ and Luxmoore LJ had a rather unfortunate habit of changing their mind. In *Fox* v. *Newcastle-Upon-Tyne Corporation*,[81] decided six months after *Lyus* v. *Stepney Borough Council*, an authority was sued in negligence for having constructed an unlit, unmarked

74 [1940] 2 KB 662, 663. 75 [1940] 2 KB 662, 666–7.
76 [1941] 1 KB 134. 77 [1941] 1 KB 134, 143.
78 [1941] 1 KB 134, 150. 79 [1941] 1 KB 134, 151.
80 [1940] 2 KB 662, 668. 81 [1941] 2 KB 120.

air-raid shelter in the middle of the street, with which the claimant cyclist had collided. The construction of the shelter had occurred after lighting restrictions had been introduced. Mackinnon LJ, with whom Luxmoore LJ agreed, held that the case was governed by the earlier decisions in *Wodehouse* v. *Levy*,[82] *Greenwood* v. *Central Service Company Limited*[83] and *Lyus* v. *Stepney Borough Council*.[84] The timing of the defendant's operations made no difference: it would have 'startling consequences' if a duty arose only in respect of obstructions created after the blackout was imposed.[85] Du Parcq LJ dissented. The principle established in *Lyus* v. *Stepney*, he pointed out, had emphasised timing. Nor were the consequences alarming – the duty simply called for 'reasonable intelligence' on the part of the authorities.[86] He also took the opportunity to endorse a narrow interpretation of *Great Central Railway* v. *Hewlett*, namely that the decision turned on the specific authority granted by the statute in question.

There seems to have been an immediate and widespread feeling that, with the decision in *Fox*, the law had taken a wrong turn. Goddard LJ called for the cases decided since 1940 to receive 'further consideration'.[87] I. C. Matson, writing in the *Modern Law Review*, argued that the logic of du Parcq LJ's dissenting judgment was compelling, and deliberately went further than Goddard LJ by saying that it was of 'paramount importance' that the law should be settled.[88] Matson also developed a point that had first been suggested in *Lyus* v. *Stepney Borough Council* by Humphreys J, which was that the legal rules were becoming detached from the expectations of those to whom they applied. As Matson put it, 'It would ill become the courts to lower the duty which in all these cases local authorities have realised (shown by the steps they have taken) to be imposed upon them in the interest of the communities they serve.'[89] The argument here deliberately slides between two senses of duty – the legal duty to pay compensatory damages, and what we might call a public or moral duty to make the authority's area safe. Essentially he was arguing that the moral duty should inform the legal duty in this context.

[82] [1940] 2 KB 561. [83] [1940] 2 KB 447. [84] [1941] 1 KB 134.

[85] *Fox* v. *Newcastle-Upon-Tyne Corporation* [1941] 2 KB 120, 124.

[86] [1941] 2 KB 120, 134.

[87] *Foster* v. *Gillingham Corporation* [1942] 1 All ER 304, 306.

[88] I. C. Matson, 'Black-Out Restrictions: Duty of Local Authorities to Light Obstructions in the Highway' (1941–1942) 5 *MLR* 248, 251.

[89] *Ibid.*, 251.

Wolfgang Friedmann took the critique a stage further.[90] He regarded the lighting restrictions cases as irretrievably conflicted, and argued that the fundamental issue had been lost sight of, that issue being 'the extent to which public authorities must remain unhampered by private liabilities in the exercise of a social function as defined by Parliament'.[91] For Friedmann, the blackout cases all fell within the well-recognised category of occupier's liability for creating a trap, and it made no difference when the obstruction in question had been created. '[O]nly a lingering of the discredited distinction between misfeasance and non-feasance' stood in the way of such a broad duty.[92] Friedmann also made an interesting point about public perceptions: 'Neither the Courts nor the public are likely to advocate any relaxation of legal duties and liabilities in favour of public authorities.'[93]

Matson had pinned his hopes on an appeal to the House of Lords in *Fox*'s case.[94] But, although leave was granted, that appeal never materialised, and it was left to the Court of Appeal, in *Fisher* v. *Ruislip-Northwood Urban District Council*, to sort things out.[95] The facts were materially identical to *Fox* v. *Newcastle-Upon-Tyne Corporation*, but the outcome was the opposite: a duty of care was owed, irrespective of the date at which the obstruction was first created. Lord Greene MR's leading speech contained a lengthy and skilful analysis of the authorities. *Morrison* v. *Lord Mayor &c of Sheffield*, he concluded, was 'manifestly right';[96] *Great Central Railway* v. *Hewlett* was binding on the Court of Appeal, but turned on the special statutory provision involved. When he turned to the Court of Appeal's decision in *Wodehouse* v. *Levy*, the range of his critique broadened. From an analytical perspective he criticised the Court's focus on a duty to *light*; the more appropriate analysis was to focus on a duty to take reasonable steps to avoid damage to the public.[97] But the broader issue was the way that the denial of a duty of care in *Wodehouse* clashed with social norms and practices. Thus, he observed that 'it would violate one's sense of good citizenship to hold that the authority could erect a refuge in an unlighted street and take no steps to warn the public of its existence'.[98] Furthermore, authorities had already demonstrated their own sense of good citizenship by lighting obstructions or painting them white. 'It is

[90] W. Friedmann, 'Statutory Powers and Legal Duties of Local Authorities' (1945) 8 *MLR* 31.

[91] *Ibid.*, 32. [92] *Ibid.*, 43. [93] *Ibid.*, 43.

[94] Matson, 'Black-Out Restrictions', 251.

[95] [1945] 1 KB 584. [96] [1945] 1 KB 584, 599.

[97] [1945] 1 KB 584, 593. [98] [1945] 1 KB 584, 593.

sometimes surprising to the lawyer', he observed, 'to find how often the practice of reasonably-minded men marches in conformity with their legal obligations.'[99] Thankfully, there was no evidence that the decision in *Wodehouse* v. *Levy* had influenced authorities' performance of their duties: 'if the view expressed in *Wodehouse* v. *Levy* were correct, and local authorities in the Metropolitan area had acted upon it (which happily they did not), the streets of London would have been littered with smashed vehicles and the bodies of their occupants.'[100] The potential for tort liability to distort an authority's performance of its role also explained why no distinction should be made between obstructions created before lighting restrictions were introduced and those created afterwards:

> I see no principle which could justify it and it would lead to the most remarkable results. A motorist who was prudent enough to select as his objective a shelter erected after the restrictions came into force could recover, while his less prudent brother could not. The spectacle of a local authority carefully lighting the one set of shelters and refraining from lighting the other (as on the argument it would be entitled to do) would not be an edifying one, and here again it is fortunate that local authorities have taken a stricter view of their obligations to the public.[101]

In conclusion, Lord Greene MR availed himself of the Court of Appeal's recently acquired power to overrule its own prior decisions[102] and 'unhesitatingly'[103] followed *Morrison* v. *Lord Mayor &c of Sheffield* in preference to *Wodehouse* v. *Levy*, *Lyus* v. *Stepney Borough Council* and *Fox* v. *Newcastle-Upon-Tyne Corporation*. Mackinnon LJ concurred, acknowledging that 'that is equivalent to saying, in the circumstances, "Peccavi"'.[104]

Both the result and the method of reaching it were significant. The court's readiness to overrule three of its own recent decisions was a dramatic illustration of the effects of the new-found flexibility introduced less than a year earlier by *Young* v. *Bristol Aeroplane Company, Limited*[105] – as A. L. Goodhart commented, with the decision in *Fisher* 'the whole picture suddenly changed'.[106] More importantly, the case said something quite striking about the kinds of reasons that would persuade the Court of Appeal to prefer one decision over another. It was not significant, for instance, which side had the larger number of supporting authorities, or

[99] [1945] 1 KB 584, 605. [100] [1945] 1 KB 584, 606.
[101] [1945] 1 KB 584, 611.
[102] *Young* v. *Bristol Aeroplane Company, Limited* [1944] 1 KB 718.
[103] *Fisher* v. *Ruislip-Northwood Urban District Council* [1945] 1 KB 584, 617.
[104] [1945] 1 KB 584, 618–19. [105] [1944] 1 KB 718.
[106] A. L. Goodhart, 'Precedents in the Court of Appeal' (1945–1947) 9 *CLJ* 349, 356.

that *Wodehouse* v. *Levy* and *Lyus* v. *Stepney Borough Council* derived direct support from the majority of the House of Lords in *Great Central Railway* v. *Hewlett*. There was not even an express allusion to the potential injustice to parties who might have relied on the trio of now overruled decisions, although we might read Lord Greene's praise for authorities' refusal to change their practices as anticipating a point about reliance. What was at the forefront of the court's reasoning was less formalistic, indeed in some ways it was an extra-legal critique of the legal rules. This could be seen most clearly in the appeal to ideals of good citizenship, and in the nightmarish vision of 'the streets of London … littered with smashed vehicles and the bodies of their occupants'. Lord Greene's awareness that he was deliberately adopting an external perspective was revealed in his comment that 'It is sometimes surprising to the lawyer to find how often the practice of reasonably-minded men marches in conformity with their legal obligations'. The military metaphor was a nice wartime touch, but the key point here was that Lord Greene clearly did not identify himself with 'the lawyer'; but if the Master of the Rolls was not a lawyer, what, exactly, was he? We might also note that Lord Greene continued to vacate his lawyer persona when he elaborated the hypothetical example of two drivers colliding with shelters erected at different times. The sardonic tone of those examples and their ridiculous effect rests on each driver *choosing* what kind of obstacle to collide with. But, as Lord Greene would obviously have known, neither of his imagined drivers would have been able to claim in that situation, because their claims would have failed either on causation of damage, or on *volenti*, or on contributory negligence (which, at that time, was a complete defence). There is a sense of playing to the gallery, at the expense of accurate – and, more compelling – legal reasoning.

The real target of Lord Greene's criticism was an approach to legal analysis that gave excessive (possibly even exclusive) emphasis to formality and precedent, without considering the impact that a rule might have on those to whom it applied. The approach that Mackinnon LJ claimed to have followed, which focussed on an 'effort to give effect to the paramount decision of the House of Lords … in *Hewlett*'s case',[107] exemplified this kind of formalism, and – on one level – it would be possible to characterise the differences between Lord Greene MR and Mackinnon LJ as a clash of judicial styles. But we might also feel that a more profound conflict was at the root of their differences. Formalism and an adherence to precedent could justify Mackinnon LJ and Luxmoore LJ in denying a duty of care

[107] [1945] 1 KB 584, 619.

where an authority had failed to mark something that had presented no danger under ordinary lighting conditions. However, where an authority had created the obstruction whilst lighting restrictions were in force, as in *Fox*'s case, precedent and formality overwhelmingly favoured a duty; yet Mackinnon LJ and Luxmoore LJ had denied liability, essentially conferring an immunity on authorities.[108] In taking this step they were giving effect to a view that public authorities should not be made liable in damages for blackout injuries. That was a view that was not only at odds with public opinion, but also with the underlying philosophy of the statutory compensation scheme for war injuries. It is not entirely surprising to find that the one exception to the broad approach to causation adopted by the courts when they interpreted the scheme was a Court of Appeal decision led by Mackinnon LJ.[109]

Whilst we can admire the stylish, confident blend of legal analysis and extra-legal rhetoric in Lord Greene's judgment in *Fisher*, we should also note its limitations. His claims about the likely consequences of denying a duty were simply assertions – motorists might have driven more carefully, or avoided all but essential journeys, if the authorities had not taken positive steps to mark potential obstacles. Nor was there any awareness in his judgment that the imposition of a duty could itself have negative consequences – for instance, by diverting the authority's resources into litigation, or encouraging it to neglect activities where no compensation would result. The analysis also assumed that 'the practice of reasonably-minded men marches in conformity with their legal obligations',[110] and that the law should reflect the obligations of 'good citizenship'.[111] This, in turn, justified the claim that treating acts and omissions differently was a mere technicality. All three assumptions were contestable – to put it mildly – but perhaps July 1945, two months after the celebration of VE Day, was the perfect time to indulge in such generalisations. For this was a time when Britain was congratulating itself on having stood united against a technically superior enemy, and would soon be creating the institutions of the welfare state. A decision emphasising good citizenship and communal responsibility for individual misfortunes was very much in tune with the times.

[108] The point can be seen nicely in Anon., 'Civilian Defense – Some Administrative and Legal Problems' (1941–1942) 55 *Harvard Law Review* 844, 857, where the discussion of *Fox* leads naturally into a discussion of the District of Columbia's exemption from liability for damage sustained in blackout accidents.

[109] *Greenfield* v. *London and North Eastern Railway Company* [1945] 1 KB 89.

[110] *Fisher* v. *Ruislip-Northwood Urban District Council* [1945] 1 KB 584, 605.

[111] [1945] 1 KB 584, 593.

VII

One further instance of tort's response to wartime conditions remains to be examined – the consequences of explosions in armaments factories. In 1914 English law had at least two general heads of tortious liability that might be relied on by claimants injured in such explosions: negligence (in the form of occupier's liability) and *Rylands* v. *Fletcher*. Factory employees also had the alternative possibility of pursuing compensation under the workmen's compensation scheme; and, if the explosion resulted from the breach of a statutory duty, a claim for full compensatory damages might well arise. In the courts the focus of attention fell on the *Rylands* v. *Fletcher* cases. The obvious attraction of such claims for claimants was that it was unnecessary to prove fault to establish liability; in a context where the dangerous characteristics of the ingredients were only partly appreciated, and where the accident might well obliterate evidence of negligence, strict liability could be crucial. As litigants were to discover, however, the ingredients of *Rylands* liability were themselves somewhat volatile.

In *Belvedere Fish Guano Company, Limited* v. *Rainham Chemical Works, Limited*[112] a violent explosion had occurred at the defendant's factory in the course of manufacturing munitions for use in the First World War. The main issue in the case concerned the personal liability of two individuals who had been closely involved in the creation of the Rainham Chemical Works company. The House of Lords held those two individuals liable on the basis that the company occupied the premises as the individuals' agents, but the decision also had a wider significance. First, in both the House of Lords and the Court of Appeal *Rylands* was seen as a broad principle. Thus, Lord Buckmaster described liability in *Rylands* as 'depend[ing] upon this – that even apart from negligence the use of land by one person in an exceptional manner that causes damage to another, and not necessarily an adjacent owner, is actionable'.[113] In the Court of Appeal Lord Sterndale MR was similarly expansive: 'a person who brings dangerous substances upon premises and carries on a dangerous trade with them is … liable if, though without negligence on his part, these substances cause injury to persons or property in their neighbourhood.'[114] Atkin LJ continued the theme:

> Where a person brings upon land of which he is in de facto possession for purposes of his business dangerous materials which would not naturally

[112] [1920] 2 KB 487; [1921] 2 AC 465. [113] [1921] 2 AC 465, 471.
[114] [1920] 2 KB 487, 499.

> be upon the land, he is under an obligation to keep those materials under control, so as not to cause mischief to his neighbours. If they do cause mischief, the neighbour has a cause of action against him for the resulting damage, though no lack of reasonable skill or care on the part of the defendant be proved.[115]

Later courts, as we will see, took a much narrower approach to the *Rylands* principle.

The second point of importance concerned the issue of non-natural use. One of the limitations of *Rylands* v. *Fletcher* liability was that the thing causing damage must have been 'not naturally there' or present under a 'non-natural user'. The former expression had been used by Blackburn J, delivering the judgment of the Court of Exchequer Chamber;[116] the latter was the phrase used by Lord Cairns in the House of Lords.[117] Lord Cairns had, perhaps, simply intended to paraphrase Blackburn J, but the nuance was potentially different. In the *Rainham Chemical Works* case Lord Buckmaster was in no doubt that the use of land to manufacture munitions was 'certainly not the common and ordinary use of the land'.[118] Although no other member of the House expressed a view on the issue, Lord Buckmaster may have been too quick to jump to this conclusion. For, whilst it was obviously true that armaments factories were not natural features of the English landscape, there was authority for the view that the assessment of non-natural use called for a less literal-minded kind of approach. The Privy Council in *Rickards* v. *Lothian*[119] had defined non-natural use as follows:

> It must be some special use bringing with it increased danger to others, and must not merely be the ordinary use of the land or such as is proper for the general benefit of the community.[120]

Rickards' case concerned a flood that had originated in domestic water supply, and the Privy Council held that the provision of such a supply fell outside the *Rylands* principle. It was, they said:

> not only reasonable, but has become, in accordance with modern sanitary views, an almost necessary feature of town life. It is recognised as being so desirable in the interests of the community that in some form or other it is usually made obligatory in civilized countries.[121]

115 [1920] 2 KB 487, 502.
116 *Rylands* v. *Fletcher* (1866) LR 1 Exch 265, 280.
117 (1868) LR 3 HL 330, 339.
118 [1921] 2 AC 465, 471.
119 [1913] AC 263.
120 [1913] AC 263, 280.
121 [1913] AC 263, 281.

This emphasis on the public interest of the activity had the potential to exclude damage caused by explosions in wartime armaments factories, but it is striking that the House of Lords thought that there was nothing in the point. Indeed, Lord Parmoor took the trouble to describe the acute crisis in explosive supply that had had to be resolved by Lord Moulton, the Director-General of explosive supply to the Ministry of Munitions.[122] By a nice coincidence it was also Lord Moulton who had delivered the opinion of the Privy Council in *Rickards*. But for Lord Parmoor, as for the rest of the House of Lords, the wartime context did not shape the legal content of the decision.

Lord Buckmaster's short dismissal of the claim that explosives manufacture in wartime might fall outside *Rylands* also seems to have failed to engage with the argument advanced by counsel. For counsel, Sir John Simon KC, did not focus his submission wholly on the interpretation of 'non-natural user'; his argument was more ambitious:

> The doctrine of *Fletcher v Rylands* does not apply where, as here, the manufacture of explosives is carried on under the direction of the Ministry of Munitions under the Regulations for the Defence of the Realm for the general benefit of the community at a time of grave national danger. Granted that in normal times the deposit of dangerous explosives would be a non-natural user of the land, in the special circumstances of this case it ought not to be so treated; and the liability arises only in the case of a non-natural user: *Madras Ry. Co. v Zemindar of Carvatenagarum*.[123]

The compression necessary in any summary of counsel's argument gives this passage a terse, almost perfunctory air. But when read together with the case that Sir John Simon had cited, it becomes far more forceful. Indeed, it becomes clear that there are two interrelated submissions here. The second relates to the interpretation of non-natural use; the first is that *Rylands* simply does not apply to the situation because of the involvement of the Ministry of Munitions and the grave national danger.

The case that Sir John Simon cited was concerned with an attempt to impose liability for damage to the claimant's railway line, which had been caused when two irrigation tanks burst their banks. The Privy Council held that *Rylands* v. *Fletcher* applied in principle to India, since it was an 'application of the maxim, *sic utere tuo ut alienum non laedas*, expressing a principle recognized in the laws of all civilized countries'.[124] There

[122] [1921] 2 AC 465, 484. [123] [1921] 2 AC 465, 467.

[124] 'Use your own property so as not to injure the property of another': (1874) LR 1 Ind App 364, 385.

was no liability on the facts, however, because the tanks were part of a 'national system of irrigation, recognized by Hindoo and Mahommedan Law, by regulations of the East India Company, and by experience older than history, as essential to the welfare, and, indeed, to the existence of a large portion of the population of India'.[125] It followed that the defendant's position was not precisely analogous to that of the private landowner in *Rylands*, who was creating the reservoir for his own gain. 'The rights and liabilities of the Defendant', concluded the Privy Council, 'appear to their Lordships much more analogous to those of persons or corporations on whom statutory powers have been conferred and statutory duties imposed.'[126] Sir John Simon's allusions to the statutory framework in the *Rainham* case were clearly aimed at making a similar point about the analogy with statutory authority. But such arguments clearly fell on deaf ears, and none of their Lordships even mentioned the *Madras Railway* case. The courts, it seemed, were far more responsive to public interest arguments abroad than at home.

We might leave the *Rainham Chemical Works* case with a slight feeling of disappointment, that it marginalised or ignored important questions of principle. But no such complaint could be made about the decisions in *Read* v. *J Lyons & Company, Limited*.[127] 'This case', said Scott LJ, giving the first judgment in the Court of Appeal, 'is elemental. It goes to the roots of the common law.'[128] The facts of the case were simple. The claimant was employed as an inspector of munitions by the armaments inspection division of the Ministry of Supply. In the course of her duties she visited the defendant's munitions factory, and was injured by the explosion of a shell. She did not allege negligence or claim under the workmen's compensation scheme;[129] rather, her claim was made either on the basis of a general principle of strict liability for ultra-hazardous activities, or on the basis that she came within *Rylands* v. *Fletcher*. Both the Court of Appeal and the House of Lords found for the defendant.

The argument that the claimant could rely on a general principle of strict liability for ultra-hazardous activities relied extensively on *The Restatement of the Law of Torts*, which had only recently become accessible to English practitioners.[130] As Scott LJ pointed out in the Court of Appeal, it was not obvious that an application of *The Restatement* would lead to

[125] (1874) LR 1 Ind App 364, 385. [126] (1874) LR 1 Ind App 364, 385–86.
[127] [1945] 1 KB 216; [1947] AC 156. [128] [1945] 1 KB 216, 224.
[129] The scheme extended to Crown employees: Workmen's Compensation Act 1897, s. 8.
[130] A. T. Denning, 'The Restatement of the Law: Its Place in the English Courts' (1951) 37 *ABAJ* 329, 329.

the defendant being made liable, since the general principle was qualified by exceptions for common usage and public duty.[131] Nevertheless, Scott LJ acknowledged the intuitive appeal of bringing together the various instances of strict liability in English tort law, but ultimately he was unconvinced. The crucial point was not so much the lack of authoritative support for such a principle, but rather that a general principle of strict liability would be at odds with the development of tort law. That development, he explained, had been set out by Oliver Wendell Holmes in *The Common Law*,[132] and consisted in a shift from absolute liability to fault. Liability for extra-hazardous acts (as opposed to activities) could be justified, but only because the defendant should have foreseen that harm would result from his acts. It was, in other words, fault-based in all but name.

In the House of Lords the general principle was rejected for less elaborate reasons. For Lord Macmillan the key point was that it asked too much: 'Your Lordships' task in this House is to decide particular cases between litigants and your Lordships are not called upon to rationalize the law of England.'[133] For Lord Uthwatt it was an issue of reasonable expectations. A 'reasonable invitee' would not expect to be guaranteed safety, he explained, so it followed that 'it is against reason that the law, whose function it is to give effect to reasonable expectations, should impose such a guarantee'.[134] It is perhaps unfair to subject a final concurring speech to too much scrutiny, but this was a rather lazy, circular assertion presented as irrefutable argument. There was no evidence of what 'reasonable' invitees to explosives factories expected, and even if it had been shown that such invitees were content to risk injury in explosions, there was no reason why the law had to reflect such expectations. On the contrary, a higher legal obligation might legitimately signal that invitees were entitled to expect that they would be safer. There was no good reason to rule out the possibility that the law could improve social behaviour.

The courts' discussion of the claimant's narrower basis of claim – namely, that she came within the principle of *Rylands* v. *Fletcher* – focussed on escape. Counsel argued that only escape from the defendant's control was needed, but the courts unanimously insisted that the escape must be from the defendant's *land*. Since the explosion in *Read*'s case had been contained within the factory, this was sufficient to dispose of the claim, but the House of Lords went on to consider the corollary, namely

[131] *Read* v. *J Lyons & Company, Limited* [1945] 1 KB 216, 226.

[132] O. W. Holmes, *The Common Law* (London, Macmillan, 1881).

[133] [1947] AC 156, 175. [134] [1947] AC 156, 186.

that *Rylands* might only apply to damage to the claimant's *land*. Although most of the judges reserved their view, there was some support for the exclusion of personal injury claims.[135]

Commentators were quick to note that the dominant theme of *Read*'s case was restriction; indeed, Wolfgang Friedmann regarded the case as a turning point in the House of Lords' attitude to tort liability.[136] T. H. Tylor speculated that the case represented a 'judicial reaction to the constant increase in legislative interference in the regulation of individual action for the benefit of society at large',[137] and it may be that the judges wanted to define their role as expounders of the common law against such welfare legislation.

In many ways the Court of Appeal's judgments are more impressive than those of the House of Lords, particularly for the way that Scott LJ addresses the argument of principle. Scott's approach was to invoke a long view of the development of fault liability, as espoused by Holmes in *The Common Law*, and to reject the argument for a general principle of strict liability because it was at odds with that development. Readers of Scott's judgment can see that Scott admired Holmes' work greatly, but the judgment only hints at the depth of feeling that Scott had for Holmes, and can – of course – give no sense of Holmes' reciprocal friendship. In fact they corresponded for over thirty years, and the earliest surviving letter – from Holmes to Scott – immediately highlights that this was a close personal relationship: 'I am so sorry and distressed at your accident that I hardly know what to write', it begins.[138] The topics on which they wrote to each other ranged from technical legal analysis to broader questions of politics and literature.[139] Scott frequently sent Holmes books and essays, on which Holmes commented appreciatively.[140] Theirs was a close epistolary friendship, characterised by mutual admiration and warmth, which Scott, at least, found intellectually inspiring. The following letter, sent

[135] [1947] AC 156, 173 (Lord Macmillan).

[136] W. Friedmann, *Law and Social Change in Contemporary Britain* (London, Stevens & Sons Limited, 1951) 93–6.

[137] T. H. Tylor, 'The Restriction of Strict Liability' (1947) 10 *MLR* 396, 402.

[138] 23 October 1903. MSS.119/3/P/HO 1 (University of Warwick).

[139] For an example of the legal analysis, see MSS.119/3/P/HO/15/2 (24 August 1926), in which Holmes delivers an extensive analysis of an essay by A. L. Goodhart.

[140] E.g. MSS.119/3/P/HO/12 (29 May 1926), warmly thanking Scott for sending Mathew, *Forensic Fables*; MSS.119/3/P/HO/23, thanking Scott for A. P. Herbert's *Misleading Cases*. Scott also sent Mathew's work to senior judges around the Commonwealth: MSS.119/3/S/LE17 (Scott to Mathew, 24 November 1927).

on hearing news of Holmes' retirement from the United States Supreme Court in 1932, gives a sense of his feelings of indebtedness:

> You have had a great career, as an illuminator of legal principle – the greatest of any living man who is or has been on the Bench in the English speaking world. You have always, since you gave me your 'Common Law' in 1897, been my chief source of inspiration. I was only yesterday seeking light in one of your decisions, on a question of trade boycott. I have striven hard to make my own your method of approach to the solution of legal problems. Those which come before me in my practice are extraordinarily varied, because my practice is so diverse: and I am constantly getting new questions – I mean facts which want a lot of thinking about in order to see what are the legal principles involved; and time after time I find myself getting help through your viewpoint of the law, and quite often from something you have written in the Common Law or some judgment. I only wish I could have seen more of you in the flesh, but it has not been possible: and your wonderful letters have helped much to keep up the contact of the mind.[141]

Counsel for the claimant in *Read* v. *J Lyons & Company* – had he read this letter – might have felt that the composition of the Court of Appeal had been rather unfortunate. There could surely have been no other Lord Justice of Appeal more resistant to the idea that what Holmes had said in *The Common Law* was not the last word.

The real objection to Holmes' theory of the development of tort was not so much that it was analytically incorrect as that it did not tell the whole story. For it was implicit in Holmes' account that once the law of tort arrived at an objective standard of fault, it was complete. No further development was called for. Other writers disagreed. Roscoe Pound, for instance, had argued that tortious liability based on fault was simply one phase of its development. Writing in 1913, he identified a further stage of legal development, which he called 'the socialisation of law', in which moral and social interests would receive greater protection than they had previously attracted.[142] The consequences of socialisation for tort would be significant – there would be restrictions on the anti-social exercise of rights and, of special importance to the theme of this chapter, a new-found role for liability without fault. As Pound explained, fault was:

141 MSS.119/3/P/HO/26 (20 January 1932). Holmes replied that Scott's letter had made him 'proud'; he also added: 'It was time to stop' (MSS.119/3/P/HO/27, 3 February 1932).

142 R. Pound, 'The End of Law as Developed in Legal Rules and Doctrines' (1913–1914) 27 *Harvard Law Review* 195, 225ff.

> an individualist ethical standard. Today there is a strong and growing tendency to revive the idea of liability without fault, not only in the form of wide responsibility for agencies employed, but in placing upon an enterprise the burden of repairing injuries without fault of him who conducts it, which are incident to the undertaking. There is a strong and growing tendency, where there is no blame on either side, to ask, in view of the exigencies of social justice who can best bear the loss, and hence to shift the loss by creating liability where there has been no fault.[143]

Thirty years later, Fleming James identified this trend in American case law. The *Rylands* doctrine, he claimed, had been used as 'a rational judicial attempt to select ultra-hazardous use of land for special treatment'.[144] No such claim could have been made about English law.

Commentators were quick to draw attention to the alternative trajectory of historical development that the claimant's argument in *Read*'s case implied. In a characteristically insightful note on the Court of Appeal's decision, Wolfgang Friedmann highlighted the distorted image of the tort landscape that was produced by a focus on fault: objective tests of fault were very close in substance to strict liability, and many industrial activities were subject to statutory duties that required no proof of fault for compensation.[145] Lord Denning, commenting on the use of *The Restatement* by the House of Lords, reported that the decision had:

> met with considerable criticism. It has been pointed out that the doctrine of 'no liability without fault' has been gradually replaced in modern times by the criterion 'On whom should the risk fall?' Judged by this criterion the proposition contained in the *Restatement* is more in accord with modern thought.[146]

No source for this modern approach was given, but Denning had recently written a Foreword to Friedmann's *Law and Social Change in Contemporary Britain*, where the principal author had made the point rather more tendentiously. 'The first and most general principle', Friedmann had written, 'is that the main function of the law of tort is the reasonable adjustment of economic risks in a capitalist – though not necessarily a capitalist – society and not the expression of certain absolute moral principles.'[147] The

[143] *Ibid.*, 233.

[144] F. James, Jr, 'Accident Liability: Some Wartime Developments' (1945–1946) 55 *Yale Law Journal* 365.

[145] W. Friedmann, 'Liability for Dangerous Activities carried out by Public Order' (1945) 8 *MLR* 248, esp. at 250.

[146] Denning, 'The Restatement of Law', 331.

[147] Friedmann, *Law and Social Change in Contemporary Britain*, 97. Denning's Foreword is at ix–x.

implication here that capitalism was only a (temporary) phase, and that the development of tort liability should be undertaken with an eye to a post-capitalist future chimed with Pound's socialisation of law. But quite how far it was from the political beliefs of the author of *The Common Law* can be seen in the following letter from Holmes to Scott:

> I am reading at the moment Tawney – 'Religion and the Rise of Capitalism', and very interesting, although he, like my friend Laski, seems to believe that a new order is coming – that capitalism departs and that they are called on to help shape the order. I am a hardened old skeptic and see no reason to wish or believe that capitalism should or will be done away with.[148]

Holmes did not link his historical claims with his broader political views. But the connection – particularly the emphasis on the individual – was not hard to see, and surely cannot have escaped the attention of his correspondent. In other words, the historical argument behind the rejection of a general principle of strict liability in *Read* v. *J Lyons & Co* was informed by a political conviction that fault-based, individualistic liability was tort's destiny.

VIII

This chapter set out to examine the influence of wartime conditions on tort liability. The results are mixed. No new torts sprang into life, and none were consigned to history by the emergency. That is not perhaps entirely surprising, given that both World Wars were – in legal developmental terms – short-lived, and that the doctrine of precedent still exercised a powerful influence. It is also worth noting that judicial conservatism in wartime might itself be seen as a form of patriotism. If, as Lord Denning half-jokingly (I think) put it, the judges of England carried the law 'in their breasts, if not in their heads',[149] the law could easily become infused with the emotions and national pride more traditionally associated with that part of the body.

The changes that took place were subtle yet significant. Some reflected the application of existing principle – as in the use of absolute privilege for tribunal proceedings, or contributory negligence in the blackout. Others, such as qualified privilege for communications to commanding officers, were more ambivalent – and looked different in different reports. The

[148] MSS.119/3/P/HO/13/1.

[149] Denning, 'The Restatement of Law', 329.

most striking developments challenged the bases of liability, and here it is particularly interesting to note the lack of judicial unanimity about how tort law should respond to war. The Court of Appeal found itself having to use its power to overrule its own decisions; and the historico-conservative individualism of *Read* v. *J Lyons & Co* was completely at odds with the quasi-empirical communitarianism of *Fisher* v. *Ruislip-Northwood Urban District Council*. The problem was that although the crisis was immediate and pressing, it was not obvious how to respond. The question posed by Lund and McDougall, in the second epigraph to this chapter, encapsulates the problem.[150] The giveaway is the adjectives, lurching as they do between *total* war, *legal* problems and the *average* man. The shift from public to private, macro to micro, and – it is tempting to suggest – central to peripheral, created a space in which differences of judgment about how tort should respond to war were both permissible and inevitable.

[150] T. Lund and E. MacDougall, 'Legislative Relief for War Injuries in England' (1943) 92 *University of Pennsylvania Law Review and American Law Register* 150.

4

Women

Ought a person, who has been made seriously ill by a shock caused intentionally or negligently by another person be entitled to recover damages even though he, – or more usually she, – has suffered no direct physical impact?

A. L. Goodhart

That a woman could seduce a man he did not doubt; it had been the theme of many poets, and people were long accustomed in the old days to make use of love philtres to seduce the affections of other people.

Darling J

I

It was, perhaps, inevitable that gender issues would play a central role in the development of tort law in the first half of the twentieth century. The legal consequences of marriage in tort liability, despite nineteenth-century reforms, remained unsatisfactorily incoherent, and still included vestiges of the theory that a married woman had no independent legal status of her own. At the same time, explicitly gender-dependent categories of liability had been created, such as the ability of a woman to sue in defamation for an imputation of unchastity without needing to prove that she had suffered loss.[1] Meanwhile, wider social and legal changes in the position of women in areas such as suffrage, education and professional opportunities raised the question of how the law of tort should respond.[2]

[1] Slander of Women Act 1891.

[2] On suffrage, the key statutes were Representation of the People Act 1918 (enfranchising women over the age of 30, subject to a property qualification) and Representation of the People Act 1928 (enfranchising all women over 21). The secondary literature is vast – one relatively recent and concise study is H. Smith, *The British Women's Suffrage Campaign 1866–1928*, 2nd edn (Harlow, Pearson, 2007). On higher education and professional opportunities there is a similar wealth of literature: J. Robinson, *Bluestockings: The Remarkable Story of the First Women to Fight for an Education* (London, Penguin, 2010) is an engaging and accessible account.

The question was particularly acute (and divisive) where the tort principles presumed female weakness and passivity.

This chapter examines how both judges and writers addressed the role of women in tort law, and pays particular attention to the arguments, language and sources that they drew on to reach their conclusions. Consideration of the Law Revision Committee's deliberations, which led to the Law Reform (Married Women and Tortfeasors) Act 1935 is deferred to Part II, where it is placed alongside assessments of the Committee's other tort-related activities.[3] Readers wanting to follow through the theme of tort law's treatment of women may, however, wish to read that chapter in conjunction with this one. It might also be helpful to make clear, at the outset, a deliberate limitation in the scope of this chapter. Several principles of tort law required claimants to have property interests in order to be able to bring claims. Thus, for instance, a claim in nuisance required that the claimant have a right of occupation of the property affected.[4] It was also held that a tenant's spouse could not claim for injuries caused by the landlord's negligent failure to repair the premises.[5] Both of these principles were likely to have a disproportionately disadvantaging effect on women, because men tended to hold proprietary interests in land, or be tenants. There was, however, nothing inherently gender-specific about the tort law principles; and by the start of our period, legislation had made it clear that married women could sue in their own right for personal injury and damage to their property.[6] This chapter does not investigate the processes of wealth distribution that led to rules requiring property interests as prerequisites for tort claims having a disproportionate impact on women.

II

Many of the peculiarities of the position of women in tort were consequences of the doctrine of the legal unity of husband and wife. Under this doctrine, the wife's existence was subordinated to her husband's for the duration of their marriage.[7] This had both procedural and substantive ramifications. Procedurally, a wife could not sue alone, and her

[3] See Chapter 12, 'Husbands'.

[4] *Malone* v. *Laskey* [1907] 2 KB 141.

[5] *Cavalier* v. *Pope* [1906] AC 428.

[6] Married Women's Property Act 1882.

[7] G. Williams, 'The Legal Unity of Husband and Wife' (1947) 10 *MLR* 16 provides a helpful overview.

husband would ordinarily be joined as co-defendant in an action against her. Substantively, and limiting the question to tort, the ramifications were more diverse; they included the rule that prevented one spouse from suing the other.[8]

The full force of the unity doctrine had been lessened by the Married Women's Property Act of 1882. Its key provisions permitted married women to bring independent actions in their own names, and to sue their husbands to protect their own separate property.[9] The general procedural incapacity of married women was, therefore, removed. But the Act had not abolished the doctrine of unity; it had merely abolished two of its instantiations. Other outgrowths of the doctrine remained in place. Thus, a husband still could not sue his wife in tort, and a wife could not sue her husband where the action did not relate to her separate property. Courts were consistently unimpressed by creative arguments about what constituted such property: lost future earnings and accrued claims for personal injury did not count.[10] The courts also resisted the suggestion that the 1882 Act removed a husband's liability for his wife's torts. The earliest decisions on the point focussed closely on the statutory wording, emphasising that the Act said that a husband 'need not' be joined as co-defendant, not that he *could not* be.[11] The same attention to language was paid by the House of Lords when determining the point in 1924, with Lord Sumner adding that the issue was 'really a project for legislation in 1924 and not a construction of the legislation of 1882'.[12] The House of Lords, however, was not unanimous. The minority of the Earl of Birkenhead LC and Viscount Cave were persuaded by an argument that seems to have been first articulated by T. Cyprian Williams, writing in the *Law Quarterly Review*, over twenty years earlier.[13] That argument placed less emphasis on the detailed wording of the Act, and paid greater attention to the underlying concepts. The essential point was that the 1882 Act, by removing a married woman's procedural incapacity, had destroyed the conceptual foundation of the unity doctrine, at least for procedural purposes. It therefore followed, by necessary implication, that a wife had a separate existence as a defendant,

[8] See further, O. Kahn-Freund, 'Inconsistencies and Injustices in the Law of Husband and Wife' (1952) 15 *MLR* 133.

[9] Sections 1 and 12 respectively.

[10] *Tinkley* v. *Tinkley* (1909) 25 TLR 264 and *Gottliffe* v. *Edelston* [1930] 2 KB 378 respectively.

[11] *Seroka* v. *Kattenburg* (1886) 17 QBD 177; *Earle* v. *Kingscote* [1900] 2 Ch 585.

[12] *Edwards* v. *Porter* [1925] AC 1.

[13] T. Cyprian Williams, 'A Husband's Liability for his Wife's Torts, and the Married Women's Property Act' (1900) 16 *LQR* 191.

and that her husband had no role in claims against her. The problem with this argument lay not in its inherent coherence, but in the way that it required an Act containing specific provisions to be read as contributing to a debate about underlying principles. This was not the first time – nor would it be the last – that the courts would be counter-suggestible when invited to embrace the *implications* of a statute.

The dominant tone in discussions of married women's tortious rights and responsibilities was thus one of detached neutrality. The technical arguments were analysed and processed efficiently enough, but there were virtually no signs of disquiet, let alone of critique. The one exception was the judgment of McCardie J in *Gottliffe* v. *Edleston*,[14] in which the technical question was whether a married woman could sue her husband for negligently inflicted pre-marital personal injury. The outcome of the case turned on whether the Married Women's Property Act provision for a wife to sue her husband to protect her separate property could be applied to an accrued claim for personal injury. McCardie J, however, seized the opportunity to advance a general critique of the law. His starting point was gender inequality, but it was the law's unequal treatment of *husbands*, not wives, that concerned him. A husband, McCardie J pointed out, was liable to pay tax on his wife's income; he was liable for the conversion of his wife's goods; and he was liable for her torts.[15] A wife had no corresponding liability in respect of her husband's possessions or activities. The immediate problem, he explained, was the short-sightedness of changes to the position of married women, which had failed to include 'the adjustments that were needed to secure a proper and adequate code for the regulation of the relations between the spouses'.[16] But the deeper structural problem was the continued existence of the unity doctrine. McCardie J found it 'difficult to see' how the doctrine could continue to apply in an era when it was acknowledged that husband and wife might well have different outlooks, interests, religious and political commitments, and so on. He then referred to the emphasis on the 'modern notion' of the assertion of individuality in the work of Lord Bryce, a jurist and Liberal politician, before adding that 'we are probably completing the transition from the family to the personal epoch of woman', and concluding that there was a 'sound sociological basis' for a 'presumption of modified unity' between spouses 'in certain respects'.[17] McCardie J then used this general critique to inform

[14] [1930] 2 KB 378. [15] [1930] 2 KB 378, 382.

[16] [1930] 2 KB 378, 383. McCardie J would, apparently, have liked to be made responsible for drafting such a code: G. Pollock, *Mr Justice McCardie* (London, John Lane, 1934) 205–6.

[17] [1930] 2 KB 378, 384–5.

his construction of the Married Women's Property Act. It would not be appropriate, he decided, to interpret the Act in a way that magnified, and exacerbated, the injustices that already existed. It followed, therefore, that a wife's accrued claim for personal injury should not be regarded as her 'separate property' for the purposes of the Act, and the claim failed.

What is significant about *Gottliffe* v. *Edelston* is not so much the result itself – although there is a certain irony about a married woman *losing* on the ground of gender equality – as the ideas and language that were being used in McCardie J's critique of the existing legal landscape. To begin with the general tone, there was an energy and determination to improve the law that earlier judicial pronouncements had notably lacked: equality was presented not merely as a matter for Parliament, but as an urgent necessity, because the current rules were at odds with social practices. The method of reasoning was also distinctive. Its starting point and driving force – the autonomy of parties to a marriage – was not a legal principle, but an observable social fact. The significance of this social fact was confirmed by the theoretical work of Lord Bryce, whom McCardie J described as having articulated the 'modern notion' of 'one's right to assert one's own individuality', thus giving the social fact the approving stamp of modernity and the moral force of a 'right'.[18] This combination of social fact and theoretical value constituted the 'sociological basis' from which McCardie J's analysis proceeded.

McCardie's method of criticising and shaping the law by reference to sociology was unique to him in this period. The word 'sociology' appears only once in the Law Reports, in a description of the work of Rudolph Steiner, and 'sociological', though slightly more frequent, is only used – except by McCardie J – to describe matters irrelevant to proper legal analysis.[19] A further, perhaps more telling indication of how far McCardie was out of sympathy with his contemporaries is provided by an article by Glanville Williams published in 1947 in the *Modern Law Review*. Williams' subject was the legal unity of husband and wife, and the question he was setting out to answer was whether it represented 'a living principle of law, from which new deductions may legitimately be drawn?'[20] Since the decision in *Gottliffe* v. *Edelston*, a husband's liability for his wife's torts had been abolished by the Law Reform (Married Women and

[18] On Bryce, see the entry by C. Harvie, 'Bryce, James Viscount Bryce (1838–1922)' in *Oxford Dictionary of National Biography*.

[19] 'Sociology': *Midland Bank Executor* v. *Harwood* [1943] Ch 422, 430. 'Sociological': *Stopes* v. *Sutherland* [1925] AC 47, 73; *In re Decision of Walker* [1944] KB 644, 652.

[20] Williams, 'The Legal Unity of Husband and Wife', 16.

Tortfeasors) Act 1935[21], but despite this, Williams' assessment of the law was timid. He gave a cursory account of *Gottliffe*'s case, which omitted any reference to McCardie J's critique, and concluded that the doctrine of unity 'ought to be used only to bolster up a decision arrived at on other grounds, and it is not in itself a satisfactory basis of decision'.[22] Despite writing in what passed for a radical law review, a dozen years after significant parliamentary pruning back of the doctrine, Williams was not prepared to endorse McCardie's view that the doctrine was impermissible in modern conditions.

The dominant attitude of quiescence towards the doctrine of unity suggests, at best, an unimaginative conservatism. At worst, it suggests that the doctrine was not seen as either fundamentally inaccurate or inappropriate, and it seems both extraordinary and disappointing that only McCardie J should have voiced the view that it was unacceptable for the law to regard a woman's identity as obliterated for the duration of her marriage. Moreover, as we shall now see, the assumptions of passivity, weakness and suggestibility inherent in the doctrine of unity informed other aspects of tort's dealings with women.

III

The legal consequences of marriage were complemented by – and ideologically consistent with – the legal consequences of interference with marriage. The central pillar of tort law's approach was a husband's action for enticement, which had a long, if exiguous history. In its eighteenth-century form it lay against anyone who either persuaded a wife to leave her husband, or encouraged a wife who had already separated from her husband to remain absent.[23] Despite the frisson of seduction in the tort's name, it was not confined to actions against sexual rivals; a husband might sue his mother-in-law,[24] brother-in-law[25] or even – in theory – an employer whose rates of pay were too good to resist.[26] The gist of the action was persuasion, not adultery.[27]

21 See further, Chapter 12.
22 Williams, 'The Legal Unity of Husband and Wife', 31.
23 *Winsmore* v. *Greenbank* (1745) Willes 577.
24 *Sanderson* v. *Hudson*, *The Times* 29 January 1923.
25 *Smith* v. *Kaye* (1904) 20 TLR 261.
26 *Place* v. *Searle* [1932] 2 KB 497, 503.
27 The common law had had an action for adultery – the claim for criminal conversation. However, this action had been abolished by the Matrimonial Causes Act 1857 s. 33.

The operation of the tort of enticement raised three legally distinct, but thematically related, issues that are central to this chapter. The first was that the action presupposed that a husband was entitled to dictate his wife's living arrangements; it was not obvious that this presupposition remained tenable at the start of the twentieth century.[28] The second issue concerned the nature of enticement itself and, in particular, how much weight ought to be given to a married woman's decision-making autonomy. Finally there was the question of who could sue: were wives just as entitled as their husbands to seek legal redress for enticement? The answers to all of these questions could not avoid invoking models of marriage, and of the ideal behaviour of a married woman.

The first twentieth-century enticement case, *Smith* v. *Kaye*,[29] indicated that, so far as the law was concerned, married women were as irresolute and pathologically suggestible as their nineteenth-century counterparts.[30] The claim was brought after the defendant had successfully persuaded his sister, who had eloped with the defendant's former coachman, to leave her marital home. Wright J's direction to the jury was careful to delineate the scope of liability for enticement:

> If Mrs Smith asked the defendants for their advice, and they merely approved of her leaving, the defendants would not be liable if they gave that advice in good faith. If the advice was gratuitous, that was, volunteered, it might be different. If the defendants persuaded her to leave, or incited her to leave, or procured her leaving, then they would be liable.[31]

The jury found for the claimant, awarding £500 (equivalent to over £50,000 today).[32]

McCardie J would later dismiss this passage – with some justification – as a rather desperate exercise in line-drawing;[33] but it is still important to register where, exactly, the lines were being placed. Only the wife who had already decided to leave and then received mere solicited *advice* affirming that decision could be seen as acting independently. Even then, it was also necessary for the defendant to have given the advice 'in good faith', a requirement which it was difficult to be entirely confident about: was only an honest expression of opinion required, or did questions of motive and disinterestedness come into play too? Unsolicited advice, on the other

[28] *R* v. *Jackson* [1891] 1 QB 671. [29] (1904) 20 TLR 261.
[30] (1904) 20 TLR 261, 263. [31] (1904) 20 TLR 261, 263.
[32] Calculated using www.thisismoney.co.uk/money/bills/article-1633409/Historic-inflation-calculator-value-money-changed-1900.html.
[33] *Place* v. *Searle* [1932] 2 KB 497, 501.

hand, 'might be different'; because the wife was not then in control of the situation, and had been taken by surprise, she could not, it seems, be assumed to have the independence of mind to resist her advisor's conclusions, despite there being no persuasion, inducement or incitement (these being dealt with in the final sentence of the passage quoted). If marriage really did make women as weak-willed and suggestible as these legal principles assumed, it was surprising that the courts were not flooded with enticement claims.

Smith v. *Kaye* was the high-water mark for the tort of enticement; later cases, with one exception, would reflect judicial reservations about both its underlying assumptions and its central concept. The tone was set by McCardie J in *Butterworth* v. *Butterworth*,[34] when he expressed doubt about enticement's continuing existence as a tort,[35] and the theme was developed more fully in *Sanderson* v. *Hudson* (by Darling J), and in *Place* v. *Searle* (by McCardie J again).

Sanderson v. *Hudson* concerned a husband's claim against his mother-in-law. Darling J seems to have kept the tone of proceedings light, at one stage asking the claimant whether he had read *The Taming of the Shrew*,[36] but in his judgment he made a significant alteration to the applicable principles. 'In the present case', he decided, 'anything which the defendant did must not only have been against the will of the plaintiff, but must have induced the wife to do that which she would not have done voluntarily. It must be proved that her will was overborne.'[37] The point about a wife's will being overborne was repeated twice more in the judgment, and it was explained that this development was a consequence of changes in the law of marriage, which allowed a wife to elect to live apart from her husband. The judge concluded that, on the facts, the wife's will had not been overborne by her mother, and the claim therefore failed.

In his judgment in *Place* v. *Searle*,[38] McCardie J applauded the decision in *Sanderson* v. *Hudson* as 'the first real recognition of the changed status of married women',[39] and took the opportunity to expand on the theme hinted at by Darling J. For McCardie J it was impossible simply to apply the principles of the tort as they had been articulated in the eighteenth

[34] [1920] P 126. [35] [1920] P 126, 130.

[36] *The Times* 27 January 1923. This report of the evidence also contained the revealing comment by the claimant that he objected to his mother-in-law treating him 'like a kaffir'. At the time of the trial both mother and daughter had returned to South Africa.

[37] *The Times* 29 January 1923. [38] [1932] 2 KB 497.

[39] [1932] 2 KB 497, 501.

century, when a wife had been seen as her husband's possession. There had been a 'revolutionary change'[40] in the position of married women since then, across fields as diverse as property ownership and political rights, which required that the principles of enticement be adapted, as Darling J had done. This was not only a matter of ideological consistency. Women's increasing involvement in political and economic life created the potential for inappropriate liabilities unless the principles were reformed: for instance, an employer who offered a married woman employment against her husband's known wishes fell within the scope of the unmodernised tort. 'The lawyer who possesses sociological vision', McCardie J declared, would be able to imagine other examples.[41] On the facts of the case the judge found that Mrs Place was a woman 'of resolute will, of independent decision, and of strong mind and physique', who had chosen to leave her husband;[42] there was, therefore, no evidence of enticement to leave to the jury.

The Court of Appeal reversed McCardie J's decision, and rejected the attempt to introduce the requirement of an overborne will. Scrutton LJ, giving the leading judgment, made it clear that he rejected the argument from revolutionary change. As he saw it, 'a husband has a right to the consortium of his wife', which generated a cause of action against a third party who unjustifiably destroyed that consortium.[43] Thus, a case like *R* v. *Jackson*,[44] which denied that a husband had a right to imprison his wife (and to which McCardie J had referred), was not part of a revolutionary change, but merely deprived a husband of one remedial enforcement option in his efforts to assert his rights. Greer LJ and Slesser LJ took the same view, also agreeing with Scrutton LJ's approval of *Smith* v. *Kaye*. It followed that there was no need to prove that the wife's will was overborne, and that there was, therefore, a case to go to the jury. The jury at this second trial, which was undefended as the defendant had emigrated to Africa, awarded £5,000 to the claimant.[45]

A reader of the official law report of *Place* v. *Searle* leaves the case with an impression of Olympian conservatism; readers of the contemporaneous report of the case in *The Times*, by contrast, would have experienced

40 [1932] 2 KB 497, 500.
41 [1932] 2 KB 497, 503.
42 [1932] 2 KB 497, 506.
43 [1932] 2 KB 497, 512.
44 [1891] 1 QB 671.
45 Pollock, *Mr Justice McCardie*, 196. It seems that Mrs Place subsequently changed her name to Searle: *The Times* 1 November 1937 in its Law Notices, records the application for a decree absolute in *Place* v. *Searle (formerly Place) and Searle*.

a peevish and highly personal tone. Scrutton LJ, it seemed, had actually begun his judgment with a disparaging attack on the parties involved:

> it was a squalid and not very interesting case, which had somehow been elevated by the newspapers into a case which afforded good copy, apparently because some ingenious counsel had considered that there was some likeness between this case and the Trojan war. Anything less like the godlike Hector and Achilles and 'the face that launched a thousand ships' he found it difficult to conceive, but the case had apparently attained great notoriety.[46]

He had brought the judgment to a close with an extraordinary attack on McCardie J:

> Mr Justice McCardie had referred to Judges with sociological knowledge. He (Lord Justice Scrutton) thought that the less sociological knowledge that was brought into the discussion of these legal questions the better. If there was to be a discussion of the relations of husbands and wives he thought it would come better from Judges who had more than theoretical knowledge of husbands and wives. He was a little surprised that a gentleman who had never been married should, as he had done in another case, have proceeded to explain the proper underclothing that ladies should wear, and he (the Lord Justice) thought that those things were better left out of the discussion of legal questions.[47]

The editorial excision of both of these passages in the Law Reports flattered Scrutton LJ, whilst also depriving readers of revealing material. The studied insult about Mrs Place's appearance, and broader contempt for the rivals for her affections, could perhaps be explained away as preliminary impatience, but the dismissiveness suggested an underlying inability to appreciate, much less empathise with, the emotional and psychological complexities in this type of situation. The attack on McCardie J was more serious. The first thing that catches the eye is the viciously personal nature of the attack: not merely McCardie J's judgment, but also his professionalism, integrity and morality are undermined. The quip about women's underwear was peculiarly gratuitous. McCardie J understood it as a reference to *Martial* v. *Frankau*,[48] in which one of the legal issues was whether certain dresses purchased by a wife came within the category of 'necessaries' for which her husband was liable to pay; there was, in other words, a legal issue about women's clothing that the judge had been required to address.[49] McCardie's response to Scrutton's attack was to threaten to

[46] *The Times* 7 May 1932. [47] *The Times* 7 May 1932, 4.

[48] *Martial and Armand, Limited* v. *Frankau, The Times* 4 November 1931, 5 November 1931 and 21 November 1931.

[49] Pollock, *Mr Justice McCardie*, 213.

withhold his trial notes from any Court of Appeal of which Scrutton LJ was a member. The Master of the Rolls had to pressure McCardie back into line, and the trial judge also faced parliamentary criticism; no one seems to have thought of reprimanding Scrutton LJ.[50] These immediate ramifications of the attack, and its gratuitous, highly personal nature, tended to obscure its deeper significance: for what Scrutton LJ had done was to attack McCardie J and all that he stood for; and what – at its most elemental – McCardie J stood for was a common law shaped by social change. For McCardie J the judicial role demanded an imaginative understanding of contemporary society; for Scrutton LJ the exact opposite was true – sociological ignorance was a judicial virtue.

By firmly excluding any requirement of overborne will, the Court of Appeal's decision in *Place* v. *Searle* seemed to have fixed the tort of enticement into a pattern of assuming female passivity and suggestibility. In the following year, however, in *Newton* v. *Hardy*,[51] it became clear that different assumptions could still be drawn upon. The case concerned a claim by a wife against her husband's married lover, and the crucial issue was whether enticement was proved. Swift J adopted the submission of counsel for the defendant that 'You do not induce a person to fall in love with you and you are not persuaded to fall in love with him; these things just happen',[52] and added that 'morally, I suppose they are equally to blame'.[53] The judge then posed the rhetorical question, 'How can I say that Mrs. Hardy enticed Newton any more than that Newton seduced Mrs. Hardy?',[54] before concluding that enticement had not been proved. The judge might, of course, have taken the view that each party enticed the other, which would have resulted in a finding for the claimant, and created a potential claim by Mr Hardy against Mr Newton; but Swift J's approach had the attraction of attributing autonomy to both parties, whilst acknowledging that neither of them was entirely in control of their emotions. There was also an evident reluctance to condemn and an effort to be sympathetic, which had been conspicuously absent from the Court of Appeal's decision in *Place* v. *Searle*. In short, Swift J provided a more realistic picture of an extramarital affair than the model assumed by the language of enticement.

[50] Pollock, *Mr Justice McCardie*, 213–16, describes the events. The mud stuck: see, for instance, E. Phillips, 'Damages for Adultery' (1981) 11 *Hong Kong Law Journal* 54, 56 n. 9, discussing *Place* v. *Searle*, and referring to McCardie J, 'the bachelor judge', having 'a curious view of sexual morality'.

[51] (1933) 149 LT 165. [52] (1933) 149 LT 165, 167.

[53] (1933) 149 LT 165, 168. [54] (1933) 149 LT 165, 168.

The final issue concerning claims for enticement raised, in an acute form, the question of how tort law dealt with women: could a wife sue for the enticement of her husband? The answer given by Darling J in *Gray* v. *Gee*[55] can perhaps be best summarised as 'yes, in theory'. The first part of that answer required the judge to address the argument, apparently seriously advanced, that a husband was not the property of his wife, but a wife was the property of her husband 'just as much … as his cattle were'.[56] Darling J could not keep a straight face: 'Do you mean an English woman or a Choctaw?' he asked.[57] Counsel then modified the argument, putting forward instead that a wife was her husband's servant. Again, the judicial response was hardly encouraging: 'Who was it said that no slave shall breathe the air of England?'[58] When counsel moved on to citing dicta of McCardie J, the judge could not resist an anecdote: 'his Lordship said that he was in Italy recently, and he had read in a newspaper a reference to Mr Justice McCardie which, translated, meant that he was "an unmarried man and impenitent"'.[59] The judgment continued in the same light-hearted vein. The idea that a husband owned his wife was illustrated by some lines from Tennyson's *Locksley Hall* and discussed with reference to Livy and bride-sales, 'an old practice which he was not altogether sure had been given up now'.[60] 'In this country', however, 'a woman was never the chattel of her husband. He had *potestas* over her and his children, but *potestas* and *proprietas* were very different things.' All this pointed towards allowing a wife to sue for enticement. However, when Darling J came to sum up to the jury, the 'in theory' aspect of his decision came to the fore. 'That a woman could seduce a man' he told them, in the passage used as an epigraph to this chapter, 'he did not doubt; it had been the theme of many poets, and people were long accustomed in the old days to make use of love philtres to seduce the affections of other people.' 'Such stories', he continued were common in the Renaissance, and he crowned his direction with the following lines from Matthew Arnold's reworking of such a story in *Tristram and Iseult*:

> That spiced magic draught,
> Which since then for ever rolls

55 (1923) 39 TLR 429.

56 (1923) 39 TLR 429, 430 (summary of the argument of Clements, counsel for the defendant).

57 (1923) 39 TLR 429, 430.

58 (1923) 39 TLR 429, 430.

59 (1923) 39 TLR 429, 430.

60 (1923) 39 TLR 429, 431. Given the frequent literary references in his decision, it may be that here Darling J was thinking of the famous opening scene in Thomas Hardy's *The Mayor of Casterbridge*.

> Through their blood, and binds their souls,
> Working love, but working teen.[61]

The jury immediately returned a verdict for the defendant.

The genial good humour, comedy and literary flourishes make *Gray* v. *Gee* read like a lost work of A. P. Herbert, although, unlike that fastidious satirist, not all the barbs hit their target: the Choctaw Nation's traditions of matrilineal property and autonomy made them an almost uniquely poor illustration of the jokey point about wives being treated like cattle.[62] But certainly, so far as broad matters of tone were concerned, mockery and disbelief were not inappropriate responses to submissions that, at least as reported, defied parody. On the other hand, the tone of ridicule was not obviously suitable for the entire case, and there is a sense that – especially in his direction to the jury – the judge became carried away by his own literary virtuosity, without pausing to consider whether the material he was citing reflected contemporary social conditions. The result is a decision of peculiar ambivalence. It manages both to assert that a married woman has the same rights as a married man; and, at the same time, to undermine that ostensible equality by saying that women seeking to enforce those rights belong to a world of fairy tales and magic potions.

IV

At the heart of the enticement cases lay the idea that the defendant was being made liable for interfering with the claimant's marital relationship, or consortium. Such interference was intentional, direct and typically self-serving, but there was no inherent reason to confine liability to such situations; indeed, prior to 1900 it was well established that a husband could recover damages against a tortfeasor who had carelessly injured his wife, and this remained the position throughout our period.[63] The damages reflected the value of the wife's assistance, society and comfort that had been lost by reason of the injury. On the face of it, the legal analysis held true whether the injured party happened to be a wife or a husband,

[61] (1923) 39 TLR 429, 431. 'Teen' here has the seventeenth-century sense of harm or injury.

[62] One recent monograph has argued that if there was a decline in the status of Choctaw women, it was due to the influence of French Catholic missionaries: M. E. Pesanttubbee, *Choctaw Women in a Chaotic World: The Clash of Cultures in the Colonial Southeast* (Albuquerque, University of New Mexico Press, 2005). See, however, the sceptical review by Greg O'Brien in (2006) 26 *Journal of the Early Republic* 346, which emphasises the continuing high status of women in Choctaw society.

[63] *Mallett* v. *Dunn* [1949] 2 KB 180.

but, as we shall now see, a wife's claim for loss of her husband's consortium was found to be constrained by policy reasons.

The leading case was *Best* v. *Samuel Fox & Co Ltd*,[64] in which the claimant's husband suffered a serious accident at work that caused him to become impotent. The claimant's counsel sought to rely on the general principle of liability for interference with consortium (which he derived from the enticement cases) and combined it with the undoubtedly correct assertion that, *mutatis mutandis*, a husband would be able to claim under such circumstances. Counsel then went on to criticise Blackstone's explanation of why a husband could claim but a wife could not, which was that a wife was 'an inferior'.[65] Without expressly endorsing Blackstone, counsel for the defendant advanced submissions that led to the same result. The enticement cases, they argued, were authority only for the liability of defendants who maliciously interfered with consortium, and a case like *Gray* v. *Gee* was best explained as an interference with contractual relations.[66] Furthermore, any successful claim required proof of a total loss of consortium, which could not be satisfied if the husband and wife were still living together. Interwoven with these submissions was a point that was not so much a legal argument as an articulation of a particular attitude: a change in public opinion could not give a wife a common law right that she had never had in the past.[67] It followed that if Bracton – which was cited to the court in its original Latin – had got the law right in the thirteenth century, that must still be the law today.[68]

The Court of Appeal unanimously rejected the claim, but was unable to agree on the question of principle. Birkett LJ was not prepared to accept that a husband had a proprietary right in the marital consortium that the wife lacked, and regarded the idea of a wife being a servant as 'impossible to reconcile ... with modern thought and modern ideas'.[69] He believed that the enticement principles could be applied to negligence, but insisted on a total loss of consortium for liability to arise. Cohen LJ and Lord Asquith of Bishopstone agreed with him on this final point, and Cohen LJ shared the distaste for Blackstone.[70] But both Cohen LJ and Lord Asquith favoured confining the underlying principles of the enticement cases to intentional interferences with consortium, and were impressed by the absence of authority for a wife's claim.

64 [1951] 2 KB 639 (CA); [1952] AC 716.

65 [1951] 2 KB 639, 646.

66 [1951] 2 KB 639, 651.

67 [1951] 2 KB 639, 650.

68 [1951] 2 KB 639, 653.

69 [1951] 2 KB 639, 663.

70 [1951] 2 KB 639, 666, describing Blackstone's explanation as 'entirely obsolete'.

When the case reached the House of Lords, counsel responded to the points raised by the Court of Appeal. The question of whether partial loss of consortium could be recovered prompted a close analysis of the Latin formulae originally used in declarations, and the broader issue of principle also received a Romanist infusion.[71] Counsel for the defendant now drew directly on the language of Bracton to assert that a husband's claim for loss of his wife's consortium was based on *potestas*: 'from early times ... a person in the potestas of another was deemed to be in an analogous position to that of the other person's property.'[72] A husband's claim, on this basis, was for interference with his *potestas* over his wife. Crucially, a wife had no *potestas* over her husband, hence the asymmetry of rights in the two spouses.

The House of Lords unanimously rejected the claim, although Lord Oaksey and Lord Reid queried whether consortium was truly indivisible. On the more important question of principle they all agreed that the enticement cases were confined to deliberate and malicious interferences, and that the availability of a claim to a husband in respect of his injured wife did not compel them to recognise a corresponding claim where the husband was injured. The husband's claim was based on a proprietary,[73] or quasi-proprietary,[74] right that was anomalous, but could only now be changed by statute. The result was an imbalance in rights, 'but', as Lord Goddard remarked, 'English law is free neither of some anomalies nor of everything illogical'.[75]

We need not disagree with this oddly self-satisfied platitude, but nor should we allow the invocation of history to draw a veil over the court's thought processes. One of the most striking features about the case is just how large history was allowed to loom. This was not *compelling* history in the sense of binding judicial precedent – there was no such precedent – it was history in the form of the language of pleadings and excerpts from textbooks, with the latter being treated with unquestioning veneration. Thus, Bracton's use of the Roman law concept of *potestas* was allowed to serve as an explanation for a husband's right to sue for loss of consortium, despite this explanation rather tendentiously assuming that English courts had received Roman law. Nor was the concept of *potestas*, as used by Bracton, subjected to any critical scrutiny. Reference to any Roman law textbook would immediately have alerted counsel and the judges to

[71] For analysis of the formulae see [1952] AC 716, 720–1.
[72] [1952] AC 716, 721. [73] [1952] AC 716, 731 (Lord Goddard).
[74] [1952] AC 716, 735 (Lord Morton). [75] [1952] AC 716, 733.

the fact that Bracton's concept of *potestas* was very different to the Roman idea; in classical Rome, under a free marriage, a wife would indeed have been subject to *potestas*, but it would have been the *potestas* of her *father*, not her husband.[76] A court with a different attitude might just as easily have dismissed these passages from Bracton and Blackstone as no more than antiquarian straws in the wind, but, for the House of Lords, 'there are no books of higher authority'.[77] The use of the present tense here was revealing.

The House of Lords was, of course, aware that it was no longer the eighteenth century, but the failure of the law to treat husbands and wives equally seemed not to worry it. Lord Goddard's remark about anomalies has already been set out; Lord Porter attempted something more sophisticated:

> Even … if it be assumed that in enticement cases the husband and wife have equal rights it does not follow that today they have equal rights and liabilities one towards the other in all respects. I do not think it possible to say that a change in the outlook of the public, however great, must inevitably be followed by a change in the law of this country. The common law is a historical development rather than a logical whole, and the fact that a particular doctrine does not logically accord with another or others is no ground for its rejection.
>
> Undoubtedly certain differences between the position of husband and wife have been extinguished or modified by Act of Parliament with the result that the general opinion of the relationship which exists between the spouses has changed, and it is quite true that modern textbooks express inconsistent opinions.[78]

Neither of these factors, however, required change in the common law.

Some aspects of this important passage invite parody – its underlying argument can be paraphrased as 'we should not complain about the common law being nonsense so long as it is old English nonsense' – but there are also more subtle themes at work. The first is the reference to 'this country'. The immediate context of the passage was not comparative, and the identity of the implied contrast remains elusive. Possibly the idea of the common law as an institutional safeguard against unchecked popular will was intended to echo Edmund Burke's well-known criticisms of

[76] For an exposition of *potestas* in Roman law see P. du Plessis, *Borkowski's Textbook of Roman Law*, 4th edn (Oxford University Press, 2010), 113ff.

[77] [1952] AC 716, 731 (Lord Goddard).

[78] [1952] AC 716, 727.

post-revolutionary popular government in France.[79] The rhetorical strategy, on the other hand, is easier to piece together – it links country, history and common law doctrine, and seems to regard the common law as an institutional expression of the national past. On this view of the common law, people who complain that the law is at odds with contemporary values are made to sound rather like a visitor to a National Trust property who bemoans the lack of Wi-Fi internet access: the criticism has a certain superficial coherence, but fundamentally misses the point about the cultural importance of the edifice. Quite how resistant to change the common law was – on this model – can be seen in the final sentence quoted. A reluctance to be swayed by divided modern textbooks was perfectly defensible – although we might also reflect that textbooks are likely to be at their most useful on controversial points, and that the common law doctrine at issue was itself founded only on Bracton and Blackstone. What is immediately more striking is that indecisive modern textbooks are categorised with Acts of Parliament promoting equality for spouses. Lord Porter did not give any explanation as to why such statutes should be disregarded when attempting to ascertain the common law, and that was a pity, because, assuming he was right to see the common law as the expression of the country's history and values, parliamentary interjections were surely compelling evidence of what those values were. Perhaps Lord Porter's answer would have been that the common law, once fixed, was unresponsive to social change, and that it was to misunderstand the nature and ideological purpose of the common law to demand anything else. It may also be the case that the deliberate positioning of the (traditional) common law in opposition to (popular) statutes provides further evidence for the influence of Burke. In any event, both the decision and the reasoning in *Best* v. *Samuel Fox & Co Ltd* highlighted where such an approach led: the common law operating as a closed system, structurally decoupled from social values.

V

Whilst the legal position of married women in tort law was patchy and unsatisfactory, a woman's reputation for sexual purity was policed assiduously. Two leading defamation cases from the period illustrate, in different ways, how this occurred.

[79] E. Burke, *Reflections on the Revolution in France* (Oxford University Press, 1993; first published in 1790).

The first, *Youssoupoff* v. *Metro-Goldwyn-Mayer Pictures, Limited*,[80] arose out of a Hollywood feature film released in the United Kingdom under a title that made clear its lack of revisionist ambitions: *Rasputin, the Mad Monk*. It was a fictionalised dramatisation of historical events, with a screenplay that would be nominated for an Academy Award,[81] and included a scene in which the writer had felt the need to make the Rasputin character less appealing by having him either rape or seduce the fiancée of his eventual assassin. In the film the assassin was a fictional character, Prince Chegodieff, but it was well known that the real-life assassin was a Russian aristocrat called Prince Youssoupoff – indeed, His Majesty had written a book about it.[82]

The Prince's wife sued the filmmakers for defamation, and her claim succeeded both at first instance and in the Court of Appeal. For our purposes, the most important feature of the case was the decision that, whether the film portrayed seduction or rape, the allegation was actionable. This, in fact, raised two distinct questions. The first was whether the allegation of being a victim of rape was defamatory. The second was that, if the film was treated as slander, the allegation would need to be brought within the category of imputations against female chastity, in order to be actionable without proof of special damage under the Slander of Women Act 1891.

At first instance Avory J seems not to have needed to deal with the first question, but he did directly address the second one.[83] Counsel for the defendant seems to have argued that the film, taken as a whole, portrayed the assassin's fiancée as a 'pure, trusting, loyal, devoted woman', and that the imputation of 'ravishment' inferred no lack of chastity, because her consent was not implied. Avory J, however, disagreed. He was particularly struck by counsel's invocation of a passage from Shakespeare's *The Rape of Lucrece*. 'That, however', observed Avory J:

> was an unfortunate reference, because he (his Lordship) had, since the beginning of the case, re-read the poem and had found one verse which was a direct authority for saying that a woman who had been ravished had been deprived of her chastity:–

[80] (1934) 50 TLR 581.

[81] Best Writing, Original Story 1934 (writer, Charles MacArthur). It lost out to William Lord's *One Way Passage*. See www.oscars.org/awards/academyawards/legacy/ceremony/6th-winners.html.

[82] F. Yusupov, *Rasputin: His Malignant Influence and His Assassination* (trans. Oswald Rayner) (London, Jonathan Cape, 1927).

[83] *The Times* 6 March 1934.

But she hath lost a dearer thing than life,
And he hath won what he would lose again:
This forced league doth force a further strife;
This momentary joy breeds months of pain;
This hot desire converts to cold disdain:
Pure Chastity is rifled of her store,
And Lust, the thief, far poorer than before.[84]

This seems to have settled the matter, for the judge then turned to the principles applicable to identifying fictional characters as real claimants.

When the case reached the Court of Appeal, only Slesser LJ addressed the general question of whether an allegation of being a rape victim was defamatory. He concluded that it was, because the category of defamatory imputations was not limited to accusations of immoral conduct; it also extended to statements that tended to make a claimant 'be shunned and avoided and that without any moral discredit on her part'.[85] A person said to have been raped came within this test because she 'has suffered in social reputation, and in opportunities of receiving respectful consideration from the world'.[86]

Slesser LJ held that the film was libel, rather than slander, so he did not need to decide whether there was an imputation of unchastity. Scrutton LJ, however, felt that the argument had to be dealt with:

> I desire to approach this argument seriously if I can, because I have great difficulty in approaching it seriously ... and this is the argument as I understand it: 'To say of a woman that she is raped does not impute unchastity.' From that we get to this, which was solemnly put forward, that to say of a woman of good character that she has been ravished by a man of the worst possible character is not defamatory. That argument was solemnly presented to the jury, and I only wish the jury could have expressed, and that we could know, what they thought of it, because it seems to me to be one of the most legal arguments that were ever addressed to, I will not say a business body, but a sensible body ... I really have no language to express my opinion of that argument.[87]

Greer LJ opted not to deal with the points separately, making only the short observation that 'If anyone printed and published the following words, "The lady who was engaged to Prince Youssoupoff had had sexual relations with the mad monk Rasputin", nobody could suggest that that was not a libel which ought to meet with serious consequences'.[88] Both he

[84] *The Times* 5 March 1934. [85] (1934) 50 TLR 581, 587.
[86] (1934) 50 TLR 581, 587. [87] (1934) 50 TLR 581, 584.
[88] (1934) 50 TLR 581, 585.

and Slesser LJ also dealt with a complaint about the trial judge's summing up, which, it was said, had failed to make sufficiently clear to the jury that an imputation of being a victim of rape should attract a lower award of damages than an imputation of having been seduced. Both appellate judges rejected the complaint. Greer LJ thought that the jury would have understood the point anyway. Slesser LJ's reasons were more elaborate:

> it was not necessary to ask the jury to entertain such speculation at all. When this woman is defamed in her sexual purity I do not think that the precise manner in which she has been despoiled of her innocence and virginity is a matter which a jury can properly be asked to consider. When I say 'properly' I do not mean it would be wrong to ask them to consider it, but the absence of any such consideration cannot, in my view, disturb the jury's ultimate finding.[89]

The result was that both the jury's verdict and its award of £25,000 damages in the Princess' favour were upheld.

The *Youssoupoff* case can seem both highly significant and frustratingly elusive at the same time. It addresses fundamentally important issues, but only obliquely, in a way that places the onus on the reader to piece things together. It can also seem a disappointing decision, because it deals with a fraught, difficult question in a rather perfunctory way. As Leslie Treiger-Bar-Am later noted, all the judges regarded the general point of principle as obvious,[90] and it does not even seem to have worried Patrick Hastings KC, the Princess' counsel; for him the real concern was Prince Youssoupoff's evidence.[91] Only Slesser LJ offered any reasoning on the general point, but his statement that a person said to have been raped 'suffered in social reputation and in opportunities of receiving respectful consideration' was simply an assertion. P. H. Winfield, noting the case in the *Law Quarterly Review*, was troubled by the assumption that such a woman would tend to be shunned and avoided;[92] W. T. S. Stallybrass went further, saying that 'Slesser L.J. takes too low a view of twentieth century society'.[93] Whether senior courts or senior common rooms provided the better vantage point for observation of twentieth-century society was a nice question, but the terms of this exchange tended to emphasise a concern with how people

89 (1934) 50 TLR 581, 588.

90 L. Treiger-Bar-Am, 'Defamation Law in a Changing Society: The Case of *Youssoupoff v Metro-Goldwyn-Mayer*' (2000) 20 *Legal Studies* 291, 299.

91 P. Hastings, *Cases in Court* (London, William Heinemann Ltd, 1949) 33.

92 P. H W[infield], untitled note (1935) 51 *LQR* 281, 282.

93 W. T. S. Stallybrass (ed.), *Salmond's Law of Torts*, 9th edn (Sweet & Maxwell, London, 1936) 399 n. (c).

actually responded, as opposed to how they or idealised right-thinking people in their positions, ought to have responded. Later courts tended to emphasise the normative dimension of the test, which has made the *Youssoupoff* decision seem, in retrospect, yet more problematic.[94]

The treatment of the chastity point presents similar difficulties. Stallybrass' comment on the decision at first instance was a terse 'sed quaere? [but query?]'.[95] The Court of Appeal's affirmation prompted more specific reflection: 'But were the women who suffered from the German soldiery in Belgium in 1914 unchaste, and does a woman who receives alimony *dum casta* [literally, 'whilst she is chaste'] lose it if she is raped?'[96] This invocation of an atrocity within recent memory, and an apparently conflicting legal rule, formed a revealing counterpoint to the material on which Avory J had relied in coming to the opposite conclusion. For, insightful as Shakespeare is about the human condition, an Elizabethan poet's dramatisation of the thought processes of a Roman heroine hardly qualified as 'authority' for the proposition that a victim of rape in 1934 was unchaste. Scrutton LJ's comments, which Stallybrass described as 'an outburst … scarcely judicial in spirit',[97] take us little further as a matter of analysis, but, because of their instinctive nature, are revealing of that judge's underlying attitude. On closer inspection two points stand out. The first is the sudden appearance of an assailant's moral character as a potentially decisive factor in the extraordinary, because not tautologous phrase, 'ravished by a man of the worst possible character'. It is difficult to be sure what inspired the introduction of this moral hierarchy of rapists; a suggestion is put forward below. The second point is the judicial use of the expression 'legal argument' as a criticism. Here we can see the same concern that motivated Greene MR in *Fisher* v. *Ruislip-Northwood Urban District Council* (discussed in Chapter 3) to make scornful remarks about lawyers being surprised by sensible rules: the judicial worry was that over-elaborate legal analysis would cut off legal rules from their social supports. It is very striking that Scrutton LJ should choose this method of legitimating the decision, because, at least to a modern reader, it is the discrepancy between morality and the legal conclusion that seems to be the

94 For two significant examples of emphasising the normative aspect of the test, which remain landmark cases today, see *Sim* v. *Stretch* [1936] 2 All ER 1237 and *Byrne* v. *Deane* [1937] 1 KB 818.

95 W. T. S. Stallybrass (ed.), *The Law of Torts: A Treatise on the English Law of Liability for Civil Injuries by Sir John Salmond*, 8th edn (London, Sweet & Maxwell, 1934) 451, n. (b).

96 Stallybrass, *Salmond's Law of Torts*, 9th edn, 452–3, n. (g).

97 *Ibid.*, 399 n. (c).

decision's weakest point. At the very least we can conclude that Scrutton LJ believed that his decision accurately reflected widely held views.

The courts' fragmentary analyses of the questions of general principle in the *Youssoupoff* case, therefore, seem to raise more problems than they solve. In particular, it remains difficult to see how the judges could have failed to distinguish between consensual and non-consensual activity when that distinction seems such an obvious difference to us. Some light can be cast on the point by considering the comment made by Slesser LJ in relation to the quantum of damages: 'When this woman is defamed in her sexual purity I do not think that the precise manner in which she has been despoiled of her innocence and virginity is a matter which a jury can properly be asked to consider.' Here 'sexual purity' is an asset that is damaged irrespective of the woman's decision to engage in sexual activity; indeed, the woman is completely passive, and her choices count for nothing. In this configuration of sexual relations, Scrutton LJ's refusal to distinguish between imputations of rape and imputations of seduction, whilst being ready to discriminate between the 'character' of rapists, has a sinister kind of coherence, since it makes the seriousness of the allegation turn on the source of the pollution rather than the woman's own role in events. It should also be pointed out that the assumptions about female sexuality that inform the decision in *Youssoupoff* v. *Metro-Goldwyn-Mayer Pictures, Limited* were by no means unique to this case. The most obvious comparator would be *Place* v. *Searle*, where, as we saw in section III of this chapter, an identically constituted Court of Appeal had upheld principles of the tort of enticement that embodied female passivity and suggestibility. Indeed, those principles of enticement assumed that women were so controlled by men that their choices were little more than illusory; if this remained the working assumption, it was easier to see why the same judges in *Youssoupoff* felt that there was, in reality, virtually nothing to choose between imputations of seduction and rape. Furthermore, this image of women as subordinate to, and dominated by, men was hardly unique to the enticement cases: as we have already seen, it permeated contemporary (tort) law more generally.

A different, but related aspect of the law's attitude to female sexuality could be seen in *Kerr* v. *Kennedy*,[98] where the question was whether an imputation of lesbianism came within the Slander of Women Act 1891 as being an attack on chastity. Asquith J held that it did, because it met both of the alternative requirements for slander to be actionable without

[98] [1942] 1 KB 409.

proof of special damage, namely, that it was 'either so obviously damaging to the financial position of the victim that pecuniary loss is almost certain, or so intrinsically outrageous that [it] ought to be actionable even if no pecuniary loss results'.[99] An imputation of unchastity 'in whatever sense of the term', the judge explained, 'falls within both of these classes, since it is calculated both to bring her into social disfavour, and, as the phrase runs, to damage her prospects in the marriage market and thereby her finances'.[100] The judge then went on to deal with the suggestion that lesbianism, not being 'prominent in the public eye' in 1890s, was not intended to be included in the Act.[101] The parliamentary draftsmen, the judge asserted, would have known of it; to assume otherwise, 'one must assume that they had little or no knowledge of the literature of the ancient world: an assumption which I make bold to repel'.[102] It followed that the claim succeeded.

Asquith J's judgment was a variation on several of the themes of this chapter. Here again the classical and literary canon was being appealed to as a store of common values and knowledge about women and their ways, although we might wonder why Asquith J's confident assertion about knowledge of ancient literature did not extend to those Members of Parliament who had voted the Bill through! We might also note that he made no claims about awareness anywhere in Parliament of actual practice. Here also was the theme of marriage as a woman's defining moment, but with the twist that a woman's value was quite literally measured by the price she could command for herself in the market. As we shall see in the next section, the related idea that a woman's core identity was derived from her relationship as a wife had a systemic influence elsewhere in tort law.

VI

The rights of people suffering terror of nervous shock (to use the contemporary terminology) would not appear, at first glance, to raise issues peculiar to female claimants. As we saw in Chapter 3, men suffered such injuries, and could be compensated for them under the war injuries payments scheme. When it came to orthodox tort litigation, however, the claimants in the reported cases were invariably women, and this is probably what prompted A. L. Goodhart to observe, in the remark used as an

99 [1942] 1 KB 409, 411.
100 [1942] 1 KB 409, 411.
101 [1942] 1 KB 409, 412.
102 [1942] 1 KB 409, 412.

epigraph to this chapter, that the question in such cases was whether 'he – or more usually she' could recover in spite of having suffered no direct physical impact.[103] Of course, it does not follow from the fact that all the reported cases concerned female claimants that only women ever brought such claims; but it is certainly true that the succession of female claimants prompted judicial generalisations about women's attitudes and priorities.

When the Divisional Court addressed the issue at the beginning of the twentieth century, the law was already in an unpromising state. The leading authority was a decision of the Privy Council that denied liability in negligence where the defendant's carelessness had almost led to the claimant being killed by an oncoming train.[104] The advice of the Privy Council gave two reasons for its decision without firmly committing itself to one or the other. The first reason was that the damage was 'too remote'; the second was that such claims should not be permitted to proceed as a matter of policy. This seemed to rule out claims for nervous shock in tort, but less than ten years after the Privy Council's decision, Wright J decided *Wilkinson* v. *Downton*,[105] in which he allowed a claim for nervous shock to the victim of a cruel practical joke. The facts of *Wilkinson* v. *Downton* could be distinguished from a case of general negligence because the defendant's state of mind was closer to intention than that of the ordinary negligence defendant, but the underlying uncertainty about whether *Wilkinson* v. *Downton* could, or should, be reintegrated into the general law of negligence would remain a destabilising side issue.[106]

In *Dulieu* v. *White & Sons*[107] the Divisional Court opted to keep *Wilkinson* v. *Downton* separate from negligence in general, but nonetheless found liability in negligence for causing nervous shock. The claimant was the wife of a publican, and was pregnant. She was behind the bar of the public house when the defendant's employees carelessly drove a horse-drawn vehicle into the building, which caused her severe shock, serious illness and to give birth prematurely. The two members of the Divisional Court reached their decision to impose liability in very different ways.

[103] A. L. Goodhart, 'The Question of Damages for Shock' in R. E. Megarry (ed.), *The Law in Action* (London, Stevens, 1954) 3.

[104] *Victorian Railway Commissioners* v. *Coultas* (1888) 13 App Cas 222.

[105] [1897] 2 QB 57.

[106] For moves to incorporate *Wilkinson* v. *Downton* into negligence see, for instance, the judgment of Atkin LJ in *Hambrook* v. *Stokes Brothers* [1925] 1 KB 141, 157; Goodhart, 'The Question of Damages for Shock', 7–8.

[107] [1901] 2 KB 669.

For Kennedy J a duty of care was clear: the driver of a van owed a duty to be careful not to injure users of the highway, property adjoining the highway and those – like the claimant – who were lawfully occupying that property. In his view this was a case of physical injury (despite it not having been caused by physical impact) and was best described as 'nervous shock'.[108] However, he went on to observe, not all 'nervous shock occasioned by negligence and producing physical injury' gave rise to liability:

> The shock, where it operates through the mind, must be a shock which arises from a reasonable fear of immediate personal injury to oneself. A. has, I conceive, no legal duty not to shock B.'s nerves by the exhibition of negligence towards C., or towards the property of B. or C.[109]

In coming to this conclusion, Kennedy J acknowledged that he was echoing views expressed in the unreported case of *Smith* v. *Johnson*; but, as he made clear, he did not agree with the earlier court's analysis that such harm was too remote. Kennedy J preferred to emphasise that, in his example, A had done nothing which could reasonably be expected to injure the claimant. This seemed to indicate that there was no duty of care owed to B, although Kennedy J did not make it absolutely clear. He concluded his analysis by doubting that public policy alone could justify excluding nervous shock claims.

Phillimore J agreed with Kennedy J in seeing the case in terms of physical damage inflicted through the mind. He parted company with Kennedy J, however, when it came to analysis of the duty of care. Kennedy J had regarded the case as being governed by the general duty owed by a road user to occupants of adjoining buildings, but for Phillimore J that general duty did not extend to not frightening others; rather, it was a duty not to cause 'a collision or some other form of direct physical damage'.[110] So far as general duties where there was no impact with the claimant were concerned, the position was uncertain:

> There are dangers sometimes from the traffic at Charing Cross which might frighten not only an inexperienced and elderly countrywoman, but an experienced and cool citizen, the ideal vir constans for whom εμπιρεια [empireia – experience] makes ανδρεία [andreia – manliness]. But if physical consequences were induced by terror so produced, it may be that there would be no cause of action.[111]

[108] [1901] 2 KB 669, 672–3. [109] [1901] 2 KB 669, 675.
[110] [1901] 2 KB 669, 684. [111] [1901] 2 KB 669, 684.

However, the crucial factor here was that the claimant, 'a pregnant woman, was in her house'.[112] Phillimore J concluded his judgment by observing that the fundamental difficulty in these kinds of cases was all about duty of care, not breach of duty, causation or remoteness.

The analysis employed by Kennedy J would be subjected to searching scrutiny by later courts, and an assessment of its strengths and weaknesses is best deferred to a discussion of those cases. The analysis of Phillimore J, by contrast, has tended to be overlooked, perhaps because of its concern with the specific facts of the case. Phillimore J's judgment, however, gestures towards a cluster of prejudices and assumptions that were being brought to bear on the question of liability for nervous shock. The dichotomies in play in the example about traffic at Charing Cross were particularly revealing: man/woman, town/country, prime of life/elderly, cool/inexperienced. The first characteristics in each pairing were joined together, as if inevitably, to create contrasting caricatures of the naive old rustic woman, and the sophisticated man about town. Given who was writing, and where the judgment was being delivered, it is not difficult to pick out the one with whom the judge would have identified himself. Equally revealing (and a familiar theme from earlier sections of this chapter) was the use of criteria taken from classical literature to assess contemporary conduct. Here the criterion was, of course, gender-specific – the Roman *vir constans* (robust man), and an educated one at that, who knew his Greek. The point here is not to criticise Phillimore J for having certain ideal characteristics in mind: in assessing whether people should be able to claim in negligence for their reactions to shocking experiences, the application of a reasonable foreseeability test demands some kind of normative measure for how a 'reasonable person' would react. Rather, the point is to bring out the assumptions from which that normative measure was being constructed. Two further dichotomies could also be perceived in the background of Phillimore J's contrasting emphasis on the home – commercial/domestic and public/private – and this should alert us to an awkwardness in Phillimore J's decision. For the fact was that the claimant was not, in any ordinary sense, the classic 'pregnant woman at home'. She was only 'at home' in the peculiar sense that she happened to live where she worked, in a business whose name conflated (and played on) the contrast between the public and the domestic. The rhetorical scheme of the judgment was founded on a series of confident dichotomies, but when it came to the decision to impose liability, it was only possible to find for

112 [1901] 2 KB 669, 684.

the claimant by ignoring the blending of opposites in the situation, and inaccurately characterising her as a housewife.

Similar ambiguities of categorisation ran through the Court of Appeal's decision in *Hambrook* v. *Stokes Brothers*,[113] which involved a claim by a husband under the Fatal Accidents Act 1846. The claimant's wife was taking the couple's three children, aged 8, 10 and 11, to school. She left them to walk the final part of the journey themselves, up a steep road round a bend (where they were out of her sight). The defendants had carelessly left an unsecured lorry at the top of the hill, with its engine running. The lorry rushed down the hill just as the children were walking up it, and crashed into a shop. The wife was understandably anxious about her children's safety, an anxiety heightened when she heard from bystanders that a little girl matching the description of her daughter had been injured. She later found her daughter in hospital. As a result of these events the wife suffered a severe haemorrhage, from which she died two months later. Branson J directed the jury that the claim could succeed only if the wife had feared for her own safety; the jury found for the defendant.

A majority of the Court of Appeal allowed the appeal. Bankes LJ focussed on the dicta of Kennedy LJ in *Dulieu* v. *White & Sons*, which, he said, did not preclude liability because they were subject to the broader principle that a duty could be based on 'what a man ought to have anticipated'.[114] Here, he continued, the defendant ought to have anticipated that if the lorry ran away, it might terrify a woman, through fear for her own safety, and it should not make a difference if a woman, instead of fearing for her own safety, feared for the safety of her children. 'Does the law say', the judge added, 'that the defendant ought reasonably to have anticipated the non-natural feeling of the timid mother, and not the natural feeling of the courageous mother? I think not.'[115] Bankes LJ concluded his judgment by making it clear that his analysis was fact-specific: it applied only to a mother who was shocked by what she saw or realised with her unaided senses, and who experienced a reasonable fear of personal injury either to herself or to her children.

Sargant LJ's dissenting judgment used the same conceptual tools as Bankes LJ's judgment, giving special emphasis to what ought to have been 'reasonably or naturally' expected.[116] Where he parted company with Bankes LJ was over what that formula entailed on the facts. For him, the defendant simply 'did not do anything which could reasonably or

[113] [1925] 1 KB 141. [114] [1925] 1 KB 141, 151.
[115] [1925] 1 KB 141, 151. [116] [1925] 1 KB 141, 163.

naturally be expected to cause the harm in question to the plaintiff'.[117] The way that the harm came about was 'new and quite unusual'.[118]

Atkin LJ reached the same conclusion as Bankes LJ, via a very different route. For him, there was no duty of care issue in the case, because duty and breach of duty had been conceded on the pleadings. The only live issue was causation, and the question, essentially, was whether specially restrictive rules applied in the shock cases. Atkin LJ concluded that no such restrictive rules did apply. He was also careful to point out that, on his view of the case, foreseeability of damage was irrelevant, since all that was needed was proof that the damage was a direct result of the breach of duty. On the issue of distinguishing between fear for oneself and fear for another, he had this to say:

> It would result in a state of the law in which a mother, shocked by fright for herself, would recover, while a mother shocked by her child being killed before her eyes could not, and in which a mother traversing the highway with a child in her arms could recover if shocked by fright for herself, while if she could be cross-examined into an admission that the fright was really for her child, she could not. In my opinion such distinctions would be discreditable to any system of jurisprudence in which they formed part.[119]

Two interrelated themes of particular importance for this chapter can be traced in *Hambrook* v. *Stokes Brothers*. There is, first, the question of the extent to which the majority decision creates a special rule for women. Certainly there are elements in the judgment of Bankes LJ that could invite us to that conclusion, but those need to be set against the analysis of Atkin LJ, in which the concern about distinguishing between mothers who fear for their own safety and mothers who fear for their children's safety was simply a concern about line-drawing in itself. Indeed, Atkin LJ would have been content to recognise claims by mere bystanders, which makes it impossible to read the decision as a whole as responding to the needs of mothers. Second, there are the competing invocations of nature and of what is natural in the judgments of Bankes LJ and Sargant LJ. In the judgment of Bankes LJ there is perhaps a consciousness that the unvarnished argument from foreseeability was shaky, hence the need to bolster it with the loaded, essentially rhetorical question (quoted above) about the natural feelings of a courageous mother. With Sargant LJ, on the other hand, what is 'reasonably and naturally to be expected' – essentially, what

117 [1925] 1 KB 141, 163. 118 [1925] 1 KB 141, 163.
119 [1925] 1 KB 141, 157.

the law demands that a defendant should anticipate – did not extend to mothers' relationships with their children. The anticipation of such relationships hardly called for an imaginative gift, nor were they statistically uncommon, and that makes Sargant LJ's comments all the more significant: for legal purposes, children and their mothers could be assumed to be absent.

As might be expected from a decision containing such a kaleidoscope of attitudes, *Hambrook* v. *Stokes Brothers* engaged, and occasionally baffled, later judges. In the Court of Session's decision in *Bourhill (or Hay)* v. *Young*,[120] Lord Mackay availed himself of an interpretive freedom his English colleagues might have envied when he pronounced that Sargant LJ's judgment 'expressed the true English view',[121] an analysis that Lord Jamieson also adopted. Both of these Scottish appellate judges were endorsing an approach taken below by Lord Robertson, who had insisted on the need for a claimant to be shocked by fear for her own safety before a claim could arise. On the facts of the case there had been no such shock, because, although the claimant had been near to the location of a fatal motorcycle accident as it took place, she had been away from the site of the impact, and standing behind a tram at the time. In the course of reaching this conclusion about the need for a fear for personal safety, Lord Robertson used, as an illustration of the kind of situation where a claim would otherwise arise, the example of a person startled by the (pre-war) firing of the one o'clock gun in Edinburgh.[122] This had echoes of Phillimore J's example in *Dulieu* v. *White & Sons* of the elderly countrywoman terrified by the traffic at Charing Cross, and made use of a similar caricature of the naivety of rustic visitors to the modern city, whilst also playing on the court's location in that very city. However, as Lord Wright would point out when *Bourhill* v. *Young* reached the House of Lords, it was not necessary to link such examples to a requirement of fear for one's own safety, because in those examples no one had been negligent, so there could not be a claim in any event.[123]

The House of Lords' consideration of *Bourhill* v. *Young* confirmed that there was no requirement of fear for injury to oneself. That conclusion left open the possibility of liability to a mother for causing her to fear for her child's safety, although the House of Lords was notably unenthusiastic

120 1941 SC 395. 121 1941 SC 395, 419.
122 1941 SC 395, 406. 123 [1943] AC 92, 109.

to endorse *Hambrook* v. *Stokes Brothers*.[124] The key factor, according to the House of Lords, was foreseeability of damage whether by shock or by physical impact. On the facts of the case, they held, damage to the claimant was not reasonably foreseeable, and the claim therefore failed. In the course of reaching this conclusion, Lord Wright took the opportunity to explore whether a defendant ought to anticipate that a claimant might suffer from the 'peculiar susceptibility' to shock through being pregnant.[125] After considering what he described as the 'extreme' hypothetical example of a claimant who started to bleed after the slightest physical contact, he decided that requiring a defendant to anticipate that a woman might be pregnant was to expect too much. The only assumption that a defendant had to make was that others were of 'a reasonably normal condition, if medical science is capable of defining it'.[126] We should note two points about this analysis. First, pregnancy is seen as the antithesis of 'normal', despite its relatively common occurrence. The crude statistical likelihood of pregnancy surely made the supposedly parallel example of a person who bled following the slightest physical contact incomparable. Second, the reasonable man never gave a moment's thought to his own origins: pregnant women did not inhabit his world; he had no obligation to anticipate their presence; they were invisible.

VII

The position of women in tort law in the first half of the twentieth century was unenviable. A wife's inability to sue in her own name had been abolished, but the cluster of prejudices that had sustained that procedural bar for so long still informed and supported other legal rules where Parliament had not intervened. Thus, equality between spouses in tort and elsewhere was a pipe dream, and the principles of the tort of enticement assumed that a married woman scarcely had a mind of her own. The law of defamation's attitude was scarcely more flattering, attributing no significance to a woman's autonomy, and measuring her reputation for sexual propriety in terms of an asset in the marriage market. As for negligence, women occasionally succeeded in claims where they could be portrayed as stereotypical housewives and mothers, but the law generally stopped short of demanding that defendants ought to contemplate that a

[124] Lord Macmillan (at 105) saw no need to consider the *Hambrook* decision; Lord Russell preferred Sargant LJ's dissent (see 103).

[125] [1943] AC 92, 109. [126] [1943] AC 92, 110.

pregnant woman or a mother might be affected by their acts. In this latter situation, the analogy between a pregnant woman and a man with an extreme form of haemophilia eloquently demonstrated how pregnancy was being categorised.

In elaborating this conception of women, tort was pushing against profound social and legislative changes, and the question has to be why this antagonism occurred. Part of the answer must lie in the tradition of legal conservatism. Thus, for instance, the continuation of the tort of enticement could be attributed to conformity with precedent. Another part of the answer might be found in the common law's traditional reluctance to treat statutes as statements of principle. This would explain the continuation of the doctrine that a husband could be sued for his wife's torts, despite the statutory abolition of the bar on a wife's right to sue in her own name. More broadly, appellate judges were still unlikely to be faced with female advocates, whose abilities might have given the judges pause before they reiterated doctrines based on the passivity and suggestibility of women. But these partial answers do not really explain the entrenched nature of some of the positions we have encountered in this chapter, such as Scrutton LJ's praise for judicial ignorance of sociology, or Lord Porter's invocation of the historical common law. In these positions there is a militant note that celebrates the law's disconnection from social values, and exults in having escaped from the politics of social change. Of course, those positions were, in themselves, abrasively political beneath their camouflage of merely doing history's bidding, as can be seen from the often threadbare support for them. Thus, lines from Shakespeare became 'authority' for legal propositions about sexual propriety; Matthew Arnold's *Tristram and Iseult* defined the causal requirements in enticement claims by women; and Bracton and Blackstone between them fixed the law immutably for all time. This form of what we might call 'authority-creep' cannot be explained away as inevitable – it shows that the judicial development of tort doctrines concerning women was being tightly constrained.

5

Children

He (the Lord Justice) did not know whether the jury were influenced by sentimental sympathy in favour of the boy.

Vaughan Williams LJ

[T]here was some conflict ... between a view which may be called the 'humanitarian' view, that a child which has no knowledge or discretion to make it capable of contributory negligence must be guarded by the landowner on whose ground it is allowed or tempted to enter, and the 'hard' or 'Draconian' view, that a child must trespass at its own risk.

Scrutton LJ

I

Children played a variety of roles in tort law, although they were almost always cast as victims of the wrongs of adults. These wrongs might be redressed by actions in the child's own name (although the legal formalities were entrusted to an adult representative, typically the parent), as was the case for injuries caused by negligence. Or the wrong might be conceptualised as being to the child's parent – as when a father sued for the seduction of his daughter – in which case the claim would be brought in the parent's name. In theory a similar choice was available to the victims of torts committed by a child: the claim might be brought against the child directly, or expressed in terms of the parent's negligent failure to control their child. The reality, however, was that only claims against parents for failure to control were pursued in the courts.[1] But whichever formal structure the litigation by or against children happened to take, the legal principles governing its outcome were imbricated in assumptions about the relationships between children, adults and the increasingly mechanised world they inhabited. Indeed, it could be said that there

[1] E.g. *Donaldson* v. *McNiven* [1952] 1 All ER 1213 (QB); [1952] 2 All ER 691 (CA).

were in substance (if not always in form) three parties to each case about children: the child, its parents and the tortfeasor.

The centrality of the parental relationship was a constant refrain in cases on matters as diverse as seduction and occupiers' liability, both of which are dealt with in detail later in this chapter. It also underpinned one of the more startling arguments advanced in relation to children in tort law, namely that a child was to be identified with his grandfather, with the consequence that the grandfather's actions were to be attributed to his grandchild. The argument was put forward by counsel for the defendant in *Oliver v. Birmingham and Midland Motor Omnibus Company Limited*,[2] where the claimant, aged four, had been crossing a road holding his grandfather's hand when the grandfather, startled by the sudden approach of the defendant's omnibus, had let go of his grandson's hand and jumped to safety. The little boy was less fortunate. The court rejected the defendant's argument about identification, and held that just as the acts of a negligent driver (or ship's captain) could not be attributed to passengers,[3] so the carelessness of carers could not be attributed to infants. It followed that the boy had not been contributorily negligent, and his claim therefore succeeded.

The decision in *Oliver*'s case affirmed, as Swift J neatly put it, that 'An infant, a day old, has rights. Nobody has the right to injure him by negligence'.[4] The question that that comment in turn suggested was whether an infant could sue for injuries inflicted prenatally. But on the question of prenatal injury, by striking contrast with today's law, there was no English authority and very little literature. The major treatment of the question was provided by Winfield, in an article published simultaneously in Toronto and Cambridge, in which he argued for a cautious recognition of the right to sue.[5] His conclusion was inspired by a decision of the Supreme Court of Canada (which had drawn on the Quebec Civil Code and Roman law), and by the similar position of Japanese, French and German law, although he thought it would be 'rash' to rely on broader civil law generalisations.[6] For Winfield the chief obstacle to a successful claim was the practical difficulty of proving causation, rather

2 [1933] 1 KB 35.

3 *Mills v. Armstrong, The Bernina* (1888) 13 App Cas 1.

4 [1933] 1 KB 35, 39.

5 P. Winfield, 'The Unborn Child' (1942) 4 *University of Toronto Law Journal* 278; (1942–1944) 8 *CLJ* 76. Subsequent references are to the *Cambridge Law Journal*.

6 Winfield thanked Kurt Lipstein for his assistance with the comparative materials (see *ibid.*, 76).

than any theoretical objections to the existence of a duty of care. Indeed, he regarded the unborn child as a legal actor for other purposes too, proposing that a claim for defamation should be available to an unborn child for an imputation of bastardy. This proposal tested to its logical limit the truism that reputation was what other people think about you, but its combination of novelty in form and archaism in substance was perhaps never very likely to come before the courts in a real case. The opposite was true of antenatal injuries to children, and such claims would eventually receive statutory recognition in the second half of the twentieth century. In other areas, however, the courts would more than make up for this absence of case law on children in tort.

II

One particularly striking line of cases concerned the tort of seduction. Claims by parents for the seduction of their children had a long and – the commentators were unanimous – unfortunate history. For Winfield, the rot had set in in the middle of the seventeenth century, when it became established that the form of action was for loss of services (*per quod servitium amisit*), the same form that was used where a servant had been improperly persuaded to leave his employment. 'The law thus made a false start', said Winfield, 'by holding that the remedy must depend not on the question "Have the family rights of the parent been injured?" but on the question "Has the parent lost the services of the child?"'[7] As Winfield went on to acknowledge, however, the loss of services requirement was not applied mechanistically to child seduction cases – on the contrary, the requirement had been virtually eliminated by being presumed in respect of children of the age of majority who lived at home.[8] In fact, child seduction claims had become the staple loss of services cases by the mid twentieth century,[9] and this prompted John Fleming, in the early 1950s, to put forward a radically different analysis of the tort's development.[10] In Fleming's view the tort had not suffered from 'an unfortunate and vicious historical twist' (as Winfield had put it[11]); rather, it was a 'classical example' of a legal institution surviving a vital transformation of its

[7] P. Winfield, *A Text-Book of the Law of Tort* (London, Sweet & Maxwell, 1937) 250–1.

[8] *Beetham* v. *James* [1937] 1 KB 527.

[9] *Attorney-General* v. *Valle-Jones* [1935] 2 KB 209, 216.

[10] J. Fleming, 'The Action Per Quod Servitium Amisit' (1952) 26 *Australian Law Journal* 122.

[11] Winfield, *A Text-Book of the Law of Tort*, 250.

social and economic substratum, and adapting itself to changed circumstances.[12] The typical strategy of adaptation involved recourse to fictions 'in order to disguise the growing gap between the new factual conditions and the inherited legal norms'.[13] On this analysis, the presumption of service started to look less like a historical accident, and more like an inevitable consequence of social change.

As Fleming acknowledged, there was never a perfect fit between law and social ideas. Indeed, parts of his article, particularly the conclusion, could be read as arguing that a less than perfect fit was a *structural feature* of the relationship between the two systems. To describe the legal-intellectual environment at such (perpetual) moments of lack of fit, he borrowed an expression of Kahn-Freund's, to suggest that the law suffered from 'a feeling of uneasiness, some sense of the unreality of the atmosphere, of the clash between "law" and "truth and substance"'.[14]

The seduction decisions from the first half of the twentieth century eloquently confirmed this sense of malaise in their application to atypical family situations. The dominant note was struck by the Irish King's Bench Division in *Hamilton* v. *Long*,[15] where a widow's action for the seduction of her daughter was met with the objection that, the claimant's husband having been alive at the time of the seduction, the claim could have been brought by him alone. Counsel for the claimant advanced two arguments to counter this objection. First, at common law the daughter's service was owed jointly to both her mother and father. Alternatively, whatever the position at common law might have been before 1882, the married women's property legislation of that year conferred on the claimant her own, independent right of action. The court rejected both arguments. As a matter of common law, the relationship of master and servant was held to exist, during the father's lifetime, 'exclusively between the father as head of the family, and the daughter as his child, and one of the household which he maintained'.[16] The argument from the statute called for more elaborate analysis. At first the Act's conferral of an independent right of action on a married woman for breach of contract seemed to offer strong support for the claimant's position. However, the court explained that while the 1882 Act had undoubtedly accomplished specific legal reforms, it had not, at a

[12] Fleming, 'The Action Per Quod Servitium Amisit', 122.

[13] *Ibid.*, 122.

[14] *Ibid.*, 123. The quotation from Kahn –Freund was from the introduction to K. Renner, *The Institutions of Private Law and Their Social Functions* (London, Routledge, Kegan and Paul, 1949) 38.

[15] [1903] 2 IR 407.

[16] [1903] 2 IR 407, 411.

stroke, transformed the status of married women. Furthermore, the conceptualisation of the relationship of parent and child as one of master and servant for the purposes of the claim did not entail that that relationship became a contractual one as a matter of law. As Lord O'Brien CJ put it, 'The relationship of master and servant, or as it is more properly described the supposed relation of master and servant, which flows from the relations of parent and child, is a mere figment of the law.'[17] The 1882 Act had no application to such fictitious contracts.

Gibson J echoed much of the analysis of Lord O'Brien CJ, but he added some comments about the married women's property legislation that were notable variations on the theme. The Act, he commented, 'cannot be regarded as disturbing the father's right to his daughter's voluntary service in a case like the present of an ordinary peasant home'. 'This humble father's common law rights to his daughter's services', he continued, 'were unaffected by property legislation in which he and his wife had no concern.'[18]

Readers of Chapter 4 of this book will not need to be told that the courts steadfastly refused the opportunity to interpret the married women's property legislation liberally; so, to the extent that it turned on the statutory construction point, *Hamilton* v. *Long* was hardly breaking new ground. But two features of the decision provide crucial signposts about the legal treatment of children. The first is the confident assertion of a traditional, hierarchical family unit, with the father as sole head of the household. The second is the ambivalent legal construction of the parental relationship – the child both is, and at the same time is acknowledged *not really to be*, the father's servant. The legal 'figment' conceals the fact that we do not know what kind of relationship the law imputes, other than that – implicitly – the father is entitled to control his children's sexual activities. There is also a third feature of *Hamilton* v. *Long* that is suggestive, although in a less direct way than the first two features. It is the insinuation in the judgment of Gibson J that ostensibly general rules might legitimately differentiate on lines of class and wealth. We shall see later in this chapter that this rather troubling proposition had a habit of resurfacing at the margins of tendentious formal legal analysis.

The Irish court's decision was enthusiastically endorsed in England by Avory J in *Peters* v. *Jones*.[19] Again, the claim concerned an atypical family, in which the claimant had adopted a teenage girl, who came to live

[17] [1903] 2 IR 407, 413. [18] [1903] 2 IR 407, 415.
[19] [1914] 2 KB 781.

with the claimant and her husband; the seduction took place when the adopted daughter was twenty-two years old, and still living in the house. The judge did not hesitate to reject the argument that the claimant, as the person *in loco parentis* to her daughter, was the appropriate person to bring the claim. 'The principle', he declared, 'on which an action for seduction can be maintained is not ... that there must be the relationship of parent and child, or any quasi-relationship of parent and child, but that the relationship necessary is merely that of master and servant.'[20] And, while the claimant lived with her husband, any servant in their household was the husband's servant.

The theme of a husband's pre-eminence in his household was reiterated in *Beetham* v. *James*,[21] in a context that underlined both the strength of the fictions at work, and the potential for claims to be manipulated by hypocritical claimants. As a matter of legal form, the claim was impeccable: it was brought by a father for the seduction of his twenty-two-year-old daughter, who was still living at home. The claim's formal integrity was complemented by the kind of telling details that could be expected to play well with a jury: the claimant 'had been happily married for 34 years', and had suffered both 'dishonour' and 'a blow caused to his pride' as a result of the defendant's sordid activities.[22] The only trouble was that the claimant was not actually married to his daughter's mother (and never had been) – a truth which inconveniently emerged during the trial. Atkinson J, however, made it clear that this revelation did not jeopardise the claim, since the daughter's duty remained 'to the parent, or person in loco parentis, in whose household the girl is living, and that is the master of the house – the one who pays the rent and household expenses'.[23] It was well that the judge added this final phrase, for, on the facts of the case, the claimant was frequently absent from home for long periods, and his partner ran the household. The judge acknowledged that more difficult cases might arise about whose household a particular establishment was – such as 'where a man was paying mere occasional visits to his mistress' (and, presumably child by that mistress).[24] But while the claimant's being unmarried was irrelevant to the success of his claim, it was not irrelevant to the quantum of damages he could claim. 'The damages could only be substantial', said Atkinson J, 'if the jury were led to believe that it was a grievous wrong done to married people, who had suffered a blow to their pride and

[20] [1914] 2 KB 781, 784.
[21] [1937] 1 KB 527.
[22] [1937] 1 KB 527, 528.
[23] [1937] 1 KB 527, 532.
[24] [1937] 1 KB 527, 533.

sense of honour ... it is the insult to the parents' pride and honour that matters.'[25]

The emphasis in these cases on the way that the form of the action for seduction did not follow its substantive social function provided compelling evidence for Fleming's diagnosis (borrowing from Kahn-Freund) of a 'clash between "law" and "truth and substance"'. The cases also provided an interesting side-light on Fleming's further observation that:

> The time lag before the relevant legal rules are reshaped so as to provide once again 'a true mirror of social relations' is usually considerable, partially due to the conservatism of a judiciary whose opinions so often reflect the current notions of a past generation, and partly by reason of our emphasis on the traditional elements of the process of legal adjudication.[26]

Fleming did not indicate how close he felt the law had moved towards becoming a true reflection of social relations, and the cases provide ambivalent evidence. On the one hand, the fictitious nature of the 'service' relationship was openly acknowledged, and there was no forensic investigation of whether services had been rendered. But, on the other hand, we might hesitate to assert that the emerging law corresponded with widely held social values. For these cases depended on a father's right to control the sexual activity of his adult daughters – a stark fact that the 'figment' of services in the legal analysis tended to conceal. Once the services analysis was stripped away, what the claim was all about, in the words of Atkinson J, was 'the insult to the parents' pride and honour'. That value has a rather Victorian ring to it – indeed it strongly echoes the criticism originally advanced of the services cases by Pollock in the 1880s – and we might wonder how widely it was shared in 1937, when wider social changes such as electoral reform had given women important rights to make choices. If there is a failure to reflect contemporary values, the blame cannot be placed solely on the judiciary, for there was a notable silence from contemporary academic authors on how the law should be developing. Winfield, for instance, simply echoed Pollock's line about the need to recognise that the claim was in reality for 'outraging [a man's] domestic feelings';[27] it was taken for granted that a legal claim under the circumstances was the appropriate response. There is a strong sense here that just as the law on the point had atrophied, so had the proposed solution, with the result that

25 [1937] 1 KB 527, 533.

26 Fleming, 'The Action Per Quod Servitium Amisit', 123.

27 Winfield, *A Text-Book of the Law of Tort*, 244; F. Pollock, *The Law of Torts* (London, Stevens and Sons, 1887) 194–5.

an author writing in 1937 could be found automatically agitating for the law to reflect Victorian values. Perhaps the law (and lawyers) find it peculiarly difficult to reflect social relations when the most useful thing the law can do is to depart from the scene altogether.

III

The principles of seduction were, in theory, just as applicable to boys as they were to girls, but there seem to have been no twentieth-century cases involving claims by the parents of boys. Conversely, the principles of negligence, to which we now turn, were also gender-neutral, but all the cases concerned boys. The overarching theme of the case law was the exuberant and imaginative ways that boys found to injure both themselves and others. For the most part, courts told defendants that they must expect boys to be boys. Thus, 'the natural mischievous tendency of boys' justified a finding that an eye injury caused by a boy employee throwing a stone at a fellow worker in the workplace arose from their employment.[28] Similarly, in *Williams* v. *Eady*[29] a schoolmaster was held liable for injuries caused to one of his pupils when a bottle containing a stick of phosphorous burst after another boy had dropped a lighted match into it. Lord Esher explained that:

> the schoolmaster was bound to take such care of his boys as a careful father would take of his boys ... he was bound to take notice of the ordinary nature of young boys, their tendency to do mischievous acts, and their propensity to meddle with anything that came their way.[30]

Perhaps the most notorious instance of what we might call the 'boys will be boys' doctrine was provided by *Lynch* v. *Nurdin*,[31] in which a seven-year-old boy was injured when he fell off the defendant's cart, which had been left unattended in the street and had proved irresistible to the claimant. The fall had come about when another boy had started to lead the horse forward, and there were, therefore, three causes of the injury: the defendant's initial abandonment of the cart, the boy's leading it forward, and the claimant's own failure to take care of his own safety. The Court of Queen's Bench held that it was no bar to the claim that the claimant was a trespasser, nor did the claimant's conduct furnish a defence of contributory negligence, since the claimant had 'merely indulged the natural instinct of a child in amusing himself with the empty cart and deserted

[28] *Clayton* v. *Hardwick Colliery Co* (1915) 85 LJ KB 292 (HL).
[29] (1893) 10 TLR 41. [30] (1893) 10 TLR 41, 42. [31] (1841) 1 QB 29.

horse'.[32] The precise legal basis of the decision was difficult to pin down, as two separate reasons were given in the following concluding passage:

> the child, acting without prudence or thought, has, however, shewn these qualities in as great a degree as he could be expected to possess them. His conduct bears no proportion to that of the defendant which produced it.[33]

This could be read as a finding that, adjusting the standard of care to reflect the claimant's age, he had not been negligent. Or, it could be read as saying that the defendant's negligence was so much more serious than the claimant's negligence that a (complete) defence of contributory negligence was inappropriate in the circumstances. Both analytical routes had the potential to open up rich new fields of claims involving adventurous boys.

By the start of the twentieth century some judges were starting to worry about a gold rush. In *McDowall* v. *Great Western Railway*[34] the Court of Appeal went out of its way to tighten the foreseeability test when it held that a railway company that was fully aware of boys habitually trespassing on its lines could not be expected to foresee that those boys might release the brakes on a stationary train. Juries seem to have been less receptive to applying the foreseeability test strictly. Thus, in *Jackson* v. *London County Council*[35] a jury found the council liable in negligence when a schoolboy attending a council-run school was hit in the eye by a ball of sand and grit thrown by a fellow-schoolboy. The assailant had picked up the materials from a wheelbarrow that had been left in the school playground. Earlier on the day of the accident the school's headmaster had noticed the barrow, and had given instructions that it should be removed as he considered it dangerous; his instructions had not been carried out, but the fact that he had given them indicated that not only was an injury to a boy foreseeable, it had actually been *foreseen*. Nevertheless, Bray J expressed a 'great doubt' as to whether there was evidence of negligence,[36] and, when the case went to the Court of Appeal, Vaughan Williams LJ observed, in the sentence used as an epigraph to this chapter, that 'He (the Lord Justice) did not know whether the jury were influenced by sentimental sympathy in favour of the boy'.[37] It seems clear from these comments that the judges had hoped that negligence liability in respect of children would be pulled back, and were disappointed by the jury's decision. But, in retrospect, it

[32] (1841) 1 QB 29, 38. [33] (1841) 1 QB 29, 39.

[34] [1903] 2 KB 331 (CA); the decision at first instance is reported at [1902] 1 KB 618.

[35] (1911) 28 TLR 66 (KB); (1912) 28 TLR 359 (CA).

[36] (1911) 28 TLR 66, 67. [37] (1912) 28 TLR 359, 360.

seems to have been asking a lot of a jury to expect it to pick up the judicial signals about the nuances of the foreseeability test, and then go on to apply the test in what was virtually a counterfactual way. In other words, judges keen to limit liability were going to need sharper doctrinal tools than a foreseeability test. Vaughan Williams LJ's comment also suggested a deeper problem: the jury might have picked up the signals, and deliberately ignored them out of 'sentimental sympathy' for the boy. The point at which careful application of principles to the specific facts of the case slid into 'sentimental sympathy' was unlikely to be easy to pin down.

IV

The inevitable tensions between boys predictably being boys, sentimental sympathy, judges trying to control juries and maintaining coherent legal analysis came to a head in cases where children were injured while playing on the defendant's land. These occupiers' liability cases added the further dimension that if the boys' exuberance had led them onto land where they had no permission to be, they were trespassers, and it was a long-standing feature of English tort law that occupiers' duties towards trespassers were extremely limited. Essentially trespassers could only recover in respect of personal injury inflicted either intentionally or recklessly. The treatment of other categories of entrant was more generous. Those whom the occupier permitted to be present for their own purposes (licensees) were owed a duty in respect of concealed dangers that the occupier knew about, and which could not have been discovered by the claimant himself using reasonable care. Invitees, who were present in pursuance of business with the occupier, were owed the more expansive duty of taking reasonable care that the premises were reasonably safe.[38] This hierarchical structure both encouraged and rewarded ingenious arguments about implicit permissions and invitations.

The facts of *Cooke* v. *Midland Great Western Railway of Ireland*[39] provided a perfect illustration of how the categories of entrant could be finessed. The claimant was a child of four, who had been injured while playing with other children on the defendant's railway turntable. The turntable stood on private land close to a public road, and the children had gained access to it through a well-worn gap in the fence. This was not the first time that children had got through: the defendant's employees knew that children were in the habit of coming onto the land and playing

[38] *Indermaur* v. *Dames* (1866) LR 1 CP 274; LR 2 CP 311. [39] [1909] AC 229.

with the turntable. At trial the jury found the defendants liable in negligence, and the question on appeal, as the House of Lords was very careful to point out, was whether there was evidence of negligence.[40] They unanimously held that there was, for a variety of reasons. Lord Macnaghten's approach was the boldest of the committee. For him, the essential question was both stark and simple:

> Would not a private individual of common sense and ordinary intelligence, placed in the position in which the company were placed, and possessing the knowledge which must be attributed to them, have seen that there was a likelihood of some injury happening to children resorting to the place and playing with the turntable, and would he not have thought it his plain duty either to put a stop to the practice altogether, or at least to take ordinary precautions to prevent such an accident as that which occurred?[41]

There was no mention here of the claimant's permission to be on the land, and further down the same page it was made clear that this omission was not an oversight: 'It cannot make very much difference', he said, 'whether the place is dedicated to the use of the public or left open by a careless owner to the invasion of children who make it their playground.' This was an analysis that cut directly across the occupier's hierarchy of duties based on the status of entrants, but – not entirely consistently – Lord Macnaghten's conclusion seemed to relocate his approach within the hierarchical structure:

> Persons may not think it worth their while to take ordinary care of their own property, and may be not compellable to do so; but it does not seem unreasonable to hold that, if they allow their property to be open to all comers, infants as well as children of maturer age, and place upon it a machine attractive to children and dangerous as a plaything, they may be responsible in damages to those who resort to it *with their tacit permission*, and who are unable, in consequence of their tender age, to take care of themselves.[42]

Leaving the question of permission, which, on a traditional analysis was the fundamental starting point, until the end of his speech, and treating it as an aside, perhaps suggested that although Lord Macnaghten was not prepared to discard the hierarchical structure altogether, he did not regard it as exercising any formative influence over the extent of legal liability.

[40] [1909] AC 229, 233 (Lord Macnaghten), 241 (Lord Collins), 242 (Lord Loreburn LC).
[41] [1909] AC 229, 234. [42] [1909] AC 229, 236 (emphasis added).

Lord Atkinson's approach was more traditional, and drew on authorities such as *Lynch* v. *Nurdin* to establish a series of propositions about the duties of the owners of machines or vehicles towards children. His starting point was that 'every person must be taken to know that young children and boys are of a very inquisitive and mischievous disposition, and are likely to meddle with whatever happens to come within their reach'. Girls, it seemed, grew up quicker. From this first proposition it followed that, if vehicles or machines were left by their owners:

> In any place where children and boys of this kind are rightfully entitled to frequent, and are not unlikely actually to frequent, unattended or unguarded and in such a state or position as to be calculated to attract or allure these boys or children to intermeddle with them, and to be dangerous if intermeddled with, then the owners of those machines or vehicles will be responsible in damages for injuries sustained by these juvenile intermeddlers through the negligence of the former in leaving their machines in such places under such conditions, even though the accident causing the injury itself be brought about by the intervention of a third party, or the injured person ... be a trespasser on the vehicle or machine at the moment the accident occurred.[43]

The outlines of the facts in *Lynch* v. *Nurdin* were clearly visible beneath this general proposition. Lord Atkinson then made it clear that the general principle applied wherever children had the legal right to go, and, on the facts of the case, the children here had the leave and licence of the railway company because its employees, despite knowing that children played on the turntable, had never driven them away. He also made an important observation about the test for what counted as a 'hidden' danger, saying that the test 'must be applied with a reasonable regard to the physical powers and mental faculties which the owner, at the time he gave the licence, knew, or ought to have known, the licensee possessed'.[44]

The basic structure of Lord Atkinson's speech was, therefore, closer to the traditional hierarchy of occupiers' duties than Lord Macnaghten's analysis, but it had several significant new features. The first was the readiness to derive a permission to remain from the failure to eject the children. The second was the use of the idea of allurement, which recognised the propensity of children to be fascinated by machinery; in an era of increasing mechanisation this point gestured to a broad expansion of liability. Perhaps most important of all was Lord Atkinson's demand that occupiers should assess what might be a hidden danger to an inquisitive child.

[43] [1909] AC 229, 237. [44] [1909] AC 229, 238.

By requiring the occupier to adopt a child's perspective, Lord Atkinson was explicitly giving the child's view of the world a legitimacy and validity that it had not obviously had before.[45] This was less a case of sentimental sympathy than an insistence that the adult's perspective must (sometimes) yield to the child's.

Like Lord Atkinson's speech, Lord Collins' analysis combined formal orthodoxy with some surprisingly novel points. Two of his observations were particularly striking. First, that there was evidence not just of a licence, but of an invitation.[46] Lord Collins did not give a detailed explanation of his reasoning on this issue, and later courts and commentators would struggle to understand how the children could be entering the land pursuant to business with the railway company.[47] We can only assume that Lord Collins must have had a broader concept of invitation in mind. Second, he held that the children to whom the invitation appealed were 'incapable of caution and therefore of contributory negligence'.[48] This was hugely significant: contributory negligence was still a complete defence, and if it had no application to curious children, defendants were deprived of a major weapon in litigation. Lord Collins was also the only member of the House of Lords to consider foreign jurisprudence, referring to *Railroad Co* v. *Stout*,[49] where the United States Supreme Court had upheld liability on similar facts. There was, in fact, a rich history of turntable cases in the United States (as Pollock hinted in a note to the Law Report[50]), in which the *Stout* decision had a controversial place, since it opted to disregard the hierarchy of occupiers' duties.[51] Further analysis of the American scene, however, would only appear in the literature.

The proceedings concluded with a short concurring speech from Lord Loreburn LC, who was at pains to emphasise the 'peculiar circumstances' of the case.[52] He perhaps foresaw the controversy that the decision might

45 Contrast *Burchell* v. *Hickisson* (1880) 50 LJ (CP) 101.

46 [1909] AC 229, 241.

47 E.g. T. Beven, *The House of Lords on the Law of Trespass to Realty and Children as Trespassers* (London, Stevens & Haynes, 1909) 39.

48 [1909] AC 229, 241.

49 (1873) 17 Wall (US) 657. The reference is at [1909] AC 229, 242.

50 [1909] AC 229, 242 n. (1).

51 See further P. Karsten, 'Explaining the Fight over the Attractive Nuisance Doctrine: A Kinder, Gentler Instrumentalism in the "Age of Formalism"' (1992) 10 *Law and History Review* 45. The distinctive importance of the *Stout* decision within this body of case law is explored in L. Green, 'Landowners' Responsibility to Children' (1948–1949) 27 *Texas Law Review* 1.

52 [1909] AC 229, 242.

provoke, although even he might have been surprised at the vehemence of some of the protagonists.

V

The initial response was mild enough. Pollock's note in the *Law Quarterly Review* anticipated that some readers might get carried away, but he preferred to emphasise the more orthodox features of the case: the fact that the children had been held to be licensees, and the decision's consistency with United States' case law.[53] Pollock's summary of the approach taken across the Atlantic to child licensees and hidden dangers was that 'licensees known to the licensor to be, by no fault of their own, incapable of exercising the caution of an ordinary man are entitled to a measure of special care in proportion to their imbecility'.[54] 'Imbecility' captured some of the legal effect, though absolutely none of the tone, of Lord Atkinson's insistence that occupiers must place themselves in the position of their child licensees; but Pollock's general view of the case was positive.

The same could emphatically not be said of Thomas Beven, whose 'elaborate pamphlet' *The House of Lords on the Law of Trespass to Realty and Children as Trespassers* appeared within nine months of the House of Lords' decision.[55] Sorrow and disbelief were mixed with sarcasm and fury in a tirade against every aspect of the decision. The tone is nicely illustrated by a tendentious summary of the decision on the second page:

> The broad proposition involved is that by English law there is a duty imposed on a landowner whose property, accessible from the highway, is infested by young children who play upon it, to take precautions that they are not exposed to any greater dangers than would befal (sic) them in a well arranged playground.[56]

The excess of 'infested' here corresponds with the exaggeration of the 'playground'. The pamphlet would manage to sustain this pitch for its entire forty-seven pages, rising to something approaching a scream in its final paragraphs. Some of Beven's complaints were about the House of Lords' use of authority – in particular what he saw as over-reliance on *Lynch* v. *Nurdin*. In Beven's view, that case should have been classified as being about an obstruction on the highway – in other words, as a case of public nuisance. But more eye-catching than these technical points were

[53] F. Pollock, (1909) 25 LQR 229. [54] Pollock, (1909) 25 LQR 229, 230.

[55] The description as an elaborate pamphlet was Pollock's: 10th edn 47.

[56] Beven, *The House of Lords on the Law of Trespass to Realty*, 4.

his apocalyptic visions of the fate of property owners if they were to be made liable for the injuries of allured children. Beven foresaw nothing less than an inversion of the natural order, in which revolting children would force riverside cranes to be fenced off, watchmen to be posted at private see-saws, fruit trees to be reinforced, old swings to be repaired, ponds to be spoiled and gardening equipment to be locked away. These heterogeneous examples embraced both machinery and natural features, and both domestic and commercial occupiers, but they were unified by their gesturing towards a pastoral vision of England that was in jeopardy. An Englishman's right to his lawnmower, no less, was at stake.[57] Slightly awkwardly, Beven was not able to provide English authority for protecting the English idyll – it was, he said 'so plain … and the principle … so obvious, that to find recorded judicial expression of their common sense is difficult'.[58] American authority was pressed into service in its place.

What, then, had caused this disastrous departure from the straight and narrow? One culprit he identified was over-elaboration of legal analysis, and another, particularly in Lord Macnaghten's speech, was the ill-advised equation of moral and legal obligations. In dealing with Lord Macnaghten's approach, Beven's critique took on a new tone. The person of common sense and ordinary intelligence – which Lord Macnaghten had used as the touchstone of a duty of care – was imagined with greater sophistication: for Beven this ordinary person, assuming he thought it his plain duty to intervene:

> and had any pretensions at all as a lawyer and a student of the common law … would assuredly not have passed from enunciating a moral obligation to concluding a legal duty … And he would certainly have repugned vigorously against the suggestion to leave to an Irish jury, with their very emotional disposition and their unbounded generosity (not least conspicuous in dealing with the land rights of their neighbours), that if they found a moral obligation they were entitled to identify it with a legal one.[59]

We might feel that the hypothetical ordinary person here was starting to be fleshed out with too many of its creator's prejudices, and in some ways the combination of Lord Macnaghten's analysis and Beven's response reveal the strategies at work behind ostensibly uncontroversial invocations of ordinary people, and of common sense. But Beven's dig about sentimental

[57] The lawnmower example is on page 17.
[58] Beven, *The House of Lords on the Law of Trespass to Realty*, 18.
[59] *Ibid.*, 28.

Irishmen, who did not understand the basic difference between law and morals, also implied a personal criticism of Lord Macnaghten, as well as of his two Irish colleagues, Lord Atkinson and Lord Collins. The Irish motif continued in the next paragraph, where Beven set out the 'truth worn threadbare – that legal duty only covers a small province of moral obligation'. 'Irish land history', he pointed out:

> contains many a crucial illustration of this truth ... For example, moral duty tells me that I am not to see my brother starve, and, in the midst of plenty, stretch out no saving hand to him; but legal duty on my part to help there is none.[60]

Here, what starts out as a rather patronising remark about what the Irish should know about their own country's history, moves dangerously close to a taunt about the potato famine. At the very least, it was an extraordinarily crass example to have chosen in this context. Beven, however, had saved up his most offensive comments for a parting shot. In a conclusion that built to its climax by recapitulating the oppressive effects of the *Cooke* decision on honest English yeomen from boat builders to fruit sellers, Beven ended with this:

> Many hundreds of pounds will be paid as blackmail ... Some of the baser sort will speculate on a new road to fortune, a provision for life for a child without anything more serious than a maiming, or the loss perchance of a limb, and little Pat, or Jerry, or Tim's 500*l* will be an allurement – let us hope not an irresistible one – as of a morning the family horde is despatched to seek the day's diversions.[61]

'Pat' and 'Jerry' signal the children's nationality immediately, but it still takes a moment to take the measure of this portrait of the Irish as venal, cynical hypocrites, eager to profit from their children's serious injuries. For Beven, it seemed, the fundamental problem with *Cooke*'s case was that it was a decision by the Irish for the Irish.

VI

It is difficult to gauge the exact extent of the influence of Beven's pamphlet. Although the *Law Quarterly Review* did not notice it, it was praised in South Africa, celebrated in Canada and reprinted verbatim in every subsequent edition of Beven's own encyclopaedic book on negligence

[60] *Ibid.*, 28–9. [61] *Ibid.*, 48.

under his editorship.[62] The editors of the posthumous fourth edition excised only 'certain passages which are either wantonly offensive or not really necessary'.[63] The pamphlet seems not to have been cited by name in court, but Farwell LJ must surely have read it (or the corresponding passage in Beven's encyclopaedia), for his judgment in *Latham* v. *R Johnson & Nephew, Limited*[64] borrowed several of Beven's key points: *Lynch* v. *Nurdin* as a case of public nuisance; the importance of distinguishing – and not following – dicta in *Cooke*; and, most tellingly, the debilitating and demoralising effect of *Cooke*'s case on landowners. Beven's book was certainly cited by and to the appellate courts in cases that worked out the consequences of the *Cooke* case.[65]

Whether they were directly influenced by Beven or not, subsequent courts focussed on the question that Beven had posed so provocatively, namely, where should the decision in *Cooke* v. *Midland Great Western Railway of Ireland* be placed? Almost immediately after the House of Lords' decision, the Court of Appeal, in *Lowery* v. *Walker*, was asked whether *Cooke* applied only to children.[66] The context was a claim for injury sustained by an adult while taking a well-established short cut across the defendant's field, and the key issue was whether the claimant was a trespasser. The Court of Appeal could not agree. Vaughan Williams LJ and Kennedy LJ held that the defendant was a trespasser, and could not derive a licence from the defendant's failure to take legal proceedings against those who used the short cut. Buckley LJ, by contrast, characterised the situation as one in which the defendant 'was allowing the public habitually to cross his field'.[67] There was also a difference of opinion about *Cooke*'s case. Buckley LJ commented that *Cooke* 'was a case of children; and there

[62] South Africa: 'well-reasoned discussion' (1909) 26 *South African Law Journal* 621; Canada: 'excellent reading both for the matter contained therein as well as being an example of the caustic and amusing style characteristic of this eminent author' (1909) 45 *Canada Law Journal ns* 625.

[63] W. J Byrne and A. D. Gibb (eds.), *Negligence in Law by Thomas Beven*, 4th edn (London, Sweet & Maxwell Ltd, 1928) 188. Particularly delicate editorial choices had to be made at p. 208 of the fourth edition: the comments about Irish juries' readiness to infringe property rights other than their own were deleted; the starvation example was left unchanged, but the reference to Irish history was removed.

[64] [1913] 1 KB 398, 403–9.

[65] *Lowery* v. *Walker* [1910] 1 KB 173, 198 (Kennedy LJ); *Schofield* v. *Mayor &c of Bolton* (1910) 26 TLR 230, 231 (citation by Mr Gibbons, counsel for the claimant).

[66] [1910] 1 KB 173. See the contrast between counsel's arguments at 176 (*Cooke* applied irrespective of the age of the claimant) and 179 (*Cooke* applied only to children).

[67] [1910] 1 KB 173, 190.

may be some difference, although not I think a material difference for the present purpose between adults and children'.[68] Kennedy LJ seemed to go further, saying that *Cooke* was a case of 'plainly limited application'; 'I do not think myself', he continued, 'that it is possible to treat cases of this kind relating to children on the same basis as cases of adults.'[69]

When the case reached the House of Lords, there was no direct comment on the *Cooke* decision, but the House of Lords showed a readiness to infer a licence to enter the land that was very much in the spirit of their earlier decision.[70] They may have hoped to signal thereby that a sympathetic receptivity to arguments about implied licences was the way to proceed, but lower courts had very different ideas. In *Jenkins* v. *Great Western Railway*,[71] for instance, the Court of Appeal engaged in a strikingly technical analysis about the geographical scope of an implied licence, and concluded that a two-year-old claimant had exceeded the permitted limits. *Schofield* v. *Mayor &c of Bolton*[72] denied liability to a similarly young claimant by putting parents – who had been notable by their absence in both the facts and legal analysis of *Cooke* – back in the spotlight. This was done in two ways. First, and most crudely, parents were given a causal responsibility. Thus, on the facts of *Schofield*, where a one-year-old had wandered onto a railway track adjacent to a children's sandpit, it was said that 'the real causa causans of the accident was the gross neglect of the mother and father' in allowing their son to play in the sandpit unsupervised.[73] As Pollock would point out, this kind of reasoning was not analytically convincing: even assuming that the parents' initial decision had been negligent, it did not follow that any carelessness by the occupier had had no causal impact. Indeed, the causation principles elaborated in cases of contributory negligence placed causal responsibility on whoever had had the last opportunity of avoiding the damage;[74] applying analogous principles to the unsupervised children cases pointed away from parental causal responsibility.

The second technique for deflecting blame to the parents was more legally sophisticated, and less open to analytical objection. It introduced conditions into the implied licence that stated young children were only to be admitted under supervision.[75] This narrowed the occupier's liability in two crucial respects. First, unaccompanied children became

[68] [1910] 1 KB 173, 193. [69] [1910] 1 KB 173, 201.
[70] [1911] AC 10. [71] [1912] 1 KB 525. [72] (1910) 26 TLR 230.
[73] (1910) 26 TLR 230, 231.
[74] F. Pollock, *The Law of Torts*, 10th edn (London, Stevens and Sons, 1916) 494–5. See further Chapter 13 in this volume.
[75] It seems to have been first used by Lindley J in *Burchell* v. *Hickisson* (1880) 50 LJ (CP) 101.

trespassers, and were, therefore, only owed a very limited duty. Second, since the occupier was entitled to assume that children would be accompanied, he did not need to concern himself about hazards that would be obvious to adults but not to young children: such hazards would be made obvious to children by the advice of their adult supervisors. At a stroke, this implied condition dispensed with the need for occupiers to imagine children's perspectives of attraction and risk. Thus, in *Schofield*'s case Farwell LJ was able to say that 'whatever the invitation of the corporation, it was not given to children who were so young as not to appreciate the danger of a passing train'.[76] Vaughan Williams LJ made a particularly revealing comment:

> The mere fact that there was no evidence that children playing in the sandpit had ever strayed on to the line showed that the invitation given by the corporation, such as it was, was not to children of such tender years, but to children who might be 'allured' by an open gate, but in fact had never been so.[77]

This unapologetically acknowledged that the implied condition of adult supervision was being imposed after the event, for the benefit of the defendant. As Hamilton LJ would later observe, the great attraction of the conditional licence was that it offered 'a way out of the dilemma' that appeared to require the courts to choose between denying liability to a child or imposing oppressively high standards of care on a licensor whose licensees were incapable of appreciating even the most obvious dangers.[78]

VII

Occupiers' liability litigation continued to revolve around the graduated duties to different classes of entrant, and the question of what constituted a hidden danger to a child licensee. Accompanying the analysis of these technical legal questions, like the repetitions of a ground bass, were constant concerns about sentimentality, about where parents fitted in and about whether special rules applied to children.

Developments in relation to the graduated duties took a variety of forms, ranging from gentle revisionism to direct challenges to the entire structure. At the lower end of the scale of ambition, there were signs in some of the judgments in *Hardy* v. *Central London Railway Company*[79]

[76] (1910) 26 TLR 230, 231. [77] (1910) 26 TLR 230, 231.
[78] *Latham* v. *R Johnson & Nephew, Limited* [1913] 1 KB 398, 414.
[79] [1920] 3 KB 459.

that different approaches to trespass would apply, depending on whether the claimant was an adult or a child. In suggesting that there might be a distinction, Bankes LJ acknowledged that he was contradicting earlier dicta, but he maintained that 'what may amount to an effective warning to an adult may be no warning at all to a child'. 'I can conceive of warnings to children so ineffective', he continued:

> either from their nature or from the absence of any attempt to enforce them, as to convey to the mind of a child the impression that no real objection was taken to what was being done. In such a case it might be possible to draw the inference that the child was allowed to be and remain under the impression that it had permission to do what it was doing.[80]

On the facts of the case, it was not necessary to explore the issue further, since the children concerned were 'fully aware of the fact that they had no right to be, and no business to be, where they were'.[81] Warrington LJ also emphasised that 'it was brought home to the children that … they were doing what was forbidden', which perhaps hinted that he might have taken a different view if there had been less clarity.[82] What was particularly striking about this point was that trespass to land was well established as a strict liability tort. Readers may recall from Chapter 2 that Pollock struggled to wrestle it into his structure of tort law for this very reason. To suggest that children would only be treated as trespassers where they appreciated that their act was wrongful was to transform the basis of liability, and was also to place the child's perspective at the heart of the analysis. This was not uncontroversial – and Scrutton LJ, as the third member of the Court of Appeal in *Hardy*, was quick to reassert the traditional approach. 'I cannot understand a use of language', he declared, 'which describes [children] as there by my leave and licence, because I do not go to the expense and trouble of always stopping them from infringing my rights, though I very frequently do so.'[83]

A further attempt at incremental revisionism (and expansion) of the categories came in cases about public parks. In such cases there was no question that, in general at least, children were lawfully present.[84] The

[80] [1920] 3 KB 459, 465–6. [81] [1920] 3 KB 459, 466.

[82] [1920] 3 KB 459, 470.

[83] [1902] 3 KB 459, 473. The passage immediately preceding this quotation referred to the unfairness of imposing a duty on owners of land containing apple trees, streams 'and other infantile joys'. This may be a conscious echo of Beven.

[84] For a potential exception, see the facts of *Purkis* v. *Walthamstow Borough Council* [1934] All ER Rep 64, where the twelve-year-old claimant was injured whilst playing in an area reserved for younger children.

difficult question was whether the children were licensees or invitees. In *Purkis* v. *Walthamstow Borough Council*[85] Maugham LJ inclined to the view that the existing categories did not do justice to the situation: 'it seems to me', he commented, 'a natural conclusion that it is the duty of the local authority to do more than what I may describe as that arising from the cold neutrality of a landowner who allows persons to visit his property.'[86]

The facts of the case meant that no further consideration of the point was necessary, but in his brief comments Maugham LJ had surely identified a fundamental shortcoming: the duty categories conceived of the interests of occupier and entrant as being opposed (unless the entrant was invited on business), but the public authority's statutory obligations created a different kind of relationship, by dictating that parks must welcome the general public. A later Court of Appeal, however, held the line that there were three categories of entrant, and three only.[87] It also rejected a rather hopeful argument that the child of a ratepayer could be seen as an invitee, with the payment of rates providing the mutual financial interest traditionally required in invitation cases. The invitation argument was certainly rather strained, but that tended to highlight the very narrow conception of the relationship between occupiers and entrants that underlay the duty categories.

The closest thing to a direct challenge to the categories was provided by *Dumbreck* v. *Robert Addie & Sons (Collieries) Limited*,[88] in which a four-year-old boy had been killed by colliery machinery. The machinery stood in a field opposite the boy's house, and was easily accessible through gaps in the hedge. The occupiers knew that children frequented the field, and that their employees' desultory attempts to warn the children off had been ineffective. A majority of the Court of Session held that a duty of care was owed, using reasoning that oscillated between rejecting the categories of duty altogether and accommodating the facts within a capacious conception of licence. Thus, the Lord President (Clyde) commented that 'One of the main reasons – if not the only reason – why, in the normal case, a trespasser is beyond the scope of any duty owed to him by the proprietor, is that the latter has no reason to suppose that people are invading his property behind his back.'[89] This implied that the categories system was being superseded by a general principle of foreseeability of harm, an

[85] [1934] All ER Rep 64. [86] [1934] All ER Rep 64, 71.

[87] *Ellis* v. *Fulham Borough Council* [1938] 1 KB 212.

[88] 1928 SC 547 (CS); [1929] AC 358 (HL).

[89] 1928 SC 547, 554.

impression that was confirmed by the Lord President's emphasis on the defenders' knowledge of presence of children near the machinery.[90] On the other hand, the Lord President also stressed that the state of disrepair of the boundary fence cast valuable light on whether an occupier truly consented to the presence of children on his land;[91] that point could only be relevant in a dispute about whether the claimant was a licensee. Lord Sands, similarly, combined some very broad statements about duties owed to the perpetrators of 'trivial and amiable'[92] trespasses, with a conclusion that, in this case, children's presence was tolerated – in other words, that they were licensees.

The House of Lords seized the opportunity to reassert the orthodoxy. There were, they insisted, three sharply differing duties owed by occupiers depending on whether the claimant was an invitee, a licensee or a trespasser. Here the claimant was a trespasser, and his claim failed. The three categories of entrant were not to be distorted out of shape, or blurred into each other. In particular, the criteria for licensees needed to be tightened up: 'it is permission that must be proved, not tolerance'.[93] That, in turn, meant that less than effective protests by the occupier were legally decisive of an entrant's status as a trespasser.

Both courts' judgments were accompanied by perennial concerns about sentiment, differential treatment of children and the role of parents. Lord Buckmaster developed the theme of the appropriate differences between law and morality, while Viscount Dunedin explained that duties owed to child licensees would be more extensive than those owed to adults, since children would be less able to identify hidden dangers.[94] In making this latter remark (which was unnecessary for the decision in the case), Lord Dunedin may have overlooked the conditional licence approach – under which children had to be accompanied by adults who would draw the children's attention to any hidden dangers. Or perhaps he had not forgotten, and intended to signal that a tightening in the licensee test could be counterbalanced by discarding implied conditions; in any event, judicial reliance on the implied condition approach seems to have tailed off after the 1920s. The obvious accompanying adult would be a child's parent, and in the Court of Session (but only in that court), counsel argued that the boy's parents had been contributorily negligent in allowing him

90 1928 SC 547, 554.
91 1928 SC 547, 553.
92 1928 SC 547, 558.
93 [1929] AC 358, 373 (Viscount Dunedin).
94 [1929] AC 358, 379 and 376 respectively.

out alone.[95] The judges' responses differed. Lord Blackburn held that the boy's father could not avoid some responsibility for the accident.[96] The Lord President, by contrast, commented that to hold the parents negligent 'would be contrary to the mode of living usual in such comparatively humble households as that to which the child belonged'.[97] There was here a rare glimmer of recognition that the performance of parenting duties might be dictated by economic necessities.

VIII

The tripartite duty structure would remain in place until legislative intervention in 1957, and the House of Lords' insistence that a licensee must be positively permitted (as opposed to merely tolerated) on the occupier's land undoubtedly curtailed the number of potential claims by children. Where children could demonstrate permission, however, a (contrastingly) liberal approach emerged to the kinds of things they should be protected against. This development was almost certainly facilitated by the ambiguous language in which the relevant dangers were defined. There were two typical expressions: 'trap' and 'allurement'. 'Trap', as Hamilton LJ put it, was 'a figure of speech, not a formula',[98] a quality that made it less than ideal as a legal test. Indeed, its legal meaning was entirely metaphorical, since a person who created a 'trap' for others in the ordinary sense of the word was setting out deliberately to injure them, and was therefore liable even if they were trespassers. 'Trap' in its legal sense denoted 'the idea of concealment and surprise of an appearance of safety under circumstances cloaking a reality of danger'.[99] 'Trap' was, however, a model of clarity when set alongside 'allurement', which could be (and was) used in three different ways. First, it could refer to a deliberate strategy of tempting the claimant's animate property to harm itself – as by placing poisoned meat in the vicinity of the claimant's dog-kennels.[100] Second, it could refer to the attractive feature of the defendant's property that had

95 1928 SC 547, 550. The argument is described as being about 'contributory negligence' by the Lord President at 556. In English legal terminology 'contributory negligence' typically refers only to a claimant's own carelessness. The Lord President's usage of 'contributory negligence' may have been distinctively Scottish, but the summary of argument does not use that expression.

96 1928 SC 547, 565.

97 1928 SC 547, 556–7.

98 *Latham* v. *R Johnson & Nephew, Limited* [1913] 1 KB 398, 415.

99 *Latham* v. *R Johnson & Nephew, Limited* [1913] 1 KB 398, 415.

100 *Townsend* v. *Wathen* (1808) 9 East 277.

tempted a child to transgress the boundaries of the defendant's property: in this sense, 'allurement' was really part of the explanation for why the child could claim to have the defendant's tacit permission to come onto the land. Third, and finally, it could refer to the surprise element in the dangerous situation. Understanding analyses of allurement required an alertness to these different senses of the word in a literature where usages were inconsistent. Thus, for instance, it took careful analytical work to appreciate why Farwell LJ could correctly distinguish sharply between 'allurement' and 'concealed trap', and Viscount Dunedin could, equally correctly, treat them as meaning the same thing.[101]

Leaving aside decisions under the conditional licence doctrine – where the trap had to be such as would take an adult by surprise – the courts showed notable sympathy for injured child claimants. Thus, in *Taylor* v. *The Corporation of Glasgow*[102] a seven-year-old licensee had died after eating the berries of a poisonous shrub that was planted in a botanical garden. In the Outer House Lord Hunter rejected the claim, emphasising that the danger was not a concealed one: 'It is well known to all who frequent botanical gardens that the plants and shrubs are not intended to be tampered with, and in particular that berries or fruit growing on trees are not to be eaten.'[103] By a majority the Court of Session reversed Lord Hunter's decision, holding that the particular berries in question, which looked like 'cherries or big black currants' constituted a trap, because they looked safe.[104] Questions of parental responsibility were prominent in the judgments, and – unlike in the conditional licence cases – were separated out from questions of permission. Both Lord Dundas (in the majority of the Court of Session) and Lord Salvesen (who dissented) regarded parental responsibility in respect of obvious risks as defining the boundary of the local authority's duty to its child licensees. The potential for joint liability seems not to have been even contemplated.

In the House of Lords, which affirmed the Court of Session's decision, Lord Shaw echoed and amplified this confident demarcation of parental and proprietorial duties, explaining that 'the municipality or owner is entitled to take into account that reasonable parents will not permit their children to be sent into the midst of unfamiliar and obvious dangers except under the protection of guardianship'.[105] This apparently

101 *Latham* v. *R Johnson & Nephew, Limited* [1913] 1 KB 398, 405, and *Robert Addie and Sons (Collieries) Limited* v. *Dumbreck* [1929] AC 358, 376 respectively.

102 1920 2 SLT 74 (OH); 1921 SC 263 (CS); [1922] 1 AC 44 (HL).

103 1920 2 SLT 74, 77. 104 1921 SC 263, 270.

105 [1922] 1 AC 44, 60.

innocuous explanation moved subtly between fact, morality and law to make its point. First, it set a norm of guardianship without reference to the financial resources, or social practices, of parents. It then, on one reading, permitted an authority to assume that that norm would always be met, even if the authority knew full well that the standard of supervision was set unrealistically high. Under such circumstances, both moral and legal responsibility then shifted solely to the parent, despite the possibility, as a matter of legal analysis, of joint liability. Lord Sumner's speech in the case was notable for its rejection of the framework of half-truths and assumptions about parents that were being used as justifications for the landscape of legal liability. For Lord Sumner, the legal position in relation to parental responsibility was neither 'settled or even … simple';[106] he had particular difficulty in identifying the supposedly causal role of parental failures to give their children better instructions about potential dangers. Such failures seemed to him to be 'too remote to be a contributory cause'.[107] Lord Sumner's cautious conclusion was that further thought (and case law) was required, but even this provisional analysis was highly significant for the purposes of this chapter, for it highlighted the way that instinctive reactions about what parents ought to be doing had shaped the forms of legal liability without being subjected to rigorous legal analysis.

In *Taylor*'s case emphasis on the specific risk of eating particular berries – as opposed to the generic risk of eating wild fruit – had benefited the claimant, since he could not have been expected to know that those particular berries were poisonous. *Ellis* v. *Fulham Borough Council*[108] illustrated that a focus on the specific risk was not always helpful to claimants, and that the court would adjust its analysis accordingly. The scene of the accident was, again, a public park. It contained a paddling pool with a sandy bottom that had been designed for the use of children like the four-year-old claimant. While paddling in the pool he cut his toe on a piece of glass embedded in the sand, and the Court of Appeal held that he could recover damages from the authority. It was not submitted that the authority actually knew about the presence of the specific piece of glass, but the Court of Appeal based its decision on the authority's appreciation that children might be injured if sharp objects were left in or near the pool. This appreciation was manifested by the presence of a notice next to the pool prohibiting sharp objects, and by the instructions given to council employees to check the pool daily for any sharp objects. The difference

[106] [1922] 1 AC 44, 66. [107] [1922] 1 AC 44, 66.
[108] [1938] 1 KB 212.

in approach to *Taylor* v. *Glasgow Corporation*, where the generic risk was disregarded, is striking, as is the difference in what the authority was entitled to assume: while parents, it seemed, could always be assumed to act reasonably and responsibly in supervising their children, no such assumptions could be made about the basic decency of the general public (or its propensity to obey notices). It is difficult not to feel that, behind the linguistic confusions of traps and allurements, the courts were striving to find remedies for sympathetic claimants.

As a conclusion to this analysis of occupiers' duties towards children we might consider Scrutton LJ's remarks, which form the second epigraph to this chapter, about the choices confronting judges in these kinds of cases. There was, he said:

> some conflict ... between a view which may be called the 'humanitarian' view, that a child which has no knowledge or discretion to make it capable of contributory negligence must be guarded by the landowner on whose ground it is allowed or tempted to enter, and the 'hard' or 'Draconian' view, that a child must trespass at its own risk and, if it is so young as not to appreciate what it is doing, it is for its parents, and not for the landowner on whose land it enters without invitation, to protect it.[109]

He agreed with Salmond that liability to infant trespassers 'will in the long run do more harm than good', and insisted that the duty should lie on parents. Scrutton's formulation of the choices was stark, and the courts seem to have worked their way to a more intermediate position than his uncompromising terms allowed for – he himself, for instance, would not have found an implied licence in *Cooke* v. *Midland Great Western Railway of Ireland*.[110] In other ways, though, Scrutton's choice of language captured something of the deeper issues at stake in these cases. In rejecting a facile 'humanitarian' approach, he made it clear that he was not merely pursuing legal purity for its own sake. He perceived a potential for tort principles to signal the acceptability of certain kinds of behaviour (specifically, in this context, ways of parenting), and, thereby, encourage such behaviour in wider society. These potential effects had to be weighed against the temptation to make it easier for injured children to sue. In this analysis, law did not mirror social relations; it *defined* them. Perhaps Scrutton LJ (and Salmond) here took too high a view of the role of law in society; but such a view, though rarely expressed so trenchantly, was implicit in many of the decisions and much of the literature.

[109] *Liddle* v. *Yorkshire (North Riding) County Council* [1934] 2 KB 101.
[110] *Hardy* v. *Central London Railway Company* [1920] 3 KB 459, 473.

IX

One final way in which the law's attitude to children was revealed was when it was forced to answer the stark question: how much is a child's life worth? This was a question that would only confront the courts in the late 1930s, after the introduction of the survival of causes of action for personal injury (in the Law Reform (Miscellaneous Provisions) Act 1934), and the House of Lords' recognition of loss of expectation of life as a distinct head of damage.[111] From the outset, children's cases were problematic. The logic of awards for loss of expectation of life was that the more life was lost, the higher the award should be.[112] But in *Rose* v. *Ford* Lord Wright commented that a very young child would not necessarily be entitled to the highest award. 'Special cases may occur', he observed, 'such as that of an infant, or an imbecile or an incurable invalid or a person involved in hopeless difficulties. The judge or jury must do the best they can.'[113] What these special cases had in common – apart from nearly perfect alliteration – was enigmatic; ascertaining the appropriate award for a child in the light of this dictum would cause particular problems for the courts.

In *Trubyfield* v. *Great Western Railway Co*[114] Greaves-Lord J modified Lord Wright's dictum when he held, in a case concerning the death of an eight-year-old girl, that a reduction in the award for a child was only appropriate for a very young infant, confronted with 'all the terrors of child life, child ailments, and the like'. A child that had 'outlived the dangers of childish ailments', however, 'may look upon an unclouded vista of life'.[115] The substantial award of £1,500 reflected this view.

The jury in *Shepherd* v. *Hunter*,[116] where the accident victim was three years old, took a rather less rosy view: they awarded £90 for loss of expectation of life, which, as Slesser LJ pointed out, worked out at £2–£3 per year.[117] A majority of the Court of Appeal held that the award was 'clearly erroneous',[118] and sent the case back for another jury to have another go. Slesser LJ offered a further gloss to Lord Wright's cryptic dictum in *Rose* v. *Ford* about the special case of infants. Lord Wright, he suggested, had not meant to displace the logic by which an infant should be entitled to

[111] On the 1934 Act see Chapter 10; awards for loss of expectation of life were recognised in *Rose* v. *Ford* [1937] AC 826.

[112] *The Aizkarai Mendi* [1938] P 263.

[113] [1937] AC 826, 850.

[114] [1937] 4 All ER 614.

[115] [1937] 4 All ER 614, 616.

[116] [1938] 2 All ER 587.

[117] [1938] 2 All ER 587, 591.

[118] [1938] 2 All ER 587, 589 (Greer LJ); Slesser LJ agreed.

a substantial award for loss of expectation of life; rather, he was saying 'that one is not necessarily driven to that conclusion when he speaks of the special case of an infant, and the case has to be considered on all reasonable views, not merely measured by a mathematical consideration that an infant will probably live longer than an adult'.[119] This seemed to suggest that, in general, large awards should be made in respect of child deaths. Slesser LJ also addressed an intriguing argument advanced by the defendants:

> Mr Lynskey suggests – I was rather surprised to hear the suggestion come from him – that the local consideration that this infant lived in Lancashire and that this was a Manchester jury might have brought about this result. I cannot think that it is a question of local consideration at all. I think that one must consider it generally. It may even be that this child would have ended its life in some very happy rural area, listening to nothing but farmyard sounds and smelling sweet odours. However that may be, I think that it is impossible to say that £90 can, on any view, be proper compensation for this loss of expectation of life.[120]

Lynskey was a Liverpudlian, with a practice on the Northern Circuit.[121] He might, therefore, have been seen as speaking with some authority about attitudes to life in the north-west of England. But his argument, and Slesser LJ's response to it, indicated two important themes that would continue to dominate the case law. The first was the question of the proper role, and autonomy, of the jury, and the extent to which inconsistency between awards was a price worth paying for the authenticity of a jury's instinctive valuation. The second theme was the broader, and potentially inflammatory point that a person's length and quality of life would be determined by environmental factors, and – as Slesser LJ hinted in his comment about the farm – on a person's social mobility. Slesser LJ's response to that point was that, essentially, it had to be disregarded, and that response from that judge was particularly telling, since Slesser LJ, as a former Labour Member of Parliament, could not have been unaware of regional variations in the distribution of wealth, and the associated impact of such variations on the health and opportunities of the population.[122] It is tempting to speculate that where the Manchester jury went 'wrong' in this case was precisely

[119] [1938] 2 All ER 587, 590. [120] [1938] 2 All ER 587, 591.

[121] G. Bryson, 'Lynskey, Sir George Justin' in *Oxford Dictionary of National Biography* (online edition).

[122] S. Cretney, 'Slesser [formerly Schloesser], Sir Henry Herman' in *Oxford Dictionary of National Biography* (online edition).

in its failure to achieve the required detachment from its own social and economic milieu.

Greer LJ essentially agreed with Slesser LJ, but the third member of the Court of Appeal, Mackinnon LJ, while not dissenting, deferred to the opinion of his colleagues only with some hesitation. He felt very reluctant to derive from the fact that he disagreed with the jury's award the conclusion that the jury was mistaken. This was a line that he would reiterate in several subsequent cases, where it would attract the support of a range of appellate judges.[123] In particular, Scott LJ developed an approach to the question in which jury awards were to be accorded special authority and respect, saying in *Bailey* v. *Howard* that:

> I see no means of arriving at any sort of quantitative scale for the guidance of judges or juries except through the gradual working out, chiefly through the common sense of juries, of the sort of figures that in English civilization of to-day are to be regarded as reasonable for damages under that particular head.[124]

Less than a month later, in *Ellis* v. *Raine*, he would spell out precisely why jury awards in respect of loss of expectation of life deserved such respect:

> the problem set the Courts of this country is one of quite extraordinary difficulty. It is, so to speak, a social question, turning on the character of English society and the whole theory of politics of this country, and that being so I consider that juries are a much better guide than the judges.[125]

Scott LJ's approach had the merits of resolving the question of jury autonomy and avoiding judicial pronouncements about the economic determinants of life expectancy at a stroke. But it soon became clear that the underlying problem had not gone away, as trial judges started to make awards that the appellate courts found unacceptable. Thus, in *Mills* v. *Stanway Coaches, Limited*[126] Greaves-Lord J was held to have awarded (at least) double the correct amount when he gave £2,000 damages for loss of expectation of life to the estate of a thirty-four-year-old mother of four. For the Court of Appeal, the judge's error was not to be found in any defective legal analysis, but rather in the fact that in *Rose* v. *Ford* £1,000 had been given for the loss of expectation of life of a younger woman. It must be doubtful whether trial judges took much comfort from Goddard LJ's instruction that 'The only guide is to be moderate'.[127]

[123] *Bailey* v. *Howard* [1939] 1 KB 453; *Ellis* v. *Raine* [1939] 2 KB 180; *Gambling* v. *Benham* [1940] 1 All ER 275.

[124] [1939] 1 KB 453, 458.

[125] [1939] 2 KB 180, 183–4.

[126] [1940] 2 KB 334.

[127] [1940] 2 KB 334, 348.

The case that finally precipitated a change in the courts' approach was *Gambling* v. *Benham*, where the accident victim was two years old. Asquith J awarded £1,200 for loss of expectation of life, which the Court of Appeal held, by a majority, was not excessive.[128] Slesser LJ professed himself to be still unsure what Lord Wright had meant in *Rose* v. *Ford*; Mackinnon LJ still felt unable to say what the correct basis of assessment was.[129] Goddard LJ, by contrast, vehemently seized the initiative, and would have substituted an award of £350. The *Rose* v. *Ford* dictum, he asserted, required the award for a young child to be 'minimised'. The reason, essentially, was that a discount for the uncertainties of life should apply:

> where one is dealing with the case of a baby, or a very young child, it is far more difficult to say what his chances of the advantages of human life are than in the case of an adult, not necessarily of full age, but grown up and embarking, or about to embark, on life, having finished his education and being about to start in some definite calling. With an infant, one does not know that its parents will live, or that it will have any education.[130]

This last sentence was, perhaps, partly inspired by the wartime context. Interestingly, Goddard LJ concluded his judgment with the indication that he would not have been so interventionist with a jury award.

The House of Lords went further than Goddard LJ, substituting an award of £200, and indicating that a very different kind of approach should be taken to such awards in future.[131] Perhaps the key point was that 'the thing to be valued is not the prospect of length of days, but the prospect of a predominantly happy life'.[132] It followed that no statistical or actuarial calculation could supply the sum to be paid, and that a court had to investigate whether 'the circumstances of the individual life were calculated to lead, on balance, to a positive measure of happiness'.[133] Courts were to disregard financial losses and gains, and social position, and should choose 'very moderate figures'. Awards for very young children would be particularly low, since 'there is necessarily so much uncertainty about the child's future that no confident estimate of prospective happiness can be made'.[134]

As commentators were quick to observe, the House of Lords had effectively changed the nature of the damages award. Otto Kahn-Freund,

[128] [1940] 1 All ER 275.
[129] [1940] 1 All ER 275, 278 and 279 respectively.
[130] [1940] 1 All ER 275, 280.
[131] *Benham* v. *Gambling* [1941] AC 157.
[132] [1941] AC 157, 166. [133] [1941] AC 157, 166.
[134] [1941] AC 157, 167.

writing in the *Modern Law Review*, offered a particularly perceptive critique of both decision itself, and the manoeuvrings that had led up to it.[135] For him, the underlying problem was that, in seeking to make an award for loss of expectation of life, the law had tried 'to overstep the boundaries of its own effectiveness, and of the limitations of judge-made law in particular'.[136] Kahn-Freund was unconvinced that it could ever be appropriate to put a financial value on human life in court proceedings – he described the attempt to do so as 'touch[ing] the borderline of blasphemy'[137] – and he subjected the mechanisms proposed by the House of Lords to a devastating critique. In relation to children he pointed out that the insistence on uncertainty as to future prospects underplayed the fact that 'the future career of the vast majority of infants was pretty well mapped out by their social environment'.[138] Similarly, the question of education (to which Goddard LJ had referred when *Gambling* v. *Benham* was heard in the Court of Appeal) was 'settled by the state'.[139] The failure to take account of social environment when assessing the expectation of happiness of adults was even more glaring, and it prompted Kahn-Freund to introduce a sarcastic note:

> All we can do is to look at the 'character and habits of the individual' and see whether they were 'calculated to lead him to a future of happiness or despondency', but we must not look further, though we may have suspected that war and peace, defeat and victory, crisis and prosperity, bad harvest and good, are not less potent elements than individual character traits and habits. The human type envisaged by Lord Simon is a self-contained monad – his prospects of contentment are ingrained in his personality, collective factors do not count.[140]

The House of Lords' insistence that financial factors must be disregarded inspired a cutting paraphrase – 'Wealth does not produce happiness, nor does poverty produce misery. This has now been laid down by high authority.' But Kahn-Freund followed up this waspishness with a careful analysis. He agreed with the result on grounds of legal policy, but deplored Lord Simon's facile statement that lawyers and judges should 'join hands with moralists and philosophers and declare that the degree of happiness to be attained by a human being does not depend on wealth and status'. 'The social philosophy which inspires this statement', commented Kahn-Freund, 'is untenable in view of the facts with which we are all familiar

[135] O. Kahn-Freund, 'Expectation of Happiness' (1941–1942) 5 *MLR* 81.
[136] *Ibid.* [137] *Ibid.*, 89. [138] *Ibid.*, 93.
[139] *Ibid.* [140] *Ibid.*, 95.

and indeed incompatible with the bulk of social legislation. The degree of happiness does depend on wealth and status, but for excellent reasons the law asks us to disregard this fact.'[141]

Kahn-Freund's coruscating commentary highlighted the way in which ideologically slanted judicial reconstructions of social relations could be used to justify legal rules. In the context of this chapter his points about children were particularly significant. For just as courts deciding occupiers' liability cases were making assumptions about the proper extent of parental supervision, and erecting those assumptions into legal principles, so courts deciding fatal accidents cases assumed that children were reliant on their parents in other ways. Indeed, we could go further and draw the parallel between the economic assumptions in the occupiers' liability cases about a family where close parental or other supervision was available, and the surely similar assumptions of Goddard LJ in *Benham* v. *Gambling* about a family providing an (implicitly private) education for its children. This was how the law imagined the family, and it made its rules accordingly.

X

Tort law dealings with children in the first half of the twentieth century offered a variety of visions of children and childhood. The seduction cases depended on the analogy between childhood and service, and assumed a father's right to exercise control over his daughters' most intimate choices. The occupiers' liability cases, by contrast, envisaged a more carefree childhood experience, where, importantly, the adult world had to be adapted to the tastes and enthusiasms of children, particularly boisterous boys. When it came to the transition to adulthood, as contemplated in the loss of expectation of life cases, the emphasis was on children's vulnerability to ailments, and their dependence on their parents to provide the education and other benefits that would lead to a happy life. Inevitably, conceptions of childhood suggested complementary conceptions of parenthood, which courts and commentators frequently articulated, whether to indicate that the parent should be sued, or – more commonly – to point out where the real blame lay.

These different conceptions of childhood and parenthood interlocked to some extent, but were not entirely consistent with each other. That is, perhaps, only to be expected in legal principles drawn from different

[141] *Ibid.*, 96.

regions of tort law, but it also seems to have reflected a certain ambivalence about children in wider society. Undoubtedly the importance of recognising the autonomy and validity of children's views of the world had been gaining support from at least the middle of the nineteenth century (when it had been given a huge spur by Dickens' adoption of the child's perspective in many of his novels[142]). This, I think, was behind the American scholar Leon Green's assertion that occupiers' liability decisions in favour of foreseeably trespassing children were made because 'Children are vital to our way of life'.[143] (It was, otherwise, a rather cryptic remark, since children are indispensable to the continuation of any way of life.) But alongside this conception of childhood as a distinctive, inherently valuable life-experience, there still existed an older conception of children as essentially small adults, legitimately subjected to economic pressures and obligations.[144] One very visible manifestation of this conception was the continuing legal obligation on children to maintain their parents, which would only be abolished in 1948.[145] Such an obligation (and the broader conception of which it formed part) made it appropriate, rather than simply distasteful, to address (for instance) the economic benefits received by parents as administrators for their children's estates in the expectation of life cases.[146] Perhaps unsurprisingly, the tort doctrines could not avoid being both influenced by, and lending their support to, these competing conceptions about the roles of parents and their children.

[142] G. Orwell, 'Charles Dickens' in G. Orwell, *Inside the Whale and Other Essays* (Victor Gollancz, London, 1940).

[143] Green, 'Landowners' Responsibility to Children', 12.

[144] C. Tuttle, 'Children' in *Oxford Encyclopaedia of Economic History*, vol. 1, 415 provides a helpful overview of the competing conceptions.

[145] M. Crowther, 'Family Responsibility and State Responsibility in Britain Before the Welfare State' (1982) 25(1) *Historical Journal* 131.

[146] E.g. *Gambling* v. *Benham* [1940] 1 All ER 275, 280: 'one is in effect ... merely giving a *solatium* to the parent for the loss of the child'.

6

Media

He desired to say that the Court had no sympathy with this class of literature, which pandered to an unhealthy taste, and as to which, the oftener it was repeated the greater was the appetite for it.

A. L. Smith MR

In the eyes of the Committee we are not an important body, much less important than the journalists. But, such as we are, we represent English literature, and I think it would do no harm if this were tactfully indicated.

E. M. Forster

I

The history of tort law as it applied to the media in the first half of the twentieth century is the history of a series of overlapping conflicts about the nature, purpose and ambitions of the law in this area. The law of defamation, which formed the focal point of the debates, seems in retrospect to have been perfectly designed to provoke such disputes. One of its key features was the distinction between libel and slander, under which written defamation was subject to more stringent rules than its spoken equivalent. This distinction did not need to await the rise of radio broadcasting to be exposed to criticism: the early nineteenth-century court that installed the distinction did so with marked reluctance, saying that it was compelled by authority to do so, and law reformers immediately began producing proposals to eliminate it.[1] When radio broadcasting started to establish itself in the 1920s as a medium of mass communication, it therefore served to intensify the existing controversy over the differential treatment of spoken and written words, rather than creating a new debate.

[1] *Thorley* v. *Lord Kerry* (1812) 4 Taunt 355. The nineteenth-century proposals to abolish the distinction are discussed in P. Mitchell, 'The Foundations of Australian Defamation Law' (2006) 28 *Sydney Law Review* 477.

A second key feature of defamation that lent itself to debate was the role of fault. In 1900 it would have been impossible to assert with any real confidence whether liability in defamation turned on fault, because over the course of the previous century both the definition of malice, and the circumstances under which it could be presumed against the defendant, had been finessed to the brink of incomprehensibility.[2] The House of Lords' most recent pronouncements on the issues in *Capital and Counties Bank* v. *George Henty & Sons*[3] were bewilderingly diverse, and – as we shall see – the confusion opened the way for decisive judicial action. The role of fault, as well as being occluded, was also fragmented: the standard of fault applicable to a writer (whatever that standard was) was different to the standard applicable to a mere distributor, such as a newsvendor. For distributors a negligence standard was to be used, although the precise standard of care and detailed duties of a distributor remained to be worked out. The growth in the number of periodicals and the volume of copies being distributed during the first half of the twentieth century made the resolution of detailed questions about a distributor's standard of care more urgent, and was also used as an argument for that standard being set low. As we shall see, this suggestion that the law should adapt itself to the way the distributors' business was organised attracted a mixed reaction.

Both the distinction between libel and slander and the principles governing fault were structural features of defamation created by the common law. A further, relatively recent feature had been introduced by statute. That was the creation of special defences for newspapers where defamatory matter was contained in contemporaneous, fair and accurate reports of parliamentary proceedings, judicial proceedings and public meetings.[4] The pressure to expand the precise coverage of these defences, so as to embrace disciplinary tribunals and administrative adjudications, was difficult to resist. But what was more debateable was the policy of giving special protection to newspapers, and – more subtly – shaping the law of defamation as if it applied only to newspapers.

Two other features of defamation law were important in bringing fundamental conflicts to the surface. The first was the role of the jury, in particular its powers to decide whether defences had succeeded and what the quantum of damages should be. These powers heightened the uncertainties

[2] P. Mitchell, *The Making of the Modern Law of Defamation* (Oxford, Hart Publishing, 2005) chapter 5.

[3] (1882) 7 App Cas 741.

[4] Mitchell, *The Making of the Modern Law of Defamation*, chapter 10.

of litigation for the parties, and served to highlight the contrasting interpretations that judges and juries might place on the same set of facts. The second feature was the scope of the tort itself, confined as it was to imputations tending to damage the claimant's reputation. This left a wide area of statements for which tort provided no redress, ranging from distressing revelations about a person's private life to profitable unauthorised use of their image. Whether defamation should be expanded to include such (loosely classified) invasions of privacy involved, of course, detailed legal analysis. But it also raised broader questions about the activities of the press, about the merits of self-regulation as against compulsion, and invited comparisons with foreign systems of law.

II

The conflicts and issues at stake in the development of tort law relating to the media may well have been debated with such vigour because the contested legal issues were often aligned with the opposing interests of powerful groups. Thus, newspaper interests pushed for the expansion of defences for newspapers; distributors argued for a standard of care that would not disrupt their methods of business. Such self-interest was only to be expected. But what made the development of media-related tort law unusual was that the interests of those affected by the law of defamation came to be regarded as legitimate motives for change. The crucial moment came during a Cabinet meeting on 1 February 1939. The subject of discussion was a libel reform Bill, which was scheduled to receive a second reading in the House of Commons. The Bill consolidated two earlier proposals – one from A. P. Herbert MP, the other from the Empire Press Union – and had been drafted by Herbert, Valentine Holmes (a prominent libel junior) and Kenneth Henderson (an influential newspaper lawyer). Its origins and authorship might have been expected to give it a certain authority, but the Lord Chancellor (Lord Maugham) assured the Cabinet that 'he had consulted a number of eminent lawyers on the matter. They were all of opinion that the Bill was a very bad Bill indeed.'[5] The Lord Chancellor wished to appoint a Committee to consider the subject of libel reform. 'He thought that owing to the technical nature of the subject, the Committee should consist largely of lawyers.' The Cabinet agreed

[5] LCO 2/3058 Law of Libel (Amendment) Bill, 1939. The file shows that the consultees were Tucker LJ and Goddard LJ.

to a Committee, but, in discussion, 'the view was expressed that ... the membership should not be restricted to members of the legal profession'.[6]

The Lord Chancellor had probably envisaged a libel reform committee along the lines of the Law Revision Committee, which had been created only five years earlier and consisted entirely of lawyers, whether in practice or academics.[7] Had the libel reform committee proposal been approved by the Cabinet without modification, the committee's personnel, proceedings and report would surely have claimed libel as a province of 'lawyer's law' – that is, law formed and developed by lawyers, using criteria derived primarily from legal practice. As a result of the Cabinet's intervention, however, both the libel committee's composition and its procedure would contrast sharply with that of the Law Revision Committee, for the libel committee included journalists, a publisher, a newspaper proprietor and an author, and would hear evidence from an impressively wide range of witnesses, including novelists, printers, newsagents and librarians. It was now being recognised that this diverse collection of people were not only objects of libel law; their experiences and proposals were also to inform how the law should be changed.

The Lord Chancellor and his Permanent Secretary, Sir Claud Schuster, diligently implemented the Cabinet's instructions. Schuster quickly identified Lord Porter (a Law Lord) as the committee's chairman, and then proceeded to pick his way carefully through the flurry of unsolicited offers that followed the announcement that a committee was being set up. Expertise was not the guiding principle, nor was seniority: one of Schuster's first decisions was to pass over both A. L. Goodhart and P. H. Winfield on the basis that they were already on another official committee. Rather, as a revealing file note makes clear, Schuster had a particular composition in mind: three barristers, two solicitors, a jurist, a newspaper proprietor, two journalists, an author and two laymen.[8] The fact that some names were filled in but others left blank showed that the process was not being driven by personalities, but by the need to get the right spread of representation. Schuster even seems to have been content to delegate some choices. As 'jurist' he appointed E. C. S. Wade, from Cambridge, on the basis of an unsolicited recommendation from Kenneth Pickthorn, the Member of Parliament for Cambridge University. Wade was in fact

[6] LCO 2/3058 Minutes of Cabinet Meeting, 1 February 1939.

[7] The Law Revision Committee's creation and contribution to tort are discussed in Chapters 9 to 13.

[8] LCO 2/3058 The note, headed 'DRAFT' is undated; it appears in the file between correspondence dated 14 February 1939 and 15 February 1939.

Pickthorn's third choice (after Winfield and Goodhart), and had never written on tort.[9] Schuster was also content to appoint E. M. Forster on the recommendation of the Society of Authors (their other suggestions were Hugh Walpole and Ernest Raymond), and Taylor on the recommendation of the Institute of Journalists.[10]

When it came to selecting the representatives from legal practice, however, Schuster went to some lengths. He had immediately filled one of the solicitors' roles with Reginald Poole, but felt less confident about the second position, and sought advice from the Solicitor General, Terence O'Connor, about appointing O. S. Hickson. O'Connor's reply that 'I think myself I would probably trust him more than most of the Solicitors I know who make a practice of defending newspapers' – a qualified endorsement if ever there was one – seems to have reassured Schuster.[11] More problematic, however, was the third position for a barrister. Norman Birkett KC and Richard O'Sullivan had been signed up, but Valentine Holmes had declined.[12] One possible candidate was G. O. Slade, but here Schuster worried that expertise might be bought at the expense of character: 'some people think he is difficult to get on with', Schuster wrote to Birkett, 'and might be a difficult and not very useful member of the Committee.'[13] Birkett sent Schuster two notes in reply. The first tended to confirm Schuster's assessment: Slade was 'very self-opinionated and can be quite stubborn over non-essentials: and has not too good a control over his temper in times of provocation. The qualities make him "difficult" at times ... I think everything would depend on how he was handled and Porter would be admirable for that!'[14] Birkett's second note, dated the following day, put things in a different light:

> At the Bench at luncheon today, Porter took me on one side and said that he hoped that I was going to be a Member of the Committee. I told him I was and he mentioned the name of Slade. I thereupon asked him his view of him, and he said that he had always got on very well with him when

[9] LCO 2/3058 Letter dated 10 February 1939 from Pickthorn to Donald Somervell (the Attorney General); Somervell forwarded the letter to Schuster. Wade's main research interest was constitutional law, on which he had published a textbook – *Constitutional Law* (London, Longmans Green and Co, 1931).

[10] LCO 2/3058 The letter from the Society of Authors is dated 16 February 1939; that from the Institute of Journalists is dated 15 February 1939.

[11] LCO 2/3058 Letter dated 10 February 1939. Hickson telegraphed his acceptance from Monte Carlo (18 February 1939).

[12] LCO 2/3058 Letter from Holmes dated 16 February 1939.

[13] LCO 2/3058 Letter dated 21 February 1939.

[14] LCO 2/3058 Letter dated 21 February 1939.

> Slade had appeared before him in the old days, and appeared to welcome him as a Member of the Committee.[15]

Slade was duly appointed.

Birkett's notes were a nice illustration of the smallness of the world of law reform, and of its club-like atmosphere; they also highlighted Lord Porter's reputation as a chairman. Perhaps more surprisingly, that seems to have been Porter's main recommendation. As he himself wrote to Schuster, 'I am not an expert on the law of libel but I will of course act as chairman on the Lord Chancellor's Committee, if he thinks I can help.'[16] Porter here was not being excessively modest: he had a reputation for commercial expertise and unfussy legal exposition, but had no libel background. It would be possible to see Schuster's choice of him as merely expressing a preference for character, but – in the context of the instruction from the Cabinet – it is surely more significant than that: what Schuster needed was someone who was not already so immersed in the complexities of libel law that he would be resistant to changing it, but who also had enough authority to hold the balance (and we might note that it was a perfectly even split) between lawyers and non-lawyers on the Committee.

As things turned out, the perfect symmetry of lawyers and non-lawyers was short-lived. Within a week of the Committee's membership being settled, Schuster was writing to Porter about including a publisher.[17] We might suspect that, despite Schuster's denials, the underlying cause of this development was a waspish letter to *The Times* from the publisher Geoffrey Faber. Bertram Christian – described by Schuster as 'a rather pompous little man, but not a bad fellow' – was appointed, and with his appointment the Committee was complete.

III

One of the most interesting, and controversial, issues on which the Committee would hear evidence was the position – both legal and practical – of distributors. In 1885, in *Emmens* v. *Pottle*,[18] the Court of Appeal seemed to have created special rules governing the liability of distributors, but both the exact content and the range of application of those rules was uncertain.[19] The Court of Appeal's decision had excused from liability the

[15] LCO 2/3058, 22 February 1939. [16] LCO 2/3058, 16 February 1939.

[17] LCO 2/3058, 14 March 1939. [18] (1885) 16 QBD 354.

[19] For an explanation of how the rules in *Emmens* v. *Pottle* differed from the earlier applicable principles, see Mitchell, *The Making of the Modern Law of Defamation*, 130–1.

vendors of a newspaper containing an article defamatory of the claimant. Crucially, as found by the jury, the defendants had no knowledge of the existence of the article; they had not been negligent in not knowing that there was 'any libel' in the newspaper; and, 'the defendants did not know that the newspaper was of such a character that it was likely to contain libellous matter, nor ought they to have known so'.[20] Lord Esher MR disavowed any intention to lay down a general rule, but made it clear that the defendant's ignorance of the libel was a necessary, but not a sufficient, condition for avoiding liability: it was also necessary to show that the defendant ought not to have known, 'which must mean, that they ought not to have known using reasonable care'.[21] What the defendant ought not to have known was not limited to the existence of the libel on the claimant; the necessary knowledge went further – the defendant ought not to have known that the paper was likely to contain 'a' libel. The word 'a' here was the crucial one; it required the defendant to consider whether the newspaper being circulated was the kind of production that was likely to libel people *in general*. It was, perhaps, not entirely clear whether Lord Esher MR intended to erect this point about the character of the publication into a condition of the defence – he had, after all, wanted to avoid laying down a general rule. But no such hesitation was visible in Bowen LJ's concurring judgment: 'I by no means intend to say', he declared, 'that the vendor of a newspaper will not be responsible for a libel contained in it, if he knows, or ought to know, that the paper is one which is likely to contain a libel.'[22]

The Court of Appeal's decision was expressly fact-specific, and that inevitably raised questions about its scope. In his (unsuccessful) submissions, the claimant in *Emmens* v. *Pottle* had emphasised the element of profit. That dimension of the situation would resurface in *Martin* v. *The Trustees of the British Museum*.[23] There the court applied the decision in *Emmens* v. *Pottle* to reach the conclusion that the British Museum was not liable for making available pamphlets containing libellous matter. The jury had found that the Museum's trustees neither knew, nor ought to have known, that the pamphlets contained libels, nor had the trustees been negligent; the jury did, however, find that the trustees had not discharged their duties with proper care, and the claimant's counsel used this finding to press for a verdict in her favour. Pollock B, however, held that there had been no evidence of negligence to go to the jury, and that

[20] (1885) 16 QBD 354, 355.
[21] (1885) 16 QBD 354, 357.
[22] (1885) 16 QBD 354, 358.
[23] (1894) 10 TLR 338.

the defendants must therefore succeed. He then proceeded to make a series of observations about the case, including the following:

> The case was admitted to be one of 'first impression' and no case had been cited even of a private individual so dealing with a book innocently in his library having been held liable as publishing a libel … It would be different if the books were sold across the counter or delivered to be sold in the street. It was laid down on the ground of social policy that if a man chose to sell books or papers he must take the consequences of his acts if he knew that they contained libellous matter.[24]

The judgment then moved on to emphasise the 'vast public duty' on the trustees, and observed that the claimants had failed 'to prove their case as against a public body'. It concluded with a discussion of the trustees' powers under the British Museum Act 1753.

The reporter may have done Pollock B a disservice, but the overwhelming impression here is of an instinctive response not yet disciplined into the form of legal analysis. The last two sentences of the passage quoted above (beginning at 'It would be different …') were particularly unfortunate. The second sentence appeared to give an illustrative example of the general proposition in the first sentence; but when Pollock B had applied the principles from *Emmens* v. *Pottle* to the case, he had affirmed that a distributor who actually knew of the presence of the libel complained of was liable, whether it happened to be a newsvendor or a library. There was, in other words, absolutely no difference between the position of a commercial distributor and a library in the situation Pollock B highlighted. If there was a distinction between a newsvendor and an institution like the British Museum – and Pollock B seemed sure that there was – it was perhaps to be found in the less onerous standard of care that might be legitimately imposed on an altruistic public body. Pollock B's own later allusions to statutory powers, and to the claim being against a public body, might suggest that his mind was moving towards this idea of a variable standard of care. But even if this was so, the jury's attitude was quite clearly different. Pollock B commented that 'There was a vast public duty cast on the trustees to receive all books sent and purchase others, and that probably influenced the findings of the jury, who thought they could not inquire into or know the character of all the books asked for and used',[25] but that impression seems impossible to reconcile with the fact that the jury found that the trustees had not discharged their duties with proper care. That finding suggested that the jury regarded the defendants' public

[24] (1894) 10 TLR 338, 339. [25] (1894) 10 TLR 338, 339.

duties as – at best – irrelevant. This would not be the last time that juries would take a higher view of a distributor's obligations than a judge felt able to endorse.

At the beginning of the twentieth century, then, the broad outlines, but little of the fine details, of the distributor's position were settled. The first case on the issue in the new century – *Vizetelly* v. *Mudie's Select Library Limited*[26] – would confirm this sense of a doctrine still in its formative stages. The libel complained of was contained in a book, *Emin Pasha: His Life and Work*, and the publications had occurred when the defendants had lent copies of this work to their subscribers. The claimant had already brought a successful action against the publishers, part of the settlement of which included an undertaking to withdraw the libel from circulation. This the publishers had done by advertising for the return of all copies in order that the offending page could be removed, and an amended substitute page inserted; but, despite subscribing to one of the journals in which the advertisement appeared, the defendants had continued to circulate the book. At the trial the defendants' managing director gave evidence as to how they dealt with the risk of libels in books they circulated. Essentially, they did nothing: they circulated so many books that it was impossible to have them all read, they employed no reader, and 'it was cheaper for them to run an occasional risk of an action than to have a reader'.[27] The jury, having been asked by Grantham J to consider 'whether the defendants had used due care in the management of their business', found a verdict for the claimant with damages of £100.

Arguments on the appeal ranged widely, with counsel for the claimant even suggesting that the *Emmens* v. *Pottle* doctrine was inapplicable, since it was a special rule for newsvendors. The more fundamental issue, however, was the standard of care required of distributors. The key point was the extent to which a distributor was obliged to inspect and investigate his wares. In the defendant's submission the nature of the business of a circulating library made it unreasonable to take positive steps about a particular title unless there was a 'special circumstance to put them on inquiry'.[28] The Court of Appeal, however, was not prepared to interpret the test of reasonable care so narrowly, holding that there was evidence of negligence in the defendant's assessment that it was cheaper to run the risk of libel than to employ readers. When it came to explaining the analytical basis of *Emmens* v. *Pottle*, however, the judges were less confident. For A. L. Smith

[26] [1900] 2 KB 170. [27] [1900] 2 KB 170, 172.
[28] [1900] 2 KB 170, 173.

LJ, the question was whether the defendants had published the libel 'as … disseminators',[29] it being implicit that some special sense of publication was involved. For Romer LJ, the doctrine was all about mitigating the hardships created by the basic rule that anyone involved in transmitting a libel 'published' it – in other words, it was about a defendant escaping liability *despite* having published. And for Vaughan Williams LJ, the doctrine was entirely unproblematic, being 'when carefully read … in consonance with the whole history of the law of libel'.[30] Junior counsel for the defendant, one T. E. Scrutton, would later repeatedly remind readers that these were three irreconcilable views.[31]

One aspect of the judgments in *Vizetelly*'s case that Scrutton LJ found more valuable was Romer LJ's restatement of the basic principles of the distributor's defence. If the distributor supplied the material 'in the ordinary way of his business', said Romer LJ:

> the nature of the business and the way in which it was conducted must be looked at; and, if he succeeds in shewing (1.) that he was innocent of any knowledge of the libel contained in the work disseminated by him, (2.) that there was nothing in the work or the circumstances under which it came to him or was disseminated by him which ought to have led him to suppose that it contained a libel, and (3.) that, when the work was disseminated by him, it was not by any negligence on his part that he did not know that it contained the libel, then, although the dissemination of the work by him was prima facie publication of it, he may nevertheless, on proof of the before-mentioned facts, be held not to have published it.[32]

What is perhaps most striking about this restatement is the way it moves from 'the libel' in part (1.) to 'a libel' in part (2.), then back to 'the libel' in part (3.). It looks as if Romer LJ was being careful to preserve the distributor's obligation to assess the general character of the work being distributed.

IV

As these principles were applied over the course of the next fifty years, a body of case law developed that crystallised the specific obligations of distributors. There was no duty to be proactive; but, if a publisher was

[29] [1900] 2 QB 170, 175 (adopting the language of Lord Esher MR in *Emmens* v. *Pottle*).
[30] [1900] 2 QB 170, 178.
[31] *Bottomley* v. *FW Woolworth and Co Limited* (1932) 48 TLR 521, 521; *Sun Life Assurance Company of Canada* v. *WH Smith and Son Limited* (1933) 150 LT Rep 211, 214.
[32] [1900] 2 QB 170, 180.

once alerted to defamatory matter about the claimant in a periodical, there seems to have been an obligation to check subsequent issues – or, at least, the next one.[33] It was also held to be negligent to operate a system of distribution in which there was no mechanism to respond to the discovery of defamatory material by one of the distributor's employees.[34] These principles were not reached by consensus. In *Batten* v. *Pall Mall Deposit and Forwarding Company* Lord Hewart CJ prefaced his direction to the jury with an expression of regret. 'If the matter had been at large', he said:

> the jury might have thought that a very complete duty should be laid on those who retailed or distributed newspapers for profit to see that none of the newspapers which they sold contained any libellous matter. If that were so, some of our newspapers might find great difficulty in getting anyone to distribute them.[35]

Here the distributors' liability principles were being attacked not in terms of their legal foundations (in respect of which they were certainly vulnerable), but in terms of their instrumental failure to further the policy goal of suppressing libellous newspapers. Whether the law of defamation ought to be furthering that goal was perhaps too controversial to be assumed, but the analysis was absolutely right to identify the potential for distributors to act as gatekeepers; and, of course, the stricter the distributor's liability, the more likely it would be to refuse to distribute dubious material.

Lord Hewart CJ also took a distinctive approach to evidence of the volume of material distributed, and the time pressure under which it was done. Judges generally seem to have been sympathetic to the argument that where a large number of different titles were being distributed to tight deadlines, little checking of the material was possible. Thus, in *Haynes* v. *de Beck*, where the distributors were the well-known firm of WH Smith, Darling J characterised the failure to spot a libel as 'a mere slip which involved no kind of moral obliquity'.[36] Similarly, in *Bottomley* v. *FW Woolworth and Co Limited*, Scrutton LJ was evidently impressed by the fact that the defendant distributed between 400 and 500 different titles of remaindered American magazines each week.[37] Such sympathy

[33] *Batten* v. *Pall Mall Deposit and Forwarding Company Ltd*, *The Times* 23 June 1927 and 24 June 1927 (KB); *The Times* 19 November 1927 (CA).

[34] *Sun Life Assurance Company of Canada* v. *WH Smith and Son Limited* (1933) 150 LT Rep 211.

[35] *The Times* 24 June 1927.

[36] (1914) 31 TLR 115, 116.

[37] (1932) 48 TLR 521, 521.

implicitly accepted the distributors' method of business as a legitimate constraint on what the law could demand. Lord Hewart CJ saw things differently. As he put it to a director of WH Smith who was giving evidence in *Hood* v. *WH Smith and Son Ltd*, 'What does it matter if the Paris Magazine reaches Birmingham or Bristol on Wednesday or Thursday?'[38] His summing up made the point explicitly. Referring to the account of the defendant's methods of business that had been given in evidence, he said:

> If the jury had not been dazzled and distracted by that narration, they might have asked themselves what was the point of that evidence. Was the point urged that, while the bigger the business the more danger there was of some defamatory matter being distributed, the bigger the business the less need there was to take care because taking care was difficult?[39]

The jury found for the claimant, awarding £350.[40] This intransigent attitude towards distributors distinguished Lord Hewart CJ from his judicial colleagues; but it seems to have been shared by juries. Darling J's comment about the distributor's 'mere slip' in *Haynes* v. *de Beck* was made in the course of explaining why he was not prepared to enforce a jury's award of damages; Scrutton LJ in *Bottomley* v. *FW Woolworth and Co Limited* described a jury's finding of negligence as 'absurd'. Juries, like Lord Hewart CJ, seem to have felt that distributors needed an incentive to be more discriminating about what was put into circulation.

V

The element of the principles governing distributors' liability that had the potential to make distributors into censors was the requirement that a defendant ought not to have known that the material distributed was likely to contain 'a libel'. This widened the focus of the inquiry from what the defendant knew, or ought to have known, about the material's coverage of the claimant to a broader assessment of the kind of writing involved. *Weldon* v. *'The Times' Book Company (Limited)*[41] provided a good illustration. There the claims arose from allegations contained in two biographies of the French composer Gounod; the defendant was sued for having

[38] *The Times* 5 November 1937. [39] *The Times* 5 November 1937, 4.

[40] Hood's success encouraged her to pursue similar claims against a bookshop in Liverpool and against Selfridges. See LCO 2/3060 Law of Libel Committee Memoranda, 'OBSERVATIONS on evidence' by E. W. Seymour, National Association of Wholesale Newsagents, dated 12 July 1939, p. 2.

[41] (1911) 28 TLR 143.

sold the books, and sought to defend itself as a distributor. The jury found for the defendant, a decision which was upheld on appeal. Cozens-Hardy MR was quick to emphasise that the authors of the books concerned were French scholars 'of the highest literary distinction'.[42] 'It was quite impossible', he continued:

> that distributing agents such as the respondents should be expected to read every book they had. There were some books as to which there might be a duty on the respondents or other distributing agents to examine them carefully because of their titles or the recognized propensity of their authors to scatter libels abroad. Beyond that the matter could not go. It was impossible to say that there was a liability to examine the contents of books like the two in question, which were by authors of high character and related to a distinguished musician who had been dead for over a quarter of a century.[43]

Here high culture, scholarship and literary distinction were being contrasted implicitly with the low culture, populism and undistinguished journalism that was the staple fare of libel cases. It might well have been true that scholarly authors of literary distinction could be expected to adopt a more restrained attitude to defamation than less scrupulous journalists. It was probably also safe to assume that professional scholarly biographers would eschew unsubstantiated allegations. But self-restraint, a measured tone and proper research were not the requirements of the legal test. The test focussed on whether the defendant ought to have known that the work distributed was likely to contain a libel, and surely the truth was that any biography – especially a carefully researched and evaluative one – was bound to contain defamatory allegations about someone. After all, there can be few biographical subjects fortunate enough to go through life experiencing nothing but the impeccable behaviour of those around them. For similar reasons it was also difficult to see how the defence could be applied literally to the distribution of any newspaper or periodical dealing with current affairs, since all such publications could not but cast aspersions on somebody.

The suspicion must be that, when courts asked whether the defendant ought to have known that the distributed material contained 'a libel', they did not quite mean what they said. Perhaps they really meant 'an actionable libel'. Certainly the reference by Cozens-Hardy MR in *Weldon*'s case to the time that had elapsed between Gounod's death and the publication pointed in that direction: allegations against individuals did not cease to

[42] (1911) 28 TLR 143, 144. [43] (1911) 28 TLR 143, 144.

be defamatory, but they did cease to be actionable after those individuals' deaths. By the same token, a rigorous scholarly biography was almost inevitably going to be defamatory, but was highly likely to be protected by defences of justification or fair comment. In other words, for works concerning living individuals at least, the legal test had become a proxy for an overall assessment of literary quality.

Two later judgments of Scrutton LJ suggested – in an uncharacteristically indecisive way – that the law might be reinterpreted so as to excuse distributors from this uncongenial exercise in literary criticism. In *Bottomley* v. *FW Woolworth and Co Limited* a jury had found the defendants negligent in distributing an issue of *Detective Story Magazine* that contained a defamatory article about the claimant. There had been nothing to alert the defendants to the presence of the offending article, but the jury found negligence in the defendants' failure to make 'a periodical examination of specimen magazines'. Horridge J refused to enter judgment for the claimant, and, on appeal, he was held to have acted correctly. 'The jury's answer', said Scrutton LJ:

> was absurd and irrelevant. If Messrs Woolworth had in fact examined specimen magazines that would have had no effect unless the libel was contained in the actual magazine which was examined. How would a periodical examination of specimen magazines show that the magazine in question contained a libel?[44]

This critical analysis assumed that the distributor's defence turned on whether the distributor ought to have anticipated the presence of the particular libel sued on. But, as we have seen, the defence included another element – that the defendant ought not to have known that the material was 'likely to contain a libel'. A distributor who undertook periodical examinations of specimen publications would have been able to form an estimate of the magazine's propensity to contain libels, from which it would have been possible to predict whether future issues were likely to contain a libel. In other words, the jury's answer was absurd and irrelevant only if the test was whether the distributor ought to have known that the publication was 'likely to contain *the* libel'. Scrutton LJ, however, then concluded his judgment by reiterating the principles laid down by Romer LJ in *Vizetelly* v. *Mudie's Select Library, Limited*, which, as we have seen, included asking whether the defendant ought to have known that the material contained 'a' libel. A year later, in *Sun Life Assurance*

[44] (1932) 48 TLR 521, 521.

Company of Canada v. *WH Smith and Son Limited*[45] Scrutton LJ would enthusiastically endorse the exposition of Bowen LJ ('a very good man to follow'[46]) in *Emmens* v. *Pottle*. Scrutton LJ paraphrased Bowen LJ's test as follows: 'the vendor of a newspaper will not be responsible for a libel contained in it if he (1) does not know, and (2) ought not to have known … that the paper is one not which did contain a libel, but which was likely to contain a libel'.[47] The glimpse of a more generous regime for distributors had vanished.

When the representative of the National Association of Wholesale Newsagents appeared before the Porter Committee, he identified distributors' liability in respect of publications likely to contain a libel as a major concern. There was both a problem of definition, and – more troublingly – the practical consequence of the rule.[48] 'It seems to us', he pointed out, 'that if a paper is allowed to be sold freely throughout the country with no restrictions on it whatever, it is rather unfair on us that the whole onus of having to decide whether the public may read it or the publisher may get it across should lie with us.'[49] In other words, the legal principles had forced distributors to act as censors. The representative also made it clear that the Association maintained a blacklist of publications that its members would not handle. This included titles such as *Paris Magazine* (the subject of the litigation in *Hood* v. *WH Smith and Son Ltd*[50]) and – spot the theme – *Paris Art*, *Paris Follies*, *Paris Gayety*, *Paris Music Hall*, *Paris Nights*, *Paris Plaisirs*, *Paris Plastique* (!), *Paris Pleasures*, *Paris Sex Appeal*, *Paris Studio* and *Paris Thrills*. There were 150 titles in total,[51] the majority of which were blacklisted on grounds of obscenity or sedition; but *Action*, the Fascist newspaper, had been blacklisted for libel, as had the *Daily Worker*.[52] The Association had a standing committee, formed within the previous three years, to which any dubious titles were referred for adding

[45] (1933) 150 LT Rep 211. [46] (1933) 150 LT Rep 211, 214.

[47] (1933) 150 LT Rep 211, 214.

[48] The problem of definition is perhaps given more emphasis in the minutes of evidence than in the witness' evidence: LCO 2/3059 Committee on the Law of Defamation. Minutes of Meetings 1939, Ninth Meeting 14 June 1939, p. 2.

[49] LCO 2/3063 Committee on the Law of Defamation. Minutes of Evidence. 14 June 1939, evidence of William Seymour, representing the National Association of Wholesale Newsagents, p. 244.

[50] *The Times* 5 November 1937.

[51] In reply to a question from E. M. Forster, the witness had estimated the list at 'fifty or sixty' (LCO 2/3063, p. 262); the actual list, produced at Forster's request, was three times this length (it can be found in LCO 2/3060 Law of Libel Committee Memoranda).

[52] LCO 2/3063, p. 256 (margin note).

to the blacklist.[53] No mechanism for removing titles from the list seems to have been called for.

The wholesale newsagents also explained that they did not rely solely on the blacklist and the standing committee to protect them. Whilst they felt doubtful about the legal effectiveness of publishers' indemnities,[54] if one issue of a publication had contained a libel, they would insist upon a 'solicitor's certificate' before distributing the next issue.[55] This was, essentially, a solicitor's undertaking that the later issue contained no libel.[56] In practice, wholesale newsagents relied on publishers to stand behind them, and impecunious publishers were, therefore, their 'greatest danger'.[57] It was not clear whether the wholesale newsagents had investigated the possibility of insurance; but the retail newsagents who appeared before the Committee had done so, and found that no policies were available.[58]

What the case law and the evidence to the Porter Committee brought out was that, far from being the peripheral parties that they might have appeared, distributors had been forced into a central role in the legal regulation of media. They would have preferred to have been treated as 'a conduit pipe' for the work of others,[59] but the combination of an open-ended reasonable care standard and consistently unsympathetic juries had created far more onerous obligations, and had spawned a correspondingly bureaucratic machinery of standing committees and blacklisting.

VI

The reasonable care standard imposed on distributors contrasted strikingly with the basis of liability for authors, editors and publishers. For these latter parties liability, from 1910 onwards, was strict. The legal question was not whether the defendant had intended, or been careless, in defaming the claimant; rather, if a (hypothetical) reasonable person

[53] LCO 2/3063, p. 240 (function of committee) and p. 252 (date of creation of committee).

[54] LCO 2/3063, p. 267 (note that Hickson, who had asked the question, seemed to disagree). The leading case, *WH Smith and Son* v. *Clinton* (1908) 99 LT 840, suggested that a libel indemnity would only be ineffective where the distributor 'knew or may be presumed to know' that he was committing an unlawful act (p. 841).

[55] LCO 2/3063, pp. 240–1.

[56] There is a sample in LCO 2/3060.

[57] LCO 2/3063, p. 267 (giving the specific example of an action against the distributor and Odhams Press for an article in *John Bull*). The remark about 'our greatest danger' is at p. 242.

[58] LCO 2/3064 Evidence of Alexander MacLaren, General Secretary of the National Federation of Retail Newsagents, Booksellers and Stationers, 12 July 1939, p. 398.

[59] LCO 2/3063, p. 263.

reading or hearing the statement would understand it to be defamatory of the claimant, an action lay. As I have explained elsewhere, the introduction of strict liability by the House of Lords' decision in *E Hulton & Co* v. *Jones* took the law in a significantly new direction, away from defamation's traditional emphasis on malice. Such a development was made possible by the law on malice having fallen into disarray, but it also seems to have been inspired by the rise of popular newspapers in the late nineteenth century.[60] Before dealing in detail with the decisions on strict liability, it is, therefore, important to set the scene by giving a sense of judicial attitudes to popular newspapers in the early twentieth century.

It would have been possible to see the proliferation of popular newspapers as a cause for celebration – here, after all, was compelling evidence of an increase in literacy and an interest in current affairs. That, however, was not the judicial view. With remarkable solidarity, judges regarded popular newspapers from the *Daily Mail* to the *Sunday Chronicle* as regrettable symptoms of a decline in taste, manners and journalistic standards. Thus, in one of the earliest twentieth century cases, *Chattell* v. *Daily Mail*,[61] arising out of a paragraph stating that the claimant, an actress, had a daughter who was also an actress, A. L. Smith MR went out of his way to say, in the quotation used as an epigraph to this chapter, that 'the Court had no sympathy with this class of literature, which pandered to an unhealthy taste, and as to which, the oftener it was repeated the greater was the appetite for it'.[62] But the senior judiciary's disapproval was as nothing compared with the jury's. Inflamed by Marshall Hall's fulminations about 'dastardly attacks by the Press on the character of individuals',[63] the jury took twenty-five minutes to make an award of £2,500 – over £250,000 in today's prices.[64] This, it should be emphasised, was for an insinuation that the claimant, who performed under her maiden name, had a teenaged daughter; from which it could be deduced (but was not stated) that the claimant was slightly older than she had claimed. Even the appellate judges felt that

[60] P. Mitchell, 'Malice in Defamation' (1998) 114 *LQR* 639; Mitchell, *The Making of the Modern Law of Defamation*, chapter 5. J. Morgan's review of *The Making of the Modern Law of Defamation* in (2006) 122 LQR 691 highlights the latter's greater emphasis on the rise of the popular press.

[61] *The Times* 16 July 1901 (news item) (QB); *The Times* 13 December 1901 (CA).

[62] *The Times* 13 December 1901.

[63] *The Times* 16 July 1901.

[64] The conversion of this, and other damages awards discussed in this chapter, to reflect current values, was done using www.thisismoney.co.uk/money/bills/article-1633409/Historic-inflation-calculator-value-money-changed-1900.html.

this award was excessive, and the award was reduced to about £100,000 in today's prices. Being a libel claimant was a lucrative role.

Judicial distaste for popular newspapers not only coloured attitudes to damages awards, it also informed the content and application of substantive principles. In *English and Scottish Co-Operative Properties Mortgage and Investment Society, Limited* v. *Odhams Press, Limited*[65] the issue was whether an article headed '*FALSE PROFIT RETURN CHARGE AGAINST SOCIETY*', and which reported that a summons had been issued against the society for making a false profit return, was capable of imputing fraud. A jury had found that it did bear that meaning, and had awarded a farthing in damages. The Court of Appeal upheld the finding on liability, and sent the case back for a reconsideration of the damages award. On the issue of meaning, Slesser LJ dealt crisply with the argument that the article meant no more than that the society had been accused of applying inappropriate principles of accountancy:

> This article was published in a popular newspaper. If the words 'false profit' in a popular newspaper mean that which is merely untrue in the technical sense that a sum has been attributed to profit which … technically should not have been so called, I do not think that would have found expression in large italicized block type as something worthy of observation by the readers of the newspaper.[66]

Mackinnon LJ's attitude was similar, and was encapsulated in his comment that 'The accurate title of the item of news published by this paper might have been something like this: "Dispute between accountants as to the proper principle of drawing up a balance sheet"'.[67]

This reasoning demonstrated a cluster of interlocking attitudes to popular newspapers and their readers. There was an obvious disapproval of both the vocabulary and presentational style of the newspaper: Mackinnon LJ almost seemed to be suggesting that newspapers ought to select only the driest and least engaging statements for their headlines; Slesser LJ seemed to be saying that only a smaller and more sober typeface was appropriate for reporting technical financial matters. This distaste for the newspaper's language and appearance was then used to inform the decision about what the words meant: such loudness and vulgarity could not be deployed to report a dispute over accountancy principles – hence, something more sinister must be being insinuated. This conclusion was

[65] [1940] 1 KB 440. [66] [1940] 1 KB 440, 452.
[67] [1940] 1 KB 440, 456–7.

affirmed by an appeal to the presumed interests of readers, who, it was assumed, could only be interested in criminality. Every step of this reasoning was contestable. There was no inherent reason why hyperbole was impermissible in a headline, nor why large italic type signified immorality. In all likelihood the responses of regular readers of the *Daily Herald* would have been desensitised by repeated exposure to such techniques and, in any event, the newspaper was actually using the language of the statute, which created a criminal offence when 'a registered society … makes a return, or wilfully furnishes information in any respect false or insufficient'.[68] As Goddard LJ mentioned in passing, it was not yet clear whether this was an offence of strict liability.[69] Nor was there any legitimate basis to assume that readers would have had no interest in a dispute about the accuracy of financial results; at the very least, it would have had an interest for mortgage-holders. It is difficult, therefore, to avoid the conclusion that what was really driving the decision was the judges' own views about the proper tone and appearance of a newspaper, combined with a patronising attitude towards the readers of such newspapers.

Even when the outcome was favourable to the newspaper, there could still be a sting of disapproval. Perhaps the best example would be *Knuppfer* v. *London Express Newspaper*, discussed in Chapter 3,[70] where one of the reasons for the defendant not being liable for a statement about a group was that such statements were so lazy and lacking in rigour that reasonable people would dismiss them as essentially meaningless. This, we might imagine, was not something that the *Express* prided itself on! For the most part, however, judicial dislike of – and juries' hostility towards – the popular press went hand in hand with the imposition of liability and high damages awards. The strict liability cases, to which we now turn, present the strongest examples.

VII

The earliest strict liability case, *Jones* v. *E Hulton & Co*,[71] contained several features that rather encouraged the expression of disapproval. The defendants had published in the *Sunday Chronicle* an article that was ostensibly comic fiction about a character called Artemus Jones. Artemus' comic foible was that, despite being an upstanding churchwarden at Peckham,

[68] Industrial and Provident Societies Act 1893 s. 62(c).
[69] [1940] 1 KB 440, 458–9. [70] See above, pp. 43–4.
[71] [1909] 2 KB 444; [1910] AC 20.

he indulged in mild loucheness and flirtation when on holiday at Dieppe. Some readers understood the character of Artemus Jones to denote the real Mr Thomas Artemus Jones, a barrister and former journalist. Jones sued, and was met with the argument that it was purely a case of accidental coincidence. Jones' counsel, the future Lord Chief Justice Gordon Hewart, effectively undermined this assertion in two ways. First, he elicited an admission from Mr Edward Hulton, the managing director of the firm that published the *Sunday Chronicle*, that Hulton had been surprised to see the name 'Artemus Jones' used in the piece, since he recognised it as the name of a former contributor.[72] Second, although the writer of the piece claimed never to have heard of Jones, we now know that Hewart's questions succeeded in badly damaging the writer's credibility, and that the writer bore a grudge against Jones that dated back to Jones' days in journalism.[73] Hence, although the case was argued in terms of whether liability in defamation was strict, the reality was that this was a bad test case. The jury's award of £1,750 – a staggering £176,000 at current values – hardly suggested that they regarded the case as one of inadvertence.

The analytical choices that ultimately persuaded the House of Lords to adopt a standard of strict liability were less than compelling. As would be pointed out later, two of the four extempore speeches contradicted themselves by endorsing both the strict liability of Lord Loreburn LC's speech and the requirement of recklessness espoused by Farwell LJ in the Court of Appeal.[74] Lord Loreburn LC's reasoning came to be seen as providing the *ratio decidendi*, and it at least had the merit of being unequivocal. The tort of defamation, he said, 'consists in using language which others knowing the circumstances would reasonably think to be defamatory of the person complaining of and injured by it'.[75] He was equally clear that this definition was not too harsh – a defendant's 'remedy', he commented, 'was to abstain from defamatory words'.[76]

Lord Loreburn LC's reasoning on the general question of strict liability made no mention of the media in general or of newspapers in particular. When he turned to the question of whether the damages awarded were excessive, however, the newspaper industry came to the fore. There were two reasons, he said, why the damages award should not be interfered

[72] (1909) 573 *House of Lords Journal, Appeal Cases* 85.

[73] P. Mitchell, 'Artemus Jones and the Press Club' (1999) 20 *Journal of Legal History* 64.

[74] *Newstead* v. *London Express Newspapers Ltd* [1940] 1 KB 377, 385–8 (Sir Wilfrid Greene MR).

[75] [1910] AC 20, 23. [76] [1910] AC 20, 24.

with. First, the jury would have been entitled to infer that there had been an element of recklessness. Second:

> the jury were entitled to say this kind of article is to be condemned. There is no tribunal more fitted to decide in regard to publications, especially publications in the newspaper Press, whether they bear the stamp and character which ought to enlist sympathy and to secure protection. If they think that the licence is not fairly used and that the tone and style of the libel is reprehensible and ought to be checked, it is for the jury to say so.[77]

This extraordinary passage promoted libel juries from assessors of compensation to ad hoc arbiters of 'tone and style', whose judgments were dictated by 'sympathy'. The allusion to misuse of 'the licence' may have been intended only as a metaphor. (There is a certain irony in discussing the intentions of the writer of a speech that established that writers' intentions were irrelevant.) But it also gestured backwards – alarmingly – to an era of press licensing; was the suggestion here that jurors could become the functional equivalent of state censors?

As the principle of strict liability was rolled out to its full extent in later cases, there was little sign of concern that either the legal rules, or the way they were being applied by juries, gave newspapers any cause for complaint. After *Jones*' case the next major landmark in strict liability was *Cassidy* v. *Daily Mirror Newspapers Limited*,[78] where the defendant had published, in its gossip column, a photograph of a Mr Corrigan with Miss Muriel Harrold,[79] together with a caption stating that their engagement had been announced. That was indeed what Mr Corrigan had told the photographer, and Miss Harrold had not demurred. Corrigan, however, was in no position to make good his promise, for he had a wife of his own already, the long-suffering Mrs Cassidy.[80] Mrs Cassidy saw the photograph and caption; so did her friends; and it was pointed out to her by other people on several occasions 'with a sneer'.[81] Mrs Cassidy sued the *Daily Mirror* for the imputation that – by implication – she could not be Mr Corrigan's wife, only his mistress. McCardie J, having observed that the *Mirror*'s 'utmost honesty' did not absolve it from liability,[82] directed

77 [1910] AC 20, 25. 78 [1929] 2 KB 331.

79 Scrutton LJ chivalrously referred to the lady as 'Miss X' ([1929] 2 KB 331, 337); she was named at the trial – *Cassidy* v. *Daily Mirror Newspapers, Limited*, *The Times* 18 January 1929.

80 Cassidy's treatment of his wife is described in the report of the evidence given on the first day of the trial – *The Times* 17 January 1929. She had petitioned for dissolution of the marriage in 1928.

81 *The Times* 17 January 1929. 82 *The Times* 17 January 1929.

the jury that the key question was how the words would be read 'by reasonably minded persons who knew the circumstances of the case'.[83] The jury took twelve minutes to return with a verdict of £500 (£27,000 today) for the claimant.

The Court of Appeal by a majority (Greer LJ dissenting) upheld the verdict. The appellants had taken two points. First, they had argued that the words were not capable of conveying the defamatory imputation, and should therefore have been withdrawn from the jury. Scrutton LJ and Russell LJ held that the defamatory meaning was one of several that could legitimately have been drawn, and that it was for the jury to choose which one they actually bore. Greer LJ dissented on this point: for him the defamatory imputation owed too much to the imagination of Mrs Cassidy's friends and acquaintances to be regarded as being conveyed by the words themselves. The appellants' second argument was that where the defamatory meaning was constructed from a combination of the words used and some special knowledge on the part of those reading or hearing them, that special knowledge had to be shared by the defendant. The majority held that, whatever the position might have been before 1910, the introduction of strict liability for defamation in *Jones* v. *E Hulton & Co Ltd* had eliminated any need for a defendant to appreciate that some special knowledge on the part of his readers had allowed them to construct a defamatory meaning from an apparently innocuous text. As a matter of deduction from the general principle in *Jones*' case, this analysis could not have been faulted.

Although it was strictly unnecessary for the decision, both Scrutton LJ and Russell LJ went on to consider how newspapers would be affected by their decision. Scrutton LJ said this:

> It is said that this decision would seriously interfere with the reasonable conduct of newspapers. I do not agree. If publishers of newspapers, who have no more rights than private persons, publish statements which may be defamatory of other people, without inquiry as to their truth, in order to make their paper attractive, they must take the consequences, if on subsequent inquiry, their statements are found to be untrue or capable of defamatory and unjustifiable inferences ... To publish statements first and inquire into their truth afterwards, may seem attractive and up to date. Only to publish after inquiry may be slow, but at any rate it would lead to accuracy and reliability.[84]

[83] *The Times* 18 January 1929. [84] [1929] 2 KB 331, 341–2.

Russell LJ was equally forthright:

> It was said that it would be a great hardship on the defendants if they were made liable in consequence of a statement innocent on its face and published by them in good faith. The answer to this appeal for sympathy seems to be to point out that, in stating to the world that Mr. Corrigan was an unmarried man (for that construction was the foundation of their liability), they in fact stated that which was false. From a business point of view no doubt it may pay them not to spend time or money in making inquiries, or verifying statements before publication; but if they had not made a false statement they would not now be suffering in damages. They are paying a price for their methods of business.[85]

Here there was none of the sympathy with established business methods and time pressures that had been expressed (by Scrutton LJ, among others) in the cases on distributors' liabilities. The implication was that if newspapers wanted to avoid such liabilities in future, they should alter their practices now. The reference in both of these paragraphs to making inquiries perhaps risked understating the position: making careful inquiries would not, in itself, be enough. It was only if the newspaper's inquiries allowed it to detect that the statement was false – and, therefore, allowed it to avoid publishing the statement altogether – that it would escape liability. Newspapers were effectively being told that nothing less than perfect accuracy would do. Scrutton LJ and Russell LJ clearly felt that the financial rewards of the newspaper business justified the law taking an intransigent attitude. But, as Greer LJ pointed out in his dissenting judgment, it was important to remember that what was being discussed was the *general* law of defamation, and it applied to all defendants, whether they were motivated by profit or not. As we shall see, others also found it difficult to resist the temptation to use hostile stereotypes about journalists and newspapers to inform their generalisations about the law of defamation.

The final landmark case on strict liability was *Newstead* v. *London Express Newspaper Limited*,[86] in which the Court of Appeal – carrying strict liability to its logical conclusion – held that even perfect accuracy was not good enough where a statement was capable of referring to someone other than its intended target. The statement in question related to the conviction for bigamy of Harold Newstead from Camberwell. That was perfectly true – a man of that name, who lived in that area, had indeed

85 [1929] 2 KB 331, 354.
86 [1939] 2 KB 317 (KB); [1940] 1 KB 377 (CA).

been convicted. But there was another man called Harold Newstead, who also lived in Camberwell; he had not committed bigamy, and he sued the newspaper for imputing that he had.

This question had troubled earlier courts, who had tended to shy away from imposing liability. Horridge J in *Shaw* v. *London Express Newspaper Ltd*[87] had felt that where a statement accurately applied to a real person, a claim by someone else with the same name as that person did not fall within the *Jones* v. *E Hulton & Co Ltd* principle. Similarly, in *DC Thomson & Co* v. *McNulty*[88] the House of Lords assumed, in the course of deciding a Scottish appeal, that proof that defamatory words were true of a real person other than the claimant would defeat the claim. The judges included Lord Atkinson, who had also decided *Jones* v. *E Hulton & Co Ltd*.[89] Even Newstead's counsel, A. T. Denning KC, sensed that a cautious approach was called for, and presented the case in terms of the defendant's negligent editing of a fuller draft report in which the bigamous Harold Newstead's home address and occupation had been given.[90] Sir Wilfrid Greene MR and du Parcq LJ, however, did not hesitate to say that the strict liability of *Jones*' case extended to this situation. Mackinnon LJ was more sceptical, but perhaps the more striking response was the jury's: they awarded a farthing in damages. If, as Lord Loreburn LC had said, the jury's true role was to express its disapproval in money, it is tempting to interpret the jury's award in *Newstead*'s case as an indication that the law had gone too far.

VIII

The previous sections have highlighted ways in which judges' and jurors' hostility to the popular press shaped the development of legal principles. But it would be misleading to suggest that the law was systematically opposed to all newspapers' interests. On the contrary, two very significant defences – concerning reports and fair criticism – explicitly took account of newspapers' positions.

No elaborate analysis was needed to identify the intended beneficiaries of sections 3 and 4 of the Law of Libel Amendment Act 1888: those sections provided defences for reports of various kinds of proceedings

[87] (1925) 41 TLR 475. [88] (1927) 71 Sol Jo 744.

[89] [1910] AC 20, 25. Lord Atkinson, along with Lord Gorrell, had agreed with both Lord Loreburn LC and Farwell LJ, thus causing some confusion about the true basis of the decision.

[90] [1940] 1 KB 377, 382–3.

in newspapers. The emphasis on newspapers was hardly surprising given the backgrounds and interests of the Act's promoters;[91] but it was, perhaps, surprising that no other entities – such as publishers of books or broadcasters – lobbied to extend the Act's protection to other publications. The form of the Act also reflected the interests of its promoters in a more subtle way, for rather than developing the law by means of general principles, the Act specified the categories of reports to which protection should attach. This drafting technique promoted certainty, albeit at the expense of flexibility if a deserving but previously overlooked instance came to light. One of the protected categories was reports of parliamentary proceedings, in respect of which there were no controversies in the first half of the twentieth century. A second category, which might have been expected to prompt more litigation, was reports of public meetings. However, after a very cautious application of the statutory provision in *Ponsford* v. *The 'Financial Times' (Limited)*,[92] there was nothing to report for the next fifty years. The category that proved to be the most controversial was reports of judicial proceedings, in respect of which a liberal and sophisticated body of case law emerged.

The statutory section provided protection for 'a fair and accurate report in any newspaper of proceedings publicly heard before any court exercising judicial authority ... if published contemporaneously with such proceedings'. As the Court of Appeal was quick to point out, the rationale underlying the section was that 'as everyone could not be in Court, it was for the public benefit that they should be informed of what took place substantially as if they were present'.[93] Hence, it followed that the report of the contents of a charge sheet that had not been read out in court proceedings fell outside the section;[94] nor was there a defence if the reporter failed to hear a significant point – such as the withdrawal of a criminal charge.[95] On the other hand, if part of the proceedings could not have been heard by a member of the public who was present, a reporter's failure to hear and report that part would not jeopardise the defence.[96]

91 See further Mitchell, *The Making of the Modern Law of Defamation*, chapter 10.

92 (1900) 16 TLR 248.

93 *Furniss* v. *The Cambridge Daily News (Limited)* (1907) 23 TLR 705, 706 (Sir Gorrell Barnes P).

94 *Furniss* v. *The Cambridge Daily News (Limited)* (1907) 23 TLR 705.

95 *Mitchell* v. *Hirst, Kidd & Rennie Ltd* [1936] 3 All ER 872.

96 *Mitchell* v. *Hirst, Kidd & Rennie Ltd* [1936] 3 All ER 872, 873: 'The report must be fair and accurate. If it could not be heard, that would be another matter' (Lawrence J).

The rationale of the defence – that reading the report should be like attending court – also inspired judicial resistance to technical points about what, strictly, 'judicial proceedings' were. Thus, in *Farmer* v. *Hyde*[97] the defendants had reported a dramatic intervention in a libel trial, when a man, whose conduct was being criticised in evidence, stood up and said to the judge: 'May I make an application? I am the Rector of Stiffkey, and I want to contradict the many lies that have been told in this Court.' Slesser LJ, with whom Greene LJ and Luxmoore J agreed, held that a broad approach to 'proceedings' was appropriate, which included something done 'which is ... related to the proceedings'.[98] Reports of 'wholly irrelevant' statements, it seemed, would not receive protection, but on the facts of the case the 'application', though irregular, was within the course of proceedings.[99]

A similar point arose in *Hope* v. *Sir W C Leng and Co (Sheffield Telegraph) (Limited)*,[100] where it was submitted – unsuccessfully – that a statement made by a litigant in court, but not in the witness box, was not part of the proceedings. Collins MR emphasised that a 'common sense' approach was needed, and indicated that 'a more liberal view of the immunity of reporters was taken now than used to be taken in former times'.[101] This attitude ensured that newspapers would not be caught out by the technical niceties of what might or might not be 'proceedings', and showed a certain sympathy for the position of journalists without legal training. But Collins MR also went further, saying that he 'entirely concurred' in the direction given by Grantham J at the trial, in which the jury's attention had been drawn to the special position of a court reporter for a daily newspaper.[102] As Collins MR went on to explain:

> The report was a report in a daily newspaper, and it was not to be judged by the same standard of accuracy which would be adopted if they were criticizing a law report of a professional law reporter. It must be regarded from the standpoint of persons whose function it was to give the public a fair account of what had taken place in a Court of justice.[103]

This approach set the tone for other courts' analyses of the question of accuracy – and reports that were neither verbatim nor detailed were nevertheless held to be protected.[104] In itself this kind of approach represented

[97] [1937] 1 KB 728.
[98] [1937] 1 KB 728, 741. [99] [1937] 1 KB 728, 743.
[100] (1907) 23 TLR 243. [101] (1907) 23 TLR 243, 245.
[102] (1907) 23 TLR 243, 244. [103] (1907) 23 TLR 243, 244.
[104] *R* v. *Evening News* [1925] 2 KB 158; *Duncan* v. *Associated Scottish Newspapers Limited* 1929 SC 14.

a significant development in the freedom of the press, as well as being an early manifestation of the principle of open justice. But the cases on accuracy, as well as those on the meaning of 'legal proceedings', also had a broader significance when seen in the context of tort law's attitude to the media. For here – unlike in the cases on strict liability – the journalist's position was at the heart of the analysis; the legitimacy and importance of the role of newspapers was being acknowledged; and the legal principles were being carefully developed so as to encourage and facilitate the performance of the newspaper's role.

It was hardly surprising that the representatives of press interests who gave evidence to the Porter Committee did not propose any structural changes to these congenial principles. They did, however, propose expansion of the statutory defences in two ways. First, they proposed to add reports of company meetings and reports of foreign court proceedings to the protected list. Second, they urged a more conceptual reform, that would extend the privilege to reports of non-judicial tribunals (such as disciplinary panels of professional associations), or at least to the republication in newspapers of the decisions promulgated by such bodies.[105] The Committee accepted all but the foreign courts proposal, rejecting the latter only because it was 'impossible' to formulate an appropriate test for the requisite standards that an institution had to meet before it could truly call itself a court.[106] In short, the privilege for reports had been, and would continue to be, a powerful illustration of tort's responsiveness to one aspect of newspapers' operations.

IX

If the development of the privilege for reports of judicial proceedings could be seen in terms of lawyers refraining from imposing their standards on journalists, the development of the defence of fair comment could be seen as lawyers restraining both themselves and juries from the temptation to

[105] Protection had been denied in *Hope* v. *I'Anson* (1901) 18 TLR 201 and *Chapman* v. *Lord Ellesmere* [1932] 2 KB 431. For an example of the press proposals, see the memorandum submitted by Kenneth Henderson on behalf of the Newspaper Proprietors Association, dated May 1939 in LCO 2/3060, pp. 12–17.

[106] *Report of the Committee on the Law of Defamation* (Cmd 7536, 1948) para. 108. The point had been raised by R. O'Sullivan KC during the Committee's questioning of Kenneth Henderson, the representative of the Newspaper Proprietors Association. O'Sullivan highlighted the difficulties of determining whether 'at the present time' (i.e. June 1939) a so-called court in Germany or the Soviet Union came within the English definition of a court. LCO 2/3063, p. 208

define the limits of criticism. The defence of fair comment was over a hundred years old by the start of the twentieth century, and it was well settled that its core application was in relation to criticisms of literary or artistic works.[107] Where exactly the defence fitted into the overall architecture of defamation was less clear. Its origins lay in the general principle that malice was necessary for liability, but was presumed against a defendant who had uttered defamatory words. The onus then fell on the defendant to rebut this presumption; proving that he had written the words complained of as part of a review of an artistic or literary performance tended to do that, because it suggested that the defendant's motive was to inform and improve public taste, rather than to injure the claimant. As the underlying test of malice first changed its meaning, then drifted into obscurity, and finally disappeared altogether in the wake of *Jones* v. *E Hulton & Co Ltd*, the defence of fair comment was left in search of a home. Eventually it was accommodated alongside the defence of justification, with which it had a rather fraught relationship, particularly when the two defences were forced together in the so-called 'rolled-up plea' (in which a defendant pleaded both justification and fair comment).[108]

So far as the core application of fair comment was concerned, the courts consistently emphasised the critic's freedom to criticise. In one of the earliest twentieth-century cases, *McQuire* v. *Western Morning News Company Ltd*,[109] the defendant's dramatic critic had written a scathing review of the claimant playwright's latest effort. A jury had found a verdict of £100 (£10,300 today) for the claimant, following a direction that suggested that the defence of fair comment would fail if the jury considered the criticism unjust. Collins MR, giving the judgment of the Court of Appeal, immediately identified that the jury had been asked the wrong question. 'One thing', he said, 'is perfectly clear, and it is that the jury have no right to substitute their own opinion of the literary merits of the work for that of the critic, or to try the "fairness" of the criticism by any such standard.'[110] Where literary work was concerned, he continued, criticism would only cease to be protected by the fair comment defence where 'it is something that passes out of the domain of criticism itself'.[111] What he meant by this, he explained, was that the criticism had to be honest and

[107] For the historical development see Mitchell, *The Making of the Modern Law of Defamation*, chapter 8.

[108] For a trenchant criticism of the rolled-up plea, see *The Aga Khan* v. *Times Publishing Company* [1924] 1 KB 675.

[109] [1903] 2 KB 100. [110] [1903] 2 KB 100, 109.

[111] [1903] 2 KB 100, 109.

to be relevant, in the sense that it stuck to the work under review.[112] Less than a year later, in *Joynt* v. *Cycle Trade Publishing Company*,[113] Vaughan Williams LJ would go out of his way to endorse these remarks.

It thus appeared that dramatic, literary and artistic critics were being carefully protected under the principles of defamation. The Court of Appeal's decision, two years later, in *Thomas* v. *Bradbury, Agnew & Co*[114] provided a reminder that the legal protection was not quite so extensive as it might have seemed. There the claim arose out of a book review in *Punch*, which described the claimant's biographical study of Sir John Robinson as 'add[ing] a new terror to death'. The review criticised the claimant for passing off his subject's witticisms as his own, for obtruding his own views and for failing to make the most of the original sources. On the face of it, it seemed to be exactly the kind of case that Collins MR had envisaged in *McQuire*'s case, when he had talked about anything within the domain of criticism being protected. The jury, however, had been persuaded to make a finding of malice. The defendants, represented on the appeal by Scrutton KC and Atkin,[115] argued that, as a matter of law, malice did not defeat the defence of fair comment. Rather, the defence was akin to justification, where malice was irrelevant. Given the defence's history, that was always going to be a difficult argument to run, even for such distinguished counsel, and the Court of Appeal duly rejected it. For Collins MR, a malicious comment was not truly a comment at all.[116]

Critics may have been disappointed by the Court of Appeal's refusal to reposition the defence of fair comment alongside justification, but they surely must have been more troubled by the alleged evidence of malice, and the jury's readiness to act on it. For all that evidence consisted of was showing that the author of the review had a 'strained relationship' with the author of the book, and that the review had been printed as an essay, not with the other reviews.[117] In his judgment, Collins MR was prepared to concede that personal animosity towards the author of a work did not automatically deprive a reviewer of the defence of fair comment – such a reviewer might legitimately bring 'a perfectly dispassionate judgment to bear upon [the claimant's] literary merits'.[118] However, 'given the existence of malice, it must be for the jury to say whether it has warped [the defendant's] judgment'.[119] Juries were, therefore, to be asked to make fine

112 [1903] 2 KB 100, 110. 113 [1904] 2 KB 292.
114 [1906] 2 KB 627. 115 At the trial Atkin had been led by Birrell KC.
116 [1906] 2 KB 627, 638. 117 [1906] 2 KB 627, 631.
118 [1906] 2 KB 627, 642. 119 [1906] 2 KB 627, 642.

judgments about the purity of the literary motives of reviewers; that must have been a particularly dismaying prospect for literary editors, where the expertise of a reviewer would often correspond with some personal acquaintance with the author of the work. And the idea that an editorial decision about whether to publish a piece as a review or as an essay could be used subsequently as evidence of malice, was disheartening and inhibiting in equal measure. It encouraged a rigid approach, in which all literary discussion was relegated to the back pages of the reviews section, and also provided a powerful deterrent for any editor who might be inclined – either from the importance of the book or the quality of the reviewer's response to it – to give greater prominence to an insightful review.

A good sense of how critics felt about the way in which the defence of fair comment applied in practice can be seen in the evidence given to the Porter Committee by the Institute of Journalists and the Critics Circle. In reply to a question from Norman Birkett KC (who was acting as chair in Lord Porter's absence), which asked whether libel law restricted journalists in their writing, the witness answered 'Yes, especially if he is a critic'.[120] Slightly later Mr B. Weller from the Institute was invited to elaborate on a personal recommendation he had made in a memorandum submitted to the Committee; that recommendation was for all libel trials to be by judge alone.[121] 'I feel very strongly upon that point', said Weller. 'After all, a judge is a trained critic, and he, surely, is a better assessor of damages than, say, a greengrocer … the average jury has no aesthetic knowledge.'[122] There seemed to be two points here – one about a judge's superior legal analytical skills, the other about a judge's higher cultural attainments. Birkett asked whether Weller was really making 'the critic's point', and Weller made clear that he was. The jury, he reiterated, was 'not a body of any particular literary quality'.[123] Birkett was obviously alarmed by the implicit contrast suggested by this statement – 'I do not want to be disrespectful about anybody', he said, 'but how many Judges are literary in the sense of the word you imply?' 'I would not presume to make any statement on that', came the – perhaps slightly embarrassed – reply.[124] Birkett was, of course, quite right that judges had no, as he put it, 'special knowledge or training in literature'.[125] But that, surely, was not what Weller was suggesting. The point was more subtle. It was that judges – by virtue of their social position and

[120] LCO 2/3064 Committee on the Law of Defamation Minutes of Evidence (Tenth–Fourteenth Days), p. 462.

[121] LCO 2/3060 Memorandum from the Institute of Journalists, p. 4.

[122] LCO 2/3064, p. 469.

[123] LCO 2/3064, p. 470.

[124] LCO 2/3064, p. 470.

[125] LCO 2/3064, p. 470.

educational background – would approach artistic criticism cases with an innate appreciation of and sympathy with the critical undertaking, which a jury would lack. Such innate sympathy could make all the difference in a case like *Thomas* v. *Bradbury, Agnew & Co.*[126] Birkett's anxiety that judges should not be placed in a false position as literary experts was perfectly understandable, but a nice light is thrown on his exchange with Weller by a letter from E. M. Forster. Forster was the Society of Authors' representative on the Committee, and he was writing to the Society's Secretary, Denys Kilham Roberts, about the difficulty of getting the Committee as a whole to acknowledge the value of literature. This was Forster's assessment: 'No one (except perhaps Porter and Birkett) realises that English literature is an important matter, not to say a national asset.'[127]

X

Up to this point, the focus of the present chapter has been on print media, particularly newspapers. An account of the tort principles governing the media in the first half of the twentieth century would, however, be incomplete if its exclusive focus was on print. For, from 1922 onwards, radio broadcasting was taking place alongside – and, to some extent, in competition with – traditional methods of mass communication.[128] There was the potential here for a range of new legal issues to be contested. For instance, was broadcast speech to be treated as libel or slander? Was a broadcaster to be regarded as a co-publisher, or merely as a distributor of the defamatory matter that had been aired? The special position of the British Broadcasting Company (and Corporation, as it became) also suggested tricky legal questions about the extent to which it might take advantage of any special rules protecting public authorities.

It is, then, rather surprising that the BBC should have left such little trace in the Law Reports. By stark contrast with the lively debates on the point in the United States, and careful appellate analysis in Australia, there was virtually no English authority on whether broadcast defamation was to be treated as libel or slander.[129] Opportunities had not been lacking,

126 [1906] 2 KB 627.

127 M. Lago and P. Furbank (eds.), *Selected Letters of E M Forster Volume Two 1921–1970* (London, Collins, 1985) 165.

128 A. Briggs, *The Golden Age of Wireless* (London, 1965) 152–9 discusses how the Corporation developed a distinctive approach to news broadcasts.

129 For the United States the literature is too voluminous to provide a comprehensive list. Three articles giving a sense of the variety of discussion are L. Vold, 'The Basis for Liability for Defamation by Radio' (1935) 19 *Minnesota Law Review* 611; G. Farnum,

but what had seemed destined to be the leading case was settled;[130] and when, in *Bergman* v. *Macadam*,[131] a case finally came to judgment, the judge seems to have assumed that the correct category was slander, without giving any reasons for that conclusion. As Winfield would caustically comment in a memorandum to the Porter Committee on the law in the United States, *Bergman* v. *Macadam* was 'worthless as reported'.[132] Members of the Porter Committee were forced to fall back on a decision of Lord Atkin *in a moot*;[133] and it speaks volumes for the state of the law in 1948 – as well as for the very different attitudes of law review editors in that era – that C. J. Hamson was able to publish a moot judgment on the point in the *Cambridge Law Journal* of that year.[134]

There was, however, even less authority on whether the BBC was a co-publisher or mere distributor of defamatory broadcasts. Again, the contrast with the United States is revealing. There vigorous discussion in courts and law reviews wrestled with how to apply the existing rules to the new technology;[135] in England both courts and writers seem never to have mentioned the point. The lack of discussion cannot be explained by the BBC's organisational structure, since a significant part of its output was delivered by outside speakers. Indeed, *Bergman* v. *Macadam* was such a case. It may be, however, that other internal factors explain why the point was never raised. Under the direction of Hilda Matheson, the Talks Department at the BBC had developed a highly interventionist editorial policy, under which even speakers as distinguished as E. M. Forster were required to produce full drafts in advance of the broadcast, and to

'Radio Defamation and the American Law Institute' (1936) 16 *Boston University Law Review* 1; and R. Donnelly, 'Defamation by Radio: A Reconsideration' (1948) 34 *Iowa Law Review* 12. For Australia see *Meldrum* v. *Australian Broadcasting Co Ltd* [1932] VLR 425, and the later reflections of Lowe J on the decision, delivered following a paper given by Mr Justice Barry: 'Radio, Television and the Law of Defamation' (1949) 23 *Australian Law Journal* 203, 220. The contrast between the Australian and American positions was discussed in J. Redmond, 'Reading from Script into Broadcasting Apparatus – Libel or Slander' (1933) 7 *Australian Law Journal* 257.

130 *Williams & Norgate Ltd* v. *BBC*, *The Times* 24 April 1926, noted at (1926) 70 Sol Jo 613.

131 *The Times* 9 October 1940.

132 LCO 2/3060 Winfield, 'American Law Relating to Defamation as a Tort', p. 2.

133 LCO 2/3062 Committee on the Law of Defamation. Minutes of Evidence, 20 (question by O'Sullivan KC).

134 C. Hamson, 'Moot Case on Defamation' (1948) 10 *CLJ* 46.

135 A sense of the progress of the debate can be seen in the following: Vold, 'The Basis For Liability For Defamation by Radio'; F. Nash, 'The Application of the Law of Libel and Slander to Radio Broadcasting' (1938) 17 *Oregon Law Review* 307; A. Newhouse, 'Defamation by Radio: A New Tort' (1938) 17 *Oregon Law Review* 314; L. Vold, 'Defamatory

revise those drafts as required.[136] There were two reasons behind this approach. The first was timing: talks needed to fit their allocated time-slots perfectly.[137] The second was tone: Matheson's ideal talk was a carefully crafted piece delivered with an air of spontaneity and intimacy that connected directly with listeners. She particularly admired H. G. Wells' talk on immortality, which Wells had transformed from a formal lecture into 'an intimate confession of faith' as a result of a chance conversation with a railway signalman.[138] Whatever the technical legal position might have been, it would have been misdescribing the broadcaster's own activities (and belittling the Talks Department) to claim that the BBC merely 'distributed' the talks of outside speakers.

A concern about misdescription may also have been behind the BBC's reluctance to avail itself of any of the legal protections available to public authorities. There is no trace of the point in the (few) cases against the BBC, and it seems to have been first raised by E. C. S. Wade in a question he put, as a member of the Porter Committee, to R. Jardine Brown, the Head of the BBC's Legal Department. Wade's specific point was that the shorter limitation periods for claims against public bodies introduced by the Public Authorities Protection Act 1893 might apply to the BBC as a 'semi-public' body.[139] Jardine Brown was surprised by the point, and asked to reply to it later, in writing. His supplemental memorandum to the Committee stated that it was 'not felt that the Public Authorities Protection Act would assist'.[140] No detailed explanation was given, but Jardine Brown may have realised that, even if the BBC could be argued to be a semi-public body for the purposes of the limitation rules, such a status would have been at odds with the Corporation's broader determination not to be seen as an organ of government, or a state broadcaster.

Jardine Brown's evidence also showed that the BBC's absence from the Law Reports did not signify that it was untroubled by the law of libel.

Interpolations in Radio Broadcasts' (1940) 88 *University of Pennsylvania Law Review* 249; R. Seitz, 'Responsibility of Radio Stations for Extemporaneous Defamation' (1940) 24 *Marquette Law Review* 117; L. Vold, 'Extemporaneous Defamation by Radio: A Rejoinder' (1941) 25 *Marquette Law Review* 57.

136 Briggs, *The Golden Age of Wireless*, 124–5. L. Hughes and E. MacLeod Walls, 'General Introduction' in M. Lago, L. Hughes and E. MacLeod Walls, *The BBC Talks of E M Forster 1929–1960 A Selected Edition* (Columbia and London, University of Missouri Press, 2008) 1–4.

137 See also the evidence of R. Jardine Brown, Head of Legal Department, BBC in LCO 2/3062, pp. 32–3.

138 Hughes and MacLeod Walls, 'General Introduction', 2.

139 LCO 2/3062, p. 15.

140 LCO 2/3060 'Supplemental Memorandum', p. 1.

Three main areas were highlighted. The first was a flow of claims based on the *Jones* v. *E Hulton & Co Ltd* principle of strict liability for defamation arising from a coincidental name. Jardine Brown gave one instance of a name shared between a claimant and a real person,[141] and another of a name shared with a fictitious character. The latter suggested that the BBC was adopting a robust attitude to such claims. It concerned a solicitors' clerk named Falder, who happened to share both the surname and profession of a character in John Galsworthy's play *Justice*. Following a BBC broadcast of the play – in which Falder commits fraud – the real Falder wrote to the BBC claiming damages for libel. Jardine Brown read out his response to the members of the Porter Committee:

> Certain facts appear to have escaped your notice which make your claim preposterous if nothing worse. The play in question, by the late John Galsworthy, is not a recent one, but was first produced in 1910, and has since then had four London revivals, the last of which was at the Playhouse in April of this year. In the Play the character Falder commits suicide. It would be a waste of time to say more.[142]

This confident dismissal seems to have had the desired effect, but it is worth noting that Jardine Brown was not on quite such strong legal ground as he seemed to think. For whilst it would, indeed, have been obvious to anyone knowing the background and history of the play that the character Falder did not refer to the real Falder, a reasonable person ignorant of such facts might easily, on hearing the play, have made the connection. Jardine Brown's analysis assumed that all listeners had the kind of literary knowledge that – as we have seen in the previous section – critics feared that ordinary jurors lacked.

Jardine Brown's forthright reply to Falder also raises, implicitly, other questions; namely, why did this bullish attitude not translate into litigation? Why were legal points that might have benefited the BBC not taken in the same assertive way? Jardine Brown's comments on the BBC's attitude to litigation, which form the second important theme in his evidence, suggest two reasons. The first is that litigation was not handled by Jardine Brown's department. The BBC carried insurance, one of the provisions of which allocated libel litigation to the firm of William Crocker and Co.[143] We do not know what Crocker's attitude was, but the insurer's priorities may well have been to achieve cost-efficient compromises rather than to take a stand on particular legal doctrines. The second reason was broader,

[141] *Lambros* v. *British Broadcasting Corporation*, *The Times* 27 June 1935 and 28 June 1935.
[142] LCO 2/3062, p. 11. [143] LCO 2/3062, p. 2.

and would have applied whether or not Jardine Brown and his department were making the decisions. 'We have the feeling', Jardine Brown explained:

> that there is a curious lack of, I was going to say, humanity towards the BBC in any mistake that it makes; that even in certain cases where it has been impossible, for some legal reason, for the Jury to award against us they have taken a very long time to come to that conclusion. We feel very strongly that there is the feeling: Here is the BBC on one side, a wealthy Corporation, with every sort of opportunity to vet and take care, and on the other side there is the unfortunate litigant; that, quite apart from the merit of the action, excessive damages are apt to be awarded. And, of course, there is another feeling in the minds of people inside the BBC, that, in some ways not to as great an extent as newspapers but to a greater extent than publishers, we have this devouring maw of broadcasting to be fed, and one does not have a great amount of time.[144]

Juries, it seemed, could be counted upon to be even-handed: they were as unsympathetic towards the broadcaster as they were towards the newspapers.

The third theme of Jardine Brown's evidence brought out how libel affected the day-to-day operations of the BBC. His particular focus was criticism. In reply to a question from Norman Birkett KC, that asked whether he considered that the right of criticism was protected, Jardine Brown replied 'I should have said not'.[145] He referred to a relatively recent decision, *Wilson* v. *British Broadcasting Corporation*,[146] in which a jury had rejected a fair comment defence and awarded £2,100 damages (£127,000 today) for a libel on the claimant's singing abilities that had been published on the letters page of the *Radio Times*. The jury's verdict on liability may well have been defensible – the letter gave specific comical examples of the claimant's alleged habit of intruding H's into certain words, but those words did not actually occur in the part the claimant had been singing. However, as Jardine Brown put it, 'our "chief grouse" … was this: It was felt very strongly that if a mistake had been made the damages were altogether in excess of any evil that mistake might have caused.'[147] The decision 'very much depressed the freedom, the right to criticise', and had led Jardine Brown to take a far stricter line than he would have liked with scripts that made strong criticisms of literature.

144 LCO 2/3062, p. 5. 145 LCO 2/3062, p. 23.

146 *The Times* 20, 21 and 22 June 1934. See also J. Dean, *Hatred, Ridicule or Contempt* (Harmondsworth, Penguin, 1963) 85–9.

147 LCO 2/3062, p. 5.

This was an aspect of tort's application to the media that was invisible in the law reports and legal textbooks, but which had fundamental and far-reaching effects.

XI

The insidious effect of libel on writers, which Jardine Brown had drawn attention to as one of several concerns, was at the heart of the Society of Authors' contribution to the Porter Committee. The Society's nominee was E. M. Forster, who was ideal for the role. By 1939, when the Committee's proceedings began, he was a celebrated novelist, having published what would be his final novel, *A Passage to India*, in 1924. He could therefore speak with great authority about the effect of libel on the creation of fiction. He also had other, less well known but equally important qualifications. For instance, he was not only a novelist – indeed, by the time that the Porter Committee was in session his output was exclusively literary journalism and non-fiction.[148] Nor was his work confined to writing: he already had significant experience as a broadcaster, and this enabled him to articulate concerns arising out of his own first-hand experience of the full range of media.[149]

A further advantage that Forster had – although it would not have seemed like an advantage at the time – was his experience as a libel defendant.[150] Both he and his publisher had been sued in 1937 for defamatory allegations made in *Abinger Harvest*, a collection of his reviews and non-fiction. The offending item was entitled 'A Flood in the Office', and was a review of a pamphlet discussing a scheme to dam the Nile.[151] The pamphlet violently criticised the scheme and its creator, Sir William Macdonald. Forster, in the course of his review, summarised the criticisms, and although at the end of the review he was careful to say that he could not offer any judgment on the merits of the scheme, he had not systematically distanced himself from the pamphleteer's polemic, and admitted to

148 E. M. Forster, *Two Cheers for Democracy* (London, Edward Arnold, 1951) collects essays, articles and broadcasts 'nearly all' (Prefatory Note) composed after 1936.

149 Hughes and MacLeod Walls, 'General Introduction'. The volume contains the text of 70 of Forster's 145 radio talks.

150 The episode is described in a statement from Edward Arnold & Co in LCO 2/3064, pp. 509–11.

151 E. M. Forster, *Abinger Harvest* (London, Edward Arnold, 1936) 277–81. For reasons which are explained in the next paragraph, only certain rare copies of the first edition contain this review.

admiring the style.[152] On its first appearance in the *Athenaeum* magazine in 1919 the review had caused no controversy; but by 1936, and unfortunately for Forster, official inquiries had concluded that the allegations in the pamphlet were unfounded. When Forster repeated those charges in *Abinger Harvest*, he therefore unwittingly exposed both himself and his publisher to liability.

The action was eventually settled by a statement in open court that acknowledged that Forster had 'unfortunately and mistakenly' repeated the pamphlet's allegations as if they were well-founded, a payment of £500 (£28,000 today), and a publisher's undertaking to recall all copies of the book and remove the offending review from it.[153] The experience left its scars. Shortly after the case Forster was invited by the trustees of T. E. Lawrence to produce an edited collection of Lawrence's letters. Forster's friendship with Lawrence made him an ideal choice, but he was alarmed by the pungency of some of the correspondence and – in view of his recent experience – asked the trustees to indemnify him against liability for libel.[154] When the trustees felt unable to do so, Forster resigned the commission. Here, then, was a distinguished author of both fiction and non-fiction, who also had experience as a broadcaster and personal knowledge of how libel affected authors.

Forster also had an additional advantage, which is more difficult to define, but which is perhaps best described as 'committee-sense'. We know, for instance, that he was aware that certain points could be made more effectively in the Society of Authors' memorandum than in his own questions, since for him to make them risked looking 'precious' and 'self-interested'.[155] He was also careful not to trespass into the areas of expertise of other committee members, and had a light touch that avoided awkward moments. In speaking of his own libel action arising from 'A Flood in the Office', for instance, there was the potential for embarrassment, since the claimant had been represented by Norman Birkett KC. When the subject arose, Birkett explained that his involvement had been confined to making the statement in open court, and Forster wittily replied: 'May I say, I had the great advantage of having you against me!'[156]

152 *Ibid.*, 281.

153 *Macdonald* v. *Edward Arnold and Co*, *The Times* 19 February 1937.

154 The friendship is recalled in E. M. Forster, 'Clouds Hill' in *Two Cheers for Democracy* (London, Penguin, 1972) 347–51.

155 Letter to Denys Kilham Roberts, 20 May 1939. Lago and Furbank, *Selected Letters of E M Forster Volume Two 1921–1970*, 165.

156 LCO 2/3064, p. 511.

From the outset Forster took an energetic approach. As he said in a letter to Denys Kilham Roberts, he did not want 'to miss any of the initial moves'.[157] He pressed Schuster to include a newspaper editor on the Committee, arguing that a newspaper proprietor would have little day-to-day experience of editorial realities.[158] Schuster refused.[159] Ironically, Lord Kemsley, the proprietor who was on the Committee, resigned shortly afterwards and suggested that his replacement should be an editor.[160] With Schuster, however, once a decision was made, it stayed made.[161] Forster had more success in shaping the approach of the Society of Authors. It is not clear whether he had any direct role in the Society's decision to confine itself to two points, namely, the liability of authors of fiction where their characters could be identified with real people, and speculative (i.e. unmeritorious) claims – although we do know that he felt very strongly about the former point.[162] But he definitely was influential in deciding how those issues should be presented. Writing to the Secretary of the Society in May 1939, he offered no comments on the legal substance of the draft memorandum, but 'I do suggest' he wrote:

> that in your preamble you should point out, as drily as possible, that an author's work has or may have an aesthetic side. It would not be necessary to point this out to a committee of Frenchmen, but an English committee is always obtuse here. The assumption hitherto, is that the author's outlook is the same as the journalist's. No one (except perhaps Porter and Birkett) realises that English literature is an important matter, not to say a national asset, and that owing to the present working of the libel laws the authors of today have not as good chance of turning out valuable work as had the authors of the past.[163]

As he summed it up, in the remark used as a second epigraph to this chapter, 'In the eyes of the Committee we are not an important body, much less important than the journalists. But, such as we are, we represent English literature, and I think it will do no harm if this were tactfully indicated.'

[157] E. M. Forster to D. Kilham Roberts, 12 April 1939. King's College Cambridge.

[158] LCO 2/3058, 3 April 1939. [159] LCO 2/3058, 4 April 1939.

[160] LCO 2/3058, 3 May 1939 (Kemsley to Schuster).

[161] LCO 2/3058, 9 May 1939 (Schuster to Porter, saying that Kemsley's replacement should be a newspaper proprietor).

[162] E. M. Forster, 'Bookshelf' (broadcast in December 1938) in *The BBC Talks of EM Forster 1929–1960* eds. M. Lago, L. Hughes and E. Macleod Wells (London and Columbia, University of Missouri Press, 2008) 138.

[163] Letter to Denys Kilham Roberts, 20 May 1939. Lago and Furbank, *Selected Letters of E M Forster Volume Two 1921–1970*, 165.

The memorandum submitted to the Porter Committee (which seems to be the only version surviving) did include a preamble on these lines, which Forster had approved.[164] Intriguingly, there is some evidence that Forster may have come to feel that the preamble did not quite strike the right note. In his own copy he annotated the following sentence – 'Such an atmosphere is not conducive to the production of the best work which our leading authors are capable of' – by a wavy underlining of 'leading'.[165] Elsewhere he highlighted important points by vertical lines in the margin. Stressing the effect only on 'leading authors', he may have felt, made the case sound too elitist, and risked sliding into the preciousness that he had been so anxious to avoid.

In the questions he posed to witnesses, Forster subtly and persuasively developed the theme of the damaging effect of libel on creativity. Thus, with the BBC's Jardine Brown, who was the Committee's first witness, he brought an insider's knowledge of the realities of broadcasting to bear on the question of script approval, and thereby encouraged the witness to reflect on the role of lawyers: 'I have a difficult course to steer between the desire to please the author, who sometimes writes strongly, and my duty to the Corporation. I do not want to spoil his broadcast; at the same time I do not want to get the BBC into difficulties.'[166] This led Forster to put his crucial point: 'I think one of the criticisms brought against your unfortunate Corporation is that the talks are sometimes timid and unenterprising. I suppose that might be attributable to the fear of libel and slander actions?' 'There is no doubt about it', replied Jardine Brown.

Forster was also able to deploy his insider's knowledge of the literary world to good effect. The Committee's second witness was Serjeant Sullivan, whose memorandum had dismissed as 'almost unknown' those cases where an author had unwittingly created a character that readers identified as a real person. Forster was quick to pick up on this. 'I felt that was perhaps a little severe', he said, 'because I happened to hear of a case this morning in which a novelist – I cannot mention his name, because the case will be coming up – had innocently chosen a name and circumstance referring to the same person. That sentence in your memorandum makes the path of the author appear to be rather more rosy than it is.'[167] The

164 LCO 2/3060 'Memorandum of the Incorporated Society of Authors, Playwrights & Composers', p. 1. Forster's approval of it can be seen in his letter to Kilham Roberts of 6 June 1939: 'I have been away ... and only today receive your letter and the draft-preamble, which I like very much' (King's College Cambridge).

165 King's College Cambridge. 166 LCO 2/3062, p. 31.

167 LCO 2/3062, p. 71.

rambling reply showed that Forster had scored a point. If, as Forster commented in a letter to Kilham Roberts, 'Serjeant Sullivan did not cut much ice', that happy result had flowed directly from Forster's questions.[168]

What might be regarded as Forster's most powerful contributions to the Committee came in relation to the Society of Authors' witnesses and the evidence of Oswald Cox. The Society's witnesses were its President (Ernest Raymond), its Secretary (Denys Kilham Roberts), his deputy (Miss Barber) and the novelist Alec Waugh. Forster was asked to take the lead in questioning them, but he was less of an inquisitor and more like the conductor of a well-orchestrated performance. He began by asking Kilham Roberts about literature as a 'national asset' (the very phrase that Forster had suggested adding to the Society's memorandum).[169] Kilham Roberts agreed that it was, indeed, a national asset, and was then invited to say how libel prevented authors from 'giving their best'.[170] Kilham Roberts had come prepared, producing the equivalent of a celebrity video link in the form of a letter from J. B. Priestley, which regretted that he could not be with them, and went on to outline how oppressive it was to risk liability for libel every time one created a fictional character. 'Both in plays and novels I have gone to extreme lengths to try and protect myself', said Priestley, 'often weakening my original plan and always spending much time that could have been better spent on other aspects of my work.'[171] Back, as it were, in the studio, Ernest Raymond agreed, and particularly drew attention to the word 'weakening' in Priestley's letter. Authors, he explained:

> think of themselves as people with a very serious contribution to make to other people's imagination. They hope that they can heighten that imagination and their one desire is to give an absolutely objective picture of the things which they see, and the threat of the libel law as it stands does produce depressing psychological inhibitions about giving that purely objective picture.[172]

At this point Forster moved from conductor to soloist in order to tell the Committee about his experience with the T. E. Lawrence letters project. Kilham Roberts added that 'the libel law has murdered, or killed a good many books'.[173] The rest of the performance continued in a similar vein, including a detailed account of the 'A Flood in the Office' controversy.

168 Lago and Furbank, *Selected Letters of E M Forster Volume Two 1921–1970*, 166.

169 LCO 2/3064, p. 502. 170 LCO 2/3064, p. 503.

171 LCO 2/3064, pp. 503–4. 172 LCO 2/3064, p. 504.

173 LCO 2/3064, p. 506. The statement by one of Forster's biographers that Forster 'extracted' this declaration from Kilham Roberts seems scarcely to do justice to Kilham Roberts'

With the Society of Authors' witnesses Forster was in the congenial position of encouraging like-minded people to express themselves. The contrast with Oswald Cox could not have been starker. Cox was the solicitor to the *Daily Telegraph*, and drew on this expertise in his evidence; but he was speaking in his personal capacity, and could not have made it clearer that he opposed any special privileges for newspapers.[174] On the issue of liability for unwittingly creating a fictional character that readers identified as a real person, he was forthright: 'the writer is being paid for what he does and is making money out of it, so it is up to him to compensate, if he does any damage.'[175] A similar approach should be applied to situations, exemplified by *Cassidy* v. *Daily Mirror Newspapers Limited*, where readers' special knowledge of a situation led them to place a defamatory meaning on otherwise innocuous language: '[The writer] is doing it for money and presumably he is making money out of if, and he should insure against any risks that he runs.'[176]

No other witness would give such prominence to the availability of insurance as a justification for imposing liability. Indeed, Cox's confident assertion about insurance rather contrasted with the hazy picture that emerged elsewhere. The BBC, for instance, did insure;[177] the retail newsagents, by contrast, would have liked cover, but were unable to obtain it.[178] Associated Newspapers (the publishers of the *Daily Mail*) chose not to insure, because some policies entitled the underwriters to insist on the insertion of apologies, and Associated Newspapers was not prepared to compromise its editorial independence.[179] Some of the most interesting evidence about insurance came from a Committee member, the publisher Bertram Christian. Having observed that libel insurance was a 'recent' development, he said to Cox: 'Every publisher desires to insure but I think you can take it from me that there are cases where it is practically impossible to do so, if the publisher has had a run of bad luck.'[180] Cox was more sanguine, suggesting that special conditions and obtaining counsel's view of the manuscript could usually resolve matters. Christian, however, was insistent, and he, surely, was in the best position to know.

enthusiastic desire to say it. P. Furbank, *E M Forster A Life, Volume Two Polycrates' Ring* (London, Secker & Warburg, 1978) 232.

174 LCO 2/3062, p. 124. 175 LCO 2/3062, pp. 112–13.

176 LCO 2/3062, p. 113. 177 LCO 2/3062, p. 2.

178 LCO 2/3064 Evidence of Alexander MacLaren, General Secretary of the National Federation of Retail Newsagents, Booksellers and Stationers, 12 July 1939, p. 398.

179 LCO 2/3063 Evidence of Kenneth Henderson, representing the Newspaper Proprietors Association, p. 211.

180 LCO 2/3062, p. 123.

Cox's view of professional writing as a purely commercial activity that should bear its own costs could not have been further from Forster's deeply held convictions about the significance of literature. When it came to Forster's turn to question Cox, however, he did not pursue the question of the inherent value of literature, but focussed instead on the practical consequences of insisting on insurance. Insurers, he astutely pointed out, would be likely to require counsel's opinion to be sought; and counsel would be likely to advise removing anything doubtful. The result would be literature that was feebler, duller, flatter. Forster also exposed the crudeness of Cox's understanding of writers' motivations in the following exchange:

Q [FORSTER]. You make two assumptions – first, that writers are always paid and, secondly, that they write to be paid. I do not think those assumptions are true.
A [COX] No, only theoretically true.
Q [FORSTER] What do you mean by 'only theoretically true'? It is practically not true, is it?
A [COX] It does not affect the argument.[181]

This confrontation enacted a fundamental difficulty about the role and purpose of libel law. It was possible to see Cox's position – as Forster did immediately afterwards – as essentially focussing on journalists to the exclusion of other authors. That, however, too readily assumed that 'journalists' and 'authors' were mutually exclusive categories, when the reality – which Forster himself embodied – was that many authors made their living from a variety of genres, from fiction, to reviewing for periodicals, to broadcasting for the BBC.[182] It was getting closer to the real issue to say that the law faced a choice between regarding writing as merely another form of commercial activity and regarding it as something inherently worthwhile. But even that does not quite capture the position. The real question was what, in Oswald Cox's slightly unhappy phrase, was 'theoretically true'? In other words, what was the version of reality that the law would commit itself to, and use to inform its future development? It was here that Cox's simplistic stereotype of writing as commerce was at its most seductive, and also, therefore, where Forster's authority and ability to articulate and marshal the arguments for a more nuanced understanding of literary activity was so crucial.

[181] LCO 2/3062, p. 143.

[182] For Forster's own slightly later assessment – anticipating the disappearance of the 'detached artist' – see 'Books in 1941' (broadcast in July 1941) in *The BBC Talks* 145.

XII

Up to this point, the analysis of the application of tort law to the media has focussed on defamation. That focus reflects the dominance of defamation in the case law, the law reviews and the reform bodies involved. An exclusive focus on defamation, however, would leave out of account the ultimately unsuccessful, but in itself quite revealing attempt to introduce a remedy for invasion of privacy.

The first immediately striking aspect of this initiative was its source. In 1929, in *Tolley* v. *JS Fry and Sons Limited*,[183] a majority of the Court of Appeal had dismissed a claim for defamation on the basis that the words complained of were not capable of bearing a defamatory meaning. What the defendants had done was to use a caricature of the claimant, who was a well-known amateur golfer, in an advertisement for their products. The claimant argued that reasonable people would assume that he had been paid for the endorsement, and that he had, therefore, been guilty of compromising his amateur status. P. H. Winfield felt that the decision highlighted an important gap in the scope of protection offered by English tort law, and quickly produced an article that argued for the recognition of a right to privacy.[184] In making this argument, Winfield drew on comparative material from India, the United States, Germany and South Africa. His key point was that 'our law probably lags behind the needs of a community in which intrusion on privacy is apt to take offensive forms owing to the modern development of instantaneous photography and of methods of advertisement which, to say the least of them, are totally indifferent to the feelings of private individuals'.[185]

Winfield's article made a compelling argument for judicial recognition of a right to privacy. But, as a final note made clear, he was not content to rely on his own efforts: he had encouraged his colleague, Professor Harold Gutteridge, to write on the protection of privacy in Continental legal systems. Gutteridge's article appeared in the next issue of the *Law Quarterly Review*.[186] He had confined himself to German and Swiss law, of which he provided a comprehensive and theoretically informed account, and also explained why *Tolley*'s case would have been decided in the claimant's favour in Germany. A shorter piece on the French law of privacy, by

[183] [1930] 1 KB 467.

[184] P. Winfield, 'Privacy' (1931) 47 *LQR* 23. The opening sentences of the article made clear that it had been prompted by the decision in *Tolley* v. *JS Fry and Sons Limited*.

[185] Winfield, 'Privacy', 30.

[186] H. Gutteridge, 'The Comparative Law of the Right to Privacy' (1931) 47 *LQR* 203.

F. P. Walton, followed Gutteridge's article.[187] It seems that all three authors must have hoped that their work might inspire the House of Lords when it came to hear the appeal in *Tolley* v. *JS Fry and Sons Limited.*

When the House of Lords' decision was handed down, Winfield, Gutteridge and Walton must have been disappointed.[188] The appeal had succeeded, but solely on the ground that the caricature was, after all, capable of bearing a defamatory meaning. The opportunity for judicial development of a tort of invasion of privacy seemed to have passed.

The announcement of the creation of the Porter Committee in 1939 reignited Winfield's enthusiasm, and he wrote to *The Times* to draw public attention to the absence of a right of privacy in English law.[189] Winfield's involvement did not stop there: he also submitted, at the Committee's request, a memorandum on libel in the United States. The memorandum focussed on the (then) recent exposition in *The Restatement of the Law of Torts* but, crucially, it did not deal with privacy, since Winfield now took the view that privacy fell outside the Committee's terms of reference.[190] Winfield's Cambridge colleagues, Harold Gutteridge and Kurt Lipstein, took a different approach. They had been commissioned to produce a memorandum on defamation in civil law systems,[191] and they produced an elegant and comprehensive account that, among many other points, highlighted the different scope of those Continental wrongs corresponding to the English tort.[192] In fact, although the memorandum was submitted in their joint names, it was entirely the work of Lipstein. The authors appear to have been working in parallel, and it is interesting to note that an incomplete, evidently abandoned draft in Gutteridge's hand had flagged up that the German law of copyright dealt with complaints like those at issue in *Tolley* v. *JS Fry and Sons Limited*; the memorandum submitted did not explicitly make this point.[193]

There was also some support for a right to privacy among witnesses. For Serjeant Sullivan, for instance, the problem was that the law had failed to keep up with certain social norms. 'It is something which among ourselves', he observed, 'we should never tolerate, that domestic affairs

187 F. Walton, 'The Comparative Law of the Right to Privacy' (1931) 47 *LQR* 219.

188 *Tolley* v. *JS Fry and Sons Limited* [1931] AC 333.

189 P. Winfield, 'The Law of Libel', letter to the Editor, *The Times* 6 February 1939.

190 LCO 2/3060 Winfield, 'American Law Relating to Defamation as a Tort', p. 8.

191 LCO 2/3059 Committee on the Law of Defamation. Minutes of Meetings. Fifth meeting, 11 May 1939.

192 H. Gutteridge and K. Lipstein, 'Defamation in European Systems of Law' *LCO* 2/3060.

193 The manuscripts of the first drafts by Lipstein and Gutteridge are transcribed in the Appendix.

should be looked into, that things perhaps long forgotten should be dug up. There is a perfectly well defined idea in the mind of a gentleman as to what he may do and what he may not do.'[194] Newspapers, however, were not gentlemen. The Newspaper Proprietors' Association witness made no bones about it. 'Does anyone get privacy?' he asked, rhetorically. 'It seems to me to be quite apart from the law of libel you have not any privacy in this country.'[195]

That was how things would remain. The Committee's report gave two reasons for making no change – the first was the difficulty of definition; the second was that the problem could be dealt with 'as one of internal discipline to be regulated by an understanding between the proprietorial and journalistic organisations. The offence is primarily one of good taste.'[196] This second reason assumed, of course, that the problem only concerned newspapers, and it is quite striking that self-regulation was now being put forward for entities that the law of defamation had traditionally disciplined so sternly. What resulted was a less than convincing patchwork of micro-management (for defamation) and laissez-faire (for privacy).

XIII

The Porter Committee's Report was completed in 1948, and was the final significant event in the development of media-related tort law in our period. Some, but not all of its proposals would be implemented in a private members' Bill in 1952.[197] Thus, after 1952 broadcast defamation was treated as libel;[198] and the creator of a fictional character that readers identified with a real person could avoid liability by showing that he neither knew, nor, had he taken reasonable care, would have known, that the words were understood to refer to the claimant, provided that he also offered to publish a suitable apology.[199] There was also an expansion in the

194 LCO 2/3062, p. 39. Sullivan at this point said that he was dealing only with defamation; however, he later (at p. 54) proposed that there should be liability for 'any publication that was offensive to the ordinary sensitiveness of a man with regard to his own doings and his own character and his occupation'. The minutes of his evidence confirm the impression that he was making a point about words being actionable beyond the scope of the current law of defamation (LCO 2/3059 Fourth meeting, 10 May 1939).

195 LCO 2/3063 Evidence of Kenneth Henderson, p. 225.

196 *Report of the Committee on the Law of Defamation* (Cmd 7536, 1948) para. 26.

197 Defamation Act 1952. A proposal to liberalise the rules of evidence applying to mitigation of damage was the main casualty.

198 Defamation Act 1952, s. 1.

199 Defamation Act 1952, s. 4.

kinds of meetings of which newspapers could publish reports,[200] and a greater flexibility was introduced to the defence of fair comment.[201]

These were less than radical changes, and reflected the Report's general satisfaction with the state of the law. That state of satisfaction was – as a chorus of commentators pointed out – very much the product of a common law lawyer's point of view.[202] Defendants would still be left to the tender mercies of hostile juries with minimal oversight from the Court of Appeal. Writers and editors would still continue to be unwilling co-adventurers in the common law's voyage of self-discovery, despite a plea for greater clarity, such as by codification (which the Porter Committee rejected). To change the metaphor, if the history of tort in its application to the media could be seen in terms of who had ownership of its rules and principles, the answer in 1950 was clear: it was the lawyers.

200 Defamation Act 1952, s. 7.

201 Defamation Act 1952, s. 6.

202 E. Hall Williams, 'Committee on the Law of Defamation: The Porter Report' (1949) 12 *MLR* 217, 223 ('very much a product of the common law outlook'); R. C. Donnelly, 'The Law of Defamation: Proposals for Reform' (1949) 33 *Minnesota Law Review* 609, 632 ('the report smacks of a rigid professionalism').

7

Roads

> If there be no obligation to restrain animals from … obstructing vehicles, the introduction of fast traffic cannot create one, and on the other hand, if there be such an obligation, the introduction of fast traffic cannot do away with it, although it makes the consequences more serious, and the obligation in that way more onerous.
>
> Pickford LJ

I

The fast traffic being introduced onto English roads was, of course, the motor car. The increase was exponential: cars went from being rare and expensive playthings at the turn of the century, to being a commonplace mode of transport by 1950. More widespread use of cars led to greater familiarity with the benefits, and social acceptance of the risks, of motoring. A useful barometer is provided by the fluctuating speed limits imposed by Parliament. In 1896 the Locomotives on Highways Act s. 4 had significantly liberated speed limits by raising them to 14 mph – the previous limits had been 4 mph in the country and 2 mph in town. The Motor Car Act of 1903 s. 9 raised that limit further, to 20 mph, and the Road Traffic Act 1930 Schedule 1 abolished speed limits for light cars altogether. A 30 mph limit for built-up areas was reintroduced by the Road Traffic Act 1934 s. 1, but it would not be until 1965 that the national speed limit of 70 mph was imposed (by the Motorways Traffic (Temporary Speed Limit) (England) Regulations).

The changes to the speed limits reflected Parliament's readiness to respond to social change (if not its susceptibility to pressure from the motoring lobby).[1] Some judges may have been tempted to emulate Parliament's responsiveness when they were applying tort principles to motor cases, but – whether judges were so tempted or not – the methods and conventions of common law development would have made it

[1] W. Plowden, *The Motor Car and Politics 1896–1970* (London, The Bodley Head, 1971).

impermissible to change the rules in the same way that Parliament could change the speed limit. Any judicial development had to be more subtle, to draw on the existing stock of common law concepts, and to appear to be the natural culmination of earlier decisions. The studied neutrality which characterises the comments of Pickford LJ quoted above was typical: the common law was not to be seen to be taking sides.

II

Courts that were invited to develop the common law in its application to novel motoring situations had a rich stock of principles and ideas to draw upon. The most orthodox route for redress was the standard action for negligence; but, in addition, there was also a potential claim for public nuisance. One example – arguably, the classic example – of public nuisance was obstruction of the highway. A defendant whose obstruction of the highway caused the claimant special damage – that is, damage distinct from the loss suffered by the community as a whole – was liable to pay compensation. 'Obstruction' was given a broad meaning – there need not be any physical blockage; some unreasonable interference with the claimant's attempt to pass along the highway was all that was needed[2] – and there was no requirement of fault. The absence of a requirement of fault was also an attraction for claimants contemplating suing for breach of statutory duty or under the rule in *Rylands* v. *Fletcher*[3] (which had not yet been confined, as it is today, to claims concerning land).[4] Nor were the relative advantages of road-related claimants limited to the wider choice of causes of action: those undertaking dangerous work on the highway owed non-delegable duties to road users. In other words, the person undertaking the work was liable not only for the torts of his employees, but also for the torts of independent contractors whom he had engaged to carry out the work.[5]

As we shall see, the availability of these different bases of claim gave courts great scope for creativity. But the existing stock of common law principles also contained some entrenched restrictions on liability, which early twentieth-century courts felt either unable or unwilling to consider. Thus, it was authoritatively established, in 1892, and not queried thereafter, that a highway authority owed no duty to take positive steps to keep

2 *Harris* v. *Mobbs* (1878) LR 3 Ex D 268.

3 (1866) LR 1 Exch 265; (1868) LR 3 HL 330.

4 Eg *Powell* v. *Fall* (1880) 5 QBD 597; *Hale* v. *Jennings Brothers* [1938] 1 All ER 579.

5 *Holliday* v. *National Telephone Company* [1899] 2 QB 392; *Pinn* v. *Rew* (1916) 32 TLR 451.

a highway in repair.[6] More controversially, it was also established that owners of animals owed no duty to prevent their livestock from escaping onto the road and causing injury to motorists and cyclists.

The first of the twentieth century cases was *Higgins* v. *Searle*,[7] which involved a claim by a motorist against the owner of a sow. The sow had escaped from her sty and was lying down at the side of the road. The claimant approached in his car from one direction, and a horse and cart approached from the other. The sow stood up suddenly, which caused the horse to shy into the claimant's path. In taking evasive action, the claimant damaged his car. He sued, and the report describes him as basing his claim 'on the ground (1) of obstruction; and (2) of negligence'.[8] The former seems to have been an informal description of public nuisance.

Despite a jury finding that there had been no negligence on the part of the defendant, the claimant's counsel argued that the defendant was liable nonetheless, since the owner of straying livestock was liable for any damage that it did. The Court of Appeal rejected this argument. For them, proof of negligence was crucial to liability. Cozens-Hardy MR described the claimant's submissions as 'an interesting argument', which sounded like a compliment; but, as every advocate knows, an argument is never both interesting and right, and Cozens-Hardy MR went on to make it clear that strict liability for damage done by straying livestock only applied to claims by landowners. Moulton LJ added that the sow could not be regarded as an obstruction, and Buckley LJ made perhaps the most striking point, when he commented that 'A person on the highway is exposed to the ordinary risks taken by those using the highway, and if an accident happens owing to those risks … no legal consequence follows'.[9] In other words, road users had to be prepared to encounter animals in their path – straying livestock were one of the 'ordinary risks' of travel. There was no sense here that roads were (or ought to be) the exclusive preserve of passing traffic.

It was implicit in the reasoning of *Higgins* v. *Searle* that if the defendant had been found negligent, the case would have been decided differently. The decision of the Divisional Court in *Jones* v. *Lee*,[10] however, cast doubt on that proposition. *Jones* v. *Lee* concerned damage done to a tandem bicycle by a horse that had escaped through the defective hedges of

[6] *Cowley* v. *Newmarket Local Board* [1892] AC 345. See also *Saunders* v. *Holborn District Board of Works* [1895] 1 QB 64, which applied the same approach to an alleged duty to maintain pavements.

[7] (1909) 100 LT 280.

[8] (1909) 100 LT 280.

[9] (1909) 100 LT 281.

[10] (1911) 106 LT 123.

its field. The trial judge found that it had been negligent for the horse's owner to place it in a field with defective hedges; he went on, however, to find that the damage to the bicycle was not the direct consequence of the negligence. Both Hamilton J and Bankes J in the Divisional Court agreed that this latter finding was decisive against the claimant. However, they seem to have disagreed over the significance of the negligence finding. For Hamilton J, the decision on lack of direct consequence made it 'unnecessary to consider what qualifications ought to have been added to this proposition to make it right in law to say that there was negligence in the sense of a breach of duty towards the plaintiff in putting the young horse, though a quiet animal, into a field the hedges of which were defective'.[11] This suggested that it was a matter of refining and fine-tuning the general proposition so as to get it completely accurate. Bankes J, by contrast, issued a forthright denial of any duty: 'by common law the owner or occupier of land adjoining a highway is under no duty to fence so as to keep his animals off the highways'.[12]

Just over a fortnight later, the same issue resurfaced in the Court of Appeal in *Ellis* v. *Banyard*,[13] where the claimant cyclist had been injured by escaping cows. The fact that the Divisional Court had so recently failed to agree was unpropitious and the Court of Appeal's judgments tended to entrench existing differences. Buckley LJ, whose contribution to *Higgins* v. *Searle* had suggested that a duty was owed, now took an absolute view against liability: 'there is at common law no obligation on the part of the owner or occupier of land who depastures cattle near a highway, to provide any fences so as to prevent the cattle from getting into the highway.'[14] It followed that, for him, it was neither here nor there whether there was evidence of carelessness on the part of the landowner.

For Kennedy LJ, by contrast, the absence of evidence of carelessness was crucial against liability. 'I desire to reserve the question of law', he continued, 'whether there is a right in existence for travellers along the highway not to have proper gates and fences except in special circumstances. It is a matter of history that it is so in the case of commons where the highway has been dedicated subject to rights of common on both sides.'[15]

The convoluted language of the first sentence is slightly problematic, but 'a right … for travellers not to have proper gates' should probably be understood as travellers having no right that landowners provide proper

[11] (1911) 106 LT 123, 125. [12] (1911) 106 LT 123, 126.
[13] (1911) 106 LT 51. [14] (1911) 106 LT 51.
[15] (1911) 106 LT 51, 53.

gates – or, in other words, the owner having an immunity in respect of damage caused by the failure to have such gates. Kennedy LJ linked this with a point that would receive more attention in subsequent cases, about the conditions subject to which a highway had been dedicated. Detailed discussion of this point is deferred to the analysis of those later cases, but at this point we should note that Kennedy LJ was talking about the conditions of dedication 'as a matter of history'; he was not proposing a role for fictions or presumptions about dedication.

Kennedy LJ then concluded his analysis as follows:

> And I should be slow to infer that because a harmless cow or sheep is allowed to get into the highway without giving rise to a cause of action that rule applies to crowds of cattle whose mass might constitute an obstruction to travellers along the highway. There may be a case of duty arising in the case of a mass or number, even of the most harmless animals which would not apply where it was only the case of a single animal.[16]

Kennedy LJ did not make it absolutely explicit, but the allusion to 'obstruction' here surely suggests that he was thinking of a claim for public nuisance. In any event, he clearly envisaged that a duty in respect of escaping animals might be owed to road users in some circumstances.

The third member of the Court of Appeal, Vaughan Williams LJ, gave two judgments. He agreed with Kennedy LJ that the fatal difficulty with the claimant's claim was the absence of evidence of carelessness. But he did not share Kennedy LJ's uncertainty about the law:

> I should be very sorry indeed to say anything in this case which might encourage the notion that there is no duty on the part of farmers or cattle dealers and others to take care and prevent cattle which are under their charge or control from going on to the highway in such a way as to obstruct the user of it and make it unsafe and dangerous to those using it ... whether you call it negligence or nuisance the action will not lie unless there has been injury to a particular person or damage to particular property, and you prove that there has been neglect of duty or that there are such facts as show that the defendant ordered such things to be done with the cattle as would necessarily result in their being a nuisance on the highways.[17]

As Vaughan Williams LJ made clear slightly later in his judgment, doing something that 'would necessarily result' in cattle being a nuisance included 'putting his cattle in such a place or position that the natural result is that they go out of that place or position and ... obstruct the

[16] (1911) 106 LT 51, 53. [17] (1911) 106 LT 51, 52.

highway'. These allusions to 'necessary' and 'natural' results suggested that a defendant could have no excuse if he failed to appreciate their likelihood. How strongly Vaughan Williams LJ felt about the point can be seen from the fact that he added the following remarks after Kennedy LJ had delivered his judgment:

> I wish to say emphatically that I do not think it is true that a farmer is entitled to turn out untended cattle on pasture adjoining a highway without a fence to such a number that they are likely to obstruct the highway by day or night without being liable to an action by those who, using the highway, are injured by the obstruction.[18]

Vaughan Williams LJ was clearly basing this analysis on the principles of public nuisance, and at first glance his argument seems compelling. For here we seem to have an obstruction of the highway causing special damage to a particular individual. The position, however, was perhaps not quite so straightforward, because the test for public nuisance given in the leading case cited by Vaughan Williams LJ was 'an act done upon any part of the highway which is not a part of the reasonable user of it'.[19] Judges like Buckley LJ and Bankes J, who firmly denied that any liability arose, might well have retorted that the straying of cattle or sheep onto a road *was* part of the reasonable user of it, and, therefore, fell outside the purview of public nuisance. In other words, behind the differences of legal analysis there were irreconcilably conflicting assumptions about the nature and function of highways: were they a safe, segregated space for travellers, or did they blend into the wider landscape and, therefore, inevitably take their character from land uses going on around them?

III

The issue was settled by the Court of Appeal's decision in *Heath's Garage Limited* v. *Hodges*, a case concerning damage to a car caused by straying sheep.[20] In the Divisional Court, counsel for the defendant had not argued that there was no duty, and Lush J had commented that he did not see how the duty could be doubted.[21] In the Court of Appeal, however, the judges enthusiastically seized on the point. Cozens-Hardy MR, giving the leading judgment, made the position absolutely clear:

[18] (1911) 106 LT 51, 54.

[19] *Harris* v. *Mobbs* (1878) LR 3 Ex D 268, 271.

[20] [1916] 2 KB 370. [21] [1916] 1 KB 206, 215–16.

> in ordinary circumstances, on an ordinary highway, it is no breach of duty not to prevent harmless animals like sheep from straying on to the highway, and it makes no difference whether the action is sought to be based on negligence or on nuisance to the highway.[22]

Pickford LJ agreed, making the point quoted as the epigraph to this chapter, that if there was no existing common law duty, the introduction of fast traffic could not create one.[23] Neville J developed the historical theme further. The first point that he dealt with was an argument by the claimant that had sought to explain the admitted absence of duty on the owner of unfenced land by a presumption that the road across such unfenced land had been dedicated subject to the risk of cattle being on it. Neville J found this explanation unconvincing because, he said, 'in the case of fenced roads, many, if not most of them must have been dedicated before they were fenced', and the subsequent erection of fencing could have done nothing to alter the terms of the dedication. Yet, on the claimant's argument, the owners of such fenced land owed duties. It was perhaps exaggerating the importance that Neville J attached to the point to describe him as having introduced a doctrine that *all* landowners were presumed to have dedicated their land subject to the implied condition that their animals retained the freedom to roam on it.[24] If anything, the gist of Neville J's point was that arguments about dedication were beside the point, because nothing could be reliably deduced from them.

Having disposed of this historical argument about dedication, Neville J then went on to deal with the central issue in the case. History again was at the forefront of his analysis:

> the experience of the centuries has shown that the presence of domestic animals upon the highway is not inconsistent with the reasonable safety of the public using the road … There is no doubt that the advent of motor cars has greatly increased the danger resulting from the presence of loose animals on the road owing to the speed at which cars travel and the difficulty shared by man and beast of avoiding them. It was only yesterday, however, that, as mechanically propelled carriages, the right of motor cars to use the roads was subject to conditions which rendered great speed unattainable, and I think that to-day those who use them must take the roads as they find them and put up themselves with such risks as the speed of their cars occasions not only to themselves but to others.[25]

22 [1916] 2 KB 370, 376. 23 [1916] 2 KB 370, 378.

24 C. Fletcher-Cooke, 'Responsibility for Animals Straying on to Highway' (1947) 10 *MLR* 324, 326.

25 [1916] 2 KB 370, 382.

He concluded his analysis by making it clear that the historical position controlled the contemporary law:

> If the character of domestic animals with regard to highways had come to be considered for the first time when roads were tarred and motor traffic abounded, it is possible that a different view might have prevailed with regard to their harmlessness on the highway, for, however strongly the instinct of self-preservation may appeal to them, their perceptions may prove inadequate to such a judgment of the speed of the prevailing traffic as will always ensure their safety and consequently the safety of the traffic; but in my opinion it is not competent to the Courts to reconsider the classification of former times and to include domestic animals of blameless antecedents in the class of dangerous animals even when wandering on the roadsides.[26]

This forthright analysis articulated a rather discouraging view of the common law's ability to respond to social change, and incorporated a quite striking attitude to developments in the legal regulation of speed. For in 1916 the speed limit was 20 mph, and it might have been thought that the common law ought to take account of the likelihood of vehicles travelling up to that speed. Neville J, however, preferred to emphasise the earlier, far more restrictive rules – he probably had in mind the Locomotives Act 1865 s. 4 limits of 4 mph in the country and 2 mph in the town – which were consistent with the traditional common law position that livestock and travellers should be left to get out of each other's way. The result was a piece of legal analysis that settled the issue, but did so in an unashamedly antiquarian fashion, and acknowledged that it was at odds with current social and legal conditions.

As car ownership increased, and the rules on permitted maximum speeds were liberalised further, the abrasive antiquarianism of the *Heath's Garage* decision irritated the courts. The House of Lords in *Brackenborough* v. *Spalding Urban District Council* was careful not to endorse the decision,[27] and the Court of Appeal in *Hughes* v. *Williams*[28] expressed its dislike of and dissatisfaction with the rule: 'ill adapted to the conditions of life in the twentieth century' was how MacKinnon LJ put it.[29] Scots judges agreed, taking the view that the decision in *Heath's Garage* was 'in conflict with what might be described as the guiding principle of the law of negligence', as expressed by Lord Atkin in *Donoghue*

[26] [1916] 2 KB 370, 383.

[27] [1942] AC 310, 316: 'Whatever view may be taken of the correctness of [*Heath's Garage*]...' (Viscount Simon LC).

[28] [1943] 1 KB 574. [29] [1943] 1 KB 574, 579.

v. *Stevenson*, and dismissing the argument from rural traditions.[30] The habit of grazing cattle at the roadside, the court held, had disappeared; there was therefore no practical reason for retaining an immunity that protected the owners of such grazing cattle.[31] The Scottish court also dealt crisply with the issue of unfenced land: 'In the great unfenced areas of the Highlands the motorist or cyclist must take the roads as he finds them.'[32]

When the House of Lords finally got the opportunity, in *Searle* v. *Wallbank*,[33] to reconsider whether owners of straying livestock might owe a duty to road users, counsel for the claimants based their claim squarely on *Donoghue* v. *Stevenson* and the general duty of care.[34] The judges, however, were not convinced, and unanimously reaffirmed the result of the *Heath's Garage* case. As in *Heath's Garage* itself, historical factors had some prominence, particularly in the speech of Lord Maugham, which examined the historical development of highways 'in order to see whether there was at any time such a state of things that a legal obligation on the owner or occupier of roadside lands to repair and maintain the adjacent hedges may be reasonably inferred'.[35] His Lordship concluded that no such state had ever existed. However, he did not allow his historical investigations to determine the matter, and went on to emphasise the difficulties in defining both the scope and content of any duty, as well as making the point that Lord Atkin's *Donoghue* v. *Stevenson* principle did not call for a duty of care to be recognised whenever there was the 'mere possibility of accident'.[36] Lord Maugham's conclusion nicely illustrated the way in which history and contemporary legal analysis were interwoven in his reasoning:

> No facts in my opinion have been established which would tend to show that farmers and others at some uncertain date in our lifetime became subject for the first time to an onerous and undefined duty to cyclists and motorists and others which never previously existed. The fact that the duty does not exist if the road is uninclosed by fences and yet that accidents are rare is, I think, strong to show that the respondent was not bound as a reasonable man to think that his failure to fill up a gap in his fence was likely to cause such an accident as the one which took place.[37]

Lord Uthwatt and Lord Thankerton concurred. Lord du Parcq reached the same conclusion, but with less ostensible emphasis on history. He rejected

[30] *Wark* v. *Steel* 1946 SLT (Sh Ct) 17, 19 (Sheriff Court of Ayr).
[31] 1946 SLT (Sh Ct) 17, 22. [32] 1946 SLT (Sh Ct) 17, 22.
[33] [1947] AC 341. [34] [1947] AC 341, 344.
[35] [1947] AC 341, 347. [36] [1947] AC 341, 351.
[37] [1947] AC 341, 353.

the idea of a general duty to fence on the ground that 'both the law and the general usage of the community have sanctioned the depasturing of cattle on unfenced land'.[38] That, perhaps, was partly a historical justification. But his next point was firmly rooted in the present: 'at least on country roads and in market towns, users of the highway, including cyclists and motorists, must be prepared to meet from time to time a stray horse or cow ... The motorist must put up with the farmer's cattle: the farmer must endure the motorist.'[39] Lord Porter's speech developed a similar theme. Travellers, he said:

> must take reasonable care to avoid what they find on the road and the obligations of the owners of beasts or of users of the highway are not ... altered by an increase in the fencing of the country or by the increase in the speed of traffic or the imposition of precautions necessary in war-time. [The accident had occurred during the hours of blackout during the Second World War.] The incidence of these changes does not ... increase the duties of farmers or the burden on agriculture by increasing the duty to fence.[40]

The speeches in *Searle* v. *Wallbank*, then, had a rather different tone and emphasis from those in the *Heath's Garage* case. For the later judges, history was not enough in and of itself; the decision to deny a duty had to be justified in contemporary terms. Some of those justifications were more convincing than others. Lord Maugham's concerns about defining the content of the duty, for instance, seemed to be more relevant to questions of breach than to the existence of the duty itself.[41] We may also feel that Lord Maugham rather stretched the concept of reasonable foreseeability of damage. But, particularly in the speeches of Lord du Parcq and Lord Porter, there were important articulations of what we might, anachronistically, identify as 'policy factors', in particular, the need for mutual tolerance between farmers and motorists, and the refusal to add to the burdens of agriculture.

These factors served to highlight that the earlier assertion that denying a duty was 'ill adapted to the conditions of life in the twentieth century' was based on certain debatable assumptions about the role of tort law.[42] The point was made more explicitly by Wolfgang Friedmann, who saw *Searle* v. *Wallbank* as representing a return to 'a more cautious and

38 [1947] AC 341, 361. 39 [1947] AC 341, 361.
40 [1947] AC 341, 357.
41 Fletcher-Cooke, 'Responsibility for Animals Straying on to Highway', 325.
42 *Hughes* v. *Williams* [1943] 1 KB 574, 579.

conservative attitude' after the expansion and innovations of the 1930s.[43] Elsewhere, commented Friedmann, 'tort has generally adjusted to the advent of industry and modern technical inventions', but it had failed to do so in *Searle*'s case, where the legal issue had been precipitated by the arrival of the motor car.[44] The contrast that Friedmann seemed to have in mind was with the extension of employers' liability, which he had examined in detail earlier in his essay.[45] But that comparison did not quite work. For in the employer's duty cases, employers who were taking advantage of industrial production methods were increasingly being made to pay compensation where those methods caused injury to their employees. In cases like *Searle* v. *Wallbank*, by contrast, the claimant was also the person taking advantage of the new technology. The two lines of cases were, in fact, consistent with each other in that they both refused to transfer the costs of new technologies away from those who were taking the benefits of them. Imposing a duty in a case like *Searle* v. *Wallbank* required the courts to go a step further. It required them to translate the social fact that motoring was having a profound and largely positive social effect into a legal policy that the rules of tort liability must be reshaped so as to prioritise the interests of motorists. But it was not at all clear why they ought to do this. The argument about 'the conditions of twentieth century life' was hardly compelling – after all, agriculture was as much part of the conditions of twentieth-century life as motoring was, although, unlike motoring, it was not *distinctively* a twentieth-century activity. The reality of the situation was that two equally legitimate twentieth-century activities had come into conflict with each other. Nor was it at all obvious that tort should promote particular technologies by spreading their costs. There were too many fundamental issues at stake for the decision in *Searle* v. *Wallbank* to be airily dismissed as mere conservatism[46] – it was, rather, a significant policy decision about the nature of rural roads.

IV

While the owner of a straying animal owed no duty to road users, the owner of an animal turned onto the highway was in a different position.[47] He did owe a duty of care, which was initially expressed as liability for

[43] W. Friedmann, *Law and Social Change in Contemporary Britain* (London, Stevens & Sons Limited, 1951) 74, 84, 95–6.

[44] *Ibid.*, 95–6. [45] *Ibid.*, 84–6.

[46] *Ibid.*, 84, and more elaborately 95–6.

[47] *Deen* v. *Davies* [1935] 2 KB 282, 293–4 (Romer LJ).

damage done in accordance with an animal's known propensities. Thus, in *Turner* v. *Coates*[48] the owner of an unbroken colt, which was being led unsecured along the highway at night, was held liable for injuries to a cyclist caused when the colt started at the cyclist's light. The House of Lords' decision in *Donoghue* v. *Stevenson*, and in particular Lord Atkin's exposition of a general test for duty of care based on reasonable foreseeability of damage to the claimant, prompted further development. In *Fardon* v. *Harcourt-Rivington*,[49] where the defendant's over-excitable dog had shattered a car window and a splinter of glass had hit the claimant in the eye, the House of Lords (including Lord Atkin) asked itself whether a reasonable person in the defendant's position ought to have anticipated injury to the claimant. It concluded that the accident was 'an extremely unlikely event',[50] which the defendant could not have been expected to anticipate. The speeches were not perhaps completely clear as to whether the House was deciding that there was no duty, or that there was no breach of duty on the facts, but all agreed that 'the ordinary duty of a person to take care' applied to such situations.[51] It followed that, from at least 1932 onwards, liability for domestic animals brought onto roads was governed by orthodox negligence principles.

The picture for damage caused by cars brought onto the roads was very different: here the courts toyed with a variety of techniques that would make life easier for the claimant, by eliminating the need to prove that the defendant had not taken reasonable care. Perhaps the boldest of these techniques was the attempt to bring cars within the principle of *Rylands* v. *Fletcher* – that is, broadly, the principle that the owner of a dangerous thing was liable, irrespective of fault, if the thing escaped and caused damage. An early indication that the courts might be receptive to this technique was given in *Powell* v. *Fall*,[52] where liability was imposed under the *Rylands* principle for damage to the claimant's hayrick caused by sparks emitted from the defendant's traction engine. The decision hinted at a loose approach to *Rylands*. Mellor J described the principle as arising 'when a man brings or uses a thing of a dangerous character on his own land',[53] but he was not deterred from applying it on the facts, where the engine was on the highway and not on the defendant's land. Bramwell LJ went further, casting aside any of the potentially limiting features

48 [1917] 1 KB 670. See also *Manton* v. *Brocklebank* [1923] 2 KB 212.
49 (1932) 146 LT 391.
50 (1932) 146 LT 391, 392.
51 (1932) 146 LT 391, 392.
52 (1880) 5 QBD 597.
53 (1880) 5 QBD 597, 599.

of *Rylands*, and relying instead on a rough and ready assertion that the owner of a dangerous machine must pay for the damage that it causes.[54]

In the early years of the twentieth century, the courts were still receptive to the theory that liability for the damage caused by a motor vehicle could be imposed without fault. The point was raised explicitly in *Gibbons* v. *The Vanguard Motorbus Co (Limited)*[55] where the defendant's bus had skidded on a wet road, mounted the pavement and then crashed into a light standard outside the claimant's premises. The trial judge found that there was no negligence by the driver, but proceeded to impose liability on the basis that the defendant had 'plac[ed] a nuisance on the highway'.[56] What made the bus a nuisance was the 'well-known fact that in certain conditions motor-omnibuses were liable to skid and that when they did so it was impossible to control them'.[57] Despite counsel's protestations that negligence was essential for liability, the Divisional Court endorsed the trial judge's analysis. The implications of this reasoning were startling; as counsel had, in vain, pointed out, 'Motor-omnibuses, ordinary omnibuses, and cabs, were all liable to skid, and if it was a nuisance, having this in view, to place them on the road, all traffic must be stopped if there were a danger of skidding.'[58] The underlying problem was that the concept of public nuisance was so inherently amorphous that it could too easily be shaped by judicial value-judgments about what ought to be driven on the roads. Since the basic question was whether the defendant's use of the highway was a reasonable one in the circumstances, there was nothing to prevent the answer being an expression of judicial prejudice.

Immediately after the decision in *Gibbons* v. *The Vanguard Motorbus Co (Limited)*, therefore, there were two potential routes to no-fault road traffic liability: *Rylands* v. *Fletcher* and public nuisance. However, the Court of Appeal's decision less than a year later, in *Wing* v. *London General Omnibus Company*,[59] would close off both avenues. The claimant, a passenger in one of the defendant's omnibuses, was injured when the omnibus skidded in wet conditions. Vaughan Williams LJ dealt with the case purely in terms of the existence of evidence of negligence, but Fletcher Moulton LJ gave careful consideration to the claimant's argument that liability flowed from placing a dangerous machine on the road. 'This cause of action', he explained, 'is of the type usually described by reference to the well-known case of *Rylands* v. *Fletcher*.'[60] The typical

[54] (1880) 5 QBD 597, 601.
[55] (1908) 25 TLR 13.
[56] (1908) 25 TLR 13, 14.
[57] (1908) 25 TLR 13, 14.
[58] (1908) 25 TLR 13, 14.
[59] [1909] 2 KB 652.
[60] [1909] 2 KB 652, 665.

Rylands case, he admitted, concerned a defendant's use of his own land, 'But I have no doubt that analogous causes of action exist when a member of the public makes undue and improper use of the right which he enjoys in common with all others of using the public highways for traffic.'[61] The crucial issue, then, was not whether a *Rylands* claim was possible for road accidents, but what conditions would be required before imposing strict liability on a vehicle's owner. Fletcher Moulton LJ made it clear that those conditions were stringent, saying that:

> If a man places on the streets vehicles so wholly unmanageable as necessarily to be a continuing danger to other vehicles either at all times or under special conditions of weather, I have no doubt that he does it at his peril, and that he is responsible for injuries arising therefrom, even though there has been no negligence in the management of his vehicle.[62]

This exposition amalgamated the public nuisance and *Rylands* v. *Fletcher* arguments. It may, technically, have preserved the claim based on *Rylands* v. *Fletcher*; but it destroyed the attraction of such a claim for accident victims, since a claimant who could show that the vehicle was 'so unmanageable as necessarily to be a continuing danger' had a compelling evidential foundation for an allegation that the owner had been negligent in permitting such a vehicle to be used on the road. After *Wing* v. *London General Omnibus Company*, in other words, the conditions for a successful *Rylands* v. *Fletcher* claim following a road accident had been set so high that there was nothing to be gained by pursuing it.

The decision in *Wing*'s case eliminated one potential use of *Rylands* v. *Fletcher* in relation to cars, but other possibilities remained. For instance, in *Musgrove* v. *Pandelis*[63] the claim concerned damage by fire, which had resulted when the defendant's chauffeur (who 'was really a clerk'[64]) had started his car and thereby accidentally ignited a small fire in the carburettor. Prompt action by the chauffeur would have avoided any damage to the claimant's property; but prompt action did not occur, and the fire spread. The courts adopted an interpretation of Fires Prevention (Metropolis) Act 1774 that made it crucial whether the situation came within *Rylands* v. *Fletcher*. Both courts held that it did. Lush J at first instance held that:

> If a man brings onto his premises a dangerous thing which is liable to cause fire, such as a motor car with petrol in it, the carburettor of which is not unlikely to get on fire when the engine is started, and a fire results,

[61] [1909] 2 KB 652, 665. [62] [1909] 2 KB 652, 665.

[63] [1919] 1 KB 314 (KB); [1919] 2 KB 43 (CA).

[64] [1919] 2 KB 43, 44.

> though without any negligence on his part, he must be held liable … for the rule is that he must keep such a thing under control at his peril.[65]

He cited *Powell* v. *Fall* (the traction engine case) in support of this proposition. In the Court of Appeal, Bankes LJ had no doubt that a motor car with a petrol tank was a dangerous thing, which the defendant had brought on to his premises;[66] Warrington LJ was perhaps more cautious, describing the car as 'potentially dangerous'.[67] Duke LJ explained that the combination of petrol 'easily convertible into flammable vapour', apparatus for producing a spark and an inexperienced employee made it 'impossible to say that this is not an instance of the principle [in *Rylands*]'.[68] A later Court of Appeal, however, in *Collingwood* v. *Home and Colonial Stores Ltd*,[69] would find this reasoning problematic, and express the hope that the House of Lords would re-examine the point. One of its concerns was that the *Rylands* principle required an 'escape' from the defendant's lands to the claimant's, but on the facts nothing seemed to have escaped.[70] That was perhaps technically true, but there was more substance to their objection that *Rylands* did not apply to 'the reasonable or ordinary use of premises', which included use as a garage.[71] Possibly this was a point where timing was important. *Musgrove* v. *Pandelis* was decided in late 1918 and early 1919, as the infrastructure of English motoring was struggling to recover from wartime neglect, vehicles were scarce and the future for motorists uncertain;[72] when the Court of Appeal in *Collingwood* expressed its reservations about *Musgrove* v. *Pandelis*, the motor car had become a familiar feature of everyday life. The greater social familiarity with, and visibility of, cars meant that it was no longer plausible for the law to classify them as uncontrollable, high-strung rarities.[73]

65 [1919] 1 KB 314, 317. 66 [1919] 2 KB 43, 47.
67 [1919] 2 KB 43, 49. 68 [1919] 2 KB 43, 51.
69 [1936] 3 All ER 200. 70 [1936] 3 All ER 200, 208 (Romer LJ).
71 [1936] 3 All ER 200, 206 (Lord Wright MR), 209 (Romer LJ). For the classic articulation of this limitation on the scope of *Rylands* v. *Fletcher*, see *Rickards* v. *Lothian* [1913] AC 263.
72 S. Cooke, *This Motoring* (London, The Automobile Association, nd) chapter XXI.
73 Car numbers had increased from 77,000 in 1918 to 1,600,000 in 1936 – see Appendix B, 'Motor Vehicles in Use, 1904–1969' in Plowden, *The Motor Car and Politics*, 456. R. Church, *The Rise and Decline of the British Motor Industry* (Basingstoke, Macmillan, 1994) 12–13 highlights the 1920s as the era when product development, coupled with widespread publicity and the introduction of instalment purchasing, caused the demand for cars to take off.

V

The failure to bring road accidents within the principle of *Rylands* v. *Fletcher* did not deter claimants' representatives from exploring other potential routes to liability that did not require proof of fault. One possibility was openly to manipulate the orthodox test for breach of duty of care, so that a finding of negligence was made despite reasonable care having been taken. Persuading a judge to go along with this strategy might sound like a tall order, but the decision in *Hutchins* v. *Maunder*[74] demonstrated how it might be done. There the claimant pedestrian had been injured when the defendant's newly acquired second-hand car drove into him. The cause of the accident was not some inattention on the driver's part; rather, the poor road surface had jolted the car so much that the steering had broken, and that had meant that the driver lost control. Counsel seems to have decided to pitch his submissions at an emotive and metaphorical level, accusing the defendant of placing 'on the public highway "a wild beast"'.[75] The judgment of Darling J adopted a more sober tone, methodically ruling out negligence by the driver, and rejecting the argument that the weakness in the steering system ought to have been detected by dismantling it. But there was then an unexpected turn – 'He (his Lordship) found, however, that to place the car on the highway in its then condition was a thing necessarily dangerous to persons who used the highway, and it amounted to negligence.'[76] Here the standard of negligence had suddenly been detached from what the defendant knew, or ought to have known, about the hidden risk of steering failure.

As the Divisional Court in *Phillips* v. *Britannia Hygienic Laundry Company, Limited*[77] would point out a couple of years later, Darling J, despite his references to 'negligence', had effectively imposed absolute liability on motorists. That, the Divisional Court held, was simply not the common law – at common law liability turned on lack of due care.[78] McCardie J also subtly highlighted that the common law did not contain particularly stringent rules for cars: he explained the principles governing liability for injury done by horses, and continued, 'In my view it is reasonably clear on principle that just as no absolute duty at common law exists as against owners of horses, so no absolute duty exists with respect

[74] (1920) 37 TLR 72. [75] (1920) 37 TLR 72.
[76] (1920) 37 TLR 72, 73. [77] [1923] 1 KB 539.
[78] [1923] 1 KB 539, 550–1 (McCardie J), 556 (Bailhache J).

to motor cars.'[79] The common law, in other words, expressed no hostility towards the new technology.

One respect in which horses were different to cars – as a matter of law – was that cars were subject to statutory regulations concerning their safety and roadworthiness. These regulations suggested yet another route to no-fault tort liability – the claim for breach of statutory duty. The existence of a claim for breach of statutory duty was in fact the main issue raised in *Phillips* v. *Britannia Hygienic Laundry Company, Limited*,[80] a case where the vehicle owner was clearly not at fault, but where the vehicle failed to comply with a statutory regulation stating that 'The motor car and all the fittings thereof shall be in such a condition as not to cause danger to any one on the motor car or on any highway.'[81] The regulations also made specific provision for tyres, brakes and lights; as McCardie J put it, if breach of these regulations was actionable as a tort, 'a serious vista of liability is opened up'.[82]

For McCardie J the key point in determining whether the regulations gave rise to a claim for breach of statutory duty was to look at whom they were intended to benefit. Previous cases on breach of statutory duty had established that it was necessary to show that the claimant was a member of the class that the statute was designed to protect. The existence of such a class was crucial – a statute designed to protect the public as a whole could not give rise to a claim for breach of statutory duty. McCardie J concluded that the regulations in question, and the Motor Car Acts pursuant to which they were passed, were 'not enacted for the benefit of any particular class of folk. They are provisions for the benefit of the whole public.'[83] It followed that no claim for breach of statutory duty was available. Bailhache J agreed with McCardie J's analysis.

The Court of Appeal upheld the Divisional Court's decision. For Bankes LJ and Younger LJ the issue seemed to be relatively straightforward: the regulations were for the benefit of the public as a whole, and they, therefore, gave rise to no claim for breach of statutory duty. Atkin LJ found the point more difficult. He was troubled by the fact that it was undoubtedly intended that the regulations should promote the safety of the travelling public. Nor was he prepared to insist on there being a defined, limited class of beneficiary as a prerequisite of liability for breach of statutory duty:

[79] [1923] 1 KB 539, 553. [80] [1923] 1 KB 539 (DC); [1923] 2 KB 832 (CA).

[81] Motor Cars (Use and Construction) Order 1904, Art. II reg. 6.

[82] [1923] 1 KB 539, 545. [83] [1923] 1 KB 539, 547.

> To my mind, and in this respect I differ from McCardie J, the question is not to be solved by considering whether or not the person aggrieved can bring himself within some special class of the community or whether he is some designated individual. The duty may be of such paramount importance that it is owed to all the public. It would be strange if a less important duty, which is owed to a section of the public, may be enforced by an action, while a more important duty owed to the public at large cannot. The right of action does not depend on whether a statutory commandment or prohibition is pronounced for the benefit of the public or for the benefit of a class.[84]

Here Atkin LJ had identified a paradox at the heart of the common law's approach to breach of statutory duty. Namely, the more pervasive and fundamental the right was, the less likely it was to qualify for protection. He went on, however, to hold that the regulations in question imposed only public duties on motorists, since it was unlikely that Parliament had intended to impose absolute duties sounding in damages. This was possibly correct; but it should also be remembered that early motoring legislation such as the Locomotives on Highways Act 1896 (under which the regulations in question had been made) manifested such an anxiety about the dangers of cars, that it would not have been contrary to the spirit of the legislation to impose absolute civil liability on motorists.

VI

Phillips v. *Britannia Hygienic Laundry Company Limited* established, therefore, that claims for breach of the statutory obligations of roadworthiness were not available to accident victims against motorists. Later, more specific, narrowly expressed provisions about pedestrian crossings would be held actionable (since they were obviously designed to protect pedestrians).[85] But even though only some regulations were actionable directly, it did not follow that the remaining regulations were irrelevant to tort liability. As McCardie J had commented in the Divisional Court in *Phillips*' case, 'the breach of a statutory regulation will usually afford prima facie evidence of negligence', although 'the Motor Car Acts and Regulations do not in themselves set the standard of care required for the purpose of civil actions'.[86] In other words, whilst there was some

[84] [1923] 2 KB 832, 841.

[85] *London Passenger Transport Board* v. *Upson* [1949] AC 155; cf. the Court of Appeal's decision in the same case, which adopted a more ambiguous position ([1947] 1 KB 930).

[86] [1923] 1 KB 539.

relationship between a breach of regulations and a failure to take reasonable care, that relationship was not dogmatic. Evidence of failure to take reasonable care in the form of a breach of statutory regulations might, it seems, be outweighed by other evidence putting that regulatory breach in a different light. Thus, to use an example McCardie J had given earlier in his judgment, a driver who drove on the wrong side of the road was in breach of the regulations and, therefore, there was prima facie evidence of negligence against him. However, if the driver had been forced to use the wrong side of the road to avoid a collision, the prima facie evidence of lack of reasonable care melted away. In this analysis it was crucial that the overarching question of lack of reasonable care could be used to control the significance of a finding that regulations had been breached.

Another decision of McCardie J, in *Wintle* v. *Bristol Tramways and Carriage Company*,[87] cast light on the related question of the significance of regulatory compliance where a defendant was accused of lack of reasonable care. The case arose out of a collision between two lorries, on a narrow road, at night. The defendant was alleged to have been negligent in only showing one light; but the Locomotives on Highways Act 1896 section 2 only required a single light to be displayed. Both the Divisional Court and the Court of Appeal held that regulatory compliance did not determine the question of lack of reasonable care, and went on to hold that there was evidence of negligence against the defendant. McCardie J's analysis was particularly revealing. The 1896 Act, he said, was not designed to lessen the obligation of a driver to take reasonable care. In the district where the accident took place it was usual for vehicles to carry two lamps, and this was not being over-cautious:

> it is frequently desirable and sometimes essential that two lights should be carried under the common law obligation to use reasonable care. The obligation must depend on the nature of the vehicle, the character of the highway, and the general circumstances.[88]

Here the responsiveness to local conditions and flexibility of the reasonable care standard was being contrasted with the centrally imposed, rigid, indiscriminate nature of the statutory regulation. There was also, at least implicitly, a point being made about the attitude that the law required drivers to adopt. It was not enough simply to obey the instruction from central government; each driver had to make an independent assessment of whether mere obedience was sufficient in the local circumstances in

[87] (1916) 116 LT 125 (DC); (1917) 117 LT 238 (CA).
[88] (1916) 116 LT 125, 126.

which he found himself. In short, compliance with statutory regulations was no more determinative of a lack of reasonable care than breach of regulations.

This was not an uncontroversial position, and in *Croston* v. *Vaughan*[89] the Court of Appeal found itself unable to agree on the correct approach. At the trial Porter J had held two drivers jointly liable for injuries caused to the claimant in a road accident. The negligence of one of them, as found by the judge, consisted in stopping suddenly and failing to give a hand signal; it was the latter finding that was to prove problematic, because the driver had relied on his rear brake light (which was in working order), and the Highway Code's section on hand signals stated that they should be given 'where mechanical indicators are not used'.[90] For Greer LJ and Scott LJ, compliance with statutory requirements was insufficient to rebut an allegation of failure to take reasonable care. As Scott LJ put it, 'the [Highway] Code and the regulations contained in Statutory Order No. 897 of 1935 [setting out the requirements for brake lights] still leave upon every driver a common law duty of taking action outside the Code and the regulations in circumstances where it becomes essential.'[91] Both judges emphasised that Porter J was an experienced driver, and the implication was that he had drawn on that experience when determining how a careful driver would have acted in the circumstances.[92] In much the same way that the courts in *Wintle*'s case had relied on the local convention of carrying two lights in order to establish a more onerous common law duty than that demanded by statute, Greer LJ and Scott LJ relied on Porter J's knowledge of motoring to impose liability in line with 'the custom of the really careful driver',[93] even though that custom went beyond the guidance in the Highway Code. The emphasis was very much on local practices and insider knowledge.

Slesser LJ, however, took a different approach. For him, the relationship between the common law and the regulations was being made too sophisticated: a driver who complied with the statutory regulations on rear brake lights had, *by definition*, given adequate warning to the car

[89] [1938] 1 KB 540.

[90] Ministry of Transport, *The Highway Code* (London, HMSO, 1935) 16.

[91] [1938] 1 KB 540, 564.

[92] [1938] 1 KB 540, 552 – Porter J 'has had great experience as a driver of cars' (Greer LJ), and 562 – 'I cannot help knowing from my own experience that Porter J is an experienced driver himself' (Scott LJ).

[93] [1938] 1 KB 540, 552.

behind.[94] It could not, therefore, be claimed that the driver had been negligent in failing also to give a hand signal, particularly as the Highway Code made it clear that hand signals were superfluous. At the heart of Slesser LJ's approach was the perspective of the defendant driver, who, in Slesser LJ's view, was entitled to say that having done what the Legislature had said was sufficient, nothing further could be required of him. This attitude was, of course, the exact opposite of the attitude underpinning the view that regulatory compliance was no more than prima facie evidence of reasonable care having been taken. Both views had their advantages. The view that saw regulatory compliance as by definition satisfying the requirements of reasonable care gave the law an attractive simplicity, and allowed a defendant to be completely clear about his obligations. The view that regulatory compliance was only prima facie evidence of care having been taken, on the other hand, encouraged a more searching, independent-minded attitude to safety, and could be tailored to the particular circumstances of the case. But perhaps more important than these relative strengths (and corresponding weaknesses) was what these different attitudes said about the relationship between regulation and tort. On Slesser LJ's view, tort standards were replaced by regulation; but, on the view of the majority of his colleagues, tort retained its own autonomous values, which might or might not coincide with those of regulation.

VII

Slesser LJ's failed attempt to create a structural relationship between regulatory compliance and breach of duty of care may well have been inspired by an earlier, successful initiative to link breach of regulations with contributory negligence. The development of contributory negligence, culminating in the Law Reform (Contributory Negligence) Act 1945 is explained in Chapter 13, but for present purposes two points about the defence in the late 1930s and early 1940s should be emphasised. First, the defence was complete (apportionment was a statutory innovation). Second, following on from the first point, the severe consequences of a finding of contributory negligence encouraged courts to finesse the principles of causation that they applied, in order to enable them to hold that a deserving claimant's carelessness had not truly contributed to his own loss. Courts' receptiveness to ingenious arguments about the underlying responsibility for an

[94] [1938] 1 KB 540, 556.

accident provided the perfect atmosphere for theories about the role that regulations might play to flourish.

The regulation at the heart of the developments in the 1930s and 1940s was the Pedestrian Crossing Places (Traffic) Provisional Regulations 1935, No. 3, which stated that 'The driver of every vehicle approaching a crossing shall, unless he can see that there is no foot passenger thereon, proceed at such a speed as to be able if necessary to stop before reaching such a crossing.'[95] The regulation said nothing directly about contributory negligence. But in *Bailey* v. *Geddes*[96] the Court of Appeal regarded it as having highly significant implications for that plea.

The claim arose from an injury suffered by the claimant pedestrian while he was attempting to cross the road. He had stepped out from behind a tram, and had been hit by the defendant's car; under ordinary circumstances the claimant would have been vulnerable to an allegation of contributory negligence. But these were not normal circumstances. The claimant was on a pedestrian crossing, and that made all the difference. Pedestrians on crossings, said Greer LJ, 'were protected by the Regulations … and were entitled to suppose that vehicles approaching the crossing would strictly obey the Regulations which were passed for the benefit of foot passengers'.[97] Here the defendant had breached Regulation 3: because the tram was in the way, he had not been able to see that there was no one on the crossing, yet he had proceeded at a speed that did not enable him to stop before reaching that crossing. It followed that, for Greer LJ, the sole cause of the accident had been the defendant's failure to obey the Regulations.

Slesser LJ's analysis went further. Having reiterated the centrality of the Regulations, he acknowledged that, as a matter of general law, contributory negligence was a defence to a claim for breach of statutory duty. However, 'these Regulations are so framed as to make it impossible, when they apply, for any such defence to be raised.'[98] As we have seen, there was nothing in the wording of the Regulations to suggest this dramatic legal consequence. Slesser LJ, however, explained that the exclusion of contributory negligence was a matter of logic, which necessarily flowed from the sequence of events:

> If the obligation on the driver of the vehicle under the Regulations is to stop outside the crossing it is impossible that what is done inside the

[95] *Bailey* v. *Geddes* [1938] 1 KB 156, 159.

[96] [1938] 1 KB 156. [97] [1938] 1 KB 156, 161.

[98] [1938] 1 KB 156, 166.

> crossing can be the fault or the negligence of the plaintiff himself, because, if the Regulations had been obeyed, there would have been no car upon the crossing at all which could, on any view, have injured the plaintiff.[99]

Scott LJ appeared to endorse Slesser LJ's reasoning, commenting that a plea of contributory negligence was 'fundamentally inconsistent with the very basis of the Regulations'.[100] Scott LJ also made the point that the rules of tort liability must not undermine the clear legislative wish that pedestrian crossings should be places of safety.[101]

Viewed purely as a matter of legal analysis, it has to be said that Slesser LJ's exposition was not entirely convincing. One obvious difficulty with it was that it seemed not to permit the conclusion that *both* a driver *and* a pedestrian could contribute to the damage by their carelessness. The logic seemed to be that once a driver had been shown to have acted unlawfully, no further legal analysis was necessary. Today we would almost certainly feel that a causal link to the injury had been established between both the driver's and the pedestrian's negligence; but that analysis is a lot more attractive today than it would have been in 1937, because today we have the legal tools to reflect joint causal responsibility in the form of the apportionment provisions of the contributory negligence legislation. For Slesser LJ, although a conclusion of joint causal responsibility was perfectly possible, its practical effect would have been to defeat the claimant's claim entirely – in reality, therefore, he was forced to choose between the claimant's fault and the defendant's fault as the cause of the injury. A second difficulty was that Slesser LJ's approach to causation was at odds with the approach developed in other contributory negligence cases where the acts of carelessness were not simultaneous. In such cases the court had elaborated the 'last opportunity' doctrine, under which causal responsibility for the damage was attributed to the party who had the last opportunity of avoiding it. In *Davies* v. *Mann*,[102] for instance, the owner of a donkey who had left it to graze at the roadside with its forefeet tied together was able to defeat an allegation of contributory negligence raised by a waggon driver who had collided with the donkey and injured it: certainly the donkey's owner had been at fault, but the waggon driver had had the last opportunity to avoid the damage. By 1937 the last opportunity doctrine had been over-elaborated to an extent that undoubtedly compromised its coherence, but its basic approach of emphasising the

99 [1938] 1 KB 156, 166.
100 [1938] 1 KB 156, 167.
101 [1938] 1 KB 156, 167.
102 (1842) 10 M & W 546.

final events in a sequence was exactly the opposite of the approach that Slesser LJ was advocating.

Perhaps more important than these analytical objections – at least for the purposes of this chapter – was the way that Slesser LJ's analysis went against the grain of the relationship between regulation and tort. We have already seen that courts were not prepared to equate the performance of statutory duties with meeting the standard of reasonable care, and that an independent-minded assessment of a situation was necessary. Here, by contrast, no awareness, let alone independent thought, was being demanded of the pedestrian, and he was entitled to rely on the assumption that others would perform their statutory duties. Such a departure from the traditional common law position may have been mandated by the introduction of protected pedestrian crossings; if so, this was a striking illustration of tort responding to policy initiatives.

The significance of *Bailey* v. *Geddes* was quickly realised, and a cluster of appellate cases explored its scope and implications. Both the court of first instance and the Court of Appeal in *Wilkinson* v. *Chetham-Strode*[103] recognised that the analysis in *Bailey* v. *Geddes* was not limited to Regulation 3 of the 1935 Regulations; it could also be applied to Regulation 5, which provided as follows:

> The driver of every vehicle at or approaching a crossing at a road intersection where traffic is for the time being controlled by a police constable or by light signals shall allow free and uninterrupted passage to every passenger who has started to go over the crossing before the driver receives the signal that he may proceed over the crossing.[104]

Any pedestrian who had 'started to go over the crossing' in these circumstances could not, it was held, be met with a plea of contributory negligence. An intricate debate then ensued over whether a pedestrian using a crossing with a pedestrian refuge in the middle of the road was still 'on the crossing' when he reached the refuge. If he was still on the crossing, then his immunity from a plea of contributory negligence extended to the second leg of his journey. The Court of Appeal held that he was not on the crossing at the halfway point: either there were two separate crossings, or, if it was all one large crossing, the refuge was not a part of the crossing, and a pedestrian at a refuge was, therefore, no longer 'on the crossing'.

While *Wilkinson* v. *Chetham-Strode* accomplished a modest expansion of the analysis from *Bailey* v. *Geddes*, the Court of Appeal's decision in

[103] [1940] 1 KB 309; [1940] 2 KB 310 (CA).

[104] *Wilkinson* v. *Chetham-Strode* [1940] 1 KB 309, 310.

Chisholm v. *London Passenger Transport Board*[105] marked out a limitation. As in *Bailey* v. *Geddes* the claim was concerned with injuries to a claimant who alleged that the defendant had been in breach of Regulation 3 (being able to stop before reaching the crossing); but the facts were not exactly the same, for in *Chisholm*'s case the claimant had stepped out onto the crossing when the defendant's vehicle was only a short distance away. At the trial Hilbery J had simply applied *Bailey* v. *Geddes*, and concluded that no defence of contributory negligence was available. The Court of Appeal, however, felt that a more discriminating approach was called for. At the heart of its reasoning was a sense of alarm about the practical implications if the trial judge was correct; for, in order to avoid being in breach of Regulation 3, drivers would have 'to slow down to almost a walking pace at every pedestrian crossing, and this would reduce the flow of traffic in a busy town to an absurdity'.[106] The solution was to interpret Regulation 3 less literally: the provision was not to apply to a pedestrian 'embarrassing' (i.e., stepping out in front of) a car, and was limited to cars that were a reasonable distance away from the crossing when the pedestrian set off across the road. Rather than seeing the Regulations as being all about protecting pedestrians, they were now seen as requiring 'reciprocal forbearance and consideration' between all road users.[107]

In late 1942 the Court of Appeal would fundamentally alter its attitude to the relationship between the Regulations and contributory negligence. The claim in *Sparks* v. *Edward Ash, Limited*[108] again concerned an injury to a pedestrian using a crossing, and again focussed on Regulation 3. But, rather than holding that proof of a breach of Regulation 3 logically excluded any defence of contributory negligence, the Regulation was held to be simply part of the context that the court should take into account when deciding whether the claimant had taken reasonable care for his own safety. A pedestrian using a crossing was, therefore, 'absolved in some degree from the insistent duty of care which he owes to motor traffic elsewhere', but not absolved entirely.[109] Some careful manoeuvring was required to explain the departure from *Bailey* v. *Geddes*. MacKinnon LJ and Goddard LJ described those parts of *Bailey*'s case that excluded contributory negligence as mere dicta. Scott LJ had a more embarrassing task: he had sat in *Bailey* v. *Geddes*, when he had said that a plea of contributory negligence was 'fundamentally inconsistent' with proof of a breach of the

[105] [1939] 1 KB 426. [106] [1939] 1 KB 426, 438 (Scott LJ).
[107] [1939] 1 KB 426, 439 (Scott LJ). [108] [1943] KB 223.
[109] [1943] KB 223, 230 (Scott LJ).

Regulations. In *Sparks* v. *Edward Ash, Limited* Scott LJ now regarded that earlier judgment as having been 'expressed ... in terms that were too universal'.[110] The result was that, after a short period where regulations had dictated tort analysis, the general common law approach had reasserted itself; there was now no structural difference between negligence claims where no regulations existed and negligence claims where regulations were also in force. The only difference was the emphasis, or nuance, that considering regulations as part of the context might introduce.

VIII

The development of tort liability in respect of roads and cars in the first half of the twentieth century inevitably reflected contemporary concerns. These concerns were not confined to Britain: the perceived advantages of roads reserved exclusively for cars would inspire the construction of the Italian *autostrada* in the 1920s and the German *Autobahnen* in the following decade.[111] Similarly, the law could not avoid becoming caught up in debates about how best to accommodate the new technology of motoring. Tort could not respond to changes in public opinion as quickly as Parliament could adjust speed limits, but perhaps it did not need to. The general judicial attitude seems to have been that new technology did not call for new legal concepts; the principles that had applied to horses could equally well apply to cars; and the common law was flexible enough to cope with the differences. Of course, there were exceptions, such as the pronouncement that storing a car in a garage was a non-natural use of land, but the overwhelming majority of decisions avoided a panic-stricken reaction against motorists. Perhaps the most difficult question that the law of tort faced was not how to analyse the facts of motoring cases, but how to accommodate itself to the Regulations governing road safety. For these regulations represented not just a different approach to attributing

110 [1943] KB 223, 231.

111 For an overview of the Italian development, see M. Moraglio, 'Real Ambition or Just Coincidence? The Italian Fascist Motorway Projects in Inter-war Europe' *The Journal of Transport History* 30(2) (2009) 168; for Germany, a good sense of the motivations surrounding the construction of *Autobahnen* is given in R. Vahrenkamp, 'Automobile Tourism and Nazi Propaganda: Constructing the Munich–Salzburg *Autobahn*, 1933–1939' *The Journal of Transport History* 27(2) (2006) 21. An extraordinarily ambitious plan for a pan-European network of motorways designed for the exclusive use of cars is analysed in A. Badenoch, 'Touring between War and Peace: Imagining the "Transcontinental Motorway" 1930–1950' *Journal of Transport History* 28(2) (2007) 192.

liability, but also a challenge to the autonomy of tort law itself. As we have seen, the issue where courts really struggled and disagreed with each other was how to define tort's attitude to statutory regulations. Ultimately a position protective of tort's autonomy was arrived at, with regulatory provisions merely fleshing out the context; and we might perhaps feel that this was one area where the placid judicial assumption that no significant changes were needed in the common law was a little too complacent.

For we should note that tort seems to have provided precious little encouragement towards improving safety standards. The point is nicely illustrated by the campaign in the 1930s to introduce a system of no-fault compensation for pedestrians injured by cyclists or motorists.[112] But perhaps a more eloquent demonstration is provided by Stenson Cooke's history of the Automobile Association. Cooke was the Association's first Secretary, and his book is a remarkable, almost unclassifiable work. The subtitle described it as 'a romantic history', but its protagonists were anonymised (being identified only in a list of 'characters' at the end), and the *Daily Express*, in some confusion, was driven to calling it 'a novel … every word of which is true'. It was in reality an example of a rather odd genre – the third person memoir – written in a style that owed something to Bertie Wooster, and it provided a lively insider's account of the extraordinary success of the Association. One continuing preoccupation was the promotion of safety, on which the Association was tireless, its activities ranging from distributing free reflectors to cyclists to supplying primary school road safety lessons.[113] The Association had significant dealings with the law, and campaigned for law reform – but neither it nor its members ever seem to have had the slightest concern with tort. Cooke refers only once to 'civil cases', and then he means contractual disputes with repairers.[114] The context of that reference is, perhaps suggestive. Cooke was discussing a proposal to extend the insurance coverage offered by the Association, and it may be that the law of tort governing motor claims had in reality become the concern of insurers rather than of motorists long before insurance was made compulsory by the Road Traffic Act 1930.[115]

[112] P. Bartrip, 'Pedestrians, Motorists, and No-Fault Compensation for Road Accidents in 1930s Britain' (2010) 31 *Journal of Legal History* 45.

[113] Cooke, *This Motoring*, at 161 and 160 respectively. Another important initiative, described at 155–7, concerned improving roadside warning signs.

[114] Cooke, *This Motoring*, 244–5.

[115] Cf. J. Spencer, 'Motor Cars and the Rule in *Rylands* v. *Fletcher*: A Chapter of Accidents in the History of Law and Motoring' (1983) 42 *CLJ* 65, 77–9, where it is argued (at 78) that 'the evidence suggests' that most motorists did not have third-party insurance before

But whatever the underlying explanation, if it was true, as Winfield once remarked, that 'where the railway slew its scores, the motor vehicle killed its hundreds',[116] it was perhaps a pity that tort law was unable or unwilling to do much about it.

the 1930 legislation. 'The evidence' relied on, however, is merely the wealth and alleged arrogance of early motorists.

116 P. Winfield, *A Text-Book of the Law of Tort* (London, Sweet & Maxwell, 1937) 209.

8

Workmen

> [T]he law lords manifested a far higher degree of legal statesmanship than the Court of Appeal has displayed in recent cases.
>
> William Robson

> The doctrine, which was said to be based on an implied term assumed to exist in 1842, cannot ... be read into the modern relationship of master and servant.
>
> Sir Stafford Cripps KC

I

The title of this chapter needs a little explanation. It is not intended to be gender-specific: the ideas it discusses applied equally to both male and female workers, although there were concerns that women tended to be ignorant of their legal rights.[1] Nor is it limited to adults; indeed, claims arising from injuries suffered by child workers raised fundamental questions about the basis of the legal doctrines that applied to them. It is, however, intended to confine the focus to injuries to manual workers (broadly defined), which is the core sense in which the word 'workmen' was understood in early cases under the workmen's compensation scheme.[2] As we shall see, English law – and, less willingly, Scots law – created and elaborated doctrines that had special reference to such injuries, often with the effect of excluding liability on the part of the workman's employer.

[1] R. Chambers, 'Some Aspects of Workmen's Compensation' (1941–1942) 5 *MLR* 113. The response by L. Hammond, 'The Administration of the Workmen's Compensation Acts' (1941–1942) 5 *MLR* 215 was more upbeat.

[2] *Simpson* v. *Ebbw Vale Steel, Iron, and Coal Company* [1905] 1 KB 453; S. Deakin, 'Tort Law and Workmen's Compensation Legislation: Complementary or Competing Models?' in T. T. Arvind and J. Steele (eds.), *Tort Law and the Legislature* (Oxford, Hart Publishing, 2013) 253, 255–6.

The primary structural feature of employers' liability for injuries suffered by their workmen was the doctrine of common employment. Also known as the fellow-servant rule, the doctrine provided that an employer was not liable for an injury to one of his employees where it was caused by a fellow employee's carelessness in the course of common work with the injured employee. From its creation in the middle of the nineteenth century to its abolition in the middle of the twentieth century, the doctrine of common employment defined the legal landscape of workplace injuries.[3] Courts tirelessly investigated the doctrine's somewhat obscure rationale and mapped its shifting boundaries. Judges also found themselves having to police attempts to circumvent the rule by bringing claims for breach of statutory duty, or of an employer's non-delegable duty. And perhaps most strikingly, the statutory system of workmen's compensation was brought into being, which provided lower levels of compensation than tort law, but was not subject to the defence of common employment.[4] Creating a parallel alternative compensation scheme may look like a rather elaborate way to draw the sting out of a troublesome common law doctrine; as trade unionists argued at the time, it would have been simpler to pass legislation to abolish the common law rule. The obvious solution was being rejected because it was not politically desirable; but, of course, the ramifications of such a radical and ambitious scheme were never likely to be exclusively political. At a theoretical level, the creation of the workmen's compensation scheme suggested interesting questions about the role and functions of tort law; at a practical level, it generated a mass of litigation that could – occasionally – touch a common law nerve. In short, the doctrine of common employment and the responses to it made up the law on injuries to workmen.

II

As the doctrine started to fall out of favour in the second quarter of the twentieth century, judges and writers started to wonder whether it was not

[3] Law Reform (Personal Injuries) Act 1948. For an overview of the Act's provisions see J. Unger, 'Law Reform (Personal Injuries) Act 1948' (1949) 12 *MLR* 347. For the involved reform process (in which common employment was almost a side-issue), see P. Bartrip, 'The impact of institutions and professions on compensation for occupational injury in England' in P. Mitchell (ed.), *The Impact of Institutions and Professions on Legal Development* (Cambridge University Press, 2012) 36, 50–5.

[4] P. Bartrip and S. Burman, *The Wounded Soldiers of Industry: Industrial Compensation Policy 1833–1897* (Oxford, Clarendon Press, 1983).

'made up' in a more pejorative sense. One writer called it a 'feeble fiction', and its origins were certainly not easy to pin down.[5] Most accounts began with *Priestley* v. *Fowler*,[6] where a butcher's boy had been injured by the collapse of his employer's overloaded cart. Lord Abinger CB's judgment denying that a duty was owed to the employee would become notorious for its alarmist tone and its proliferation of examples where similar duties would be owed:

> He who is responsible by his general duty, or by the terms of his contract, for all the consequences of negligence in a matter in which he is the principal, is responsible for the negligence of his inferior agents. If the owner of the carriage is therefore responsible for the sufficiency of his carriage to his servant, he is responsible for the negligence of his coach-maker, or his harnessmaker, or his coachman. The footman, therefore, who rides behind the carriage, may have an action against his master for a defect in the carriage owing to the negligence of the coach-maker, or for a defect in the harness arising from the negligence of the harness-maker, or for drunkenness, neglect, or want of skill in the coachman; nor is there any reason why the principle should not, if applicable in this class of cases, extend to many others. The master, for example, would be liable to the servant for the negligence of the chambermaid, for putting him into a damp bed; for that of the upholsterer, for sending in a crazy bedstead, whereby he was made to fall down while asleep and injure himself; for the negligence of the cook, in not properly cleaning the copper vessels used in the kitchen: of the butcher, in supplying the family with meat of a quality injurious to the health; of the builder, for a defect in the foundation of the house, whereby it fell, and injured both the master and the servant by the ruins.[7]

This kind of analysis was hardly out of the ordinary for a court that, as Cornish and Clark put it, looked to 'the impact upon the domestic responsibilities of the pater familias'.[8] Later judges would queue up to criticise the legal analysis, invariably pointing out that Lord Abinger CB had erroneously assumed that the master was liable for the negligence of independent contractors.[9] On the law as it stood in 1837, however, Lord Abinger CB was not mistaken: it was not until 1840 that vicarious liability

[5] J. Gold, 'Common Employment' (1937) 1 *MLR* 228.

[6] (1837) 3 M & W 1.

[7] (1837) 3 M & W 1, 5–6.

[8] W. Cornish and G. Clark, *Law and Society in England 1750–1950* (London, Sweet & Maxwell, 1989) 491.

[9] Eg *Fanton* v. *Denville* [1932] 2 KB 309, 315–16 (Scrutton LJ); *Radcliffe* v. *Ribble Motor Services Limited* [1939] AC 215, 238–9 (Lord Wright).

would be limited to the torts of 'servants'.[10] More to the point, *Priestley* v. *Fowler* could not be relied upon as *authority* for the fellow-servant rule, for the simple reason that there was no allegation of negligence by a fellow servant in the case.[11] What the judgment did provide, however, was an articulation of the relationship between masters and servants in which the doctrine of common employment could take root. Two passages were particularly forthright. First, the servant 'may, if he thinks fit, decline any service in which he reasonably apprehends injury to himself: and in most of the cases in which danger may be incurred, if not in all, he is just as likely to be acquainted with the probability and extent of it as the master'.[12] Second, shortly afterwards, 'to allow this sort of action to prevail would be encouragement to the servant to omit that diligence and caution which he is in duty bound to exercise on the behalf of his master, to protect him against the misconduct or negligence of others who serve him'.[13] The first sentence generalised, and idealised, the working relationship, entirely leaving out of account an employee's financial dependency on his employer. The second sentence, not entirely consistently with the first, gestured towards the incentives that might dictate a servant's performance of his duties, identifying the availability of a tort claim as a distorting factor. What was perhaps most striking about this was the idea that the servant would be encouraged to allow himself to be injured by the prospect of being able to sue; we might feel that only a lawyer, who had never actually suffered serious injury, would regard a tort claim in that way.

Other judges on both sides of the Atlantic evidently shared Lord Abinger's worldview,[14] and in 1858 the House of Lords laid down the authoritative statement of the common employment doctrine in *Bartonshill Coal Company* v. *Reid*.[15] 'When the workman contracts to do work of any particular sort', said Lord Cranworth LC:

> he knows, or ought to know, to what risks he is exposing himself: he knows, if such be the nature of the risk, that want of care on the part of a fellow-workman may be injurious or fatal to him, and that against such want of care his employer cannot by possibility protect him … Principle,

[10] Cornish and Clark, *Law and Society in England 1750–1950*, 491.

[11] See *Baker* v. *James Brothers and Sons, Limited* [1921] 2 KB 674, 679; P. Winfield, 'The Abolition of the Doctrine of Common Employment' (1949) 10 *CLJ* 191, 191.

[12] *Priestley* v. *Fowler* (1837) 3 M & W 1, 6.

[13] (1837) 3 M & W 1, 7.

[14] *Hutchinson* v. *York, Newcastle and Berwick Railway Co* (1850) 5 Exch 343; *Farwell* v. *Boston and Worcester Railroad Corporation* (1842) 4 Metcalf 49.

[15] (1858) 3 Macq 282.

> therefore, seems to me opposed to the doctrine that the responsibility of a master for the ill consequences of his servant's negligence is applicable to the demand made by a fellow-workman in respect of evil resulting from the carelessness of a fellow-workman when engaged in common work.[16]

The decision in the *Bartonshill Coal* case brought Scots law into line with the English position, and firmly based the doctrine on voluntary exposure to risk. As Lord Cranworth LC had put it, that exposure had come about when 'the workman contracts to do work', but that left open whether the contract was essential or merely an incidental detail. If, for instance, two workmen employed by different employers were collaborating on a task, the risk of injury from the negligence of one of them might be obvious, but could the doctrine of common employment still be invoked? The House of Lords' answer, in *Johnson* v. *WH Lindsay & Co*[17] was a resounding 'no'. As Lord Herschell put it:

> if the exemption results … from the injured person having undertaken, as between himself and the person he sues, to bear the risk of his fellow-servant's negligence, it can never be applicable where there is no relationship between the parties from which such an undertaking can be implied.[18]

The crucial word was the last one – for none of these cases ever had (or, in the future, would) concern express waivers of liability agreed to by workmen. This was, rather, an implied term, derived from the contractual relationship between the parties. Indeed, by the start of the twentieth century it was difficult to see how it could be justified on any other basis, since in the course of the 1890s the House of Lords had gone out of its way to emphasise that the defence of voluntary assumption of risk required proof that the risk in question had been willingly undertaken. Mere knowledge of the risk coupled with a continuation of the claimant's activity was not enough.[19] Only the contractual analysis permitted the conclusion that the risk of damage from a fellow servant's negligence lay on the employee.

III

The earliest twentieth-century cases on common employment exhibited a flourishing doctrine that the courts were applying with confidence to the general run of workplace injuries. Factual nuances that might seem to stand in the way of implying a term that the employee took the risk

[16] (1858) 3 Macq 282, 284. [17] [1891] AC 371.
[18] [1891] AC 371, 378. [19] *Smith* v. *Baker* [1891] AC 325.

were briskly swept aside. Thus, an argument by no less a figure than J. R. Atkin KC, that common employment could not apply where the contract contained express terms about risk, was unhesitatingly dismissed. 'We are here', said Collins MR, 'dealing with a positive rule of law with regard to the relation of employer and employed, which is really based upon considerations incidental to that relation rather than on any actual intention inferred to have existed in the minds of the parties in the particular case.'[20]

Two cases later the same year would take a similar position. Both concerned the negligent failure to give proper instructions to a fifteen-year-old employee, who suffered injury as a result. In *Cribb* v. *Kynoch, Limited*[21] the main issue was whether a master could delegate responsibility for giving proper instructions to workers, but the court also dealt with an argument that the claimant, as a fifteen-year-old, would not have been aware of the risks from fellow servants. The court held that that did not matter: 'The rule is that the master as between him and his servant has not agreed to be responsible for the negligence of a fellow-servant.'[22] *Young* v. *Hoffmann Manufacturing Company Limited*[23] elaborated on this position. As in *Cribb*'s case, counsel for the claimant argued that the claimant's young age was inconsistent with him having undertaken the risk of injury by a fellow servant. The Court of Appeal, however, made it very clear that counsel's argument made 'an impossible suggestion':[24] it was neither here nor there that the child had not contemplated the risk – the common employment doctrine imported 'stipulations and provisions usual in the particular trade, and such as a master may reasonably impose as a protection to himself'.[25] Sir Gorrell Barnes P added that the common employment doctrine came within the principles for implying contractual terms set out in the classic case of *The Moorcock*.[26] This was doubly revealing. It indicated that the courts regarded common employment as a contractual doctrine, and an orthodox one at that. It also highlighted what kind of implied term the courts had in mind, for, in the passage that Sir Gorrell Barnes P quoted from *The Moorcock*, Bowen LJ spoke of the 'presumed intention of the parties' and the demands of 'business efficacy'.[27] On this analysis, the fact that the worker was fifteen years old and, there-

[20] *Burr* v. *Theatre Royal, Drury Lane, Limited* [1907] 1 KB 544, 555.
[21] [1907] 2 KB 548. [22] [1907] 2 KB 548, 562.
[23] [1907] 2 KB 646. [24] [1907] 2 KB 646, 650 (Cozens-Hardy MR).
[25] [1907] 2 KB 646, 650–1. [26] (1889) 14 PD 64.
[27] [1907] 2 KB 646, 652–3.

fore, unlikely to consider what risks of damage he might be bearing, was simply irrelevant. This was a term implied as a matter of law, not fact.

What gives terms implied in law their claim to legitimacy is not that they are giving expression to what the parties intended to promise but were too forgetful or flustered to say; rather, terms implied in law reflect a normative judgment about the content of the kind of contract before the court. They are often inspired by an assessment of who is best placed to avoid a risk – as, for instance, in the implied terms as to quality in sale of goods – and inevitably draw on judicial assumptions about how the contract in question should operate. The doctrine of common employment fitted perfectly into this category: it relied on an assessment of who was best placed to avoid the risk in order to fashion a generalised contractual term for employment relationships. It even, ironically, could be said to promote Bowen LJ's 'business efficacy' in the sense that businesses were relieved of liability to their employees, and therefore made more profitable. In formal terms, the doctrine of common employment could not be faulted.

In terms of its substantive content, however, by the late 1930s the doctrine had come to appear controversial. Lord Wright in *Wilsons & Clyde Coal Company, Limited* v. *English*[28] commented that the doctrine was 'well-established, but illogical',[29] and in *Radcliffe* v. *Ribble Motor Services Limited*[30] the House of Lords was invited either to abolish or limit it. Abolition was felt to be impossible, as the doctrine had been laid down by the House of Lords in *Bartonshill Coal Company* v. *Reid*, and implicitly acknowledged in statutes such as the workmen's compensation legislation. Limitation, by contrast, was available, and was achieved by paying close attention to the concept of 'common work'. This was an aspect of the doctrine that had hitherto attracted very little judicial analysis, and the House of Lords was happy to fill the gap, supplying a test that the injured workman and the workman causing the damage 'must be employed in common work, that is, work which necessarily and naturally or in the usual course involves juxtaposition, local or casual, of the fellow employees and exposure to the risk of negligence of one affecting the other'.[31] On the facts of the case a coach driver who happened to be injured by another coach driver from the same firm in the course of a journey was held to fall outside the doctrine: each driver was engaged in an independent task.

[28] [1938] AC 57. [29] [1938] AC 57, 79.
[30] [1939] AC 215. [31] [1939] AC 215, 249 (Lord Wright).

While the detailed reasoning on 'common work' was practically significant,[32] the House of Lords' general tone of disapproval dominated its decision. Both Lord Atkin and Lord Wright undertook pained analyses of the authorities on common employment, and were unimpressed by what they found. *Priestley* v. *Fowler* was alarmist, emotional and badly reasoned. Lord Atkin said that he 'appreciate[d] the vigour and literary style'[33] of Shaw CJ's influential exposition of common employment in *Farwell* v. *Boston and Worcester Railroad Corporation*,[34] but that was all he appreciated. Lord Wright found it a one-sided view of public policy, which included the incomprehensible claim that wages invariably reflected risks undertaken by the worker.[35] Lord Macmillan avoided detailed analysis, but his assessment was no more cheerful.

To the extent that it was possible to reduce the House of Lords' objections to a single complaint, it was this: common employment had lost touch with its roots as an implied term. Thus, for Lord Atkin, courts had attempted to state the limits of the doctrine 'as an objective rule of law without having regard to its foundation in the implied contract of the workman'.[36] Lord Macmillan observed that:

> The danger attendant on all doctrines which are founded on presumptions, implications or fictions originally thought to be equitable is that they are apt to be extended by a process of logical development which loses sight of their origin and carries them far beyond the reach of any such justification as they may have originally possessed.[37]

Lord Wright seemed to have the same point in mind when he criticised Collins MR for having suggested in *Burr* v. *Theatre Royal, Drury Lane, Limited* that 'the doctrine of common employment' should be placed 'on an abstract rule'.[38] What Lord Wright thought was the correct approach is hinted at towards the end of his speech, where he imagined a driver's response if a proposed implied term had been expressly put to him.

These would surely have been compelling criticisms if the doctrine of common employment had been based on an implied term in fact – that is, an implied term that helpfully articulated what the parties had meant to say. But, as we have seen, common employment was not being justified in those terms; it was being justified as an implied term in law. Surely

[32] Contrast the outcomes in *Miller* v. *Glasgow Corporation* [1947] AC 368 and *Glasgow Corporation* v. *Bruce* [1948] AC 79.

[33] [1939] AC 215, 228.

[34] (1842) 4 Metcalf 49.

[35] *Radcliffe* v. *Ribble Motor Services Limited* [1939] AC 215, 241.

[36] [1939] AC 215, 230.

[37] [1939] AC 215, 235.

[38] [1939] AC 215, 247.

what was objectionable about the doctrine was not its failure to reflect the parties' actual intentions, but the normative assertions that it made. Thus, even if it was sometimes true that the workman might be better placed than his employer to avoid the risk of injury, did that justify an implied term that treated the workman as if he was *always* better placed? Furthermore, should being best placed to avoid the risk determine who bore that risk? The disparity in the financial resources of the parties might make it more appropriate to place the risk on the employer. Evolving ideas of employers' responsibilities to their workers, as manifested in the workmen's compensation legislation (and elsewhere), might also inform the content of any proposed term. This was what Sir Stafford Cripps KC, as counsel for the claimant in the *Radcliffe* case, was suggesting when he said, in the sentence used as an epigraph to this chapter, that 'the doctrine, which was said to be based on an implied term assumed to exist in 1842, cannot … be read into the modern relationship of master and servant'.[39] The judges, by contrast, seemed to be focussing on criticising the doctrine for failing to be something that it was not.

Cripps' argument also hinted at a deeper problem with the law's development. Assuming that the doctrine of common employment properly expressed the law's attitude to employment relationships in the mid nineteenth century, was that attitude to be fixed in the common law for all time? The House of Lords' answer that the doctrine was too well established to be abolished suggested that the law was, indeed, permanently set: it was incapable of registering whether terms previously implied in law continued to reflect contemporary understandings of the parties' relationship. The terms Cripps used were also suggestive in another way: 'the modern relationship of master and servant' was an oxymoron. The 'modern relationship' was that of employer and employee, although the older idiom of 'master and servant' would still remain a valid description for those in domestic service. As it turned out, Cripps was making his submissions in *Radcliffe*'s case just as the number of workers employed in domestic service was entering a rapid and terminal decline, so it would have been ill-advised to develop the law to reflect the norms of domestic service.[40] What was more problematic was that 'master and servant' had, at least historically, denoted a hierarchical relationship of status. To put the question in terms of 'servants' suing 'masters' risked making an

[39] [1939] AC 215, 217.

[40] The number of private domestic servants declined by two-thirds between 1939 and 1941. See R. McKibbin, *Classes and Cultures: England 1918–1951* (Oxford University Press, 1998) 109.

action by an employee sound like a piece of impertinent insubordination by an individual who needed to be taught his place. We might recall that when, in *Priestley* v. *Fowler*,[41] Lord Abinger CB chose illustrations of how the world would be turned upside down by imposing a duty of care on masters, all his examples concerned claims by *domestic* servants. Trying to develop the law to reflect the social conditions and understandings of the 1930s in the shadow of such anachronistic and historically freighted terminology made the task doubly difficult.

IV

The judicial exposition of common employment in the first half of the twentieth century indicated that the outlook for legal development in this area was bleak. The doctrine may have been, as Joseph Gold said, a 'feeble fiction', but it had an all too real grip on the common law.[42] Common employment, however, was not the whole story – elsewhere exceptions to the doctrine were created, and flourished.

One of those exceptions was the tort of breach of statutory duty. In 1898 the Court of Appeal had held, in *Groves* v. *Lord Wimborne*,[43] that the defence of common employment was unavailable where a worker had been injured by machinery that, in breach of the occupier's statutory duty, had not been securely fenced.[44] Crucially, the statutory obligation was placed upon the occupier personally, which allowed the courts to say that a breach of it fell outside the doctrine of common employment, because the doctrine was all about the risk of a third party's breach of duty. Here, by contrast, the employer was being made accountable for a breach of his own duty.[45] The (appellate) courts would take a consistently uncompromising approach to the duty to fence machinery over the course of the next fifty years, and there was a similar attitude to the condition of premises.[46] There was even support for the view that civil liability for breach of statutory duty was more extensive than criminal liability under the same

[41] (1837) 3 M & W 1. See above, at 211.

[42] Gold, 'Common Employment', 228.

[43] [1898] 2 QB 402. [44] Factory and Workshop Act 1878, s. 5.

[45] *David* v. *Britannic Merthyr Coal Company* [1909] 2 KB 146, 157 (Fletcher Moulton LJ).

[46] On machinery, see *Wing* v. *Soar* (1926) [1938] 1 KB 379; *Carey* v. *Ocean Coal Company, Limited* [1938] 1 KB 365; *Vowles* v. *Armstrong-Siddeley Motors Ltd* [1938] 4 All ER 796. On premises, the most striking decision is perhaps *James Nimmo and Company Limited* v. *Connell* [1924] AC 595.

legislation, since statutory defences to criminal prosecutions might not apply to civil claims.[47]

That was not to say, however, that employers' liability for breach of statutory duty was limitless. In *Groves* v. *Lord Wimborne* itself Vaughan Williams LJ had indicated that contributory negligence was a defence to breach of statutory duty claims, and his view was regarded by the Court of Appeal in *Dew* v. *United British Steamship Co*[48] as settling the point. But it soon became clear that the issue was not quite so straightforward as it had first appeared. The High Court of Australia, in *Bourke* v. *Butterfield and Lewis Limited*,[49] had taken a more sophisticated approach when deciding a case in which a worker's foot had become trapped in unfenced machinery. The majority judgment of Knox CJ, Gavan Duffy J and Starke J had sought to identify the principles governing contributory negligence as a defence to breach of statutory duty by appealing to the same statutory intention that created the claim for breach of statutory duty in the first place. 'It would be unreasonable', they said:

> to attribute to Parliament an intention to impose upon the employer responsibility for an injury which the employee deliberately invites, whether by adopting the means of inflicting it, or by rejecting the means of avoiding it, or for an injury which has happened because the employee deliberately took an unnecessary risk not in the interests of the employer, but for his own purposes. It is not easy to frame an exact formula; but it may be said that the employer is responsible for the negligence, but not for the misconduct, of his employee.[50]

Here, the employee's act of momentarily resting his foot on a stationary machine fell short of such misconduct.

Isaacs J placed less emphasis on statutory intention, and was more concerned with the High Court's obligations to society as a whole. 'The Court', he observed, 'no less than the Parliament whose words we have to interpret, is a living organism of the same society, broadly conscious of its industrial activities and the evils intended to be met, and fully seized of the corporate sense of the community in regard to them.'[51] This led him to conclude that contributory negligence as a defence was inconsistent with the claim for failure to fence dangerous machinery, as required by statute. For Isaacs J the factory owner's position verged on hypocrisy:

[47] *David* v. *Britannic Merthyr Coal Company* [1909] 2 KB 146, 162 (Fletcher Moulton LJ); *Riddell* v. *Reid* [1943] AC 1, 11 (Lord Thankerton), 25 (Lord Wright), 30–2 (Lord Porter).

[48] (1928) 98 LJ (KB) 88.

[49] (1926) 38 CLR 354.

[50] (1926) 38 CLR 354, 360.

[51] (1926) 38 CLR 354, 369.

he was seeking to criticise the employee for a failure to take reasonable care, while having created working conditions where precisely such lapses were inevitable.[52] However, like the majority, Isaacs J did not consider that the employer's liability was unlimited: wilful misuse of machinery or acts entirely outside the sphere of employment were the employee's own responsibility.

It is possible that Higgins J, in his short concurring judgment, intended to go further than either the majority or Isaacs J. Since this was a claim for breach of statutory duty rather than negligence, he argued, contributory negligence could have no relevance.[53] It seems, however, that Higgins J would not have favoured disregarding actions by the employee that broke the chain of causation. Such actions could probably be described as 'misconduct', and almost certainly as 'wilful misconduct', so it would seem that Higgins J was not far from agreeing in substance with his colleagues' expositions.

Bourke v. *Butterfield and Lewis Limited* was brought to the attention of Lawrence J in *Flower* v. *Ebbw Vale Steel, Iron & Coal Company, Limited.*[54] Like *Bourke*'s case, the facts in *Flower*'s case involved an injury to a workman caused by machinery that was not securely fenced. Lawrence J was evidently troubled by the Australian decision, saying that it was inconsistent with English authority, and adding that:

> Much of the reasoning of the learned Judges in High Court of Australia appears to me to ignore the true limits of the doctrine of contributory negligence and to assume that the doctrine demands of a workman in a factory a higher degree of care than an ordinary prudent workman in a factory would show.[55]

Lawrence J then hinted at how the standard of contributory negligence could be adapted to factory conditions when he said that 'the tribunal of fact has to take into account all the circumstances of work in a factory and … it is not for every risky thing which a workman in a factory may do in his familiarity with the machinery that a plaintiff ought to be held guilty of contributory negligence.'[56]

The Court of Appeal preferred to avoid the issue.[57] For them the availability of contributory negligence as a defence in claims for breach of statutory duty was established by Court of Appeal authority, and only the House of Lords could change the law. When the case reached the House of

[52] (1926) 38 CLR 354, 369. [53] (1926) 38 CLR 354, 376.
[54] [1934] 2 KB 132. [55] [1934] 2 KB 132, 139.
[56] [1934] 2 KB 132, 140. [57] [1934] 2 KB 132.

Lords, however, it was disposed of on the basis that there was no evidence of contributory negligence on the part of the claimant.[58] Lord Wright, however, addressed the legal position. He praised Lawrence J's explanation of the standard of contributory negligence, commenting that when Lawrence J made it clear that a workman was not to be liable for 'every risky thing', he 'was carefully distinguishing between what may not very precisely be called an error of judgment of the workman and something which he describes as contributory negligence'.[59] More controversially, Lord Wright also suggested that the majority judgment in *Bourke*'s case 'seems to embody a rule little, if at all, different from what Lawrence J adopted'.[60]

Less than a year later, in *Craze* v. *Meyer-Dumore Bottlers' Equipment Co Ltd*[61] the Court of Appeal had to admit that, on the authorities, it had no choice but to recognise contributory negligence as a defence to breach of statutory duty. Greer LJ suggested that he reached this conclusion with regret. Lord Wright in *Flower*'s case, he commented:

> indicated that there might be some doubt – I think that is the effect of his speech – as to whether the ordinary rule of contributory negligence could properly be held to apply to a case where the complaint is breach of statutory duty. Although I do not suppose it matters, that point of view is one which has considerable weight because, apart from the authorities, one would rather suppose that the necessity for guarding machinery and the necessity for a statutory provision to the effect that dangerous machinery should be guarded was accepted, and the intention of the legislature was that there should be protection, not merely for the purpose of protecting careful workpeople, because it is not the very careful workpeople that want protection, but it is those who are not careful who do want protection.[62]

Here Greer LJ was surely correct to say that Lord Wright in *Flower*'s case was not merely making a point about the standard of care in contributory negligence. What Wright was advocating – the 'misconduct' test – effectively disapplied the contributory negligence defence (in any orthodox form) from claims for breach of statutory duty. Greer LJ's reasons for agreeing with Lord Wright showed that he must have been influenced by the majority's judgment in *Bourke*'s case, and it is striking that, rather than limiting himself to the point about authority, he should have gone out of

[58] [1936] AC 206. [59] [1936] AC 206, 214.
[60] [1936] AC 206, 216. [61] [1936] 2 All ER 1150.
[62] [1936] 2 All ER 1150, 1153.

his way to urge that development of the principles of breach of statutory duty should be inspired by the social policies underlying legislation.

V

When the House of Lords finally settled the point, three years later in *Caswell* v. *Powell Duffryn Associated Collieries, Limited*,[63] analytical orthodoxy trumped Antipodean appeals to legislative intentions. The context was, yet again, a failure to fence dangerous machinery securely. On the facts the House of Lords held that the claimant had not been contributorily negligent; but, unlike in *Flower*'s case, the judges went on to address the question of principle. For Lord Atkin the key point was that a successful claim for breach of statutory duty required proof of causation of damage; contributory negligence could not be irrelevant to such a claim since it went to causation. Nor was contributory negligence limited to claims for negligence – after all, Lord Atkin pointed out, *Butterfield* v. *Forrester*[64] was a landmark decision on contributory negligence that had been given on a claim for public nuisance. Lord Atkin concluded his speech by emphasising that the test for contributory negligence must be sensitive to the factual context:

> the care to be expected of the plaintiff in the circumstances will vary with the circumstances; and … a different degree of care may well be expected from a workman in a factory or a mine from that which might be taken by an ordinary man not exposed continually to the noise, strain, and manifold risks of factory or mine.[65]

Lord Thankerton agreed with Lord Atkin, and Lord Macmillan, Lord Wright and Lord Porter reached the same conclusion. Lord Wright made it clear that his agreement was less than wholehearted:

> If the matter had been free from authority, I should, I think, have thought it simpler to hold that a workman's claim for injury caused by breach of the employer's statutory duty to fence and like duties, is only barred by blameworthy conduct on the man's part of such gravity and so directly causing the accident as in the judgment of the judge or jury to be properly described as the substantial cause of the accident.[66]

This was a surprising attitude to have adopted. There was, of course, authority, but it was not *binding* authority. So far as the House of Lords was

[63] [1940] AC 152. [64] (1809) 11 East 60.
[65] [1940] AC 152, 166. [66] [1940] AC 152, 178.

concerned, the question was open – as the Court of Appeal had pointed out more than once.[67] Furthermore, there was persuasive authority in the shape of the High Court of Australia's decision. Deference to authority was, therefore, unnecessary, and also seems to have been uncharacteristic for Lord Wright.[68] We might wonder whether this was not another occasion on which Lord Atkin's ability to bring his colleagues into line was in play.[69]

One issue on which Lord Wright's agreement with Lord Atkin was unqualified was the fact-sensitivity of the contributory negligence test. 'What is all-important', said Lord Wright:

> is to adapt the standard of negligence to the facts, and to give due regard to the actual conditions under which men work in a factory or mine, to the long hours and the fatigue, to the slackening of attention which naturally comes from constant repetition of the same operation, to the noise and confusion in which the man works, to his pre-occupation in what he is actually doing at the cost perhaps of some inattention to his own safety.[70]

Lord Porter's speech echoed this sentiment.[71]

What was perhaps most significant about these observations on the application of the contributory negligence test was their perspective – their willingness to enter into working conditions, and to imagine the physical and mental toil taken by repetitive manual labour. The contrast with Lord Abinger CB's schematic, cynical analysis in *Priestley* v. *Fowler* of servants' willingness to expose themselves to risks was particularly striking. Here the law was being open to industrial conditions, even if it was not going as far as the Australian High Court in allowing those conditions to prompt radical doctrinal innovation.

VI

In the background of Lord Atkin's, Lord Wright's and Lord Porter's speeches in *Caswell*'s case was an argument about the nature of claims for

67 *Flower* v. *Ebbw Vale Steel, Iron & Coal Company, Limited* [1934] 2 KB 132, 147 (Scrutton LJ), 150 (Maugham LJ), 154 (Talbot J); *Craze* v. *Meyer-Dumore Bottlers' Equipment Co Ltd* [1936] 2 All ER 1150, 1153 (Greer LJ), 1154 (Greene LJ), 1155 (Scott LJ).

68 N. Duxbury, 'Lord Wright and Innovative Traditionalism' (2009) 59 *University of Toronto Law Journal* 265, 278–85.

69 For the most famous example, see A. Rodger, 'Lord Macmillan's Speech in *Donoghue* v *Stevenson*' (1992) 108 *LQR* 236.

70 *Caswell* v. *Powell Duffryn Associated Collieries, Limited* [1940] AC 152, 178–9.

71 [1940] AC 152, 187.

breach of statutory duty. If such claims were not based on negligence, it was said, the claimant's contributory negligence must be irrelevant. This was, essentially, the argument that had appealed to Higgins J when, in *Bourke* v. *Butterfield and Lewis Limited*, he had held that contributory negligence did not apply to claims for breach of statutory duty. As we have seen in the previous section, Lord Atkin rejected the premise that contributory negligence was relevant only to claims based on negligence. Lord Wright and Lord Porter were non-committal: neither was prepared to decide the case on what Lord Wright called a 'technical ground'.[72] Lord Macmillan, however, took a very different attitude to the argument, asserting forthrightly that:

> a civil action for damages in respect of an accident to a miner alleged to be due to a breach of statutory duty on the part of his employers must, in my opinion, be based upon negligence and be subject to the general principles of law which govern actions of damages for negligence.[73]

At first sight Lord Macmillan's position looks counter-intuitive. One of the defining features of a claim in negligence is the requirement of proving that the defendant failed to take reasonable care: liability is fault-based. In claims for breach of statutory duty, by contrast, the claimant needs only to show that he has suffered damage as the result of a breach of statutory duty that was imposed to protect people in his position: liability is strict. To say that liability for breach of statutory duty is a kind of liability for negligence is – on the face of it – to confuse fundamentally different torts.

Behind Lord Macmillan's view, however, there was a rich literature. One of the earliest expositions of the idea that a breach of statutory duty was equivalent to negligence was provided by Fletcher Moulton LJ in his controversial judgment in *David* v. *Britannic Merthyr Coal Company*.[74] The case arose from a mining accident caused by an outrageous disregard of the statutory duties protecting miners. Fletcher Moulton LJ had no hesitation in finding that a miner's widow could maintain an action for breach of statutory duty, and added that:

> the effect of this view of the statute is that breaches of its provisions become statutorily equivalent to negligence, and this appears to me to correspond precisely with the history and object of such legislation. It has often been pointed out that such legislation aims only at imposing

[72] [1940] AC 152, 178. [73] [1940] AC 152, 167.
[74] [1909] 2 KB 146.

> on all that which prudent and considerate employers will do of their own accord. By embodying in the provisions of an Act ... those precautions which it is advised should be observed in the management of these dangerous undertakings the Legislature erects a standard of carefulness and requires all who carry them on to come up to that standard. It no longer is left to the chance opinion of a jury to decide whether these precautions may properly be omitted. The Legislature decides the question for them.[75]

What is perhaps most eye-catching about Fletcher Moulton's analysis here is that he makes the statutory duties into a superior version of the classic negligence test, from which the unpredictability of jury verdicts has been eliminated. There was no sense here – unlike the cases on road safety discussed in the previous chapter – that breach of statutory duty was merely *evidence* of negligence that might be outweighed by counter-indications of carefulness.

Other members of the Court of Appeal in *David* v. *Britannic Merthyr Coal Company*, and the House of Lords in the same case,[76] did not find it necessary to endorse Fletcher Moulton LJ's views. On the facts of the case, nothing turned on whether the claim for breach of statutory duty was regarded as a species of negligence. In the late 1920s, however, a context would come to light in which it was absolutely crucial whether breach of statutory duty was appropriately categorised as a claim for negligence.

That context was the interpretation of the Workmen's Compensation Act 1925 s. 29(1), which stated that:

> When the injury was caused by the personal negligence or wilful act of the employer or of some person for whose act or default the employer is responsible, nothing in this Act shall affect any civil liability of the employer, but in that case the workman may, at his option, either claim compensation under this Act or take proceedings independently of this Act; but the employer shall not be liable to pay compensation for injury to a workman by accident arising out of and in the course of the employment both independently of and also under this Act, and shall not be liable to any proceedings independently of this Act, except in case of such personal negligence or wilful act as aforesaid.

If claims for breach of an employer's statutory duty were not for 'the personal negligence or wilful act of the employer or of some person for whose act or default the employer is responsible', they were barred by the subsection.

[75] [1909] 2 KB 146, 164.

[76] *Britannic Merthyr Coal Company, Limited* v. *David* [1910] AC 74.

The Court of Appeal, in a series of decisions culminating in *Rudd* v. *Elder Dempster and Company, Limited*[77] held that s. 29(1) did indeed bar claims for an employer's breach of statutory duty. 'My difficulty', Scrutton LJ commented, 'has been to see what other meaning can be given to these words.'[78] The history of the subsection provided only ambivalent indications. It had formed section 1 of the original Workmen's Compensation Act 1897, and that date was significant, because *Groves* v. *Lord Wimborne*, the leading case establishing an employer's liability for breach of statutory duty, had not been decided until 1898. The statutory provision may, therefore, have been drafted without having claims for breach of statutory duty in mind. The *Groves* decision, unfortunately, offered no guidance on how to interpret it – the legislation was not cited, since the events giving rise to the claim, and, indeed, the Court of Appeal's decision, preceded the coming into force of the Act. Only three days separated the latter two events, so if it was true that the section barred claims against employers for breaches of statutory duty, the Court of Appeal's decision was obsolete before it was even reported.[79] This was a somewhat surprising conclusion, but one that the Court of Appeal in the 1920s felt unable to avoid.

The House of Lords in *Lochgelly Iron and Coal Company, Limited* v. *M'Mullan*[80] felt able to take a different approach, holding unanimously that an action for an employer's breach of statutory duty was a claim for 'personal negligence' under s. 29. Lord Atkin's reasoning encapsulated the House of Lords' position. A breach of an employer's statutory duty relating to safety, he said:

> constitutes negligence ... All that is necessary to show is a duty to take care to avoid injuring; and if the particular care to be taken is prescribed by statute, and the duty to the injured person to take the care is likewise imposed by statute, and the breach is proved, all the essentials of negligence are present.[81]

This was a rather formalist account of negligence, in which the existence of a duty, a breach and damage was of primary importance; the content of these components was, on this account, irrelevant. This, we should remember, was the same judge who had made so much of the substantive

[77] [1933] 1 KB 566. The earlier cases were *Bennett* v. *Whitehead* [1926] 2 KB 380 and *Higgins* v. *Harrison* 25 BWCC 113.

[78] [1933] 1 KB 566, 587.

[79] On the timings see Scrutton LJ in *Rudd* v. *Elder Dempster and Company, Limited* [1933] 1 KB 566, 569 and 581.

[80] [1934] AC 1. [81] [1934] AC 1, 9.

content of duties of care in *Donoghue* v. *Stevenson* two years earlier. Lord Warrington echoed Lord Atkin's reasoning, adding that 'personal negligence means nothing more than neglect on the part of the person concerned to perform the duty imposed on him for the protection of the pursuer amongst others'.[82] The move here from 'negligence' to 'neglect' was almost a play on words; like Lord Atkin's reasoning, it glossed over the fact that liability for breach of statutory duty was strict.

While Lord Macmillan regarded the argument that an employer's breach of statutory duty was not personal negligence as 'untenable',[83] Lord Wright, who gave the final speech in the case, found the point more difficult. Something of Lord Wright's equivocation comes through in the following passage:

> In such a case as the present the liability is something which goes beyond and is on a different plane from the liability for breach of a duty under the ordinary law, apart from the statute, because not only is the duty one which cannot be delegated but, whereas at the ordinary law the standard of duty must be fixed by the verdict of a jury, the statutory duty is conclusively fixed by the statute. But the duty is the same kind in this respect, that it is a duty to take care and precautions for the safety of the workmen; it is a duty to take care which is owed to the workman, and which if broken constitutes negligent conduct for which, if damage ensues to the workman affected, damages are recoverable. Hence the breach of such a duty as that in question has been, I think, correctly described as statutory negligence.[84]

The two most important words here were 'I think' in the final sentence. Lord Wright was clearly alive to the substantive contrast between negligence and breach of statutory duty, but was prepared to allow a formalist account of negligence to decide the case. His reasoning could be summarised as saying that claims for breach of statutory duty had enough in common with claims for negligence to be categorised as negligence. But Lord Wright's unease was palpable: he went on to claim that the statutory duties provided 'conclusive evidence of negligence', which was an attempt to bring the substantive requirements for the two torts together.[85] In support of this position he could only cite Fletcher Moulton LJ's controversial exposition in *David* v. *Britannic Merthyr Coal Company* (discussed above). A second case he cited, the Ontario decision in *Thompson* v. *Wright*, said that breach of statutory duty was 'per se evidence of negligence'.[86] This

[82] [1934] AC 1, 14. [83] [1934] AC 1, 18.
[84] [1934] AC 1, 23. [85] [1934] AC 1, 27.
[86] (1892) 22 Ont Rep 127.

was a far weaker claim than the claim that breach of statutory duty was *conclusive* evidence of negligence, for the simple reason that anything less than conclusive evidence could be rebutted by countervailing evidence. There was nothing special about breach of statutory duty if it was merely inconclusive evidence of negligence – and it was clearly impossible to claim that such inconclusive evidence made negligence and breach of statutory duty substantively identical.

Lord Wright's was the last speech to be delivered in *Lochgelly Iron and Coal Company Limited* v. *M'Mullan*, but it would not be his last word on the subject. When he returned to the point, in *Caswell* v. *Powell Duffryn Associated Collieries, Limited*,[87] it was obvious that he was still troubled. 'I do not think that an action for breach of statutory duty such as that in question is completely or accurately described as an action in negligence', he said. 'It is a common law action based on the purpose of the statute to protect the workman, and belongs to the category often described as that of cases of strict or absolute liability.' 'The cause of action', he continued, 'is sometimes described as statutory negligence and it is said that negligence is conclusively presumed.'[88] A reference to and single sentence summary of the *Lochgelly* case followed. This suggestive, but rather elusive passage indicated a significant change in Lord Wright's thinking. The first sentence, if taken to its logical conclusion, and having particular regard to accuracy of description, meant that the *Lochgelly* case was wrongly decided. The third sentence, which seemed to be nothing more than a neutral piece of reportage, was striking for what it left out. For the person who had most recently said that breaches of statutory duty provided conclusive evidence of negligence was Lord Wright himself. Now, of course it would not have been proper for Lord Wright to say 'in what, let's be frank, was one of my finest moments, I said …'; but to disown his own previous position is surely revealing, especially as the implication is that people who make assertions about 'statutory negligence' have failed to carry through the legal analysis properly. This seems to have been an unfortunate, and uncomfortable, situation for Lord Wright, in which his instinctive sympathy for injured workmen conflicted with his commitment to clarity of legal analysis. Ultimately, it seems, the lawyerly commitment prevailed, but only once it was too late.

[87] [1940] AC 152. [88] [1940] AC 152, 177–8.

VII

Lord Wright would also find himself at the forefront of developments in the closely related field of employers' common law duties. These duties were significant for the same reasons that an employer's statutory duties were significant, namely, that they fell outside the defence of common employment. To put the point in the language of implied terms, the employer impliedly undertook to perform his common law duties, and was, therefore, liable if those duties were not performed.

The major contrast between an employer's common law and statutory duties was that while statutory duties were defined by a text, common law duties were constrained only by judicial creativity. By the beginning of the twentieth century such creativity had allowed the law to reach the position where an employer's common law duties required the careful selection of employees, and that reasonable care had been taken to furnish those employees with adequate material and resources to carry out the work. Perhaps the most important – and certainly the most influential – nineteenth-century exposition of employers' common law duties was provided by Lord Cairns LC in *Wilson* v. *Merry & Cunningham*.[89] There the claimant's husband had been killed in a mining accident caused by a build-up of methane. The build-up was due to the erection of a temporary scaffold in the mine, which interfered with the circulation of air. It was held that the claim was barred by the defence of common employment, and in the course of reaching this conclusion Lord Cairns LC delivered what would become a classic passage:

> The master is not, and cannot be, liable to his servant unless there be negligence on the part of the master in that which he, the master, has contracted or undertaken with his servant to do. The master has not contracted or undertaken to execute in person the work connected with his business. The result of an obligation on the master personally to execute the work connected with his business, in place of being beneficial, might be disastrous to his servants, for the master might be incompetent to perform the work … But what the master is, in my opinion, bound to his servant to do, in the event of his not personally superintending and directing the work, is to select proper and competent persons to do so, and to furnish them with adequate materials and resources for the work. When he has done this, he has, in my opinion, done all that he is bound to do.[90]

[89] (1868) LR 1 HL Sc 326. [90] (1868) LR 1 HL Sc 326, 332.

Here the scope of the common employment defence was being firmly grounded in its contractual rationale: the employer was liable for no more than he had (impliedly) promised to do. Lord Cairns LC was assuming that such promises would relate only to the performance of tasks – hence the point about an employer not undertaking to do something he was incompetent to do – but that was not the only way such undertakings could be conceptualised. Lord Colonsay's speech in the same case, which received far less attention than Lord Cairns' exposition, struck a different note: 'there are duties', he said, 'incumbent on masters with reference to the safety of labourers in mines and factories, on the fulfilment of which labourers are entitled to rely, and for the failure in which the master may be responsible.'[91] In Lord Colonsay's approach, the employer's personal competence was irrelevant: certain duties *and responsibilities* went with the role of employer. The language of 'incumbency' also hinted at how Lord Colonsay would have resolved an inherent tension in Lord Cairns' position. For if we accepted that an employer's common law duties were no more than his contractual commitments, there was nothing to stop an employer divesting himself of all responsibility by the use of an express term to that effect. Intermediate positions were also easy to imagine, in which an employer made an employee responsible for the provision of adequate materials for the work; it seemed to follow, on Lord Cairns' analysis, that the employer would then no longer be liable for failures to supply adequate materials. Lord Colonsay's approach, by contrast, suggested that responsibility for duties relating to safety remained with the employer.

The bigger question lurking in the background was whether the role of employer carried an irreducible minimum of responsibility. This was never going to be an easy question to answer, but it was made doubly difficult by industrial development and terminological conservatism. As Lord Colonsay had recognised in *Wilson* v. *Merry & Cunningham*, the 'constantly-increasing scale' of industrial enterprises had created managerial levels and hierarchies of workers that had not previously existed.[92] These new enterprises had come about through what Lord Colonsay called 'new combinations and applications of industry'.[93] This was an extremely rare judicial acknowledgement of the role of capital, and it gestured towards a fundamental difficulty with the language in which the courts were trying to make sense of the situation. For the courts were persisting in talking about the liability of a 'master', when the reality was that the capitalist

[91] (1868) LR 1 HL Sc 326, 344. [92] (1868) LR 1 HL Sc 326, 343.
[93] (1868) LR 1 HL Sc 326, 343.

employer pretended no expertise, no 'mastery', in the business. This dissonance between the employer's role and the language used to describe it made possible Lord Cairns' otherwise paradoxical point about the master who was personally incompetent to carry on his own business. It could also be seen in situations where courts were being invited to develop the content of an employer's common law duties. Thus, in *Young* v. *Hoffmann Manufacturing Company Limited*[94] it was argued that the employer's duties included a duty to give proper instructions in how to do the work. In rejecting this argument Sir Gorrell Barnes P said:

> It is practically impossible for the employers themselves in most works to give the necessary instructions to inexperienced workmen as to the work they have to do, and the mode in which they should do it. It seems unreasonable to imply that the master has undertaken to do so. The result of an obligation on the part of the master personally to instruct might, as Lord Cairns said in [*Wilson* v. *Merry & Cunningham*] of the execution of the work, be disastrous to the servant, for he might be incompetent personally to instruct.[95]

What is particularly noticeable about this passage, if we pay close attention to the language, is the switch from 'employers' and 'workmen' in the first sentence, to 'master' and 'servant' in the second two. It was almost as if the judge felt it necessary to make clear that he was really concerned with employers of workmen in factories before reverting back to the traditional terminology. This was a wise precaution, because it might otherwise have been all too easy to be misled by the terminology into thinking that the defining quality of a 'master' was his experience and expertise, and deducing from that defining quality that his role required him to instruct his employees. The other striking point about the passage is the way that it appeals to contemporary industrial practice as the basis for developing the law. It was clear that the judge was adopting the position of Lord Cairns LC in *Wilson*'s case, namely, that an employer's liability was logically inseparable from a personal undertaking to carry out the task. It followed that, where it was impractical for an employer to give instructions in person, no obligation in relation to instructions could be implied, and the employer could not, therefore, be liable for a failure to instruct. There was no sense here of Lord Colonsay's approach, under which – assuming that the obligation could be implied – an employer would remain responsible for a failure to give proper instructions irrespective of internal arrangements for delegating the task of instruction. This emphasis on industrial

[94] [1907] 2 KB 646. [95] [1907] 2 KB 646, 655–6.

practice, it should be noted, had the potential to discriminate perversely between different employers: the more removed and the less expert the employer, the less likely it was that the courts would find that a personal obligation towards his workers could be implied. The obvious beneficiaries of such an approach were capitalist entrepreneurs.

A certain unease about relying on industrial practice as the touchstone for employers' common law duties could be seen in the Privy Council's advice in *Toronto Power Company* v. *Paskwan*.[96] The claimant's husband had been killed when a block fell from a crane at his workplace; a jury found the defendant employers negligent in having failed to provide a safety device, or failing to employ a signalman who could have spotted the danger before the accident occurred. The claim therefore fitted under the heading of failure to provide adequate materials for the work; but the defendants argued that, by employing competent engineers to decide what materials were needed, they had performed all their obligations. Counsel for the defendants sought to draw an analogy with the position on giving instructions, but the Privy Council as unpersuaded: giving instructions, said Sir Arthur Channell, 'is a matter which it is fairly obvious must in almost all cases be done for the master by others'. The supply of plant, he continued:

> stands on a rather different footing. It is true that the master does not warrant the plant, and if there is a latent defect which could not be detected by reasonable examination, or if in the course of working plant becomes defective and the defect is not brought to the master's knowledge and could not by reasonable diligence have been discovered by him, the master is not liable, and, further, a master is not bound at once to adopt all the latest improvements and appliances. It is a question of fact in each case, was it in the circumstances a want of reasonable care not to have adopted them.[97]

This analysis succeeded in preserving an employer's common law duty to supply adequate material, but did so on a worryingly fragile basis. The analysis seemed to say that what distinguished instructions to employees from provision of materials was that the former were commonly delegated. Perhaps it was true – although the Privy Council provided no supporting evidence – that the selection of material was typically undertaken by the employer in person. But if that was the practice, the Privy Council's reasoning gave employers every incentive to change it immediately. A more robust rationale was hinted at earlier in the advice, where

[96] [1915] AC 734. [97] [1915] AC 734, 738.

it was said that 'the providing proper plant, [*sic*] as distinguished from its subsequent care, is especially within the province of the master rather than of his servants'.[98] This was an ambiguous statement. Read descriptively, it merely pointed out the employer's ability to control what plant was acquired; but read normatively – a reading that the use of 'especially' might encourage – it marked out an area of legal responsibility from which the employer could not escape.

VIII

When the Court of Appeal came to decide the important case of *Fanton* v. *Denville*[99] in 1932, employers' common law duties were, therefore, precariously poised. The facts were unusual – an actor had been injured during rehearsal by a feature of the set – but the legal questions, articulated by Scrutton LJ at the start of his judgment, were utterly familiar. First, did an employer warrant that the plant and property of his business were safe, or was he only liable for a failure to take reasonable care? Second, if he was only liable for a failure to take reasonable care, could he perform that duty by delegating it to employees whom he had taken reasonable care in appointing? The Court of Appeal unanimously held that the duty only required reasonable care to be taken, and that it could be performed by delegation to a competent employee. Scrutton LJ reached this conclusion on the basis of authority – no English case, he said, had imposed liability on an employer who had delegated his duty in respect of proper plant to a competent employee. *Toronto Power Company* v. *Paskwan*, which was not an English case, should, said Scrutton LJ, be seen as an instance of an employer sanctioning an improper system. Greer LJ took a more straightforward approach to the *Toronto Power* case: it was only of persuasive authority, and he was not persuaded by it. On the broader question, by contrast with Scrutton LJ's reasoning, Greer LJ was not content to rely on authority. For him, the key concept was 'personal negligence':

> even in cases where the negligence relied on by the plaintiff consists of negligence in the supply or maintenance of plant or machinery, the employer is only liable if personal negligence is proved, and … if the failure to supply or maintain the plant or machinery in a safe condition is due to the negligence of the manager to whom the duty has been entrusted by the employer, the employer is not responsible unless it can be shown that

[98] [1915] AC 734, 738. [99] [1932] 2 KB 309.

> he failed to use reasonable care to select a competent manager, or that he has in some way been guilty of personal negligence.[100]

Slesser LJ agreed that an employer who delegated his duty in respect of plant and machinery to a competent employee was not liable.

The Court of Appeal gave the impression that its hands were tied by earlier authority; but the truth was that the existence of a duty in respect of proper plant, responsibility for which could not be delegated, was supported by powerful dicta in the House of Lords and by a decision of the Privy Council.[101] The cases said to preclude the recognition of the duty all predated these decisions.[102] Perhaps more interesting was Greer LJ's attempt to rationalise the position by appealing to the concept of 'personal negligence'. This had a certain superficial attraction, but on closer analysis was little more than a restatement of the underlying question, namely, what responsibilities were incumbent in the employer's position? Nevertheless, and whatever the merits of the decision, *Fanton* v. *Denville* undoubtedly narrowed the scope of employers' common law duties.

That narrowing, however, proved to be only temporary. In *Wilsons & Clyde Coal Company, Limited* v. *English*[103] the House of Lords overruled *Fanton* v. *Denville* and reasserted broad categories of employers' duties. Like so many of the employers' liability cases, the claim arose out of an accident in a coal mine, when the claimant was crushed by machinery that had been suddenly put into motion without warning. The trial judge held that the defenders (this was a Scottish case) had not provided a safe system of working, and imposed liability; the Court of Session agreed. Counsel for the defenders on the appeal to the House of Lords argued, following *Fanton* v. *Denville*, that an employer could be liable only for personal negligence. Counsel for the claimant was not called on. That gave away the result of the appeal, but no one could have predicted the vehemence with which the speeches were expressed.

Lord Thankerton set the tone. 'The fallacy in the appellant's argument', he said:

> lies in the view that the master, being under a duty to take due care in the provision of a reasonably safe system of working, is absolved from that

100 [1932] 2 KB 309, 327–8.

101 Dicta: *Wilson* v. *Merry & Cunningham* (1868) LR 1 HL Sc 326, 332 (Lord Cairns LC), 344 (Lord Colonsay); *Smith* v. *Baker* [1891] AC 325. Decision of the Privy Council: *Toronto Power Company* v. *Paskwan* [1915] AC 734.

102 *Wigmore* v. *Jay* (1850) 5 Ex 354; *Potts* v. *Port Carlisle Dock and Ry Co* (1860) 8 WR 524.

103 [1938] AC 57.

> duty by the appointment of a competent person to perform the duty. In my opinion the master cannot 'delegate' his duty in this sense, though he may appoint some one, as his agent in the discharge of the duty, for whom he will remain responsible under the maxim respondeat superior.[104]

Lord Macmillan was equally forthright: 'the provision of a safe system of working in a colliery is an obligation of the owner of the colliery. He cannot divest himself of this duty, though he may ... perform it through the agency of an employee.'[105] Lord Wright's speech was more analytically elaborate, but no less emphatic, than what had gone before it. His immediate target was *Fanton* v. *Denville*, which he described as contradicting 'the settled authorities binding on this House'.[106] This directly contradicted statements in *Fanton*'s case itself, which purported to be following authority. But perhaps the most interesting case that Lord Wright drew attention to was one decided after *Fanton* v. *Denville* (and which the Court of Appeal could not, therefore, be reprimanded for disregarding). That case was *Lochgelly Iron and Coal Company, Limited* v. *M'Mullan*, in which the House of Lords had held that a claim for breach of statutory duty was a claim for 'personal negligence' under the Workmen's Compensation Act 1925 s. 29. What Lord Wright wanted to emphasise was that, in the same way that statutory duties were imposed on employers with the result that they were liable for any breaches, 'the same principle, in my opinion, applies to those fundamental obligations of a contract of employment which lie outside the doctrine of common employment, and for the performance of which employers are absolutely responsible'.[107] 'When I use the word absolutely', he continued, 'I do not mean that employers warrant the adequacy of plant, or the competence of fellow-employees, or the propriety of the system of work. The obligation is fulfilled by the exercise of due care and skill. But it is not fulfilled by entrusting its fulfilment to employees, even though selected with due care and skill.'

The employer's fundamental obligations, he explained, were threefold – to appoint competent staff, to provide adequate material and resources, and to operate a safe system of work. Lord Maugham agreed, particularly associating himself with Lord Wright's criticisms of *Fanton* v. *Denville*.

The employer's threefold common law duties were, therefore, firmly established as falling outside the doctrine of common employment. The decision won plaudits from commentators, with William Robson writing admiringly, in the sentence used as an epigraph to this chapter, of

[104] [1938] AC 57, 64–5. [105] [1938] AC 57, 75.
[106] [1938] AC 57, 76. [107] [1938] AC 57, 78.

the House of Lords' statesmanlike approach. How the House of Lords had achieved this success was striking. As there had been no appellate argument on behalf of the successful claimant, the speeches must have reflected a strength of feeling that already existed. Part of the explanation for that strength of feeling may be that two of the Law Lords were Scots – Lord Thankerton and Lord Macmillan – and the Scots had a particularly troubled relationship with the doctrine of common employment. As Lord Macmillan would remind his colleagues two years later in *Radcliffe* v. *Ribble Motor Services Ltd*, the Scots courts had initially resisted the common employment doctrine, only to have it imposed upon them by the House of Lords' decision in *Bartonshill Coal Co* v. *Reid*.[108] Both Lord Macmillan and his compatriot jumped at the chance to narrow the doctrine's scope. On the other hand, Lord Thankerton and Lord Macmillan could not claim to be representing current Scottish judicial opinion. It was true that there had been Scottish criticism of *Fanton* v. *Denville* in *Bain* v. *Fife Coal Company, Limited*;[109] Lord Thankerton quoted Lord Justice-Clerk Aitchison's comment that *Fanton*'s case 'appears to me to be a startling whittling down of the duties which the law has hitherto recognised, at any rate in Scotland, as attaching to a master towards his servant'.[110] But what Lord Thankerton did not mention was that Lord Justice-Clerk Aitchison's colleagues did not support him on this point, and went out of their way to say so.

Lord Wright's approach cannot, of course, be explained by Scottish patriotism. His background might perhaps have been influential in another way, for he had grown up in an industrial part of the north-east of England, and, as we have seen earlier, felt an instinctive sympathy for injured workers. But closer to the surface of his analysis was a point about language. His sensitivity to particular words was apparent from the outset of his speech, when he observed that the case concerned 'the obligation of an employer towards his employees, to use the more modern terminology'.[111] He continued to use that modern terminology, departing from it only once, in the following passage:

> [Common employment] is explained on the ground that the employee by his contract of employment agrees with his employer to assume the risk of

[108] [1939] AC 215, 235 – 'fastening upon the law of Scotland a principle as distasteful as it was alien to Scottish jurisprudence'.

[109] 1935 SC 681. [110] 1935 SC 681, 693.

[111] *Wilsons & Clyde Coal Company, Limited* v. *English* [1938] AC 57, 76–7.

> his fellow-servant's negligence. The principle is stated, with little regard to reality or to modern ideas of economics or industrial conditions, to be that this particular risk is included in the agreed remuneration. This result is stated rather as a dogma to flow logically from the relation of master and servant.[112]

Here 'master and servant' is used deliberately to underline the anachronistic and unrealistic nature of the doctrine. Lord Wright clearly felt that it was important to get away from ideas of 'master and servant', and his speech in the *Wilsons* case illustrates one benefit of doing so. For it is difficult to think of 'servants' being entitled to insist on their 'master' owing them non-negotiable obligations; that is not how we think relationships of subservience work. In the same way, talking about a 'master' suggested a single individual; and it seems not unreasonable only to require individuals to take reasonable care in respect of their own acts. Misdescribing the relationship set the legal analysis on the wrong path. The truth was that employers were often not single individuals but corporations, within which safety responsibilities were delegated away from those who took the financial benefits. As Lord Wright recognised, the common law could learn from statutory regulations by imposing duties for the performance of which an employer remained responsible. This was legitimate precisely because the employee was not a servant, and his employer was not a master.

IX

Throughout the first half of the twentieth century, tort claims were not an injured workman's sole avenue of legal redress. Alongside the tort system operated the system of workmen's compensation, which had been introduced in 1897, and would continue in force until 1948. The workmen's compensation legislation created a system of intimidating complexity, which judicial interpretation would render yet more labyrinthine.[113] But its basic philosophy was simple: it required employers to compensate their employees for injuries suffered at work, irrespective of the employer's fault.

[112] [1938] AC 57, 80.

[113] R. Merkin and J. Steele, *Insurance and Law of Obligations* (Oxford University Press, 2013) 9.4 gives an invaluable outline of the key changes to the scheme during its lifetime. See also Bartrip, 'The impact of institutions and professions on compensation for occupational injury in England', 48–50.

No one could have accused the workmen's compensation scheme of duplicating existing remedies. Indeed, it could be said, with only a little exaggeration, that the common law's basic philosophy was precisely the opposite of the compensation scheme's. The availability of remedies under the compensation scheme puts the cases discussed in this chapter in a rather different light. It is perhaps difficult to understand their existence at all, because the compensation system's rules strongly incentivised an injured workman to choose between a common law and statutory compensation claim: it was, technically, possible to have compensation assessed under the scheme following the failure of a claim against the employer at common law, but the court was 'at liberty to deduct from such compensation all the costs which, in its judgment have been caused by the plaintiff bringing the action instead of proceeding under [the Workmen's Compensation] Act'.[114] Why, we might ask, would any well-advised claimant spurn the guaranteed award under the compensation scheme in favour of a difficult journey through the hostile terrain of the common law? The answer was simple: money. Payments under the compensation scheme did not aspire to compensate the injured workman in full; they merely replaced some of his lost earnings for a fixed period. Injured workmen therefore faced an unenviable choice: settle for less under the compensation scheme, or risk losing everything in the common law casino.

There is little to suggest that the two parallel systems of compensation influenced each other. In a recent study, Simon Deakin was able to identify only one positive instance of influence – on the narrow question of whether a nurse was an employee.[115] There was also a short-lived influence on causation in tort, exercised by the workmen's compensation decision in *Harwood* v. *Wyken Colliery Company*;[116] but that influence came to an end when the House of Lords decided that the underlying aims of the workmen's compensation scheme made decisions under it unreliable guides to common law principles.[117] The sense that the two systems were just too different to be able to tell each other anything useful also came through powerfully in the textbooks. As we saw in Chapter 2, Pollock regarded the workmen's compensation scheme as simply not tort, and sent readers away to other works. Winfield became embroiled in a debate with Landon

114 Workmen's Compensation Act 1897 s. 1(4); re-enacted as Workmen's Compensation Act 1925 s. 29(2).

115 Deakin, 'Tort Law and Workmen's Compensation Legislation, 260.

116 [1913] 2 KB 158.

117 *Baker* v. *Willoughby* [1970] AC 467, criticised in *Jobling* v. *Associated Dairies Ltd* [1982] AC 794.

about the exclusion of workmen's compensation from tort textbooks, but neither writer was prepared to say that the workmen's compensation material cast any light on tort principles.

Judges, to the extent that they mentioned the workmen's compensation scheme in tort cases at all (which was rare), seemed to regard the scheme's existence as a reason to reaffirm their commitment to doctrinal purity. A good example of this judicial attitude was the comment of Lawrence J in *Flower* v. *Ebbw Vale Steel, Iron & Coal Company, Limited* when, encouraged by counsel to take a more relaxed attitude to evidence of contributory negligence by a workman:

> I was invited to consider how a jury would have regarded the question, but I cannot think I ought to allow any consideration of the sympathy which every one must feel for a good workman who has lost his hand to influence my decision. Such considerations are, I think, adequately provided for by the Workmen's Compensation Act, 1925, under which the plaintiff is entitled to a weekly payment of 30s a week.[118]

The scheme, on this view, was not only compensating for workplace injuries, it was compensating for the common law's limitations as well.

There was much to compensate for: the common law had remained notably impermeable to social and legislative changes, maintaining a doctrinal consistency that might have been admirable on a different subject. At the centre of this attitude of intransigence was the doctrine of common employment, which, despite the flimsiest of foundations, established itself as a defining feature of the legal landscape. Exceptions to common employment eventually flourished, but exceptions could only take you so far. Robson, in the epigraph to this chapter, was quick the praise the House of Lords' statesmanship in developing one of those exceptions, and was implicitly critical of the Court of Appeal's inertia. That was certainly true for the particular topic – employers' common law duties – that Robson was discussing, and his choice of plaudit was striking. For 'statesmanship', even with its qualifying adjective of 'legal', sounded dangerously close to 'political leadership', and the House of Lords in its judicial capacity might not have welcomed being associated with either element. Nor, if we broaden out the assessment slightly, could the House of Lords have been accused of consistent statesmanship. Its attempts to evade making difficult decisions – as in *Flower* v. *Ebbw Vale Steel, Iron & Coal Company,*

[118] [1934] 2 KB 132, 140. See also *Cribb* v. *Kynoch, Limited* [1907] 2 KB 548, 562, where Bray J draws attention to the 'very large remedies' under the Workmen's Compensation Act, for which the claimant would have been better advised to opt.

Limited[119] when it dodged an important question of principle by making an additional finding of fact – recall the strategies of *Yes Minister*'s Jim Hacker, but could not be mistaken for any kind of statesmanship. Lord Wright's determination to contribute something of more lasting significance in that case marked him out, as did his later attempts to rationalise the categorisation of claims for breach of statutory duty, and to redefine the vocabulary in which the issues could be discussed. But even he had to accept the limitations on his ability to bring the law into line with contemporary values: there was just too much history to be able to make a fresh start.

[119] [1936] AC 206.

PART II

9

The Law Revision Committee

I

Until the mid 1930s, the statutory development of tort law was sporadic and piecemeal. Parliament might very occasionally have been willing to reverse the effect of a judicial decision – as it did in the Directors Liability Act 1890, which removed the need to prove fraud against the publishers of false statements in company prospectuses.[1] It might also be susceptible to intensive lobbying, as it was when press interests secured the passage of the Newspaper Libel and Registration Act 1881 and the Law of Libel Amendment Act 1888.[2] But systematic statutory development was, for practical purposes, non-existent. Indeed, in 1901 one writer began an article on the rule that there was no contribution between tortfeasors with a quotation from Lord Herschell LC, which stated that the rule was not founded on 'any principle of justice or equity, or even of public policy'.[3] 'Were law reform a possibility in this country', the author continued, 'this dictum of Lord Herschell's might lead to the removal by legislation from our law of the principle so criticized. But the Legislature undertakes nothing so unwillingly as the reform of the Common Law.'[4]

There were two interrelated reasons for this lack of legislative interest. The first was that there was no government department or other official body with responsibility for the reform of private law. Insofar as it was within the remit of any government minister, it belonged to the Lord Chancellor as part of his overall responsibility for the legal system. The Lord Chancellor's Office, however, was small,[5] and its administrative burden both extensive and diverse – including responsibility for all judicial

[1] Reversing *Derry* v. *Peek* (1889) 14 App. Cas. 337.

[2] See further, P. Mitchell, *The Making of the Modern Law of Defamation* (Oxford and Portland, OR, Hart Publishing, 2005) 261–8.

[3] *Palmer* v. *Wick and Pulteneytown Steam Shipping Company, Limited* [1894] AC 318.

[4] J. Fischer Williams, 'The Rule in *Merryweather* v. *Nixan*' (1901) 17 *LQR* 293, 293.

[5] Lord Schuster, 'The Office of the Lord Chancellor' (1948–1950) 10 *CLJ* 175, 188–9 (describing the moves to appoint a full-time Permanent Secretary in the mid 1880s).

appointments and much ecclesiastical patronage.[6] The Chancellor personally was also heavily burdened – being required to conduct parliamentary business in the House of Lords, sit as a judge and act as chief legal advisor to the government.[7] Lord Birkenhead, for instance, dealt with the pressure of work by delegating the drafting of his judgments;[8] Lord Haldane argued for the redistribution of some of the Chancellor's responsibilities to a new Ministry of Justice.[9] There was, in short, no practical opportunity for the Chancellor or his Office to develop proposals to reform the law of tort.

As a consequence – and this was the second reason for a lack of statutory reform – any legislative reform of tort would have to compete with other parliamentary business. Without the priority accorded to government Bills, a reform measure would have to be taken up by a Member of Parliament personally, and then be steered through successfully as a Private Members' Bill. Such initiatives were not impossible – for instance, the Defamation Act 1952 was a Private Members' Bill – but their success required luck (there is a ballot to select which Bills will be considered by Parliament) and a receptive House of Commons. Neither could be guaranteed.

Little could be done to alter the high volume of parliamentary business. But the lack of departmental responsibility for private law reform could be addressed. The most significant attempt to do so came in Lord Haldane's proposals, developed from 1915 onwards, for a Ministry of Justice.[10] Haldane had become Lord Chancellor following a highly successful period as Secretary of State for War, where his major achievement had been reform of the Army.[11] He was dismayed by the paucity of secretarial support in the Lord Chancellor's Office and overwhelmed by the burden that fell on him personally.[12] His response was to modernise the

[6] Jean Graham Hall and Douglas F. Martin, *Yes, Lord Chancellor: A Biography of Lord Schuster* (Chichester, Barry Rose, 2003) 32–3 gives a list of the Chancellor's then (2003) current responsibilities.

[7] J. H. Baker, *An Introduction to English Legal History*, 4th edn (London, Butterworths, 2002) 111.

[8] Hall and Martin, *Yes, Lord Chancellor*, 117, identifying Roland Burrows as Birkenhead's assistant.

[9] G. Drewry, 'Lord Haldane's Ministry of Justice – Stillborn or Strangled at Birth?' (1983) 61 *Public Administration* 396, particularly at 405 (setting out Haldane's proposed role for the Lord Chancellor following such a reform).

[10] Drewry, 'Lord Haldane's Ministry of Justice'.

[11] Winston Churchill was expected to implement similar reforms as First Lord of the Admiralty: R. Jenkins, *Churchill* (London, Macmillan, 2001) 214.

[12] Drewry, 'Lord Haldane's Ministry of Justice', 400–1.

secretariat and to attempt to rationalise the Chancellor's functions by transferring some of them to a new Ministry of Justice. One particular advantage of the new Ministry would be that it could take a proactive role in law reform.[13]

The Law Society enthusiastically supported the proposal, but the Bar Council was against it. It appears that the Bar Council's opposition was, extraordinarily, orchestrated by Sir Claud Schuster, the Permanent Secretary of the Lord Chancellor's Office.[14] Schuster was against the proposal for a variety of reasons, but, insofar as law reform was concerned, he had one basic point: a Ministry of Justice would make no difference. As he explained in a letter to Sir Phillip Gregory, the author of the Bar Council's report, politicians were no longer interested in matters of law reform; 'social reform'[15] was what mattered to them. Schuster made the same point in an essay written by him, although published under the name of Lord Birkenhead, when he argued that the real cause of a lack of law reform was 'congestion of parliamentary business'.[16] There was, in his view, little opportunity and no inclination towards reform.

Haldane's tenure as Lord Chancellor was brief, and his proposed Ministry of Justice never materialised. But it would be a mistake to dismiss the proposal as inconsequential. So far as law reform was concerned, it highlighted an important gap in departmental responsibilities; others would subsequently draw attention to the need for that gap to be filled. Furthermore, the spectre of a Ministry of Justice, hovering in the background, was to be a spur to Schuster's own creation of the Law Revision Committee. If law reform was being seen to be done already, there would be no point creating a new department to carry out the same work.

II

The immediate catalyst for the creation of the Law Revision Committee came, in late December 1932, in the form of a motion in the House of Commons by an obscure Welsh MP, Llewellyn-Jones, 'That, in the opinion of this House, it is desirable that steps be taken to inquire into the defects in the system of law and legal procedures in England and Wales and into the measures for removing these defects'.[17] In a wide-ranging speech, Llewellyn-Jones invoked the spirit of Bentham,[18] and identified

[13] *Ibid.*, 405. [14] *Ibid.*, 404. [15] *Ibid.* [16] *Ibid.*, 407.

[17] Hansard's Parliamentary Debates, Fifth Series, Commons, vol. 273, col. 1105 (21 December 1932).

[18] *Ibid.*

various defects, both procedural and substantive, which he felt called for a remedy. Among the substantive defects were the liability of a husband for the torts of his wife,[19] and the rule that a personal action died with the person;[20] both subjects were to be considered subsequently by the Law Revision Committee. Llewellyn-Jones was not, however, proposing the mere creation of a committee; he was far more ambitious – only wholesale codification would solve the underlying problem.[21] Llewellyn-Jones was followed in the debate by Donald Somervell MP, who also called for further codification[22] and suggested that law reform should be the responsibility of the Solicitor General.[23] Somervell also made the point that law reform proposals had little chance of success unless they were government Bills.[24] The motion was carried.

Of course, the motion being carried was not a bad thing. It was hardly surprising that Members of Parliament were, on the whole, opposed to injustice. But, in itself, the motion achieved very little: the problem had always been not whether law reform was a good idea, but how it could be accomplished. Wholesale codification was not an obviously practical solution.

What made the debate and resulting motion more than a mere parliamentary platitude was the decision by Somervell, once the debate had been reported, to send the report of it to Sir Claud Schuster. Schuster was quick to pour cold water on the issue of codification. He outlined some of the practical difficulties (in terms of time and expertise), and then added: 'Lastly, and most important obstacle of all, there remains the House of Commons. Whatever Party is in power, the Whips interpose an obstacle, which can very seldom be overcome, in the way of this type of legislation. It takes time and does not gain any Parliamentary votes.'[25] On the fifth page of his reply to Somervell he dealt with reforming legislation:

> When it comes to amending the law as distinct from codifying and consolidating it, the difficulty becomes insuperable. However large a staff I commanded, I should still be shy of introducing Bills such as those referred to in the speeches of those which preceded you in the debate as, for example, about married women and their rights and obligations,

[19] *Ibid.*, col. 1107. [20] *Ibid.*, cols. 1107–8.
[21] *Ibid.*, col. 1109. [22] *Ibid.*, col. 1134. [23] *Ibid.*, col. 1133.
[24] *Ibid.*, col. 1134: 'We all know that legislation has very little chance in this House unless it has the backing of a Government Department.'
[25] LCO 2/3565 Law Revision Committee, Personnel of Committee and Terms of Reference, 13 January 1933 (Schuster to Somervell).

> because there is not the slightest chance that any such Bill when drafted would pass through Parliament, and one gets weary of ploughing the sand.[26]

Schuster's letter was an emphatic assertion of an entrenched position. But Somervell was undeterred. He sent Schuster an eight-page note of 'the kind of things I think ought to be done',[27] which included an examination of the rule that a personal action died with the person, and the principle that the loss should lie where it fell when a contract was frustrated. Both subjects would be considered by the Law Revision Committee.[28] Perhaps more importantly, though, Somervell for the first time broached the idea of a committee:

> it might be a good idea to bring the recommendations of the Department before a committee on which there might be a panel of M.P.'s with legal qualifications from all parties with co-opted Law Lords or Judges and practitioners specially qualified to deal with the matter under discussion – not too large, but it might greatly facilitate the subsequent course of a bill if it had got the approval of a committee of this kind.[29]

Schuster's reply, the following day, showed a very significant change of position on his part:

> my mind has been for a long time running on the same lines as yours in this matter ... But while the lines on which my mind has been running have been parallel with yours, they have not been completely convergent. I am not greatly in love with your proposal for a panel of legal M.P.s, and I greatly doubt whether you would find at the Bar a substantial number of people who share your views. The Bar Council is a hopeless body ... What I now propose – and have indeed had it in my mind for a long time – is the constitution by the Lord Chancellor of a Standing Committee comprising Judges, members of the Bar and members of the Law Society as well as one or two persons of experience from the outside world.[30]

Schuster obviously had some preliminary ideas about the personnel of the Committee, for he concluded his letter by saying that further progress could not be made until the Hanworth Committee on the Business of the Courts had finished its deliberations. Overnight, literally, Schuster had

[26] *Ibid.* [27] *Ibid.*, 27 February 1933 (Somervell to Schuster).

[28] For the reform of the law on the consequences of frustration see P. Mitchell, '*Fibrosa Spolka Akcyjna v. Fairbairn Lawson Combe Barbour Ltd (1942)*' in C. Mitchell and P. Mitchell (eds.), *Landmark Cases in the Law of Restitution* (Oxford and Portland, OR, Hart Publishing, 2006) 247.

[29] LCO 2/3565, 27 February 1933 (Somervell to Schuster).

[30] *Ibid.*, 24 February 1933 (Schuster to Somervell).

moved from entrenched opposition to law reform initiatives to a position where he was not only in favour, but had also identified both the mechanism and the personnel. Why exactly he had changed his mind is difficult to identify. One factor may have been Somervell's evident determination; but, on the other hand, he had seen off equally determined attempts to create a Ministry of Justice. Perhaps Schuster's real concern was that Somervell might take his ideas elsewhere (Somervell had, for instance, mentioned the Solicitor General in his parliamentary speech); it would be better, Schuster might have thought, to control the initiative directly rather than risk a rival encroaching on the Lord Chancellor's territory. Schuster might also have been alert to the possibility that blocking Somervell might trigger off further lobbying for a Ministry of Justice. He was winning the battle against such a Ministry, but it was risky to open up another front. He may even have seen the Committee as a way of further undermining proposals for the new Ministry: since part of the role of the new Ministry of Justice was to reform private law, if private law reform was going ahead elsewhere, there would be no need for another Ministry to do the same job. Tactically, assuming control of the undertaking made sense.

III

Eight months later, as the work of the Hanworth Committee was drawing to a close, Schuster wrote to its Chairman. 'The Lord Chancellor', he said, 'has long had it in mind to appoint a Standing Committee (the membership of which he might review from time to time) to advise him as to substantive amendments in the law … He, of course, does not refer to questions where any political issue arises.'[31] This was the first time that the Lord Chancellor himself had made an appearance; even then, Schuster was speaking on his behalf, and we might guess that the Lord Chancellor 'had it in mind' because Schuster had put it there. Nevertheless, the Lord Chancellor could easily have blocked the move, and it was fortunate that the Chancellor at that time – Lord Sankey – was reform-minded.[32] It may well also have helped that, around the time the Committee was being contemplated, Harold Laski, an influential left-wing intellectual, had written in praise of Sankey's reformist instincts.[33]

[31] *Ibid.*, 31 October 1933 (Schuster to Hanworth).

[32] See generally R. F. V. Heuston, *Lives of the Lord Chancellors 1885–1940* (Oxford: Clarendon Press, 1964) 497–535.

[33] H. Laski, 'Justice and the Law' in *Studies in Law and Politics* (London, 1932) 276, especially at 295, describing Sankey as a person who 'cares profoundly for ideals of legal

The first two of the four topics Schuster proposed for the committee in his letter to Hanworth were:

(1) The doctrine of no contribution between tort-feasors. (*Merryweather* v. *Nixan*, with special reference to the remarks of Herschell LC in *Palmer* v. *Wick etc.* [1894] AC 318.)
(2) The legal maxim actio personalis moritur cum persona.[34]

The second two were the liability of a husband for his wife's torts, and the recovery of interest in civil proceedings. There is nothing to suggest that there was consultation over any of these subjects beyond the confines of the Lord Chancellor's Office.

Schuster invited Hanworth to chair the committee, and to use the same personnel as those who had been on the Business of the Courts Committee. Hanworth accepted, but had concerns about the personnel, commenting that 'we should need some heavier metal from the point of pure law added to it'.[35] Hanworth's concerns were anticipated by John Foster, who was subsequently to become Secretary to the Committee, and whom Schuster had consulted over the Committee's membership. 'The Committee', he wrote to Schuster:

> I think should include two good academics and I would suggest Prof Goodhart and Amos. Goodhart is really an exceptionally brilliant man, has I think practiced in America and would be very valuable on such a committee. The advantage of having Amos would be that he would fulfil the role of a paid secretariat. He would do a tremendous amount of hard work and research and his experience as a judge in Egypt would be valuable.
>
> There should be someone from Graham-Harrison's office [Parliamentary Counsel] say Rowlatt. It would also be useful to have assistance in the House to explain the proposed amendments of the law. Turton and WS Morrison would do well for that. Add one solicitor plus a good county court judge say Hargreaves, a Master and sprinkle with judges and counsel.
>
> My selection would be
>
> Tomlin – Wright – Swift – Greene – Schuster – Porter – (Schiller?) – Goodhart – Amos – (Gutteridge?) – Turton – Morrison – Geoffrey Russell(?) – Hargreaves – Master Ball – Rowlatt.[36]

reform'. Laski sent Sankey a copy of the book, which Sankey enjoyed (Heuston, *Lives of the Lord Chancellors 1885–1940*, 511).

[34] *Ibid.*

[35] LCO 2/3565, 9 December 1933 (Hanworth to Schuster).

[36] *Ibid.*, 10 November 1933 (Foster to Schuster).

This was the first direct allusion to academic involvement. It was also the first (and last) suggestion that a parliamentary draftsman should participate.

Schuster's reply to Hanworth made clear that, whilst he was prepared to modify the personnel to include academics, he had his own very definite ideas about who they should be:

> I agree that it would be well to strengthen the Committee on the purely legal side. But it is not very easy to find pure lawyers who are also easy to work with and free from crankiness. Among the Oxford men, I have sat on a Committee with Holdsworth and found him impossible. I do not think very highly of Zulueta. Brierly is excellent, but his strength lies rather in international law than in English Common Law. Of all the teachers, professors and leaders whom I have met in recent years, I prefer Gutteridge, McNair and Wade, all of whom are Cambridge men.[37]

Ultimately invitations were sent to Gutteridge and McNair, along with Lord Wright, Romer LJ, Swift J, Goddard J, Wilfrid Lewis, Reginald Poole and W. E. Mortimer. Only Lewis refused. Porter J, Asquith KC, O'Connor KC and Topham KC were appointed shortly afterwards. So far as the appointments from the world of practice were concerned, there was little to be surprised about, although provincial solicitors pointed out that they were unrepresented.[38] The academic appointees, however, call for a little more comment, because at first sight their selection looks almost eccentric. Gutteridge was the Professor of Comparative Law at Cambridge; McNair was a lecturer at the same university who, within a couple of years, was to become Whewell Professor of International Law. Neither could have been described as a common law specialist, although McNair's early interest had been in common law.[39] More obvious academic common law specialists were not difficult to identify – Holdsworth, Goodhart, Winfield, Stallybrass, to name but four – yet Schuster made what proved to be excellent choices. Part of the reason for this slightly surprising success was that academic specialism was less extreme than it is today – as rapidly became apparent, both Gutteridge and McNair were impressively expert on the common law issues confronting the committee. A second reason, hinted at in Schuster's correspondence, was that they were adept at contributing to committees. Gutteridge had been on the Lord Chancellor's committee on the enforcement of foreign judgments (1932), and legal education

[37] *Ibid.*, 11 December 1933 (Schuster to Hanworth).

[38] *Ibid.*, 2 February 1934 (Hanworth to Schuster).

[39] R. Y. Jennings, 'McNair, Arnold Duncan (1885–1975)' in *Oxford Dictionary of National Biography* (online edition, 2004–2008).

(1932–1933), among others.[40] McNair was less experienced, but his service as secretary to Lord Sankey's Coal Commission (1919)[41] must have been valuable. Schuster (rightly, in hindsight) set great store by such proven temperamental ability. As things turned out, Gutteridge and McNair, having been included almost as an afterthought, were to exert far more influence, and make more decisive contributions, than anyone could have expected.

[40] McNair, 'Gutteridge, Harold Cooke (1876–1953)' in *Oxford Dictionary of National Biography* (online edition, 2004–2008).

[41] Jennings, 'McNair, Arnold Duncan (1885–1975)'.

10

Death

I

The first topic which the Law Revision Committee was asked to address, and the first on which it reported, was the maxim *actio personalis cum persona moritur*. The effect of this maxim was that if a personal action lay, for instance, for negligently causing personal injury, either the death of the victim or of the tortfeasor brought the action to an end. By 1934 certain exceptions had been made – the maxim did not, for instance, apply to contractual claims – but it continued to apply to claims for personal injury and for defamation. The continuing application to personal injury claims was proving particularly unfortunate, because of its consequences for the victims of road accidents: if the victim was killed by a driver's negligence the claim abated. An alternative claim was available to the victim's dependants, at that time closely defined under the Fatal Accidents Act (Lord Campbell's Act) 1846, for loss of dependency, but their claims hardly reflected the damage caused. More seriously, the death of the tortfeasor prevented any claim arising against either the individual driver or his insurer. The application of the maxim, therefore, undermined a recent parliamentary initiative to make third-party motor insurance compulsory.[1] The problem became more acute as the number of road accidents increased. As McNair commented to an audience of students a year later, 'What really gave actuality and urgency to this topic, is the intensity of road warfare which characterises the age in which we live.'[2]

The application of the *actio personalis* maxim was, therefore, an ideal first topic. It was an esoteric artefact of private law, which lacked political controversy, but which, at the same time, was causing injustice. Furthermore, its revision had been urged both by

[1] Road Traffic Act 1930 s. 35.
[2] A. D. McNair, 'The Work of the Law Revision Committee' (1935) 15 *Bell Yard* 34.

Llewellyn-Jones MP and Somervell MP in their parliamentary and private communications.[3]

However, the Committee was not asked only to consider the *actio personalis* maxim, it was also asked to consider 'the rule in *Baker* v. *Bolton*'. This additional factor required the Committee to look at the distinct, but related, rule that the death of a person could not give rise to a cause of action. In the leading case, where the claimant's wife had been killed by the negligence of the defendant stagecoach proprietor, Lord Ellenborough was reported as asserting that: 'In a civil Court, the death of a human being could not be complained of as an injury, and in this case the damages, as to the plaintiff's wife, must stop with the period of her existence.'[4] The claimant, it was held, could only recover for 'the bruises which the plaintiff had himself sustained, and the loss of his wife's society, and the distress of mind he had suffered on her account, from the time of the accident till the moment of her dissolution'[5]. The rule was not entirely convincing – it was, perhaps, intelligible as part of the broader idea that proceedings for a felony should take precedence over a civil claim[6] – and there had been attempts to challenge it. Most notably, the House of Lords in *The Amerika*[7] had been invited to abolish it, but, rather disappointingly, their Lordships seemed content to have it continue for no better reason than its historical longevity.[8] The argument for abolition, commented Lord Sumner, 'was really an appeal to this House in its legislative, rather then judicial capacity'.[9]

Attempts to circumvent the rule had been more fruitful. Most significantly the Court of Appeal had held that *Baker* v. *Bolton* did not apply where the death was as a result of a breach of contract, since the death itself was not a necessary part of the cause of action.[10] This distinction between liability and quantum had further potential, as highlighted in *The Amerika*. There, at first instance and in the Court of Appeal[11] (although

3 Llewellyn-Jones: Hansard's Parliamentary Debates, Fifth Series, Commons, vol. 273, cols. 1107–8 (21 December 1932); Somervell: LCO 2/3565, 27 February 1933 (Somervell to Schuster, p. 1 of Note).

4 *Baker* v. *Bolton* (1808) 1 Camp 493.

5 *Baker* v. *Bolton* (1808) 1 Camp 493.

6 W. Holdsworth, 'The Origin of the Rule in *Baker* v. *Bolton*' (1916) 32 *LQR* 431.

7 *Admiralty Commissioners* v. *Owners of Steamship Amerika* [1917] AC 38.

8 Winfield commented that 'Upon what ground, except that of *vis inertiae*, the judgments proceeded is not easy to see'. P. H. Winfield, 'Death as Affecting Liability in Tort' (1929) 29 *Columbia Law Review* 239.

9 [1917] AC 38, 60.

10 *Jackson* v. *Watson and Sons* [1909] 2 KB 193.

11 *The Amerika* [1914] P 167.

not in the House of Lords), counsel argued that where the defendants' ship had negligently collided with the claimants' submarine, causing the loss of both submarine and crew, *Baker* v. *Bolton* did not bar a claim for the loss of the crew's services. The cause of action, counsel argued, was made complete by the property damage to the submarine; the lost services were consequential on that damage.[12] The submission was rejected by both courts[13] and, as we have seen, the House of Lords flatly reasserted the general rule.

In 1934, therefore, the rule in *Baker* v. *Bolton* was still good law. Like the *actio personalis* maxim, it was not widely admired, but unlike the maxim, it was not causing obvious injustice. In fact, the initiative to add *Baker* v. *Bolton* to the Committee's terms of reference came from McNair who, with his acceptance of appointment to the Committee, enclosed the following note:

> Professor Holdsworth's article on the rule in *Baker* v. *Bolton* ... shows the possible confusion of the rule with *actio personalis* etc and although that rule has been deeply cut into by statute I have the feeling that the Committee could make a better job of this item if *Baker* v. *Bolton* were included, as there is a tendency to construe terms of reference strictly.[14]

We might observe here that, whilst McNair's amendment could be accommodated, the author of the leading article on the subject could not be.

II

The drafting of the Committee's report on the subject seems to have proceeded smoothly. The first draft, apparently prepared by Wright, Gutteridge, McNair and Porter,[15] was, both in structure and content, very similar to the final draft. The key proposals were that the *actio personalis* maxim should not apply to personal injury claims, 'but the damages should be proportioned either to the loss to the estate or the loss to the dependants or both heads of loss together in certain cases'.[16] The Committee also recommended the abolition of the rule in *Baker* v. *Bolton*.[17] In one respect, however, the first and final drafts were very different. In the final draft the

12 [1914] P 167, 177.

13 [1914] P 167, 177–8 (Sir Samuel Evans P), 188 (Kennedy LJ), 190 (Scrutton LJ).

14 LCO 2/3565, 17 December 1933 (McNair to Schuster).

15 These are the four names on the cover of the Lord Chancellor's Office file: LCO 2/1968 Actio Personalis.

16 Law Revision Committee, Interim Report (London, 1934) Cmd 4540 at para. 13.

17 *Ibid.*, at para. 15(e).

Committee recommended that the *actio personalis* maxim should continue to apply in 'purely personal' actions, such as defamation.[18] Earlier drafts of the report, by contrast, stated that:

> in actions which are regarded as purely personal, such as defamation, we think that the Law should be changed so that the action should not abate by reason of the death of the person defamed, but in such cases the jury should be directed to give damages to compensate the injury to the deceased's estate.
>
> In other words, we think that in all cases there should no longer be any Rule of law such as actio personalis.[19]

The change, so as to exclude personal actions, was only made in the penultimate draft of the report, but unfortunately there is no correspondence to indicate what prompted it. It seems difficult to fault the original proposal analytically, and a similar reform had been advocated by Llewellyn-Jones[20] and Somervell.[21] Perhaps the concern was that such a reform had the potential for controversy, which could bog down any legislative realisation of the report's proposals. If that was the reason, it seems most likely that it would have been advanced by Schuster, who was a member of the Committee; he, as we have already seen, was acutely aware of the difficulties of getting law reform measures through Parliament.

III

The legislative process began with Schuster's instructions to Maurice Gwyer, first parliamentary counsel. However, right from the very start of the process it was made clear that the Bill should not be a mere reflection of the Committee's report. Referring to the Committee's recommendation to abolish the rule in *Baker* v. *Bolton*, Schuster wrote that:

> The Lord Chancellor thinks that it would be impossible to carry legislation which in effect conferred upon the master a right of action in respect of damage suffered by him through the death of his servant without at the same time creating a new cause of action for a servant who is damaged through the death of his master. To include such an enactment would be to create a new cause of action altogether and to arouse considerable controversy. The Lord Chancellor proposes, therefore, that the Bill should

[18] *Ibid.*, at para. 14.

[19] LCO 2/1968.

[20] Hansard's Parliamentary Debates, Fifth Series, vol. 273, HC, col. 1108 (21 December 1932).

[21] LCO 2/3565, 27 February 1933 (Somervell to Schuster) at p. 3, para. (6).

> not interfere with the present law as respects claims by a master against a wrong doer who has caused the death of a servant and thus deprived the master of the benefit of his services.[22]

The first draft of the Bill, delivered three weeks later, showed that translating the Committee's remaining proposals into legislation would not be straightforward. As the draftsman explained in an accompanying note to Schuster, he had been troubled by the Committee's bland statement that 'damages should be "limited (sic) either to the loss to the estate or the loss to the dependants, or both heads of loss together"'.[23] 'To express the limitation in terms of loss to the estate', he explained, 'would not, I think, carry out what the Committee intend … in some cases it might well be that the result of the tortious act or breach of contract might be a gain rather than a loss to the estate, e.g. where a man killed had, by reason of life policies, been worth more dead than alive.'[24]

The result was clause 1(2) of the draft Bill, which provided as follows:

> Where a cause of action survives as aforesaid for the benefit of the estate of a deceased person, the damages recoverable for the benefit of the estate of that person:–
>
> (a) shall not include any vindictive damages;
> (b) shall not include any sum in respect of the mental or bodily suffering of that person before his death;
> (c) in the case of a breach of promise to marry shall be limited to such damage, if any, to the estate of that person as flows from the breach of promise to marry;
> (d) where the death of that person has been caused by the act or omission which gives rise to the cause of action, may include a sum in respect of funeral expenses but, save as aforesaid, shall be calculated without reference to any loss or gain caused to the estate by his death.[25]

The Bill, and the draftsman's comments, were forwarded to Lord Wright, who replied immediately:

> I always felt the drafting would be very difficult. I am not sure I am satisfied with the present draft … Wouldn't it be wise to send a copy to Porter, Gutteridge and McNair and we can have a conference sometime soon.[26]

[22] LCO 2/1974 Law Reform (Miscellaneous Provisions) Bill 1934, 27 March 1934 (Schuster to Gwyer).

[23] *Ibid.*, 17 April 1934 (Ram to Schuster). The wording in the Report was, in fact, 'proportioned either to the loss to the estate', etc. Ram's quotation was, therefore, strictly inaccurate, but the sense of his paraphrase was correct.

[24] *Ibid.* [25] *Ibid.*

[26] *Ibid.*, 19 April 1934 (Wright to Napier).

Porter seems not to have responded, but Gutteridge did, on behalf of himself and McNair. 'McNair and I', he wrote to Schuster:

> have been through the Law Reform Bill carefully & there is one matter which troubles us because we feel it might give rise to doubt hereafter.
>
> I imagine, however, that it is not our business to criticise the Bill & we do not propose, therefore, to pursue the matter.[27]

Schuster's reply was highly significant:

> If I may say so, I certainly think that, whether it is your business or not to criticise the Bill, any criticisms which you may have to make will be of the greatest assistance. The Bill was thrown together rather hastily with the intention of amending it, if necessary, before introduction, and there are several points upon which I am not myself completely satisfied.[28]

This prompted an extensive, four-page critique from the two Cambridge academics.

What Gutteridge and McNair had to say was important, and is considered further below. But we should also note that the legislative process was taking a very surprising turn. The initial problem had arisen because Schuster had chosen to ignore the suggestion that someone from the Office of the Parliamentary Counsel should be on the Law Revision Committee. There were probably good objective reasons for that, although there could also have been a territorial concern about who would be in control. At any rate, the result was that there was a rather awkward gap between the Committee's recommendations and the specific legislative language in which they would have to be realised. On the face of it, that was a problem that the Lord Chancellor's Office and the parliamentary draftsman would have to sort out between them. But that was not how Schuster proceeded. His decision to consult Lord Wright was, in itself, an interesting one: he was not referring even this fundamental matter back to the Committee, nor was he asking for the view of its chairman, Lord Hanworth. Once Wright had brought in Gutteridge and McNair, and Schuster had overridden their diffidence, a completely different picture emerged. The official status of Wright, Gutteridge and McNair was that they were merely three members of a committee (of fourteen) that had completed its duties when it delivered its report; but that official status (reflected in Gutteridge's comment that 'it is not our business to criticise the Bill') was now irrelevant. Now they were the inner circle, drafting the Bill.

27 *Ibid.*, 23 April 1934 (Gutteridge to Schuster).

28 *Ibid.*, 24 April 1934 (Schuster to Gutteridge).

IV

Gutteridge and McNair's critique drew attention to three important points. The first was the omission of *Baker* v. *Bolton*.[29] On this point, Schuster was more forthcoming with Gutteridge than he had been in his instructions to the parliamentary draftsman:

> As regards Baker v. Bolton the omission was deliberate. You may remember that we had some discussion on this matter in the Committee and that O'Connor reserved to himself the liberty to move an amendment giving to the servant a cause of action for the death of his master. As to accept such an amendment would be a far-reaching innovation in the law and to resist it would entail a very awkward Parliamentary discussion, it seems best to leave the thing out altogether.[30]

'O'Connor' here was Sir Terence O'Connor, Conservative Member of Parliament and future Solicitor General.[31] He, it seems, was anticipating the political sensitivities that might be stirred up by a law reform proposal allowing an employer to recover for the financial loss caused by the death of his employee. The concern was easy to understand, for the proposal had obvious ideological resonances. It effectively saw employees as their employer's valuable property, and treated them as a dehumanised, fungible mass, whose *raison d'être* was the creation of profit. A Conservative government supporting such a measure would obviously be vulnerable to the accusation that it was showing its true political colours, and O'Connor's suggestion to allow a claim in the converse situation – where an employee suffered loss as the result of the death of his employer – was perhaps designed to neutralise such political antagonism, rather than to provoke it. But, for Schuster, the prospect of political point-scoring was to be avoided at all costs. There is no reason to think that Gutteridge kept back this information from McNair and, assuming McNair did know, it casts an interesting light on his statement – in a lecture in 1935 – that 'For reasons not known to me' the rule in *Baker* v. *Bolton* had not been abolished.[32] He could only have been describing what, officially, his state of knowledge, as a mere Committee member, should have been.

[29] *Ibid.*, 27 April 1934 ('Law Reform (Miscellaneous Provisions) Bill; Note by H. C. Gutteridge & A. D. McNair), para. 2.

[30] *Ibid.*, 28 April 1934 (Schuster to Gutteridge).

[31] For a summary of O'Connor's career, see his obituary in *The Times*, 9 May 1940.

[32] McNair, 'The Work of the Law Revision Committee', 40.

Gutteridge and McNair's second point related to clause 1(4) of the draft Bill. This provided as follows:

> Where a person dies in the interval elapsing between a wrongful act or omission and the suffering of damage by another person by reason of that act or omission, there shall be deemed for the purposes of this Act to have been in existence before his death such cause of action against him, if any, as would have existed if his death had occurred after the suffering of the damage.[33]

The academics were concerned that, as it stood, the clause would not include instantaneous deaths, for instance, in road accidents; in such cases, they argued, there might be no 'interval' between the wrongful act and the damage suffered by the claimant. Schuster forwarded Gutteridge and McNair's comments to the draftsman,[34] Granville Ram, who responded at length.[35] The point about instantaneous deaths, he argued, 'was not a good one' and was 'based on a misapprehension'. 'In the illustration they give', he continued:

> as to the motor accident they seem to assume that the 'wrongful act or omission' is the accident itself – i.e. the actual impact – or at any rate they assume that the impact must always have synchronized with the 'wrongful act or omission': but surely the 'wrongful act or omission' is not the impact but that which caused the impact – e.g. the excessive speed or the failure to keep a proper look out – and the cause must always have preceded the effect! Whatever 'A' did, or omitted to do, which resulted in damage to 'B', must have been done or omitted before 'A' died, for dead men can neither act nor omit.[36]

This rather pompous response was missing the point. Mere carelessness in itself could not be characterised as a 'wrongful' (or tortious) act until it had caused damage – the damage was what made it wrongful. It was, therefore, inaccurate to assert, as Ram did, that the wrongful act must always, as a matter of logic, precede the damage.

Ram, however, went on to say that he was 'impressed by the consideration that if this subsection has created difficulties in their [Gutteridge's and McNair's] minds it is still more likely to do so in the minds of other people'.[37] He was, therefore, prepared to amend the subsection if a better formula could be found. Following meetings with Lord Wright (which Ram

[33] LCO 2/1974. [34] LCO 2/1974, 28 April 1934 (Schuster to Ram).
[35] *Ibid.*, 4 May 1934 (Ram to Schuster).
[36] *Ibid.*, p. 1. [37] *Ibid.*, p. 2.

requested[38]), and Gutteridge and McNair (which Schuster arranged[39]), Ram did find a new formula, which became s. 1(4) of the Act:

> Where damage has been suffered by reason of any act or omission in respect of which a cause of action would have subsisted against any person if that person had not died before or at the same time as the damage was suffered, there shall be deemed, for the purposes of this Act, to have been subsisting against him before his death such cause of action in respect of that act or omission as would have subsisted if he had died after the damage was suffered.

Despite the hopes of all concerned, however, the problem of instantaneous death did not go away. In *Morgan* v. *Scoulding*[40] counsel argued that where the claimant had died instantaneously, the cause of action never 'vested' in him (as required by s. 1 of the Act), and could not therefore be enforced by his estate. This argument seemed to overlook the provisions of s. 1(4). Lewis J rejected it for a different reason, taking very much the same approach that Ram had adopted in his response to Gutteridge and McNair: 'The cause of action was not the death, but the negligence of the defendant in colliding with the deceased man on his motor-cycle.'[41] The point was also taken up by C. K. Allen in the *Law Quarterly Review*,[42] without reference to *Morgan* v. *Scoulding*. In fact, the answer to the whole problem was supplied by A. L. Goodhart in an understated editorial response to Allen. 'With all due respect to Dr. Allen's ingenious argument', he wrote:

> we suggest that there need be no difficulty if we realize that in fact there is no such thing as 'instantaneous death'. Even when a man is shot there is an instant of time between the moment when the bullet strikes the surface of his body and when it enters his heart. During that moment the right of action for [loss of] 'expectation' [of life] is vested in him. This may seem not unlike the subtlety of the 'scintilla juris', but when a purely technical point is raised it is not unfair to meet it with an equally technical one.[43]

The existence of that interval, however brief, would have allowed the original clause 1(4) to work perfectly; it also allowed the cause of action to 'vest' for the benefit of the claimant's estate.

[38] *Ibid.*, p. 5.

[39] *Ibid.*, 5 May 1934 (Schuster to Gutteridge): 'I will try and arrange the meeting between Ram and Wright for which the former asks: but no doubt it would be of assistance to Ram if he could simultaneously or at some other time see McNair and yourself.'

[40] [1938] 1 KB 786.

[41] [1938] 1 KB 786, 790.

[42] C. K. Allen, 'Is Life a Boon?' (1941) 57 *LQR* 462, 462–3.

[43] (1941) 57 *LQR* 465.

Gutteridge and McNair's third point related to the Bill's provisions for the assessment of damage to the estate. They were particularly troubled by the statement in s. 1(2)(d) that the damages were to be 'calculated without reference to any loss or gain caused to the estate by his death'. This, they feared, might exclude earnings that the tort victim would have received in the future, but now would not. For instance, they said, an artist might be killed before completing a picture for which he had been promised £500. 'According to the Report [of the Law Revision Committee] his personal representatives ought to recover £500';[44] but, under the Bill, this was not clear. Here Gutteridge and McNair had identified a fundamental difficulty that would trouble both Parliament and the courts, and take nearly half a century to resolve.

Meanwhile, Wright had also had the chance to consider the Bill, and wrote to Schuster's deputy at the Lord Chancellor's Office in terms that cast light both on the content of the Act and on Wright's role in the process:

> A message at the P[rivy] C[ouncil] tomorrow will reach me: but I shall come to the H[ouse of] L[ords] soon after 4/W
>
> Dear Napier,
>
> I am not sure if the 2nd Reading of the Law Reform bill is still planned (?) for tomorrow evening. I shall come over from the Privy Council in any case.
>
> I enclose a note from Gutteridge & McNair which the draftsman might look at & consider. I have been thinking independently of the same matters.
>
> As to (1)(2), as it stands I am not sure that it is not entirely negative: that is that it states what damages are not recoverable but not what are, that is except funeral expenses in (d). I think there should be a clearer statement of the affirmative proposition, viz that in general the damages shall be such as would compensate for damage caused to the estate – e.g. like cases under 26(1)(2) of the Administration of Estates Act 1925, or cases like taking coal or trespass as in Phillips v Humphrey [*Philips* v. *Homfray* (1871) LR 6 Ch App 770.] or causing subsidence, or fraud: then the negatives can follow (a)(b)(c) – (d) is more difficult because the Fatal Accidents Act will still operate in cases under (d) – damages there should be calculated without reference to gain to the estate eg insurance policies but what about loss? e.g. loss of a valuable contract or premature termination of a valuable life interest. Perhaps the best way would be to limit (d) to cases where damages are awarded under the Fatal Accidents Act – leaving all the cases of death caused by wrongful act to come under the general terms of the Bill, as I think it should be amended in respect of damages.

[44] LCO 2/1974, 27 April 1934 (Gutteridge and McNair to Schuster).

> Is it now superfluous to add as in the A[dministration of] E[states] A[ct], any damages recovered shall be part of the personal estate of the deceased? I haven't time to examine the point.
>
> As to 1(4) I think on the whole after some changes of mind that it would be better to provide for the case where the wrongdoer dies at the moment of the wrongful act which could be done by inserting 'dies at the moment of the wrongful act or omission causing damage or in the interval elapsing'. Quaere would it be better to put instead of 'before the death' simply [']at the moment of the wrongful act or omission[']?
>
> I make these suggestions for the consideration of the draftsman who has admirably done a very difficult job.[45]

So far as the content of the Act was concerned, Wright's major suggestion was to include an 'affirmative proposition' about the measure of damages. That seemed a sensible suggestion, but, as Wright's letter makes clear, what he envisaged would have referred to other statutory provisions or case law analogies: it would have sounded rather more like an academic commentary or judicial exposition than a statutory section. His suggestion for cl. 1(4), on the other hand, was a definite improvement: it made far clearer what that subsection was really about. We should also, in this connection, note Wright's changes of mind: this would not be the last time that he would be in two minds about this statute.

So far as Wright's contribution to the process was concerned, the letter brings out several important dimensions. First, it gives a vivid picture of his multiple roles. His day job was as a Law Lord; his second job was as a legislator; and he was moonlighting as a consultant to the parliamentary draftsman. The letter gives a sense of him (physically) rushing from one job to another. It also provides impressive evidence of the detailed attention that he was prepared to give to the legislation. Second, the letter shows an admirable lack of self-importance: it is presented as a supplement to Gutteridge and McNair's critique, and Wright makes no assumptions that his changes will be incorporated. His praise for the draftsman was appreciatively received. These qualities would ensure that he would continue to be at the very centre of private law reform initiatives.

Ram responded to Gutteridge, McNair and Wright in one document.[46] As he pointed out, Gutteridge and McNair's point about 'loss to the estate' was linked to Wright's point about an 'affirmative proposition': any 'affirmative proposition' would have to address the question of lost future earnings. That question, Ram said:

[45] LCO 2/1974, 30 April 1934 (Wright to Napier).

[46] LCO 2/1974, 4 May 1934 (Ram to Schuster).

> is the most difficult point in connection with the Bill and I confess to being in some doubt as to the exact intention of the Committee. It never occurred to me that the Committee would have desired that in such a case as that put in the [Gutteridge and McNair] memorandum the executors should recover the £500 as damages.[47]

He then delivered a compelling analysis of Gutteridge and McNair's artist example:

> The illustration taken by Gutteridge and McNair is a plausible one, but its plausibility rests upon the tacit assumption that the loss to the artist's estate is to be estimated by comparing his pecuniary position at the date of death with what his pecuniary position would have been a week later. But why only a week later? Why not a month later or a year later? by which time he might well have spent the whole of the £500, so that no part of it would have remained in his estate.
>
> If the principle is to be that the estate is entitled to moneys which the deceased might have been expected to earn if he had lived, I do not see where one is to stop. Take a civil servant, in good health, with a salary of £200 a year, who is run over and killed at the age of 30. It would be reasonable to assume that if he had lived he would have received at least £5,000 in salary and pension. Clearly that cannot all be regarded as a loss to the estate, for if he had lived he would have had to have spent most of it on food and lodging. Examples of the difficulties which such a principle would lead to might be multiplied indefinitely.[48]

These difficulties, he concluded, made any 'affirmative proposition' impossible.

Meetings between Ram's deputy[49] and Wright, and Ram, Gutteridge and McNair followed. They resulted in amendments from Ram that reflected the final form of the Act. The subsection was still basically negative; however, the reference to pain and bodily suffering of the deceased person had now been deleted, and the part dealing with gains or losses to the estate now read as follows:

> (c) where the death of that person has been caused by the act or omission which gives rise to the cause of action, [damages recoverable for the benefit of the estate] shall be calculated without reference to any loss or gain to his estate consequent on his death, except that a sum in respect of funeral expenses may be included.

[47] LCO 2/1974, 4 May 1934 (Ram to Schuster).

[48] LCO 2/1974, 4 May 1934 (Ram to Schuster), pp. 3–4.

[49] Ram himself was ill. LCO 2/1974, 10 May 1934 (Ram to Schuster).

Ram's covering letter to Schuster indicated how central Gutteridge, McNair and Wright had become:

> As a result of these conversations … these [amendments] will satisfy Lord Wright. I think they will also satisfy Gutteridge and McNair so far as they go, but Gutteridge and McNair wanted some affirmative statement as to the measure of damages. Lord Wright on further consideration decided against attempting any such affirmative statement, and personally I think it would be safer not to.[50]

The assumption was that their approval was needed before the amendments were made.[51]

V

These very detailed exchanges were taking place under time pressure, created by the fact that the first draft of the Bill had already been introduced into the House of Lords by the Lord Chancellor, and the second reading was pending. That took place on 2 May 1934, and the Committee stage, at which the amendments were made, followed twelve days later. On the second reading, the Lord Chancellor introduced the Bill with a speech adorned with lengthy quotations from Holdsworth.[52] The only controversy arose out of the exclusion of defamation from the reforms;[53] but, as the Lord Chancellor pointed out, 'The only difficulty is that the question of allowing an action for a libel on a dead man is a controversial one.'[54]

The Committee stage, however, was to prove more acrimonious. The Lord Chancellor introduced the amendments with the comment that they were 'of a very technical character and are little more than drafting alterations'. 'The Government are much indebted to the gentlemen who have drawn attention to these matters', he continued, 'and I should like to express our obligation to … Lord Wright for the great help he has given in assisting to draft the new clauses.'[55] He then set out what he believed was recoverable under the Bill as 'loss to the estate':

[50] LCO 2/1974, 10 May 1934 (Ram to Schuster).

[51] See also Ram's letter to Schuster on 28 June 1934, where, discussing further amendments to the Law Reform (Miscellaneous Provisions) Bill, Ram says: 'I have had some correspondence with Gutteridge and McNair with regard to the substance of these amendments and they are in favour … Would you like me to send them copies of these amendments, or do you think they have now been consulted enough?'

[52] Hansard's Parliamentary Debates, Fifth Series, HL, vol. 91, 2 May 1934, col. 988 at 990.

[53] *Ibid.*, cols. 994–5 (Lord Danesfort).

[54] *Ibid.*, col. 995.

[55] Hansard's Parliamentary Debates, Fifth Series, HL, vol. 92, 14 May 1934, cols. 332–3.

> The ... result ... would be that no damages are recoverable at all except out-of-pocket expenses incurred before death and, by express provision, funeral expenses. The result of this will be to give adequate damages in the case of death.[56]

These 'merely technical' amendments, however, troubled Lord Danesfort, who had earlier questioned the exclusion of defamation from the Bill. What, he asked, happened to the deceased's lost future earnings? What exactly did the clause excluding losses and gains to the estate mean?[57] Lord Wright intervened:

> The difficulty which the Committee, and I speak as a member, had to face was this, that it is almost impossible to determine what would have been the loss to the estate in such a case as the noble Lord has put, of a surgeon being killed in an accident, by trying to calculate what the position would have been if the surgeon had lived. The man would have been expending money for his own purposes. He might have expended everything that he earned, in any way which was convenient to him. In those circumstances it seemed impossible to equate the position in the case of death with the ordinary position of a personal injury case, and it was found impossible to produce any formula which would be a satisfactory direction to a jury in such a case.[58]

Lord Danesfort, however, was unpersuaded. Surely, he argued, the same difficulty was faced, and overcome, every time an assessment of damages for loss of dependency under Lord Campbell's Act took place.

This prompted an extraordinary reply from Lord Hanworth:

> I hope the noble Lord will not take that view ... nobody who has not given continuous attention to the problems involved can speak with any authority. I must say that the Committee who have been dealing with this have been considering it for weeks, and parsing every single word. It is important that every word should be parsed and considered in making an alteration of this sort. It is not a matter on which you can bring a fresh mind, in the course of the last few minutes to bear ... I do hope that the Lord Chancellor will not feel embarrassed by a criticism which cannot ... have had the same close scrutiny that has been given to this matter by the Committee.[59]

56 *Ibid.*, 333. Cf. the briefing notes that had been prepared for the Lord Chancellor by his officials: 'This result gives a more niggardly measure of damage than the Committee intended and than it seems desirable.' LCO 2/1974, undated (filed between letters dated 10 May 1934 and 13 May 1934).

57 Hansard's Parliamentary Debates, Fifth Series, HL, vol. 92, 14 May 1934, col. 333.

58 *Ibid.*, col. 334. 59 *Ibid.*, col. 335.

The amendment was agreed to; the other amendments passed without debate.

These proceedings at the Committee stage were remarkable. Wright was presented as the architect of the Bill, with Gutteridge and McNair only acknowledged as 'the gentlemen' in the shadows. There was, of course, nothing wrong in acknowledging the hard work of others, but as things turned out, the acknowledgment created an expectation that Wright would defend his own work. In doing so, Wright effectively took over as Lord Chancellor. The terms in which Wright defended the Bill were also striking. He referred to the difficulty faced by 'the Committee' in devising a suitable formula. Presumably by this he meant the Law Revision Committee (there was no other possible committee); but, assuming that he did mean the Law Revision Committee, that was rather misleading. As we have seen, the Committee had not gone into how 'loss to the estate' should be defined; indeed, it was precisely the Committee's failure to do so that had created the problem.

Hanworth's speech in support of Wright took things to a new level. Its dominant note was one of resentment – who did Lord Danesfort think he was? – and his remark that 'a fresh mind' was inappropriate on matters such as this was worthy of the script of a political satire. What is particularly ironic about Hanworth's contemptuous contribution is that, in fact, Wright was privately worrying that the Bill had got it wrong. The day before the Committee stage, Wright had written to Napier (Schuster's deputy) in terms that must have caused alarm in the Lord Chancellor's Office:

> Dear Napier,
>
> We live and learn and I am learning how difficult the draftsman's work may be. That is specially so when broad changes are being made in the general ideas that have sprung up in centuries of the common law. To attempt to be too precise in the new rules would, I think, be fatal. We can't attempt to provide against every possibility: we must trust to the Judges giving a beneficial interpretation in accordance with the main purpose of the Act: if anything goes wrong there must be amendment, that could, I imagine, easily be done in some other Bill or Act rendered necessary by the activities of the Law Revision Committee … The real problem that bothered me in the committee, and still bothers me, is whether loss of earning capacity consequent on death should not be recoverable – a jury could, it is said, estimate that loss, just as in a case of partial or total incapacity. A surgeon or painter loses his right hand but survives: a jury will award him damages: why not in the same way for the benefit of the estate if his earning capacity is ended by death? … On the whole I think it would

> be impossible to define in the Act the considerations necessary to determine the amount of the loss to the estate consequent on the death. I think the Committee would accept this view.[60]

Danesfort's 'fresh mind' had in fact hit upon the Bill's key structural weakness. It was exactly the kind of point that called for parliamentary discussion.

The Bill's passage through the Commons was less eventful. The Bill was introduced by Sir Donald Somervell MP, who was now the Solicitor General.[61] Only four other members of Parliament spoke, three of them lawyers, and none of them had any criticisms to make. One of them commented that the Bill was 'entirely a non-party matter';[62] another, not unconnectedly, regretted that so few members were interested in it.[63] One minor amendment was made – permitting the recovery of funeral expenses in a claim under Lord Campbell's Act – which was passed by the Lords without opposition. The first of the Law Revision Committee's proposals had now become law.

The progression from reference to the Committee to statute book had been accomplished in a peculiar and distinctive way. The Committee's proposal had been in broad, general terms, leaving the details of the statutory language to be worked out later. Those linguistic details raised major questions of principle, but, rather than either leaving it to the parliamentary draftsman or referring questions to the full Committee, an inner circle of Gutteridge, McNair and Wright had been consulted. Those three individuals came to exert an extraordinarily powerful influence over the content of the legislation; but they were exercising this influence in a completely unofficial fashion, as consultants. The official influences over the shape of legislation – the parliamentary draftsman and the Houses of Parliament – took a subordinate role. The draftsman did so out of choice; the House of Commons out of indifference; and the House of Lords was, in effect, told to mind its own business. All the really important developments were happening off the official stage. As things turned out, this peculiar and distinctive pattern was to become the typical way of giving effect to the Law Revision Committee's proposals.

[60] LCO 2/1974, 13 May 1934 (Wright to Napier).

[61] Hansard's Parliamentary Debates, Fifth Series, Commons, vol. 290 15 June 1934, col. 2111.

[62] *Ibid.*, col. 2116 (Major Milner).

[63] *Ibid.*, col. 2119 (Major Llewellin).

VI

The subsequent history of the Act underlined Lord Wright's point that it was impossible to anticipate everything. In November 1934 in *Flint* v. *Lovell*[64] the Court of Appeal held, by a majority, that a claimant who had suffered personal injury through the defendant's negligence could recover for loss of 'the prospect of an enjoyable, vigorous and happy old age'.[65] The chief analytical obstacle to such an award was that it was difficult to reconcile with *Baker* v. *Bolton*.[66] There it had been said that death could not in itself give rise to a cause of action; here the Court of Appeal seemed to be making an award because death would come sooner. Greer LJ dealt with this obstacle by emphasising that *Baker* v. *Bolton*, as confirmed in *The Amerika*,[67] dealt with the different situation where a claimant was seeking to recover damage 'by reason of the death of another'.[68] He also echoed the House of Lords' historical justification for the rule, and argued that this justified giving the rule a narrow reading.[69] Slesser LJ also emphasised the rule's narrow scope, saying that it only applied where there was a felony with which the civil action merged.[70] On the facts, which concerned a road accident, there was no such felony.[71] Roche LJ, dissenting, held that an award for loss of expectation of life was inconsistent with *Baker* v. *Bolton*.

Flint's case highlighted that the *Baker* v. *Bolton* rule, unless it could be distinguished, had the potential to restrict common law development. In *Rose* v. *Ford*,[72] decided by the Court of Appeal less than a year later, that potential was realised. Essentially the question was whether damages for loss of expectation of life could be recovered by executors under the 1934 Act when the tort victim had died as a result of the defendant's negligence. The Court of Appeal, again by a majority, held not. This was something of a surprise – after all, the claimant had been deprived of expectation of life in the most emphatic way imaginable – but it was held that the rule in *Baker* v. *Bolton* excluded recovery. Slesser LJ explained that the 1934

[64] [1935] 1 KB 354.

[65] [1935] 1 KB 354, 355 (Acton J at first instance, whose decision was affirmed by the Court of Appeal).

[66] (1808) 1 Camp. 493.

[67] *Admiralty Commissioners* v. *Owners of Steamship Amerika* [1917] AC 38.

[68] *Flint* v. *Lovell* [1935] 1 KB 354, 358.

[69] [1935] 1 KB 354, 359.

[70] [1935] 1 KB 354, 364.

[71] [1935] 1 KB 354, 365.

[72] [1936] 1 KB 90.

Act did not alter the *Baker* v. *Bolton* principle that 'the right of action is merged in the felony'.[73] When the claimant died, he continued:

> the wrongful act of the defendant became a felony, and to award damages to the estate on this head would in fact be to award damages in respect of the felony of causing her death at any rate if the conditions of criminal culpability ... were satisfied.

However, Slesser LJ also added that it was not necessary to show that the defendant's act had amounted to manslaughter: 'Whether it did or did not do so would depend on whether the degree of negligence constituted the killing manslaughter, an inquiry which I do not think the 1934 Act required the Court to make.'[74] Here Slesser LJ was moving slightly, but significantly, from the position he had adopted in *Flint* v. *Lovell*. In the earlier case he had said that a felony must occur for the *Baker* v. *Bolton* rule to apply; now he was saying that the fact that there *might* have been gross negligence (and, therefore, manslaughter) was enough. Greene LJ concurred in this result without setting out his own reasons.

When *Rose* v. *Ford* reached the House of Lords[75] the Court of Appeal's decision was reversed, and its reliance on *Baker* v. *Bolton* sharply criticised. *Baker* v. *Bolton*, Lord Atkin said, 'had no application to the death of a supposed plaintiff'.[76] Furthermore, the reasons given to support it were unsatisfactory. 'I see no reason', asserted Lord Atkin, 'for extending the illogical doctrine of *The Amerika* to any case where it does not clearly apply. As to the supposed foundation of the doctrine in the law relating to felony I will only say that if the rule is really based on the relevant death being due to felony, it should long ago have been relegated to a museum.'[77] Lord Thankerton concurred, and Lord Russell took a similar view. Lord Wright's speech was particularly interesting, for he went out of his way to attack the Court of Appeal's fundamental approach:

> I venture respectfully to think that the view of the Court of Appeal illustrates a tendency common in construing an Act which changes the law, that is, to minimize or neutralize its operation by introducing notions taken from or inspired by the old law which the words of the Act were intended to abrogate and did abrogate.[78]

'The same tendency', he added, was shown in the Court of Appeal's 'references to a dogma of somewhat obscure import and uncertain application,

[73] [1936] 1 KB 90, 107. [74] [1936] 1 KB 90, 108.
[75] [1937] AC 826. [76] [1937] AC 826, 833.
[77] [1937] AC 826, 834. [78] [1937] AC 826, 846.

that in civil court the death of a human being cannot be complained of as an injury'.[79] Lord Wright was clearly frustrated by the Court of Appeal's failure to adopt the kind of 'generous interpretation' that he had hoped for when the Bill was being passed into law. It may also have crossed his mind that, had the full recommendations of his Committee been implemented, the rule in *Baker* v. *Bolton* would have been abolished, and the Court of Appeal could not have been tempted into error. At any rate, at least his position as a Law Lord meant that he could, authoritatively, make clear what he had meant in his statute.

The final speech was delivered by Lord Roche, who had, as Roche LJ, been persuaded in *Flint* v. *Lovell* that it was inconsistent with *Baker* v. *Bolton* ever to award damages for loss of expectation of life. His Lordship now professed to be 'satisfied' by the arguments that 'the doubts [he had expressed in *Flint* v. *Lovell*] are of insufficient force to debar the plaintiff from his remedy here'.[80] However, as his speech unfolded, it became clear that his satisfaction was not unqualified. The rule in *Baker* v. *Bolton*, he felt, could be confined to cases where the claimant was basing his claim on the death of a third party; here, that was not the case – the claim was by the deceased's representative, and the damage due to death was only one head of the damages claimed. But, so far as the wider question was concerned, it was clear that Lord Roche was unconvinced. What had changed between *Flint*'s case and *Rose* v. *Ford* was, rather, his conviction that he could do anything about it. As he put it:

> I am unable to see that it is the duty or the right of your Lordships, sitting in a judicial capacity, either to enter upon a task of rendering the law uniform and consistent where lack of uniformity and consistency may manifest itself at present, or for the sake of uniformity to extend the rule to cases and circumstances not actually within its scope.[81]

The fact that Parliament had chosen not to abolish the rule in *Baker* v. *Bolton* had, therefore, not ultimately prevented the development of damages for loss of expectation of life. But it had been a close thing. If the litigation in *Rose* v. *Ford* had not been driven by insurance companies in search of an authoritative ruling,[82] the Court of Appeal's majority judgment could easily have remained undisturbed.

[79] [1937] AC 826, 846. [80] [1937] AC 826, 854.

[81] [1937] AC 826, 857.

[82] *Rose* v. *Ford* [1936] 1 KB 90, 102: the claimant's counsel 'frankly stated that he was acting for one or more insurance companies who desired to have the questions involved in this case finally determined by the House of Lords' (per Greer LJ).

VII

The other major question that arose in litigation under the Act was how, precisely, to quantify 'loss to the estate'. Two points proved particularly problematic. The first was whether s. 1(2)(c)'s stipulation that damages were to be 'calculated without reference to any loss or gain to [the deceased's] estate consequent on his death' excluded recovery for income which the deceased would have received had he not died. As has been shown, Wright, Gutteridge, McNair and Ram were keenly aware of this point, and the final version of the legislation had been framed with the intention of excluding recovery. The immediate judicial reaction was that this aim had been achieved. In *Slater* v. *Spreag*,[83] decided in June 1935, a claim for lost future earnings had been pleaded, but was not pursued at the trial; nevertheless, MacKinnon J expressed the opinion that it was excluded by s. 1(2)(c).[84] Three months later, however, a more cautious approach was taken by the Court of Appeal in *Rose* v. *Ford*,[85] with Greene LJ commenting that s. 1(2)(c) was aimed at losses such as the deceased having been the tenant for life of valuable property.[86] The same doubts could be seen when the case reached the House of Lords. Lord Atkin, never a judge to be cautious for the sake of it, refused to give an opinion on whether s. 1(2)(c) excluded the recovery of lost future income.[87] The only other comment on the subsection came from Lord Wright:

> s.1, sub-s.2(c) is especially significant, because it particularizes certain classes of losses and gains. It presupposes that damages may in general be calculated where death has been caused by the wrong, but excludes from the calculation losses or gains to the estate consequent on the death. I need not examine the full scope of this proviso, which is not directly material in this appeal. Obvious instances of what are referred to are such items as, on the one side, insurance moneys falling due on death, and, on the other, annuities ceasing on death.[88]

Taken out of context this was a fairly unremarkable example of judicial caution. But, given the context of Lord Wright's involvement with the 1934 Act at all levels of its inception and parliamentary passage, it was highly significant. Lord Wright had been a central, if not *the* central figure in shaping s. 1; he was on record in *Hansard* defending the effect of s. 1(2)(c) in excluding lost future earnings; but he was not now prepared to

[83] [1936] 1 KB 83. [84] [1936] 1 KB 83, 87.
[85] [1936] 1 KB 90. [86] [1936] 1 KB 90, 110.
[87] *Rose* v. *Ford* [1937] AC 826, 835.
[88] [1937] AC 826, 842.

assert that the section achieved what he knew it had been carefully crafted to achieve. There is, of course, one obvious explanation for his apparently inconsistent attitude, and that is his ambivalence – manifested most clearly in his letter the day before the Committee stage of the Bill[89] – about whether the exclusion of lost future earnings was right. He may well have thought that, if the courts held that lost future earnings were recoverable, that would not be such a bad thing. In the event the courts did so hold, explaining s. 1(2)(c) as relating to insurance payments, annuities and the like.[90] But the change was short-lived: Parliament swiftly moved to add s. 1(2)(a)(ii), which stated that damages under the Act could not include 'any damages for loss of income in respect of any period after that person's death'.[91] It had taken virtually half a century, but the point was finally settled.

The second problematic question in assessing 'loss to the estate' was what effect, if any, a successful claim under Lord Campbell's Act would have. It was not immediately obvious that there was an overlap at all. Lord Campbell's Act gave a claim to a list of dependants on the deceased tort victim, under which they recovered the value of their lost dependency; the 1934 Act gave a claim to the deceased's personal representative, for loss to the estate. Different claimants were claiming for different losses. But where the victim died intestate, this strict legal analysis started to look unrealistic. In such circumstances the deceased's personal representative was typically his dependent spouse; and the beneficiaries of his estate were his spouse and their children. The point became of particular practical significance once the House of Lords had recognised, in *Rose* v. *Ford*,[92] that a claim under the 1934 Act could include an amount for the deceased's lost expectation of life. This was a significant sum, even after the House of Lords' later plea – in *Benham* v. *Gambling*[93] – for judges and juries to be moderate in assessing it. There was also a difficulty over lost future earnings: the deceased would have supported his family using his earnings, but those earnings might also be recoverable under the 1934 Act. Did that require a deduction from the 1934 Act award, so that it would, in effect, represent only that part of the deceased's lost future earnings that he would have spent on himself? As we have seen, the position on the recovery of lost future earnings remained uncertain, so this difficulty was not brought to the surface in the cases. But it is interesting to note that

[89] See above, n. 60. [90] *Gammell* v. *Wilson* [1982] AC 227.

[91] Administration of Justice Act 1982 ss. 4(2), 73.

[92] [1937] AC 826. [93] [1941] AC 157. See further Chapter 5, section IX.

Ram was well aware of it, and used it as an argument against allowing any recovery of lost future earnings under the 1934 Act.[94]

The answer to these difficulties emerged only gradually. A first attempt was made by Lord Wright in his speech in *Rose* v. *Ford*. His view was that a jury assessing damages for loss of the deceased's expectation of life under the 1934 Act should take into account any award made under Lord Campbell's Act. This was necessary, he explained, because:

> one of the fruits of continued life is generally provision for dependants. If that provision is made good by awards under the Fatal Accidents Act, the loss consequent on the shortening of life may be deemed to be pro tanto reduced.[95]

Conversely, although without endorsing Lord Wright's detailed explanation, the Court of Appeal held that where the same parties will benefit from both a 1934 Act claim and a claim under Lord Campbell's Act, the amount of the 1934 Act claim was to be deducted from the Lord Campbell's Act claim.[96] If the 1934 Act damages were greater than those awarded under Lord Campbell's Act, the award under Lord Campbell's Act should be zero. Like Lord Wright, the Court of Appeal was concerned about duplication; but unlike Lord Wright, it did not explain why the two awards were duplicates. In fact, it was not clear that they were duplicates in cases where the 1934 Act claim was essentially for the deceased's loss of expectation of life. That award was for the deceased's own lost asset; and Lord Wright's attempt to link it with loss of dependency was, it is submitted, more ingenious than sound. Lord Wright's explanation was also vulnerable to the criticism that it gave a financial dimension to awards for loss of expectation of life; for instance, it might seem to follow that if the deceased had a large number of dependants, he should receive a higher award. This was at odds with several judicial statements that the award for loss of expectation of life was not connected with financial circumstances.[97] Furthermore, even if part of an award for loss of expectation of life reflected the lost pleasure of providing for one's family, that could not be true of the whole award. Other parts of the award reflected the loss of other pleasures; Lord Wright's explanation, if implemented accurately, required the award for loss of expectation of life to be apportioned, and only the part relating to the lost pleasure of supporting dependants to be

[94] See above, n. 48. [95] [1937] AC 826, 853.

[96] *Ellis* v. *Raine* [1939] 2 KB 180.

[97] *Trubyfield* v. *Great Western Railway Co* [1937] 4 All ER 614; *Benham* v. *Gambling* [1941] AC 157, 167.

set off against any claim under Lord Campbell's Act. Given the difficulties courts experienced in fixing a global sum for loss of expectation of life,[98] such apportionment would almost certainly have been unworkable.

A more convincing explanation was eventually found in *Davies* v. *Powell Duffryn Associated Collieries, Limited*.[99] It was based, not on a precise analytical point about duplication, but on the fact that Lord Campbell's Act required any financial benefits to dependants arising from the death (apart from insurance[100]) to be taken into account in assessing damages. An award under the 1934 Act would be such a benefit. The position was, therefore, clarified; but it was still not perfect. The provision in Lord Campbell's Act worked well if a claim under the 1934 Act had already been brought. But if it had not, courts hearing a claim under Lord Campbell's Act were placed in a dilemma: should they assume that a 1934 Act claim would be brought, or not? If they assumed that it would be brought, they would be reducing their award to reflect an event that might well never happen. If, on the other hand, they assumed that no 1934 Act claim would be brought, full damages would be awarded under Lord Campbell's Act, and the claimant was then free to bring a 1934 Act claim, which would yield precisely the kind of benefit that should have been set off against the Lord Campbell's Act damages. Crucially, there was no provision in the 1934 Act to allow an award made under it to be reduced as a consequence of an award made to the deceased's dependants.[101] The House of Lords held that the court should 'always take into account the possibility of … proceedings [under the 1934 Act] and make allowance accordingly'.[102] This would, in effect, encourage both claims to be brought simultaneously. It was not a particularly elegant solution, but it was probably the best available given the state of the legislation.

98 E.g. *Shepherd* v. *Hunter* [1938] 2 All ER 587, 589 (Greer LJ), 591 (MacKinnon LJ); *Bailey* v. *Howard* [1939] 1 KB 453, 458 (Scott LJ), 459 (MacKinnon LJ); *Ellis* v. *Raine* [1939] 2 KB 180, 183 (Scott LJ).

99 [1942] AC 601.

100 Fatal Accidents (Damages) Act 1908.

101 [1942] AC 601, 615–16 (Lord Wright).

102 [1942] AC 601, 608 (Lord Russell).

11

Contribution

I

The second tort topic to be considered by the Law Revision Committee was the rule that there was no contribution between tortfeasors. Like the *actio personalis* maxim, which the Committee had dealt with in its first report, the no contribution rule had a long history. It had been recognised at least since the late eighteenth century, when it had been set out by Kenyon CJ in *Merryweather* v. *Nixan*.[1] The case concerned two parties who had been found jointly liable for damage to the reversionary estate in a mill; one of the causes of action successfully relied upon against them had been in trover (it would now be described as an action for conversion). The claimant in that action had levied the whole sum against Merryweather (as he was perfectly entitled to do); Merryweather paid in full, and was now seeking reimbursement of half the amount from Nixan. At trial Merryweather was nonsuited, a decision upheld by the Court of King's Bench. Lord Kenyon CJ was reported as saying that:

> he had never before heard of such an action being brought, where the former recovery was for a tort: that the distinction was clear between this case and that of a joint judgment against several defendants in an action of assumpsit: and that this decision would not affect cases of indemnity, where one man employed another to do acts, not unlawful in themselves, for the purpose of asserting a right.[2]

As the second clause in this quotation made clear, the no contribution rule was confined to tort cases. The final clause hinted at some of the difficulties that would arise in seeking to pin down its exact scope.

Lord Kenyon's exposition of the rule appeared to apply to all torts, whatever the state of mind of the tortfeasor. But it quickly became clear that the rule was not to have such universal application. Thus, in *Adamson*

[1] (1799) 8 TR 186. [2] (1799) 8 TR 186.

v. *Jarvis*[3] it was held that an auctioneer had a right to claim contribution from a party who had exposed the auctioneer to liability in conversion by instructing him to sell goods that the party had misrepresented that he owned. Best CJ observed that: 'from reason, justice, and sound policy, the rule that wrong-doers cannot have redress or contribution against each other is confined to cases where the person seeking redress must be presumed to have known that he was doing an unlawful act.'[4] The same theme could be seen in *Betts* v. *Gibbins*,[5] where Lord Denman CJ said that: 'The general rule is, that between wrongdoers there is neither indemnity nor contribution: the exception is, where the act is not clearly illegal in itself.'[6]

But whilst the general rule and its limited application were well settled by 1935, none of the cases explained why the rule was felt to be necessary.[7] That omission was rectified by the editors of *Smith's Leading Cases*, who treated *Merryweather* v. *Nixan* as an application of the maxim *ex turpi causa non oritur actio*.[8] The joint tortfeasor pursuing contribution from another was seen as having to assert his own tortious act as the basis of the other's liability; the *ex turpi* maxim prohibited him from doing so. To modern eyes this does not seem very convincing, because today we think of contribution as a free-standing obligation created by a court's decision to impose joint liability; in modern law, in other words, we think of the claim as arising from the liability, not the tort.[9] But this is not how nineteenth-century lawyers saw it. To them, the basis of contribution was an implied contractual obligation to pay half of the loss;[10] as a matter of public policy, no such contract should be implied to adjust the consequences of a wrong.

The rule that there could be no contribution between tortfeasors was not, therefore, without foundation, although the implied contract

3 (1827) 4 Bing 66. 4 (1827) 4 Bing 66, 73.

5 (1834) 2 Ad & E 57. 6 (1834) 2 Ad. & E. 57, 74.

7 See especially Lord Herschell LC's comment on the 'meagre' reasoning in *Merryweather* v. *Nixan* in *Palmer* v. *Wick and Pulteneytown Steam Shipping Company, Limited* [1894] AC 318, 324.

8 J. Fischer Williams, 'The Rule in *Merryweather* v. *Nixan*' (1901) 17 *LQR* 293.

9 See, e.g. A. Burrows, *The Law of Restitution*, 2nd edn (London, Butterworths, 2002) 290–1.

10 E.g. *Palmer* v. *Wick and Pulteneytown Steam Shipping Company, Limited* [1894] AC 318, 333: '"tort" in its strictest meaning, as it seems to me, ought to exclude the right of contribution which would imply a presumed contract to subscribe towards the commission of a wrong' (Lord Halsbury); *WH Smith and Son* v. *Clinton* (1908) 99 LT 840, 841: 'It was very early discussed whether there was any implied contractual relation between two tortfeasors, so as to entitle one to contribution against the other' (Coleridge J).

foundation was starting to look rather shaky by the 1930s.[11] This, however, did not make the rule immune from criticism, and in *Palmer* v. *Wick and Pulteneytown Steam Shipping Company, Limited*,[12] a Scottish appeal to the House of Lords, Lord Herschell LC remarked, in relation to *Merryweather* v. *Nixan*, that:

> It is now too late to question that decision in this country; but when I am asked to hold it to be part of the law of Scotland, I am bound to say that it does not appear to me to be founded on any principle of justice or equity, or even of public policy, which justifies its extension to the jurisprudence of other countries.[13]

It was this passage to which the attention of the Law Revision Committee was drawn by its terms of reference.[14] Interestingly, however, the case as a whole demonstrated a more ambivalent attitude towards the no contribution rule than that single quotation suggested. Lord Halsbury, whilst not wanting to question the Scottish position, indicated that in his view *Merryweather* v. *Nixan* was correct, adding that '"tort" in its strictest meaning, as it seems to me, ought to exclude the right of contribution which would imply a presumed contract to subscribe towards the commission of a wrong'.[15] Even Lord Herschell LC himself suggested that future development in England need not necessitate the overruling of *Merryweather* v. *Nixan*: in his view claims for negligence did not involve conscious wrongdoing, and therefore fell within the exception to the no contribution rule.[16] If Lord Herschell LC's approach had been implemented, the rule in *Merryweather* v. *Nixan* would have been marginalised to such an extent that its continued existence would not have presented any great practical difficulties. But that did not happen. As a result, the topic was very suitable for consideration by the Law Revision Committee.

II

Responsibility for the first draft of the report seems to have been delegated to a small group – Goddard, Swift, Asquith and Topham – led

[11] For criticism of the implied contract basis of obligations see, e.g. Lord Wright, '*Sinclair* v. *Brougham*' in *Legal Essays and Addresses* (Cambridge University Press, 1939) 1.

[12] [1894] AC 318. [13] [1894] AC 318, 324.

[14] Law Revision Committee, *Third Interim Report*, Cmd 4637 (1934), para. 1.

[15] [1894] AC 318, 333. [16] [1894] AC 318, 323–4.

by Goddard.[17] The first draft it produced contained much material that would survive to the final version. Thus, it described the no contribution rule as being 'of obscure and uncertain origin',[18] as being based on *Merryweather* v. *Nixan* and as having limited scope. It recommended that 'the common law rule should be altered as speedily as possible',[19] and it also recommended that the alteration should apply not only to joint tortfeasors in the strict sense, but also to situations where two tortfeasors had independently contributed to the same damage. 'This is the position', the report pointed out, 'which frequently arises where the plaintiff sustains a single damage from the combined negligence of two motor car drivers, and recovers judgment against both.'[20] In short, the damages should be apportioned between the tortfeasors in all such cases.

This was a coherent basic structure, and contained sensible suggestions for reform. It was, however, rather disappointing in its account of the basis of the rule. As we have seen, it was not a rule that made no sense; on the contrary, it was a rule that flowed from certain assumptions about the nature of contribution. The drafting committee's failure to address these assumptions, and, in particular, its failure to engage with the idea that contribution was based on an implied contract, was something of a missed opportunity. The implied contract theory underlay many other categories of liability, but its inherent artificiality and the unnecessary limitations it imposed were increasingly coming to be recognised.[21] A critical assessment by the Law Revision Committee might have accelerated its rejection and replacement by more coherent ideas of unjust enrichment. In this connection it is tempting to speculate what the report might have said if Wright and Gutteridge had not been allocated to the *actio personalis* team. Wright, who has been described as 'the leading advocate of the existence of a law of restitution',[22] was influential in the destruction

[17] The four names were those listed on the cover of the relevant Lord Chancellor's Office file LCO 2/1967, Law Revision Committee. Contribution between joint tortfeasors. Goddard sent the first draft to Schuster, with a covering letter stating that it was from 'my Group' (Goddard to Schuster, 13 March 1934).

[18] Law Revision Committee, *Third Interim Report*, Cmd 4637 (1934), 4.

[19] *Ibid.*, 5. [20] *Ibid.*, 5–6.

[21] D. Ibbetson, *A Historical Introduction to the Law of Obligations* (Oxford University Press, 1999) 284–93.

[22] E. McKendrick, 'Frustration, Restitution and Loss Apportionment' in A. Burrows (ed.), *Essays on the Law of Restitution* (Oxford, Clarendon Press, 1991) 147, 153 n. 31. Lord Wright's admiring and enthusiastic review of the American *Restatement of the Law of Restitution* vividly illustrates his views: Lord Wright, 'Restatement of the Law of Restitution' in *Legal Essays and Addresses* (Cambridge University Press, 1939) 34;

of the implied contract theory;[23] Gutteridge had written on comparative English and French unjust enrichment.[24] It is difficult to believe that they would not have had something to say on the subject.

Having advocated a new rule of apportionment, the first draft of the report went on to consider how the rule should be implemented and what exceptions should be made to it. The recommendations on both points would undergo significant modifications as the report moved through its various drafts.

So far as implementation was concerned, the first draft struck a rather cautious note:

> We have not considered whether alteration is desirable in the rule established by Greenlands v Wilmshurst[25] ... that damages for a joint tort cannot be assessed separately against each defendant, nor whether it would be desirable to adopt Admiralty rules as to apportionment of damages (cf. The Maritime Conventions Act 1911, sects. 1, 2 & 3) to collisions on land, as these questions seem to be beyond our terms of reference.[26]

Behind this rather mundane-looking sentence there loomed a fundamental issue of principle. As the sentence indicated, the Court of Appeal in *Greenlands, Ltd* v. *Wilmshurst* had held that a finding of joint liability was logically inconsistent with a verdict that assessed each tortfeasor's liability separately: there had to be a single, total award against all the defendants. In a system where contribution between tortfeasors was not permitted, a court assessing damages in a joint tortfeasance case could, therefore, have no further role once it had ascertained the total quantum of damages. The Law Revision Committee, however, was planning to change the system in a way which would clearly require courts to make separate assessments for individual defendants. The question was whether these individual assessments should replace the existing joint award, or simply be in addition to it. This was not a mere question of procedure. If liability remained joint, a claimant need only sue one tortfeasor successfully in order to recover the damages in full; the onus was then on the tortfeasor to find, and proceed against, the other tortfeasors. If, on the other hand, liability was only to

the review had first appeared in (1937) 51 *Harvard Law Review* 369. For an overview of Lord Wright's contribution in this area see N. Duxbury, 'Lord Wright and Innovative Traditionalism' (2009) 59 *University of Toronto Law Journal* 265, 307–20.

23 See e.g. his speech in *Fibrosa Spolka Akcyjna* v. *Fairbairn Lawson Combe Barbour Ltd* [1943] AC 32, 61–4.

24 H. Gutteridge and R. David, 'The Doctrine of Unjustified Enrichment' (1933–1935) 5 *CLJ* 204.

25 [1913] 3 KB 507 (CA). 26 LCO 2/1967.

be assessed by way of individual awards against individual defendants, it was up to the claimant to track down, and proceed against, the whole set of defendants. As the first draft hinted, this was an issue that had received attention in the Admiralty jurisdiction, where it had been held that an innocent vessel was entitled to recover damages in full against one of two negligent vessels that had caused her loss.[27] But, as the rather cryptic allusion to the Maritime Conventions Act 1911 suggested, there was also a further question. The Admiralty method was to divide the total loss suffered equally; the 1911 Act, in contrast, provided that where two ships were both at fault in a collision with each other, the liability of each vessel was only to be 'in proportion to the degree in which each vessel was in fault'.[28]

Evidently the first draft was circulated to the Committee as a whole, for Gutteridge and McNair promptly produced a lengthy critique of it. They suggested that the passage quoted above needed strengthening:

> The question of the severance or apportionment of damages in cases of a joint tort appears to us to be so closely connected with that of the right of contribution as to require more than a mere reference to its existence. As Lord Sumner (then Hamilton LJ) said in Greenlands v Wilmhurst [*sic*] ... 'the unity of the verdict and of the judgment when the tort is joint is founded on and must stand with the legal theory of the liability of joint tortfeasors'. It might seem at first sight that the hardships created by the rule of non-contribution could be obviated by severing or apportioning the damages, but this would in our view merely be to replace one form of injustice by another. We do not think that a defendant should in the case of a joint tort be allowed to plead that his contribution to the injury is less than that of his fellow wrongdoers. The logical consequence of this would be to oblige the plaintiff to join all the tortfeasors in his action and this might place him in a very difficult position. It may be added that the draft Report does in fact, though without giving any reasons, negative any alteration of the rule in Greenlands v. Wilmhurst ... We therefore suggest that the third para on page 2 should read as follows:–
>
> 'Though the matter may, perhaps, be outside the terms of our reference, in a strict sense, we have considered whether it is desirable that the rule that damages for a joint tort cannot be separated (Greenlands v Wilmshurst ...) or to adopt the Admiralty rule as to the apportionment of damages (vide the Maritime Conventions Act, 1911, Sects 1, 2 and 3). But for two reasons we do not recommend any alteration of the existing law in either of the above directions:–

[27] *Owners of the Steamship Devonshire* v. *Owners of the Barge Leslie* [1912] AC 634.

[28] Maritime Conventions Act 1911, s. 1(1). See further M. Slade (ed.), *A Treatise on the Law of Collisions at Sea by R G Marsden*, 7th edn (London, Stevens and Sons, 1919) chapter VI (the first edition to appear after the 1911 Act).

(a) If damages can be severed or apportioned, as the case may be, a plaintiff whose action is founded on a joint tort will virtually be compelled to sue all the tortfeasors, which would in many cases inflict on the plaintiff serious inconvenience, delay and expense; e.g. where one of the joint tortfeasors is out of the jurisdiction or is evading service.

(b) It would be difficult, if not impossible, to assess damages according to the degree of guilt against one tortfeasor if the others have not been brought before the Court.

Therefore we think that it would be undesirable to alter the existing rule which enables a plaintiff to recover the full quantum of his damages from anyone of several joint tortfeasors. We suggest that in any amendment of the law it should be made clear that a plaintiff need not sue more than one joint feasor and that he can recover compensation in full against him.'[29]

Gutteridge asked that, subject to Schuster's approval, their commentary be circulated.[30] But this request had already been overtaken by events: the day before Gutteridge made it, the working group on the non-contribution report had met and revised the controversial passage. It now read as follows:

> The question ... arises whether the contribution by all the wrongdoers should be equal, or whether the Court should have the power to apportion the liability.
>
> It would hardly be possible to apportion the liability by way of contribution between the wrongdoers without altering the rule established in Greenlands v Wilmshurst ... that damages for a joint tort cannot be assessed separately against each Defendant.
>
> The alteration of this rule is hardly within the terms of our reference but we think that there are many cases where such an apportionment might fairly be made, more particularly it might be desirable to adapt Admiralty Rules as to apportionment of damages (cf. The Maritime Conventions Act 1, 2 & 3) to collisions on land.[31]

This was taking a different line to the one advocated in Gutteridge and McNair's (uncirculated) critique. They therefore revised their comments, and circulated the following:

> To substitute the following ...
>
> 'The question then arises whether the contribution by all the wrongdoers should be equal or whether the Court should have power to apportion the damages according to the degree of fault.

[29] LCO 2/1967, 15 April 1934 (Gutteridge and McNair to Fletcher (LCO typist)), 2–3.

[30] LCO 2/1967, 17 April 1934.

[31] LCO 2/1967 Amended report of Sub-Committee, dated 16 April 1934.

> We should like to find some way of giving effect to the latter principle, while maintaining the integrity of the rules that a plaintiff is not compelled to join all the tortfeasors and that damages for a joint tort cannot be assessed separately against each defendant (Greenlands v Wilmshurst ...). We regard it as essential that the plaintiff should not suffer any embarrassment by reason of the apportionment between the defendants of the damages, which is purely their own concern; if he were compelled to join all the tortfeasors, he would in many cases suffer serious inconvenience, delay or expense, e.g. where one of them is out of the jurisdiction or evading service; the plaintiff must be allowed to sue one or more of the tortfeasors and recover all his damages against any one whom he may select; after that and subject to that the Court might fairly in our opinion have power to make some apportionment of damages, either equally or upon the principle of the Maritime Conventions Act 1911, Sections 1, 2 & 3.
>
> This last point is hardly within our terms of reference, and we refrain at this stage from elaborating it further. We are however if desired, prepared to examine it again. But in any case we regard it as essential that any amendment of the law should make it clear that a plaintiff need not sue more than one joint tortfeasor and that he can recover his damages in full against any one of them.'[32]

Their comments on *Greenlands* v. *Wilmshurst* were perhaps best seen as based on the concern that the report should not be misunderstood. Clearly, if apportionment were to be introduced, some modification of the rule that damages could not be assessed against individual tortfeasors would have to be made. That was, perhaps, as much as the report intended to say. But the language used was rather loose, and could have been read as going further, as recommending the introduction of several liability. As Gutteridge and McNair pointed out, replacing a system of joint liability with a system of several liability was to replace one injustice with another. Eventually, in the penultimate draft of the report, all reference to *Greenlands* v. *Wilmshurst* would be deleted.

Gutteridge and McNair's comments on the adoption of Admiralty practice, by contrast, could only be seen in terms of a difference of opinion. They were not prepared to endorse either equal division or apportionment according to fault. Nor, evidently, did they agree to the specific suggestion that the Admiralty rule of apportionment according to fault should apply to collisions on land, thereby leaving it open for a different approach to apply to other accidents. Their suggestion that the report should say that the matter was outside the terms of reference was, perhaps, meant as a form of words to hide the disagreement.

[32] LCO 2/1967, 1 May 1934 (Gutteridge to Fletcher).

Gutteridge and McNair's revised amendments were circulated for discussion at a meeting of the full committee two days later. Unfortunately we have no record of what was said at that meeting, but subsequent evidence suggests that there was an inconclusive battle over apportionment. The wording of the draft report was not changed; but three weeks later the Secretary to the Committee was inviting Poole and Mortimer (two solicitors on the Committee) to give their views on apportionment.[33] This they did, in a memorandum arguing strongly against equal divisions between tortfeasors. Their main point was that equal shares were unfair, since the moral culpability of joint tortfeasors might be very different. What was needed, in their view, was a reform that allowed a court the freedom to reflect that moral culpability in its assessment of the damage. They also made a point of disagreeing with Gutteridge and McNair over whether the question was within the Committee's terms of reference: 'In view of the important bearing which this question has upon the whole problem of joint tortfeasors', they wrote, 'it is submitted that an amendment of this rule would be properly within the scope of the terms of reference of the Committee.'[34]

A further Committee meeting was held, which resulted in a further amended draft. The crucial passage now read as follows:

> The question then arises whether the contribution by all the wrongdoers should be equal, or whether the Court should have the power to apportion the liability.
>
> We think that there are many cases where such an apportionment might fairly be made, more particularly it might be desirable to adapt Admiralty practice as to apportionment of contribution if and when apportionment is claimed by one tortfeasor against another. But the apportionment, even to the extent of indemnity, should be left to the decision of the judge. Cf. The Maritime Conventions Act 1911, Sect 3.[35]

Clearly Poole and Mortimer's view had prevailed, both in relation to the terms of reference and, more importantly, in relation to the general principle of apportionment of damage according to fault. The removal of the reference to collisions on land was, it is submitted, particularly fortunate: that suggestion opened up the possibility of a different apportionment regime for traffic accidents without giving any good reason for such special treatment.

33 LCO 2/1967, 28 May 1934 (Foster to Poole and Mortimer).

34 LCO 2/1967 'JOINT TORTFEASORS; Observations on Draft Report', 30 May 1934 (Poole and Mortimer to Foster).

35 LCO 2/1967 Draft marked '4th Draft of Report'.

The other point on which the report underwent significant revision was in its treatment of possible exceptions to the new right of contribution between tortfeasors. In the first draft, the report dealt with situations where the tort was also a crime as follows:

> It would probably not be advisable to introduce any exception merely because the tort is also a crime. To do so would presumably prevent any right to contribution arising where the tort was a libel. Then in the case of an accident caused by the concurrent negligence of two drivers it would, it is submitted, be undesirable to have the question as to whether the driver was guilty of the misdemeanour of driving [*sic*], or of the felony of manslaughter, fought in a civil proceeding between the drivers.[36]

Gutteridge and McNair commented that:

> We accept this view, but we feel that it is not one which will gain immediate acceptance in all quarters and we think the case for it might be put more strongly.
>
> One is tempted, at first sight, to draw a distinction on grounds of public policy, between a crime which is committed wantonly and deliberately and one which is committed inadvertently ... or between a crime which involves a guilty mind and one which does not ... and to permit a right of contribution only in the second alternative in each of these cases. But when one attempts to define the basis of any such distinction, it becomes clearly impossible, so that one is reluctantly driven to regard as the only practicable course the one advocated in the draft Report, namely, to make no exception even in the case of the most serious crimes – even when the plaintiff's causa is turpissima. We suggest that this is a better ground than those advanced in the draft Report. The question of felonious guilt must be determined in civil actions when the defendant or the court takes the point that the plaintiff should prosecute for the felony before suing for the tort.[37]

They went on to suggest a form of words for the report:

> We have considered whether an exception to our recommendation ought not to be made in the case where the tort is also a crime. At first sight public policy might appear to demand that such an exception should be made at any rate when the crime is wanton and deliberate and not merely

[36] LCO 2/1967. The 'misdemeanour of driving' must refer to the offence of reckless or dangerous driving created by s. 11 Road Traffic Act 1930. The difficulty in distinguishing between manslaughter and reckless or dangerous driving was highlighted by s. 34 Road Traffic Act 1934, which permitted a person indicted for manslaughter to be convicted under s. 11 instead. The position is illuminatingly explained by E. Woodward and J. Chambers, *Woodward's Road Traffic Acts and Orders 1930–1934* (London, Eyre & Spottiswoode, 1934) 109–10.

[37] LCO 2/1967, 15 April 1934, 3 (Gutteridge to Fletcher).

> the result of inadvertence. We have, however, come to the conclusion that it is impracticable to draw such a distinction and that any attempt to exclude from our recommendation torts which are also crimes would produce anomalies (such as would result from the fact that libel may be a crime while slander is not) and uncertainties which it would be undesirable to introduce. Accordingly our recommendation is made without qualification.[38]

The next draft of the report incorporated that suggestion word for word,[39] adding as an example of an anomaly that negligent driving might sometimes amount to a felony. That was how the report would remain in its final form. There was a certain irony about it being the academic members of the Committee who made the point about how the rule would operate in practice. But, as we have seen already, those involved with the Law Revision Committee rarely operated within the parameters that their official role or status implied.

III

The Committee reported in July 1934; three months later Schuster was pressing Ram to start work on a Bill.[40] It was clear from the outset that both men contemplated that, as with the *actio personalis* legislation, there would be consultation. But they were not, perhaps, in complete agreement over how extensive that consultation should be. Ram wrote to Schuster mentioning 'the usual consultation and correspondence with *some* of the members of the Law Revision Committee';[41] Schuster replied that 'the members of the Committee will no doubt want to discuss the Clauses'.[42] Ram, however, responded that 'I hope that when I have had time to prepare a draft some members of the Committee will give me the benefit of their criticisms'.[43] Even after preparation of the Bill had been delayed by the pressure of other work, and Schuster was referring to the Lord Chancellor being 'now extremely anxious'[44] to get things moving, there was no question of abandoning the consultation process. As Ram pointed out, the style of the Committee's report meant that 'a great deal will have to be done in working out details which the Committee naturally regarded

[38] LCO 2/1967, 3–4. [39] LCO 2/1967, marked as 2nd Draft.

[40] LCO 2/1976 Law Revision Committee. Legislation to give effect to the Third Interim Report of the Law Revision Committee relating to the doctrine of no contribution between tort-feasors. 15 October 1934 (Schuster to Ram).

[41] LCO 2/1976, 18 October 1934 (Ram to Schuster) (emphasis added).

[42] LCO 2/1976, 19 October 1934 (Schuster to Ram).

[43] LCO 2/1976, 14 November 1934 (Ram to Schuster).

[44] LCO 2/1976, 1 March 1935 (Schuster to Ram).

as outside their functions'.[45] Further Committee involvement was indispensable if the Bill was to achieve what the Committee wanted.

Readers will perhaps not be surprised to learn that, even before a first draft of the Bill existed, Gutteridge and McNair had been lined up to comment on it.[46] But they might be surprised to learn that Ram was not even prepared to show the Bill to anyone else until he had received Gutteridge and McNair's comments.[47] The two academics had now become so central to the process that it was felt that no progress could be made without their input. Just how important Gutteridge and McNair had become can be seen in a covering letter that Ram set to Schuster with copies of a revised draft Bill:

> I enclose six copies of a draft of the Torts Bill which has been revised in the light of observations sent me by Gutteridge, McNair and Master Valentine Ball.
>
> You will notice that the revised draft contains new provisions which were not in the earlier draft, namely, subsections (3), (4) and (5) of clause 1, and clause 2. These are all points which have occurred to me personally and my 'commentators' have not yet had an opportunity of considering them.[48]

This was, in effect, to split the Bill into two – the approved and the unapproved. Unapproved material was, Ram wanted to make clear, subject to change. Quite how much it was subject to change was illustrated by the fate of Ram's new material. Clause 1(5) introduced statutory definitions, which were evidently found unobjectionable by the commentators. Clauses 1(3),[49] 1(4)[50] and 2,[51] however, which Ram had flagged as his own unaided work, did not

45 LCO 2/1976, 8 March 1935 (Ram to Schuster).

46 LCO 2/1976, 25 March 1935 (Schuster to Gutteridge).

47 LCO 2/1977 Law Revision Committee. Legislation giving effect to the *Third Report* ... and the *Fourth Report*. 18 April 1935 (Ram to Schuster): 'I thought it well not to trouble you with the draft until I have received the observations of Gutteridge and McNair with regard to it.'

48 LCO 2/1976, 13 May 1935 (Ram to Schuster).

49 'Where judgment is given against any tort-feasor entitled to recover contribution under this section any sums ordered to be paid by any person by way of contribution shall, unless otherwise ordered by the court, be a debt due from that person to the person entitled to recover under the judgment and not to the tort-feasor entitled to the contribution; and the amount recoverable under the judgment shall be reduced by an amount equal to the sums so paid.' LCO 2/1976, 13 May 1935.

50 'An order directing any tort-feasor to make contribution in respect of any damage or exempting any tort-feasor from his liability to make contribution in respect thereof shall be a bar to any action against that tortfeasor in respect of that damage.' *Ibid.*

51 'Where in any action judgment is given against two or more tort-feasors liable in respect of the same damage (whether as joint tort-feasors or otherwise) the court shall, subject as herein provided, have power to apportion between those tort-feasors the amount of

escape unscathed. There is no record of Gutteridge and McNair's comments, but their general gist can be gathered from Ram's reply:

> you will see that in the revised draft I have cut out altogether what used to be subsections (3) and (4) of Clause 1 and the whole of Clause 2. I feel I ought to apologise for having troubled you with these rather jejune provisions. They were put in at a time when I was much pressed with other work, and on reflection I have come to the conclusion that they ought not to have been there at all.[52]

This almost grovelling apology, coupled with excuses, tells us several interesting things. Clearly Gutteridge and McNair had not felt the need to hold back in criticising the draftsman's efforts; it was difficult to believe that they could be the same people who, a year earlier, had told Schuster it was 'probably not [their] business'[53] to criticise Bills. Furthermore, it was clear that their trenchant criticism was not resented or considered inappropriate; on the contrary, it was welcomed. Third, there was an odd contrast with their role in the Law Revision Committee. As we have seen, as members of the Committee they made various suggestions for reform that were not adopted in the final report; as unofficial consultants to the draftsman, however, their word was law. That no one else enjoyed such special influence was highlighted by a letter from Somervell (the Solicitor General) to Ram, in which Somervell mentioned that in relation to the 1934 Act one of the members of the Law Revision Committee had 'suggested ... that it would be useful if they were allowed or asked to consider the draft Bill at some stage in the proceedings'.[54] This, Somervell thought, was a good idea. Ram's slightly evasive reply was that 'some, at least, of the members of the Committee'[55] had been consulted.

the damages awarded, having regard to the extent of their respective responsibilities for the damage, and to exempt any of them from liability to pay the whole or any part of that amount: Provided that if at any time the court is satisfied that default has been made by any of those tort-feasors in paying the amount payable by him under any such apportionment as aforesaid, the court shall have power to make such fresh apportionment between any of the other tort-feasors (including any previously exempted from liability) as may be found by the court to be just and equitable.' *Ibid.*

[52] LCO 2/1977, 24 May 1935 (Ram to Gutteridge).

[53] See Chapter 10, n. 27.

[54] LCO 2/1977, 9 May 1935 (Somervell to Ram).

[55] LCO 2/1977, 10 May 1935.

IV

The draft Bill on contribution between tortfeasors was combined with a Bill to implement the Law Revision Committee's proposals on the legal position of married women.[56] The provisions on contribution were in the form in which they ultimately passed into law, and attracted very little parliamentary attention, none of it critical.[57] Intriguingly, though, behind the scenes things were less than serene. The first hint of trouble came in a letter from Lord Hanworth to the Lord Chancellor the day after the Bill had been introduced into the House of Lords. The typed part of Hanworth's letter merely congratulated the Lord Chancellor on the introduction of the Bill; but in manuscript he had added, 'Let me know if you hear of any possible objectors beginning with the first letter of the alphabet in sequence!', and had marked the letter 'Personal'.[58] Less than a week later, a letter from Schuster to Ram revealed to whom Hanworth had been cryptically alluding: 'Atkin, I understand, intends to move an amendment relating to the tort feasors part relating to criminal responsibility, but we shall certainly oppose this and be able to defeat it.'[59] Schuster sounded confident. But his confidence was shattered when Hanworth revealed that he planned to table an amendment to change the Bill's current title from Law Reform (Miscellaneous Provisions) Bill to something more informative.[60] Schuster wrote to the Lord Chancellor from Lord Wright's country home in a state of some agitation:

> Hanworth's amendment is very inopportune. He has had all the drafts of the Bill and could have taken the point at any time.
>
> The present title is cumbrous and there seems to be no reason why it should not be changed. But if the amendment is made in Committee there must be a Report stage; we shall lose time, and present a flank to Atkin.[61]

Hanworth, however, did not delay. He successfully moved his amendment, but the anticipated attack from Lord Atkin did not materialise. Once again, the parliamentary passage of a law reform Bill had turned out to be a formality.

56 Law Revision Committee, *Fourth Interim Report*, Cmd 4770 (1934).

57 E.g. Major Milner, Hansard's Parliamentary Debates, Fifth Series, House of Commons, vol. 304, col. 120: 'a very useful alteration in the law' (8 July 1935); this was the only comment made by the House of Commons on the contribution provisions.

58 LCO 2/1977, 1 June 1935 (Hanworth to Hailsham).

59 LCO 2/1977, 6 June 1935 (Schuster to Ram).

60 LCO 2/1977, 14 June 1935 (Hanworth to Schuster).

61 LCO 2/1977, 14 June 1935 (Schuster to Hailsham).

The subsequent history of the contribution provisions in the Law Reform (Married Women and Tortfeasors) Act 1935 was relatively untroubled. The main point of controversy related to the Court of Appeal's powers to alter the levels of apportionment fixed by trial courts. This was quickly resolved by following the approach taken to apportionment in Admiralty cases:[62] namely, alteration should only occur where there had clearly been some mistake.[63] Rather more troubling were signs that judges were approaching apportionment inconsistently. Denning J felt able to make a broad apportionment under the statute;[64] Hilbery J, however, insisted that a narrower approach, focussed more on causation, was required, and apportioned liability equally despite widely differing degrees of fault in the two tortfeasors were concerned.[65] Perhaps the broad language of the statute made such individual differences of approach inevitable; but it was a pity that, the point having been thrashed out in the Law Revision Committee, it then had to be thrashed out again in the courts and the textbooks.[66] Perhaps if Poole and Mortimer (the architects of the proposal that apportionment should be linked to fault) had been consulted by the draftsman, some more emphatic form of statutory language might have been found.

[62] *British Fame (Owners)* v. *Macgregor (Owners), The Macgregor* [1943] AC 197, disapproving a wider approach taken in *The Testbank* [1942] P 75.

[63] *Ingram* v. *United Automobile Service, Limited* [1943] 1 KB 612.

[64] *Whitby* v. *Burt, Boulton and Hayward Limited* [1947] 1 KB 918.

[65] *Collins* v. *Hertfordshire County Council* [1947] 1 KB 598.

[66] E.g. P. Winfield, *A Text-book of the Law of Tort*, 4th edn (London, Sweet & Maxwell, 1948) 172: 'It seems reasonable to regard "responsibility" [in the Act] as referring to the moral accountability of a person, and, indeed, that is one of the meanings given in the English dictionary.' That Winfield was responding to *Collins* v. *Hertfordshire County Council* can be seen from the fact that this passage did not appear in earlier editions of his book (see, e.g., 3rd edn (London, Sweet & Maxwell, 1946) 168).

12

Husbands

It is to be hoped that the value of an Act will not be measured by the length of the discussion concerning it in Parliament.

J. F.

I

A husband's liability for his wife's torts had attracted the attention of law reformers long before the subject was considered by the Law Revision Committee in 1934. The common law position was that under the doctrine of coverture, when a woman married her existence became merged with that of her husband. He became owner of her property; if she was sued in tort, her husband had to be joined as a party; and he was liable to pay damages. It might have been possible to interpret the Married Women's Property Act 1882 as abolishing the husband's liability, since it provided that a married woman was liable for her own torts, and her husband 'need not' be joined in any proceedings against her. As we saw in Chapter 4, however, the courts took a more cautious approach. 'Need not', they said, was not the same as 'may not': it followed that the 1882 Act had left open the option for husbands to be joined in proceedings for torts committed by their wives.

The decision of the House of Lords in *Edwards* v. *Porter*[1] settled, as a matter of authority, that the 1882 Act had not abolished a husband's liability for his wife's torts. Almost immediately there were moves to reverse the decision by legislation. Lord Danesfort, whom we have already seen taking a keen interest in law reform,[2] put down a question for debate in the House of Lords that asked 'whether in view of the wide legislative

[1] [1925] AC 1.

[2] See Chapter 10 pp. 264–7 on the Law Reform (Miscellaneous Provisions) Act 1934 and the pedestrians' no-fault liability scheme discussed on p. 207, the campaign for which was led by Danesfort.

changes that have been made in recent years in the status and rights of married women [the government] will appoint a Select Committee to consider the state of the law concerning the liabilities of a married man in respect of the torts and debts of his wife'.[3] A letter from Danesfort to the Lord Chancellor revealed that he did not really have a Select Committee in mind. 'The general opinion in favour of a change in the law on this point', he wrote, 'appears to be so unanimous, that possibly you may not think it necessary to have any enquiry on the subject by Select Committee or otherwise – & I need hardly say that if you shd find it possible to introduce early legislation on the point, I should be completely satisfied.'[4]

Danesfort's wish was granted. Just over a week after the Lords' debate on the motion for a Select Committee, Sir Claud Schuster was writing to the parliamentary draftsman about a Bill to abolish a husband's liability for his wife's torts. The Lord Chancellor 'thinks that this can be done in a one Clause Bill', said Schuster.[5]

A one-clause Bill was duly drafted. It provided as follows:

(1) The husband of a married woman shall not as such be liable to be sued or be made a party to any action or legal proceeding brought against her in respect of any tort committed by her, whether before or after the marriage; …
(2) … a husband or wife shall be entitled to sue the other for a tort.

An accompanying note from the draftsman highlighted that this brevity had come at a cost. Of the five points he raised, two would have continuing significance. First, there was the question of how exactly to pinpoint the liability that was being abolished. 'The husband must of course be liable for his wife if she acted as his agent, or if they were joint tortfeasors. It is submitted that the words "as such" would be sufficient to keep alive this liability.' Second, there was the scope of the reform. Subsection (2) permitted actions between spouses, but the draftsman was not sure whether this was desired by the Lord Chancellor.

The second point was dealt with quickly: the Lord Chancellor did *not* want to allow spouses to sue each other. Subsection (2) was therefore removed. As for how best to pinpoint the liability being abolished, the draftsman's suggestion was approved, and the 'as such' formulation was incorporated into the Married Women (Torts) Bill 1925. Progress, however, then stalled. The Bill was dropped after its second reading in

[3] LCO 2/777 Married Women (Torts) Bill 1925; question dated 6 May 1925.
[4] LCO 2/777, 2 May 1925. [5] LCO 2/777, 14 May 1925.

the House of Commons in December 1925; the explanation given was that there was too much other competing business.[6] A Bill in identical terms dated 1930 was produced; but that, too, went nowhere. By October 1933 the Law Society, having previously expressed concerns about the measure, was lobbying for its reintroduction.[7] In these circumstances it was, perhaps, strictly unnecessary to refer the point to the Law Revision Committee – the problem seemed to be one of political prioritisation more than anything else – but the Lord Chancellor may have felt that a Committee report would give the reform a new momentum.

II

The Law Revision Committee's report duly recommended the abolition of a husband's liability for his wife's torts.[8] As it recognised, the 'real questions' for it to consider were whether the changes introduced by the married women's property legislation should be carried further, so as to assimilate 'the position of the married woman to that of a man'.[9] Much of the report was given to explaining the historical background, and when it came to the crucial question of reform, the analysis was almost perfunctory. The key case was, of course, *Edwards* v. *Porter*, in which the House of Lords had held by a majority that a husband's liability for his wife's torts was not affected by the married women's property legislation. 'We', said the report's authors, 'respectfully agree with [the minority] view, and, in any case, think that the day has now come when a married woman should alone answer for her own liabilities, whether in contract or in tort, as if she were not married.'[10] 'It is not necessary', the report continued:

> for us to decide whether the explanation of the rule adopted by the majority in *Edwards* v. *Porter* is to be found in the fact that formerly the wife's property vested in her husband, or, as Viscount Cave preferred to say, in *Edwards* v. *Porter* ... '*in that legal unity between husband and wife which existed when the rule was formulated, and which in those days rendered it inconceivable to a lawyer that a married woman should sue or be sued alone*', or whether the explanation is to be found elsewhere. Whatever

[6] I. Kerman, *The Reform of the Law of Married Women Having Particular Regard to their Husbands and Creditors; A Paper Read at the Provincial Meeting of the Law Society held at Oxford on the 26th and 27th September 1933* (London, Solicitors' Law Stationery Society Limited, 1933) 8.

[7] LCO 2/777. Contrast the letters of 10 July 1925 and 24 October 1933.

[8] Law Revision Committee, *Fourth Interim Report*, Cmd 4770, 1934.

[9] *Ibid*., para. 4.

[10] *Ibid*., para. 14.

> may be the explanation, we are of opinion that it should now be made clear by legislation that a husband, as such, is under no liability for his wife's torts.[11]

The report's mild-mannered detachment in this crucial passage was the product of careful consideration. Until its final draft, the report's tone had been more impatient. Earlier drafts had stated that 'the day is passed when a married woman should answer for her own liabilities'. This implicit rebuke to Parliament and the courts was only toned down to 'the day has now come …' at the last moment.[12] The earliest drafts also took a more confident line with the common law rules, including the following sentence:

> In old days when in law her husband acquired actually or potentially all her property, the position may have been different. But now this is no longer the law; she has her own property, cessante ratione legis cessat ipsa lex.[13]

In later drafts this was replaced with the more neutral position that it was 'not necessary' to identify the common law rationale for a husband's tort liability.[14] A note on the draft attributes this alteration to A. D. McNair. Unfortunately it gives no indication of McNair's thinking; but one obvious explanation would be the desire to avoid a technical debate about the historical foundations of the common law doctrine. McNair may have felt that incautious generalisations about the basis for the rule could encourage attacks on the reform proposal itself. Blandness and diffidence were less likely to provoke objections.

The report did not confine itself to a husband's liability for his wife's torts. It also, as required by its terms of reference, considered 'the form of judgment in *Scott* v. *Morley*'.[15] This was essentially a point about a married woman being liable only to the extent of her 'separate property', the latter concept being defined in the married women's property legislation. The Committee proposed to do away with the concept of 'separate property' altogether, and to make a married woman subject to the same legal processes – including bankruptcy – that were available against men and

[11] *Ibid.*, para. 15.

[12] LCO 29/46 Law Revision Committee Fourth Interim Report (Married Women's Liability) Signed Copy, where the amendment is made in manuscript.

[13] LCO 2/1969 Liability of husband for wife's torts. Report second draft page 9 (dated July 1934).

[14] LCO 2/1969 Report third draft (dated October 1934) inserts the passage beginning 'It is not necessary …'.

[15] *Scott* v. *Morley* (1887) 20 QBD 120.

unmarried women.[16] Had the report stopped there, it would have dutifully carried out its task as defined by its terms of reference; but it went further in two respects. First, it proposed the abolition of restraints on anticipation; second, it suggested that the rule that a husband was liable to pay tax on his wife's income should be revisited.

The first of these additional topics was relatively esoteric, but symbolically significant. Restraints on anticipation were used when property was settled on a married woman; they prevented the woman from disposing of the property, or income accruing from it, during her marriage, or from charging the property with liabilities falling due in the future. The doctrine applied only to married women, and the Committee regarded it as objectionable for a variety of reasons, including its unmeritorious deployment against creditors and, 'incidentally', its potential to prevent a woman raising capital for her own purposes.[17] The proposal was that future use of such restraints should be prohibited by statute.[18]

In relation to income tax, the Committee realised that it could not make a firm proposal – since the matter fell outside its terms of reference – but that did not deter it from discussing the point. 'If a married woman is to be placed', it said:

> in respect of her property and her contractual liability, in the same position as a feme sole [i.e. single woman], it is at least worthy of consideration whether the hardship, which in some cases now falls upon a husband in respect of his wife's income, should not be obviated by repealing the proviso to rule 16 of the General Rules under the Income Tax Act 1918 … whereby the '*profits*' of a married woman living with her husband are deemed to be the '*profits*' of the husband and are assessed and charged in his name and not in the name of the wife.[19]

This passage was a very late addition to the report.[20] Both it and the analysis of restraints on anticipation reflected a dissatisfaction with the piecemeal implementation of a principle of gender equality. That dissatisfaction may well have been inspired by an extraordinarily persuasive memorandum that had been submitted – unsolicited – by the Equal Rights Committee, an umbrella group of women's organisations. As the covering letter explained, 'The Memorandum … expresses the view that any change in the law dealing with torts should only by dealt with along

[16] Law Revision Committee, *Fourth Interim Report*, Cmd. 4770, 1934, paras. 16–19.

[17] *Ibid.*, paras. 20–1. [18] *Ibid.*, para. 22. [19] *Ibid.*, para. 24.

[20] LCO 29/46. The passage is added in manuscript at p. 9, with a note at p. 12 indicating where it should be inserted.

with other changes in the law relating to married women.'[21] The memorandum itself not only expressed that view, it also provided compelling reasons to adopt it.

The memorandum began with a powerful critique of a husband's liability for his wife's torts:

> We submit that a married woman should be put in exactly the same position as a man or a single woman with respect to any wrong she may do and her husband should cease to be liable for her torts. It is unjust that he should be made to pay damages for a wrong done by another and for which he is in no way responsible, for example, for his wife's libel or for her negligence which has damaged a third party. And it is treating a woman disrespectfully to make another, her husband, liable for her wrongful acts as if she were his horse or his dog. This attitude to the married woman is obsolete, and the law which gives effect to it should be abolished.[22]

This abolition was not, however, sufficient in itself. It should be accompanied by the abolition of any rules preventing the enforcement of a judgment against a married woman. In particular, bankruptcy laws should apply to married women in the same way as they applied to men, and restraints on anticipation should be prohibited. The arguments against restraints on anticipation were of two kinds. First, the restraint 'is a means by which the married woman can escape responsibility and evade her obligations'.[23] Second:

> The restraint is a disadvantage to the woman herself. It makes it impossible for her even when she is a rich woman to make contracts with respect to property affected by it. It limits her power to go into business and to help her family as she thinks desirable. And it makes her a troublesome and sometimes dangerous person to do business with.[24]

Finally, the memorandum argued that any legislation should expressly abolish the common law doctrine of coverture. 'We see in the responsibility of a husband for the torts of his wife', it concluded, 'an acceptance of the doctrine that the personality of the wife is merged in that of her husband – a doctrine we repudiate.'[25]

It is impossible to ignore the similarities between the Equal Rights Committee's memorandum and the Law Revision Committee's report. Both emphasised the procedural consequences that must flow from

[21] LCO 2/1969, 29 June 1934. [22] LCO 2/1969 MEMORANDUM, 1.
[23] LCO 2/1969 MEMORANDUM, 2. [24] LCO 2/1969 MEMORANDUM, 3.
[25] LCO 2/1969 MEMORANDUM, 5.

abolishing the husband's tort liability. Both also emphasised that there were two distinct grounds to object to restraints on anticipation, although where the memorandum gave equal weight to the interests of creditors and the financial autonomy of married women, the report emphasised the former and regarded the later as an 'incidental' point. Perhaps most importantly, both expressed the sense that husbands' tort liability had to be seen as part of a wider picture, not as a distinct issue in itself.

On the other hand, there were certain striking differences between the memorandum and the report. One can be seen by contrasting their recommendations: the report was not prepared to call for the abolition of the underlying common law principle of merger. There is nothing to suggest that the Law Revision Committee ever even considered the possibility; if they did, they might well have been daunted by the sheer number of instances where the principle had generated distinct rules of law.[26] A second, more fundamental difference was one of perspective. It is hinted at in the contrasting emphases given to the arguments against restraints on anticipation, but comes through most clearly in the analysis of husbands' tort liability. The early draft of the report, as we have seen, had argued that abolition of a husband's tort liability was appropriate because whereas 'in old days' the husband had control over his wife's property and could therefore pay damages for her torts out of that property, he now had no such rights. This was an argument about fairness to *the husband*. Later drafts of the report took a more neutral position, but never came close to acknowledging the wife's perspective, namely, that it was treating a woman 'disrespectfully', as if she were a dog, to make her husband liable for her torts. The Equal Rights Committee's memorandum would be one of the very few voices articulating what the legal rules implied about the status of women; no other source would manage to do so with such dispassion and precision.

III

The transition from report to Bill was characterised by political manoeuvring and the influence of external consultants. Within a couple of weeks of giving instructions for the drafting of a Bill, Sir Claud Schuster was turning his mind to potential political obstacles and, in particular, to securing the support of female Members of Parliament. His overtures to Marjorie Graves MP were welcomed, but what Graves told him about

[26] G. Williams, 'The Legal Unity of Husband and Wife' (1947) 10 *MLR* 16.

her female colleagues caused him some disquiet. According to Schuster's memorandum of their meeting, Graves:

> thought that the attempts made or threatened by the Advanced Women's Groups should not be taken very seriously. They exercise no influence in the House of Commons. She herself realised and the other Members, with the exception of Lady Astor and Miss Rathbone, would also realise that some of the matters put forward by the Advanced women were outside the scope of the Report, and that others, though possibly within the scope, were best left alone since it would be impossible to obtain unanimity upon them.[27]

This created a dilemma, which Schuster placed before the Lord Chancellor: should all women MPs be invited to discuss the reform with the Lord Chancellor, or should only five or six of the less volatile Members be included? Graves' instinct was to pursue the latter course, and take the risk of antagonising those who were not invited; but Schuster was apprehensive:

> I told her that this seemed to me to raise a great difficulty. It was necessary for us to assure the Whips that the Bill would not arouse controversy or take up time. We could not do this if we knew that Lady Astor and Miss Rathbone would oppose on the ground that it did not go far enough. Miss Graves thought that it was just possible that some influence might be brought to bear on Lady Astor, but she thought Miss Rathbone beyond all argument.[28]

The Lord Chancellor opted to include all women MPs in his invitation. In the event Lady Astor was unable to attend, and Schuster was able to report that the MPs 'showed a very reasonable spirit in discussing the proposals'.[29] But it was not all plain sailing. There was some 'not very forcible criticism' that the abolition of restraints on anticipation was not retrospective, although 'even Miss Rathbone indicated that she saw the difficulties and would not press the matter'. 'But', continued Schuster, 'she asked whether it would not be possible somewhat to simplify the method whereby the Court exercises its power to lift the restraint under section 169 of the Law of Property Act 1925.' This section gave courts the power to set aside restraints on anticipation 'if [the court] thinks fit, where it appears to the court to be for her benefit … with her consent'. The Lord

[27] LCO 2/1977 'MEMORANDUM', 23 January 1935.
[28] LCO 2/1977 'MEMORANDUM', p. 2.
[29] LCO 2/1977 Letter from Schuster to Lord Hanworth MR dated 20 February 1935.

Chancellor promised to look into the point, and Schuster sought guidance from Lord Hanworth MR (as the Law Revision Committee's Chairman).

The question was evidently referred to Romer LJ (who had been a member of the subcommittee that drafted the report).[30] He professed himself to be baffled by Rathbone's query:

> I do not understand in what respect Miss Rathbone thinks the method requires simplification. For so far as the method goes it is simplification itself. Nor is the expense incurred in getting the power exercised at all out of the way in view of the fact that it is the Court that has to exercise the power, and that it will only do so upon a full and frank statement of the circumstances of the particular case before it ... I should imagine ... that [Rathbone] would like to see the powers of the Court in relation to binding the married woman's interest somewhat extended in favour of the married woman's creditors ... I would, however, in this connection point out that, as section 169 of the Law of Property Act 1925 now stands, the power of the Court can only be exercised with the consent of the married woman. It may be considered desirable to amend the law in this respect, and let the Court, in future, be the sole judge of what is for her benefit. Except for this I cannot think that the section requires any alteration.[31]

Romer's comments prompted an immediate response from Schuster to Hanworth:

> In all the circumstances, the Lord Chancellor thinks that the wisest course will be not to embody in the Bill any proposal empowering the Court to act without the woman's consent. He greatly doubts whether Miss Rathbone would understand the point. Probably both she and the left wing women, with whom she sometimes acts, would regard such a provision as an aggravation of the situation. They look not to practical matters but to theory; and in theory they will say, why is the woman to be thus subjected to the will of the Court when the man is not. This is, of course, a childish observation, but that is no reason why they should not make it.[32]

Schuster then wrote to Rathbone, assuring her that the Lord Chancellor 'has consulted those who are best fitted to advise him with respect to the practice of the Chancery Division ... and he is assured that, so far as the method goes, it is simplification itself'.[33]

[30] LCO 2/1969. The other subcommittee members (listed on the file) were Wright, Goddard, Poole, Schuster and McNair.

[31] LCO 2/1977 Memorandum from Romer LJ enclosed in a letter from Lord Hanworth MR to Lord Sankey LC, dated 19 March 1935.

[32] LCO 2/1977, 20 March 1935.

[33] LCO 2/1977, 20 March 1935.

What immediately catches the eye in this exchange of correspondence is Schuster's obnoxious and patronising attitude towards 'left wing women'. Underlying – and supporting – that attitude was a manifest failure by both Schuster and Romer to grasp the broader point that Rathbone was making, for her point about simplifying the process under s. 169 was clearly being made in the context of a woman's right to control and dispose of her own property. The kind of simplification she had in mind was surely along the lines of giving greater (perhaps, even, generally decisive) weight to a woman's desire to be able to deal freely with her own assets. Romer LJ's comments made it very clear that he did not see the issue in those terms at all, hence his observation that 'I should imagine … that she would like to see the powers of the court in relation to binding the married woman's interest somewhat extended in favour of the married woman's creditors'. That was, of course, true in a sense, but it was a way of stating the question that completely eliminated the importance of the woman's autonomy. Similarly, Romer LJ's suggested change in the law, which rendered the woman's wishes irrelevant and left matters exclusively to the judgment of the court, would have been anathema to Rathbone. Schuster was surely wide of the mark when he said that she would not have understood the point – she would have understood it, and grasped its ideological implications, only too well. Indeed, both Romer LJ and Schuster showed such an almost implausible lack of understanding of Rathbone's basic position that it is tempting to wonder whether they were not being deliberately obtuse.

Other consultants' suggestions fared better. As soon as a draft Bill was ready, the draftsman sent it to Gutteridge and McNair in Cambridge. The draft clause dealing with a husband's tort liability stated that:

> the husband of a married woman shall not as such be liable –
> (a) for any tort committed by her … otherwise than as his agent, whether committed … before or after the marriage; or
> (b) to be sued or made a party to any legal proceeding brought in respect of any such tort.[34]

This provision was very similar to the Married Women (Torts) Bill of 1925, and perhaps owed something to the Law Revision Committee's statement that 'a husband, as such, is under no liability for his wife's torts'.[35] Gutteridge and McNair, however, expressed their unease about

[34] LCO 2/1977 Bill enclosed with letter dated 9 April 1935 from Granville Ram to Schuster.

[35] Law Revision Committee, *Fourth Interim Report*, Cmd. 4770, 1934, para. 15.

the section, 'and in particular the words "as such"'.[36] The draftsman was quick to act. When he circulated a second draft Bill, the clause had been altered to read:

> the husband of a married woman shall not, by reason only of his being her husband, be liable –
> (a) in respect of any tort committed by her whether before or after the marriage ...; or
> (b) to be sued, or made a party to any legal proceeding brought, in respect of any such tort.

That was the final form that the legislation would take. The draftsman also attached a table, setting out Gutteridge and McNair's comments in the left-hand column and his own responses on the right. Against the comments on the section dealing with husbands' tort liability, he had written 'I have derived much assistance from the points raised'. Gutteridge and McNair's critique had again been an acknowledged and indispensable part of the reform process.

IV

In obtaining Cabinet approval to bring forward a Bill to abolish husbands' liability, the Lord Chancellor had assured his colleagues that 'the Bill could be regarded as non-controversial'.[37] The Bill's reception in both Houses of Parliament bore out that description. In the House of Lords, the Earl of Listowel welcomed the Bill unreservedly:

> It is a very great relief, I think, to all married men – and I speak for them because I am a married man myself – to know that they will no longer be liable to legal proceedings if their wife's dog attacks a harmless stranger in the street, if in casual conversation she casts an aspersion on an acquaintance which is regarded as cause for a slander case, or equally if, in writing in a letter or newspaper, she introduces some remark which makes her subject to a case of libel. It is a very great relief to all married men, I think, to have that weight removed from their minds, and I speak in their name, regardless of the Party to which they may belong when I voice their gratitude.[38]

There was no other comment on the substantive provisions of the Bill. The House of Commons took a similar line, with only one MP querying

[36] LCO 2/1977 Notes attached to draft Bill, with covering letter dated 8 May 1935.

[37] LCO 2/1977, 14 May 1935.

[38] LCO 2/1978 HL Deb., 5 June 1935, cols. 303–4.

whether the law offered sufficient protection to married women.[39] Perhaps what was most striking about the debate in the Commons was the fact that no female Member of Parliament spoke. That might, perhaps, be seen as vindicating Schuster's strategy of consulting female MPs in advance, and thereby neutralising any opposition in Parliament. In any case, the fact that the consultation had taken place, and had been well attended, showed that the absence of female speakers in the debate was not due to their indifference to the reforms being proposed.

To observers not privy to the Lord Chancellor's efforts behind the scenes, however, the anodyne parliamentary proceedings were troubling. Pollock objected, in the tenth edition of his *Principles of Contract*, that the Act had been passed without discussion. This drew from an anonymous reviewer in *The Bell Yard* the response that:

> This comment is unusual and obscure, but it will be remembered that Lord Hanworth's Committee issued a report on which the Act was based. It may seem a recommendation that an Act was passed as the result of the proposals of a small but expert body instead of being subjected to last minute and ill-informed amendments.[40]

The reviewer concluded with the sentence used as an epigraph to this chapter: 'It is to be hoped that the value of an Act will not be measured by the length of the discussion concerning it in Parliament.'

The review was signed only with the initials 'J. F.'; it is virtually certain to have been written by John Foster, who was one of the editors of the journal in which it appeared[41] and who, as the Secretary to the Law Revision Committee, would have been particularly attentive to comments on the Committee's reforms. His review highlighted certain characteristic features of the law reform process, which were not confined to the husbands' liability proposals. The key point was that Parliament's role was being marginalised; indeed, any parliamentary amendments were seen as an impertinent interference with the work of the real law-makers, that is, the experts who manned the law reform committees and the Lord Chancellor's Office. The quality and coherence of legislation might be protected as a result; but the problem – as Pollock sensed – was that everything took place off-stage. In a reform such as the abolition of husbands' tort liability this was particularly unfortunate. For, despite the reform

[39] LCO 2/1978 HC Deb. 8 July 1935 col. 124 (Mr Caporn).

[40] (1936) 18 *Bell Yard* 44. Pollock's comments were in F. Pollock, *Principles of Contract*, 10th edn (London, Stevens, 1936) vii, 85.

[41] (1936) 18 *Bell Yard* 1.

itself being technical, its ideological implications for the status and autonomy of married women were hugely significant. Yet there was nowhere in the reform process, as it was being managed by the Lord Chancellor's Office, where those points could be publicly made.

We might conclude this examination of the abolition of husbands' tort liability by reflecting that even the title of the statute concealed its real effect. As originally introduced, the Bill was entitled 'Law Reform (Miscellaneous Provisions)', which was uninformative rather than misleading. But an amendment by Lord Hanworth changed the title so as to introduce the reference to 'Married Women'. It was true that the Bill did contain provisions concerning married women,[42] but the central reform was all about married *men*, as the Earl of Listowel had pointed out in the Lords' debate, and textbook writers such as Stallybrass and Winfield would explain to students.[43] Winfield's portrayal of the hardship that the Act was designed to remedy was particularly striking:

> it might well be less expensive for a man to keep a dog with a savage temper than to marry a wife with a venomous tongue; he could kill the animal, he could not even lock up the woman, and while he was not liable for the dog's bites unless he knew its evil disposition, ignorance of his wife's vices was no excuse.[44]

The comparison here between liability for a dog and liability for a wife recalled the criticisms of the law advanced by the Equal Rights Committee in its memorandum to the Law Revision Committee. But where the memorandum pointed out how objectionable it was to impose liability for a wife as if she were a dog, Winfield's perspective emphasised that a husband lacked the legal rights of control – he could not 'even' lock her up – that would justify imposing liability. The reform was sound because it corrected this imbalance between a man's legal rights and his legal liabilities. Winfield, like most of those involved in the reform process, saw this as an Act for husbands in all but name.

[42] Section 1 restated that married women could be sued in tort; section 2 abolished the 'separate property' concept that had been introduced by the married women's property legislation.

[43] W. T. Stallybrass (ed.), *Salmond on the Law of Torts*, 9th edn (London, Sweet & Maxwell, 1936) 73–4; P. H. Winfield, *A Text-Book of the Law of Tort* (London, Sweet & Maxwell, 1937) 110–11.

[44] Winfield, *A Text-Book on the Law of Tort*, 110. The passage was a slightly expanded version of P. H. Winfield, 'The Law of Tort, 1885–1935' (1935) 51 *LQR* 249, 251.

13

Contributory negligence

I

The final topic on tort that the Law Revision Committee considered was contributory negligence. Whilst the initiative to look at the *actio personalis* maxim and contribution between tortfeasors had come from within the Lord Chancellor's Office, the suggestion to examine contributory negligence came from Lord Wright,[1] who was now the Committee's chairman. Wright also proposed recruiting two new Committee members to assist him: Stallybrass (Oxford) and Winfield (Cambridge).[2] Along with Goodhart (who had joined in 1936),[3] Gutteridge and McNair, they constituted a powerful academic faction. Indeed, Gutteridge, McNair and Goodhart were asked to approve the terms of reference,[4] which were settled as follows:

> Whether, and if so, in what respect the doctrine of Contributory Negligence requires modification, and in particular to consider the following enactments bearing upon that doctrine.
>
> (a) In so far as the provisions of the Convention for the Unification of certain Rules of Law respecting Collisions signed at Brussels on the 23rd September, 1910, may permit, the Rule applicable to collisions at sea in Section 1 of the Maritime Conventions Act, 1911.
>
> (b) The Rule contained in Section 6 of the Law Reform (Married Women and Tortfeasors) Act, 1935, regarding contribution between joint tortfeasors.[5]

We have already considered the contribution between tortfeasors rule. The Maritime Conventions Act 1911 s. 1 provided as follows:

1 LCO 2/1989 Law Revision Committee. Extended terms of reference. 2 April 1937 (Wright to Schuster).
2 LCO 2/1989.
3 LCO 2/3565 Law Revision Committee. Personnel of Committee and Terms of Reference 7 July 1936.
4 LCO 2/1989, 10 April 1937 (Foster to Schuster).
5 Law Revision Committee, *Eighth Report (Contributory Negligence)*, Cmd 6032 (1939), 3.

> Where, by the fault of two or more vessels, damage or loss is caused to one or more of those vessels, to their cargoes or freight, or to any property on board, the liability to make good the damage or loss shall be in proportion to the degree in which each vessel was in fault:
>
> Provided that –
>
> (a) if, having regard to all the circumstances of the case, it is not possible to establish different degrees of fault, the liability shall be apportioned equally; and
> (b) nothing in this section shall operate so as to render any vessel liable for any loss or damage to which her fault has not contributed; and
> (c) nothing in this section shall affect the liability of a person under a contract of carriage.

The common theme linking these two statutory provisions was the apportionment of damage according to the fault of the respective parties. The defence of contributory negligence at common law, by contrast, did not allow for apportionment. As the Committee's Report put it (rather archly, since the Committee itself had devised the question it was asked):

> From the mention of these two Acts in the Reference to the Committee it is clear that they are asked to consider whether it would not be advisable that the plaintiff and defendant if both are responsible for causing the damage should, as in Admiralty practice, share the liability in proportion as they are at fault rather than that in accordance with the Common Law Rule neither should be able to recover against the other.[6]

II

On the face of it, the Committee had a simple question to consider: should contributory negligence be a complete or only a partial defence? Behind that simple question, however, lurked a more complicated problem. During the course of the nineteenth and early twentieth centuries the straightforward proposition that contributory negligence was a complete defence had become qualified by refinements concerning when, exactly, a person's lack of care could have been said to 'contribute' to his own damage. The most important refinement had been developed by Parke B in *Bridge* v. *The Grand Junction Railway*[7] and, more famously, in *Davies* v. *Mann*.[8] In *Davies'* case the claimant owned a donkey; he had tied the donkey's forefeet together and then turned it onto a public highway, to

[6] *Ibid.*, 5.
[7] *Bridge* v. *The Grand Junction Railway* (1838) 3 M & W 244.
[8] (1842) 10 M & W 546.

graze at the roadside. The defendant's waggon came along the highway 'at a smartish pace'[9] and knocked the donkey down. Erskine J directed the jury as follows:

> though the act of the plaintiff in leaving the donkey on the highway so fettered as to prevent his getting out of the way of carriages travelling along it, might be illegal, still, if the proximate cause of the injury was attributable to the want of proper conduct on the part of the driver of the waggon, the action was maintainable against the defendant ... if they [i.e., the jury] thought that the accident might have been avoided by the exercise of ordinary care on the part of the driver, to find for the plaintiff.[10]

The jury found for the claimant, awarding 40s damages. The defendant moved for a retrial on the ground of misdirection, but his motion failed. Parke B said:

> the negligence which is to preclude a plaintiff from recovering in an action of this nature, must be such as that he could, by ordinary care, have avoided the consequence of the defendant's negligence.[11]

Gurney and Rolfe BB concurred; Lord Abinger CB gave judgment in similar terms.

The decision in *Davies* v. *Mann* set out a rule that was to attract both extensive and repeated judicial analysis. Some of that analysis would be prompted by the difficulty of comparing its rather odd factual situation with other, more orthodox events such as collisions between ships.[12] But there was also an ambiguity about the decision that went right to the core of the defence of contributory negligence: was *Davies* v. *Mann* setting out a special rule for cases of contributory negligence, or was it applying the general principles of causation to these particular facts? There was support for the former interpretation in Parke B's allusion to 'an action of this nature'; but, on the other hand, the direction to the jury, which Parke B had approved, spoke of 'proximate cause'. If the case really was an application of the general principles of causation, those principles were being used in quite a striking way – in particular, they seemed to be allowing very little scope for any idea of concurrent causes. That might be justified by a desire to avoid the harsh consequences of a claimant losing his action

[9] (1842) 10 M & W 546, 547. [10] (1842) 10 M & W 546, 547.

[11] (1842) 10 M & W 546, 548–9.

[12] E.g. *Boy Andrew (Owners)* v. *St Rognvald (Owners) (The Boy Andrew)* [1948] AC 140: 'One may well ask: Which of these two vessels corresponds to the hobbled donkey?' (per Viscount Simon at 149).

completely; but it was hardly a convincing piece of legal analysis on its own terms.

As the nineteenth century wore on, it became clear that other consequences might flow from viewing contributory negligence as an aspect of causation. For instance, since the burden of proof of causation was on the claimant, it could be said that, therefore, the burden of proof in respect of contributory negligence must also be on the claimant. The House of Lords rejected the Court of Appeal's attempt to introduce this principle, saying that contributory negligence was a defence, and the burden of proving defences was on defendants.[13] Similarly, in *Radley* v. *London and North Western Railway Company*[14] Lord Penzance seemed to be making the point that contributory negligence was more than a mere matter of causation when he said that: 'though the Plaintiff may have been guilty of negligence, and although that negligence may, in fact, have contributed to the accident, yet if the Defendant could in the result, by the exercise of ordinary care and diligence, have avoided the mischief which happened, the Plaintiff's negligence will not excuse him.'[15] The contrast drawn between contribution to the accident 'in fact' and the legal disregard of such contribution highlighted that a special rule of law was involved.

On another occasion, however, the House of Lords had not managed such clarity or unanimity when trying to decide whether a verdict for a defendant could be directed as a matter of law on the ground of the claimant's contributory negligence.[16] Two Law Lords (of a panel of seven) had seen the point as being about proof of causation; three had seen it as being analogous to the rule that a finding of negligence could not be directed *against* a defendant; and the final two had seen it in terms of the claimant proving the defendant's defence by his own evidence. Behind these differences lay a fundamental conceptual uncertainty about where contributory negligence belonged in the scheme of analysis.

III

Conceptual clarity is not necessary for legal development, and the twentieth century saw a significant elaboration of the ideas put forward in *Davies* v. *Mann*. In *British Columbia Electric Railway Company, Limited* v.

[13] *Wakelin* v. *London and South Western Railway Company* (1886) 12 App Cas 41.
[14] (1876) 1 App Cas 754.
[15] (1876) 1 App Cas 754, 759.
[16] *Dublin, Wicklow and Wexford Railway* v. *Slattery* (1878) 3 App Cas 1155. See also G. Tilley, 'Directed Verdicts of Contributory Negligence' (1935) 51 *LQR* 500.

Loach[17] the Privy Council had to decide whether a defence of contributory negligence was available to a railway company whose engine had collided with the victim's wagon on a level crossing. It was clear that the accident victim had been negligent in failing to keep a proper look-out as the wagon was driven onto the railway tracks. But matters were complicated by the fact that the engine's failure to stop in time was due to a defective brake, which the railway company had negligently failed to detect before the engine began its day's work. The trial judge held that the defence of contributory negligence succeeded, because 'On the question of ultimate negligence, that negligence must arise on the conditions as existing at the time of the accident'.[18] Here, the trial judge had observed, there had been no opportunity to mend the brake between the moment that the engine driver saw the wagon on the level crossing and moment of the collision.

The trial judge's allusion to 'ultimate negligence' reflected current Canadian terminology,[19] and echoed the language of 'proximate cause' that had been used in *Davies* v. *Mann*. As Lord Sumner explained in the course of giving the advice of the Privy Council, it was a reference to the 'last opportunity' rule: whoever had the last opportunity of avoiding the damage through the exercise of reasonable care should be regarded as the sole cause of that damage. This rule seemed to require a strictly chronological analysis of events. That was what the trial judge had done. But the Privy Council held that such a strict approach was inappropriate: 'If … the same conduct which constituted the primary negligence is repeated or continued, and is the reason why the defendant does not avoid the consequences of the plaintiff's negligence at and after the time when the duty to do so arises, why should it not be also the "ultimate" negligence which makes the defendant liable?'[20] Thus, where a defendant's negligence preceded the claimant's own negligence, the defendant would still be regarded as having had the 'last opportunity' if his negligence incapacitated him from being able to take advantage of a later opportunity to avoid the damage. The defendant was still to be regarded as having had an 'opportunity' to avoid the damage, even though the damage was, in fact, inevitable when that opportunity arose.

Lord Sumner concluded the Privy Council's advice by describing the law as 'plain enough', and explaining its rationale:

> The inquiry is a judicial inquiry. It does not always follow the historical method and begin at the beginning. Very often it is more convenient to

[17] [1916] 1 AC 719. [18] [1916] 1 AC 719, 723.
[19] [1916] 1 AC 719, 725. [20] [1916] 1 AC 719, 726.

> begin at the end, that is at the accident, and work back along the line of events that led up to it. The ... inquiry ... is in search not merely of a causal agency but of the responsible agent.[21]

It was difficult to reconcile either this description or the rationale with the earlier analysis. The last opportunity test now required consideration of illusory opportunities as well as genuine opportunities. As one judicial commentator observed in 1922, the test was 'an intellectual tyranny, giving rise to confusion, embarrassment and injustice';[22] it perplexed juries. Furthermore, it was not obviously consistent with earlier decisions, most notably *Davies* v. *Mann* itself. There it could have been said that the claimant's negligent decision to leave the donkey unattended in the highway incapacitated him from taking the opportunity of pulling the donkey out of the way of the defendant's wagon. In other words, if the Privy Council was right, *Davies* v. *Mann* was wrong. As for Lord Sumner's claim that the test identified 'the responsible agent', that was belied by the outcome in both *Davies* v. *Mann* and the *British Columbia* case: in both cases both parties were clearly responsible agents. The legal test was being deliberately manipulated to avoid this obvious conclusion in order to avoid depriving the claimant of a remedy.

Two House of Lords cases within two years of each other illustrated how unpredictable and unstable the analysis had become. In the first, *Swadling* v. *Cooper*,[23] a motorist and motorcyclist had collided at a crossroads and the motorcyclist had been killed; the evidence was that each would have had only a second to see the other.[24] The House of Lords held that the trial judge's failure to mention the last opportunity test in his direction to the jury had not amounted to a misdirection. That test, they held, was suitable only for cases where 'there was a substantial interval of time between the initial negligence of the defendant or of the plaintiff respectively and the negligence which was the proximate cause of the injury'.[25] But, they continued, 'there are other cases in which the negligence of the parties is contemporaneous or so nearly contemporaneous as to make it impossible to say that either could have avoided the consequences of the other's negligence, and in which both have contributed to the accident'.[26] The facts of the case before them, they held, were of this second type.

In the second case, *McLean* v. *Bell*,[27] a car had run over a pedestrian as she crossed the street from behind a tram-car. The House of Lords upheld

[21] [1916] 1 AC 719, 727.

[22] J. O'Connor, 'Contributory Negligence' (1922) 38 *LQR* 17.

[23] [1931] AC 1. [24] [1931] AC 1, 11. [25] [1931] AC 1, 10.

[26] [1931] AC 1, 10. [27] (1932) 147 LT 262.

the jury's verdict for the pedestrian, saying that they had been entitled to find that the motorist could have avoided the accident. Lord Wright, giving the only reasoned speech, went out of his way to affirm the views expressed by the Privy Council in *British Columbia Electric Railway Company Limited* v. *Loach*. 'In one sense', explained Lord Wright:

> but for the negligence of the pursuer … in attempting to cross the road, she would not have been struck, and as a matter simply of causation her acts formed a necessary element in the final result, since without them no accident could have occurred. The decision, however, of the case must turn not simply on causation, but on responsibility; the plaintiff's negligence may be what is often called 'causa sine qua non', yet as regards responsibility it becomes merely evidential or matter of narrative, if the defendant acting reasonably could and ought to have avoided the collision … What has been called the last opportunity may in such cases need to be determined.[28]

Both cases concerned very similar, everyday accidents. In the first the last opportunity question was held to be so irrelevant that it did not need to be mentioned; in the second it was decisive. Possibly the facts might have been distinguishable, in that in the second case there was more than a single second for the motorist to take action; but even if all the facts were assumed in the claimant's favour, it could not have been more than a couple of seconds. A legal rule under which those extra seconds made all the difference between victory and defeat was not obviously defensible.

IV

The alternative approach to contributory negligence, which the terms of reference had invited the Law Revision Committee to consider, was that taken by the Courts of Admiralty. Those courts had nearly thirty years' experience of apportioning damage according to the respective fault of the parties pursuant to the provisions of the Maritime Conventions Act 1911. It is interesting, and important, to note that before 1911 a very different approach had prevailed, under which any ship in breach of the relevant statutory regulations was deemed to be in fault; if both colliding ships were deemed to be in fault, the loss was shared equally.[29] The law changed when the United Kingdom became a signatory to the Brussels Convention

[28] (1932) 147 LT 262, 264.

[29] Merchant Shipping Act 1873. For one important leading case see *Stoomvaart Maatschappy Nederland* v. *Peninsular and Oriental Steam Navigation Company* (1880) 5 App Cas 876.

on Collisions at Sea (1910), the provisions of which required liability to be apportioned according to fault. The Convention was, in turn, a reflection of a changing civil law approach across Continental Europe, which had settled on apportionment according to fault as the most satisfactory method.[30] The approach in Admiralty was, therefore, a forced experiment derived from civil law that had proved successful enough to be considered for use elsewhere.

The most obvious benefit of the Admiralty approach was that a finding of contributory negligence did not bar the claim. There was, therefore, no temptation for the courts to distort their analysis of causation in order to avoid injustice. As Lord Birkenhead LC put it in *Admiralty Commissioners v. Owners of SS Volute (The Volute)*:[31]

> the question of contributory negligence must be dealt with somewhat broadly and upon common-sense principles as a jury would probably deal with it. And while, no doubt, where a clear line can be drawn, the subsequent negligence is the only one to look to, there are cases in which the two acts come so closely together, and the second act of negligence is so mixed up with the state of things brought about by the first act, that the party secondly negligent, while not held free from blame … might … invoke the prior negligence as being part of the cause of the collision so as to make it a case of contribution. And the Maritime Conventions Act with its provisions for nice qualifications as to the quantum of blame and the proportions in which contribution is to be made may be taken as to some extent declaratory of the Admiralty rule in this respect.[32]

The final sentence did not perhaps quite do justice to the liberating effect that the 1911 Act had had upon the analysis of causation, but Lord Birkenhead's application of the broad common-sense principles to the facts of the case provided a nice illustration. What had happened was that an Admiralty ship was escorting a convoy led by the *Volute*; the *Volute* changed course without warning and the Admiralty ship, seeking to avoid a collision, failed to do so because its helm jammed. As we have seen above, similar facts in *British Columbia Electric Railway* gave rise to involved discussions about missed illusory opportunities. Lord Birkenhead LC, by contrast, could simply say that there was no sufficient

[30] F. Lawson, 'Notes on the History of Tort in the Civil Law' (1940) 22 *Journal of Comparative Legislation and International Law* third series 136, 142–4 traces the rule to the Austrian Civil Code 1811; R. Zimmermann, *The Law of Obligations: Roman Foundations of the Civilian Tradition* (Oxford University Press, 1996) 1048.

[31] [1922] AC 129. [32] [1922] AC 129, 144.

separation of 'time, place or circumstance'[33] to make it right to disregard the negligence of the *Volute*. Damages would, therefore, be apportioned.

The Admiralty courts, therefore, had a greater incentive than their common law counterparts to deal with contributory negligence in a straightforward way. But they did not have complete freedom of movement, because they had to work within the existing common law precedents, such as *Davies* v. *Mann*. The difficulties this caused were illustrated in *The Eurymedon*,[34] in which the Court of Appeal delivered judgment soon after the Law Revision Committee had started to meet.

The facts, as in so many contributory negligence cases, were unremarkable. Two ships collided on the Thames at 6 a.m. one January morning; the *Eurymedon* was sailing up the river, the *Corstar* had been moored at the side of the river, but had negligently been allowed to drift into the fairway. Each shipowner sued the other, and the question for the Court of Appeal was whether the *Corstar*'s negligence was to be regarded as contributory negligence. The Court of Appeal unanimously agreed that it did amount to contributory negligence, but offered three very different explanations for its conclusion.

Greer LJ said that the legal principles applicable had to be derived from *Davies* v. *Mann*, and set out five propositions. The first three, dealing with situations where one party saw or ought to have seen the other's negligence closely mirrored the leading case. The fourth, however, struck a different note: 'But if the negligence of both parties to the litigation continues right up to the moment of collision, whether on land or on sea, each party is to blame for the collision.'[35] The fifth proposition was closely linked to the fourth, and stated that if one party's negligence induced the other to make a negligent mistake that led to the damage, both parties should be regarded as being at fault. The facts of the case, Greer LJ held, came within this fifth proposition, because, by allowing herself to drift into the fairway, the *Corstar* had led the *Eurymedon* to mistake her lights for something else.

Slesser LJ took a different approach. He too recognised that the central question was how, if at all, *Davies* v. *Mann* could be distinguished. He held that it could be distinguished, because the *Corstar* could at all times have used its engines to correct the drift, but it did not do so; it had, therefore, 'by [its] own negligence denied [itself] the opportunity of avoiding the accident'.[36] In coming to this conclusion Slesser LJ relied on *British*

[33] [1922] AC 129, 145. [34] [1938] P 41.
[35] [1938] P 41, 50. [36] [1938] P 41, 54.

Columbia Electric Railway Company, which, he said, had previously been doubted, but now, following the House of Lords' decision in *McLean* v. *Bell*, could not be questioned.[37]

Yet a third approach was adopted by Scott LJ. He first dealt with the facts, and concluded that, as a matter of common sense, both ships were to blame. He then proceeded to consider whether the legal rules prevented this common-sense conclusion from being affirmed as a matter of law, and dealt first with *Davies* v. *Mann*. He made it clear that, in his view, much of the elaboration of the earlier case law was unconvincing:

> I confess to a feeling that much of the litigation which has taken place in the past upon this type of question has arisen through a tendency to substitute a too philosophical analysis of causation for a broad estimate of responsibility in the legal sense.[38]

In particular, there had been a mistaken tendency to focus on the last link of a chain of causation, when the real question – that of legal responsibility – depended on other factors. He cited the *British Columbia* case in support of the point, and then came to the real thrust of his judgment: 'the spirit of the proportional rule … calls for the sort of wide view of joint responsibility which Lord Birkenhead [in *The Volute*] thought right'.[39] The judgment concluded on a fascinating comparative note:

> From my experience of the views of Continental jurists about the proportional rule I feel sure that the broad view of the proportional rule is their view … I do not, of course, suggest that we should judicially mould English law by reference to foreign practice; but that we should in a branch of law covered by international convention preserve uniformity is an obvious advantage, if it is judicially possible.[40]

Since Scott LJ (along with Lord Sterndale) had signed the Brussels Convention on behalf of the United Kingdom, this final note had considerable resonance.[41]

The Court of Appeal's decision in *The Eurymedon* must have given the Law Revision Committee food for thought. One striking point was simply how complex the law had become: an ordinary, almost mundane set of facts prompted three different analyses. The main cause of that complexity was how to accommodate the last opportunity test within an apportionment regime. On this point Scott LJ's frank recognition that the cases

[37] [1938] P 41, 54. [38] [1938] P 41, 58.
[39] [1938] P 41, 60. [40] [1938] P 41, 61.
[41] *Sparks* v. *Edward Ash, Limited* [1943] 1 All ER 1, 10 (per Scott LJ) (not fully reported in [1943] KB 223).

had become over-elaborate was perhaps the only sensible way forward, but it meant that his analysis would not be consistent with precedent. Greer LJ, on the other hand, claimed to be deriving all of his legal propositions from the authorities, but his fourth proposition was inconsistent with *Davies* v. *Mann* itself, where the consequences of each party's negligence had continued down to the time of the damage, but only one party had been held liable. A similar struggle with the authorities could be seen in the contrasting uses of the *British Columbia* case. Slesser LJ used it as the basis for an ingenious argument about last opportunities, which was very much in the spirit of the Privy Council's reasoning. Scott LJ used it to support a point about the analysis of causation needing to be less technical; that was almost exactly the opposite of the Privy Council's approach, but, in so far as the result on the facts was concerned, it did support Scott LJ's point that the last negligent actor was not necessarily the sole cause. To put it more broadly, *The Eurymedon* made it clear that it would not be adequate for the Law Revision Committee merely to recommend apportionment; a workable law reform proposal would have to consider how to integrate rules inspired by the absence of apportionment within any new apportionment regime. That, in turn, would have to involve some analysis of the extent to which the existing rules embodied wider principles of causation.

V

The task fell, in the first instance, to the drafting committee of the contributory negligence group: Porter, Winfield, Stallybrass and Goodhart.[42] Their solution to the problems evidently convinced their colleagues on the Committee as a whole, for there was no alteration to the report between its first and its final versions.

Right at the start of the report it was made clear that the Committee favoured apportionment as the 'fairer' method of dealing with contributory negligence; 'but', the report continued, 'the matter is not without its complications', and the remainder of it set out to deal with them.[43]

The first difficult question was whether contributory negligence imposed more stringent requirements than the general principles of causation. This, as we have seen, was a question that had troubled nineteenth-century

[42] LCO 2/1992 Law Revision Committee (Eighth Report). Note of meeting held on 21 July 1937.

[43] Law Revision Committee, *Eighth Report*, Cmd 6032 (1939), 5.

courts. The Committee essentially dealt with the point as a terminological one: 'The use of the word "contributory" would seem to indicate that the negligence contributed to something. The use of the word "contributory" ought to mean that the negligence is part of the cause of the accident.'[44] Judicial suggestions that the last opportunity rule in fact went beyond ordinary causal requirements – in particular, Lord Penzance's comments in *Radley* v. *London and North Western Railway Company*[45] – were dismissed as a 'looser sense'[46] of 'contributory negligence'. This was, of course, a perfectly good position to adopt, but it removed the option of saying that the last opportunity rules should be jettisoned as having no basis in causation. Instead, the Committee would have to explain how those rules could be reconciled with general causal principles.

This the Committee proceeded to do, setting out in some detail the facts and reasoning in *Davies* v. *Mann*,[47] several subsequent cases and *The Eurymedon*.[48] The extent of the Committee's commitment to supporting the existing authorities could be seen in its criticism of Greer LJ's fourth proposition in *The Eurymedon*;[49] this proposition, it commented, 'appears to be somewhat too widely stated. It overlooks the fact that in all the cases quoted, the negligence of the other party continued up to the moment when the accident occurred, though at that moment he was not guilty of any fresh act of negligence.'[50]

However, having set out the common law position in some detail, the report then began to hint that not all of the cases could be supported to their fullest extent. The application of the same causal principles in Admiralty, it noted, had not always yielded the same results. Quotations from *The Volute*[51] and Scott LJ in *The Eurymedon*[52] followed, which talked about the need for a common-sense approach to causation, and 'a broad estimate of responsibility in the legal sense'.[53] These set the scene for a highly significant repositioning of two common law leading cases. 'Similar observations', the report went on:

> have been made by the Judicial Committee of the Privy Council in [*British Columbia Electric Railway Company Limited* v. *Loach*] in a judgment delivered by Lord Sumner … And by Lord Wright in *McLean* v. *Bell* … In

[44] *Ibid.*, 6. [45] (1876) 1 App Cas 754, quoted above at n. 15.
[46] Law Revision Committee, *Eighth Report*, Cmd 6032 (1939), 6.
[47] (1842) 10 M & W 546. [48] [1938] P 41.
[49] [1938] P 41, 50 (quoted above at n. 35).
[50] Law Revision Committee, *Eighth Report*, Cmd 6032 (1939), 14.
[51] [1922] AC 129 (quoted above at n. 32).
[52] [1938] P 41. [53] [1938] P 41, 58.

> both cases stress is laid upon the necessity for finding the cause which the law regards as having brought about the mischief, not necessarily regarding the act last done as having alone to be regarded, not taking too narrow a view in determining what the cause is.[54]

This was a radical, and not obviously convincing, reinterpretation of these two cases. As we have seen, the *British Columbia* case added a further level of artificial complexity to an already rigid rule; *McLean* v. *Bell* underlined the difficulties and injustices inevitable in applying the last opportunity doctrine to road accidents. Both cases could have been described as the chief culprits in making the law of contributory negligence unpredictable and unconvincing; but in the report, with the aid of careful quotation, they could be presented as showing the way forward.

The report then went on to advocate the 'common-sense' approach to causation, as approved in Admiralty, and concluded that:

> For those reasons, while we recommend that the principle of apportioning the loss to the fault should be adopted at Common Law, we do not recommend any change in the method of ascertaining whose the fault may be, nor any abrogation of what has been somewhat inaptly called the 'last opportunity rule'. In truth there is no such rule – the question, as in all questions of liability for a tortious act, is not who had the last opportunity of avoiding the mischief, but whose act caused the wrong? Sometimes the answer may be found, as in *Davies* v. *Mann* ... by answering the former question, but in other cases, as in *The Eurymedon* ... such an answer is not conclusive.[55]

We may note that the Committee at this point chose not to refer to Lord Wright's endorsement of the phrase 'last opportunity' in *McLean* v. *Bell*[56] – that, clearly, was one of the less helpful passages in his speech. Perhaps more significantly, the paragraph quoted above did not really provide a very good answer to the question of how *Davies* v. *Mann* would fit within an apportionment regime. It was all very well to say that sometimes the last opportunity would be decisive, sometimes not, but when would that be? Adding that *Davies* v. *Mann* would apply to cases like *Davies* v. *Mann* hardly took things further, and bringing in *The Eurymedon* made things worse. There, it will be remembered, Slesser LJ had regarded *Davies* v. *Mann* as decisive, and had identified the last opportunity of avoiding damage as being with the *Corstar*; Greer LJ had claimed to be applying *Davies* v. *Mann*, but in fact had decided the case by applying a legal

[54] Law Revision Committee, *Eighth Report*, Cmd 6032 (1939), 15–16.
[55] *Ibid.*, 16. [56] (1932) 147 LT 262 at 264 (quoted above at n. 27).

proposition that was inconsistent with it. Only Scott LJ had suggested that the last opportunity doctrine was 'too philosophical'[57] (i.e. wrong). Perhaps it was Scott LJ's approach that the Committee meant to endorse; but greater clarity on this crucial point was needed.

The penultimate section of the report dealt with broader benefits of and objections to an apportionment regime. The major benefit identified was that English common law would be assimilated to the laws of other countries, from France to China. The major objection was that there might be an increase in litigation; but, the Committee argued, comparative evidence suggested that this was unlikely:

> The experience in Ontario, where such a rule has been in existence since 1924 is that the total amount of damages recovered by plaintiffs is not increased to any marked extent. The increase in the number of cases in which damages have been obtained is said to have been offset to a large extent by the decrease in the amount of damages awarded in those cases where the plaintiff's negligence has contributed to the result, and this contention seems to be borne out by the fact that the Canadian insurance rates have not increased in recent years.[58]

Finally, the report turned to the question of the precise scope of any reform. Essentially it recommended that apportionment should apply wherever there was currently a defence of contributory negligence; but it should not apply to workmen's compensation claims.[59] As things turned out, this latter, apparently very minor point would assume great significance in the legislative process.

VI

The Law Revision Committee's report on contributory negligence was, then, significantly different to the Committee's earlier reports on tort topics. One major difference was that, unlike the earlier reports, the contributory negligence report sought to give a historical explanation for the current position. That might well have been prompted by Winfield, whose approach to current law controversies and law reform had always been coloured by the importance of understanding the historical position.[60]

[57] [1938] P 41, 58. [58] Law Revision Committee, *Eighth Report*, Cmd 6032 (1939), 17–18

[59] See J. Steele, 'Law Reform (Contributory Negligence) Act 1945: Collisions of a Different Sort' in T. Arvind and J. Steele (eds.), *Tort Law and the Legislature* (Oxford, Hart Publishing, 2013) 159, 171, which draws attention to the Report's failure to deal with industrial accident cases in its discussion of principles.

[60] E.g. P. Winfield, 'Law Reform' (1928) 44 *LQR* 289, 295–9 (his inaugural lecture as Rouse Ball Professor of English Law at the University of Cambridge).

A second major difference was that this report advocated (indeed, to be workable, had to advocate) not only a legislative change, but also a fundamental change in judicial assumptions about causation. In this respect there is a strikingly close resemblance between the line taken in the report and the line taken in a memorandum submitted to the Committee by Langton J.[61] That memorandum, entitled 'Contributory Negligence at Common Law and Admiralty', set out to explore 'the practical effects of the administration of the Law in the Common Law and the Admiralty side respectively'.[62] Its major point was that, whilst *Davies* v. *Mann* and the cases applying it had made the common law very complicated, no such difficulty existed in practice in Admiralty. 'There are a few cases (very few in my experience)', he explained:

> in which the 'clear line' referred to in the judgment of Lord Birkenhead in the 'Volute' … can be discerned and acted upon. So far as my experience extends there has been in every one of these few cases one or both of the following two factors present:
> (a) a substantial interval of time between the first negligence of the Plaintiff and the last and culminating negligence of the Defendant, and/or
> (b) the fact that one of the vessels concerned was at anchor, moored, or otherwise held by wind and tide in a more or less fixed position.[63]

In other words, 'in Admiralty, the work proceeds upon the understanding that in the vast majority of cases there is no room at all for the application of the doctrine to be found in Davies v Mann'.[64] Langton J's conclusion was particularly powerful:

> To sum up I would suggest that at Common Law, as in Admiralty, it would make both for more simple and more substantial justice if the Admiralty rule as to the effect of contributory negligence were given a universal application. The doctrine to be found in Davies v Mann cannot and ought not to be abolished, but it is a doctrine to be very sparingly applied, and in my view can be usefully confined to a very small class of cases. Wherever two vehicles are concerned, whether on sea or land, which possess full scope and power of movement, there is no room for this doctrine unless such an interval of time exists between the two negligences which caused the collision that there can be no manner of doubt that the Defendant

[61] LCO 2/1992 and LCO 2/1973, undated but marked as circulated to the contributory negligence subcommittee on 27 February 1939. The memorandum is anonymous, but the author refers to *The Kate* (1934) 54 Ll L Rep 120 and *The Framlington Court* (1936) 56 Ll L Rep 200 as 'two decisions of my own'.

[62] LCO 2/1992 and LCO 2/1973, 1. [63] *Ibid*., 1. [64] *Ibid*., 2

> could have easily avoided the collision not withstanding the negligence of the Plaintiff.[65]

Two points may be made about this memorandum. The first is that it was clearly very influential on the report. The second is that it gives far clearer guidance as to when to apply *Davies* v. *Mann* than the report did; the Committee may have felt that it had no standing to tell judges what to do, but the report would have dealt more convincingly with this crucial point if it had borrowed more extensively from Langton.

The third major difference between the contributory negligence report and the Committee's early reports on tort subjects was its comparative theme. The general references to civil law were perhaps more decorative than functional; but the same could not have been said of the Ontario material. This was used to rebut a significant (if speculative) argument against reform, but its source was a mystery. In fact the source was unimpeachable: it was Hartley McNairn, the Superintendent of Insurance in the Ontario Department of Insurance, who had written to A. L. Goodhart as follows:

> A copy of your letter of October 10th addressed to John D. Falconbridge, K.C.[66] dealing with the subject of contributory negligence was forwarded to me under date of October 25th, for attention and reply.
>
> Upon receipt of the above mentioned communication I made some enquiry and the replies have only recently come to hand …
>
> Coming now to your specific four questions:–
>
> (1) 'Has the Ontario statute proved satisfactory in practice?'
> From the various replies received it would appear that the Ontario statute has worked out generally satisfactory in practice.
>
> (2) 'Do you think any amendments are desirable?'
> I have received replies from three eminent counsel suggesting amendments to the 'Negligence Act' (Ontario) and the replies received are appended to this letter …
>
> (3) 'Has it increased the amount of damages recovered to a striking degree?'
> General opinion appears to be that the contributory 'Negligence Act' has increased the amount of damages recovered in Ontario. However, one eminent counsel here thinks that the statute has not

[65] *Ibid.*, 3.

[66] John D. Falconbridge was Dean of Osgoode Hall Law School and an important scholar in conflicts of law. For an assessment of his work, where he is described as a 'towering' figure, see R. Risk, 'Canadian Law Teachers in the 1930s: "When the World Was Turned Upside Down"' in R. Risk, *A History of Canadian Legal Thought: Collected Essays* (Toronto, Osgoode Society for Legal History, 2006) 341, 351–3.

> increased the amount of damages recovered and I quote that part of his letter which is appended hereto …
>
> (4) 'Have the insurance companies increased their rates since it came into force? From a practical standpoint this is the most important point. Do you know whether any of the insurance companies have issued statements or reports on the effect of the statute?'
>
> Third party insurance premium rates (public liability and property damage) are at present, lower than they were during the years 1929 and 1930. Comparing 1930 policy year experience with 1936 policy year as filed by all insurers, the loss-cost in Ontario has not varied to any extent as regards public liability insurance, but insurance on property damage has shown a slight decline in loss-cost due to a slight decline in the amount of the average claim.
>
> In Ontario, of course, motor vehicle liability insurance is not compulsory and the experience on insured cars only represents experience on one-half of vehicles licensed under the provisions of the Highway Traffic Act.[67]

Perhaps the first thing that stands out about this letter is the remarkable readiness to assist Goodhart in his research: McNairn had, effectively, conducted a survey on his behalf and was forwarding the results. It was a method of obtaining information that perhaps only Goodhart, with his unique Anglo-American prestige and contacts, could have pulled off. The second striking point emerges when one puts McNairn's letter alongside the relevant passages of the Committee's report: they do not say the same thing! The report states that the Ontario legislation has not increased the level of damages; but McNairn's letter indicates that this was a minority view. Perhaps more significantly, the report's general assertion about insurance premiums contrasts with McNairn's far more cautious assessment. In England motor insurance was compulsory, and that rather undermined any comparison with the voluntary system in Ontario. It might have been more informative – but less persuasive – to share McNairn's reservations with readers of the report.

VII

The Committee delivered its report in June 1939. Understandably, given the world political situation, implementing it was not a priority. Nothing more was heard of it until March 1943, when a question about legislation was tabled in the House of Commons inspired by the remarks of

[67] LCO 2/1992 (also copied in LCO 2/1973) McNairn to Goodhart, 15 December 1937.

Scott LJ in *Sparks* v. *Edward Ash, Limited*,[68] which highlighted the need for a proportional rule.[69] Whether prompted by Scott LJ or not, the Lord Chancellor (now Lord Simon) was on the case: he asked the Legislation Committee for authority to bring in a Bill implementing both the Law Revision Committee's recommendations on the consequences of frustration of contract (the priority), and its recommendations on contributory negligence.[70] The Legislation Committee agreed, remarking that such a Bill 'would probably be non-controversial'.[71]

Just over a month later, a first draft was ready. The clause dealing with contributory negligence was clause 3; its most important provisions were as follows:

> (1) Where, as the result of the fault of two or more persons, damage (including loss of life or personal injury) is caused to one or more of those persons, the defence of contributory negligence shall not lie against any of those persons, but the liability in respect of the whole of the damage so caused shall be apportioned among those persons according to the degree in which each of those persons was at fault:
>
> Provided that this subsection shall not affect the liability of any person under any contract or shall be construed as imposing upon any person any liability from which he is exempted or against which he has a good defence (other than the defence of contributory negligence) by virtue of any contract or otherwise …
>
> (7) In this section the expression 'fault' means negligence, breach of statutory duty, or other act or omission giving rise to a liability in tort, and also includes any lack of care, whether there is a duty or not, which would apart from this section give rise to the defence of contributory negligence.[72]

The draftsman, Harold Kent, explained to the Lord Chancellor that he had had difficulty with the definition of 'fault':

> Clause 3 presents a good many difficult features, especially the definition of 'fault' … Contributory negligence may not itself be an actionable

[68] [1943] 1 All ER 1 (fully reported); [1943] KB 223 (incompletely reported).

[69] LCO 2/1993 Law Revision Committee. 23 March 1943 (note to Schuster from Attorney-General's office).

[70] LCO 2/1993, 24 March 1943 (Simon's memorandum to the Legislation Committee). The Law Revision Committee's proposals on the consequences of frustrated contracts are dealt with in its *Seventh Interim Report (Rule in Chandler* v. *Webster)*, Cmd 6009 (1939). For the development and implementation of these proposals see P. Mitchell, '*Fibrosa Spolka Akcyjna* v. *Fairbairn Lawson Combe Barbour*' in C. Mitchell and P. Mitchell (eds.), *Landmark Cases in the Law of Restitution* (Oxford: Hart Publishing, 2006), 247.

[71] LCO 2/1993 Minutes of War Cabinet Legislation Committee, 30 March 1943.

[72] LCO 2/1993, 4 May 1943.

> wrong, because it may consist of a lack of care in circumstances which do not give rise to a duty of care: at least this seems the better view of the authorities which are numerous. The clause, therefore, ought not to make a person who has only been guilty of this kind of negligence liable for any damage suffered by another party, but only ought to determine the extent to which he can recover for damage suffered by him. I think that the clause is all right in this respect, because directly the negligence results in damage to another person it becomes actionable in itself and not merely a defence available to the other party; but the point requires consideration.[73]

In the second draft, dated 1 June 1943, that definition had assumed the shape that it was to have in the final legislation:

> 'fault' means negligence, breach of statutory duty, or other act or omission which gives rise to a liability in tort or would, apart from this section, give rise to the defence of contributory negligence.[74]

Ironically, given the anxious scrutiny lavished on other provisions, Kent's claim that the clause was 'all right' was never seriously questioned in the legislative process. Only Lord Wright commented on it, and that was to note, approvingly, its inclusion of breach of statutory duty.[75] In fact, as later cases and commentators would highlight, it actually required deft judicial interpretation to work sensibly. Essentially, the definition had to be split up, the first half (up to 'liability in tort') applying to the defendant's fault, the remainder to the claimant's fault.[76] Otherwise two unwanted consequences would occur: it would appear that a person could be made liable if his contributory negligence injured someone else, whether or not the requirements of tortious liability were satisfied; and it would also appear that if a claimant committed a tort that led to him being injured, there would be a defence of contributory negligence. For instance, a claimant's assault could prompt a battery in response. It had never been suggested that contributory negligence could be a defence to an intentional tort; but a literal application of the subsection would lead to that result.[77]

[73] LCO 2/1993 Covering letter attached to first draft of Bill.

[74] LCO 2/1993, 1 June 1943; subsections renumbered, so this appears as subsection (8).

[75] LCO 2/1993, 5 June 1943 (Wright to Simon); the addition of breach of statutory duty reflected the House of Lords' decision in *Caswell* v. *Powell Duffryn Associated Collieries, Limited* [1940] AC 152.

[76] *Standard Chartered Bank* v. *Pakistan National Shipping Corporation (Nos 2 and 4)* [2003] 1 AC 959.

[77] For support for the idea that contributory negligence might include committing a tort, whether or not it has been recognised as giving rise to a defence of contributory negligence, see *Murphy* v. *Culhane* [1977] QB 94, 99 (per Lord Denning MR);

So far as the general principle of subclause (1) was concerned, it was not quite in final form: later the formula of apportionment according to 'degree of fault' would change. Meanwhile, however, the Bill rather lost its momentum. Somervell, now the Attorney General, came up with the odd idea that fifty/fifty apportionment, as had been the position in Admiralty before 1911, would work better for road accidents than apportionment according to fault.[78] Schuster and a colleague had to waste their time heading off this eccentric suggestion.[79] More damagingly for the Bill's long-term prospects, the draftsman became fascinated – obsessed is perhaps not too strong a word – by what the position should be if the claimant's injury had come about as the result of his own negligence and the result of two or more defendants. As he explained in his covering letter accompanying the second draft of the Bill:

> I have drafted a new subsection (5) for your consideration, to meet part of the awkward problem discussed at the conference. I gather that Lord Porter's view now is that in the Admiralty division the difficulty of the absent ship (or owner thereof) is not a practical one. I feel, however, that in running down cases there is a considerable danger of one of the negligent parties not being before the court, e.g. where the driver of a motor car drives straight away from the scene of an accident and is never traced, and that we cannot avoid an express provision to deal with the point.[80]

The subsection provided as follows:

> Where it appears to the court by or before whom an apportionment of liability is to be made under this section that the damage in question was partly caused by the fault of a person who cannot be ascertained or who cannot be made a party to the proceedings, it shall apportion, or direct the apportionment of, the whole of the liability among such of the persons at fault as are before the court, according to their respective degrees of fault, and, if proceedings are subsequently taken against any person who was not a party to the earlier proceedings and his fault is established, the court shall make such adjustment of the respective liabilities of the parties to the earlier proceedings as it thinks just.

Forsikringsaktieselskapet Vesta v. *Butcher* [1989] AC 852, 862 (per O'Connor LJ); *Alliance and Leicester Building Society Ltd* v. *Edgestop Ltd* [1994] 2 All ER 38, 50 (per Mummery J). However, it is submitted that the House of Lords' decision in the *Standard Chartered* case (see previous note), has implicitly disapproved these suggestions.

[78] LCO 2/1993, 12 May 1943 (Somervell to Schuster).

[79] LCO 2/1993, 14 May 1943 (Schuster to Coldstream); 17 May 1943 (Coldstream's reply).

[80] LCO 2/1993, 1 June 1943 (Kent to Simon).

It remained in the same form in the third draft, which Lord Simon circulated to the Law Lords for comments.[81] This move on Simon's part was not, as his covering letter made clear, merely for information. He hoped to draw out any objections to the Bill before it was introduced into the House of Lords and, thereby, be able to steer the Bill through smoothly: 'it will be very unfortunate', he wrote to the Law Lords, 'if when the Bill comes to be discussed there are differences of view as to the way to carry the reforms out'.[82]

Lord Wright responded immediately, and went out of his way to applaud Simon's strategy: 'I think it is very desirable', he wrote, 'that if there are differences of opinion on the Bill among the pundits, they should be settled by agreement out of court.'[83] In this mixed metaphor the Law Lords were seen first as jurists, then as litigants; it is striking that they were not seen as legislators, who ought to discuss publicly the legislation proposed. As with previous law reform Bills, care was being taken to control the process in advance. Not surprisingly, Wright was very uneasy about Kent's new subsection: 'It is not perhaps likely to happen often. It would and might involve re-opening of a matter settled in the main proceedings. Is it necessary or desirable? I am not clear about it.'[84] Kent, however, seems to have been tenacious, and the clause remained.

Things were, therefore, progressing, albeit slowly, towards a Law Reform (Frustrated Contracts and Contributory Negligence) Act 1943. On 10 June 1943, however, out of the blue, this progress came to an abrupt halt. The nature of the obstruction and Simon's evident disappointment are both evident in his letter to the Lord President:

> I have seen this morning a letter from Maxwell[85] which raises a serious difficulty about one of the paragraphs of my Bill dealing with contributory negligence. He points out that under the Workmen's Compensation Acts, a workman who fails in his common law action 'against the employer' (as he will fail under the present law if his own negligence has contributed to the accident) is given the right, notwithstanding that he has taken the wrong proceedings, to get an award on Workmen's Compensation Act terms from the same tribunal. This is, of course, in practice a very valuable

[81] LCO 2/1993, 4 June 1943. The subsections had again been renumbered – it was now cl. 3(2).

[82] LCO 2/1993, 4 June 1943.

[83] LCO 2/1993, 5 June 1943 (Wright to Simon).

[84] LCO 2/1993, 5 June 1943 (Wright to Simon).

[85] Sir Alexander Maxwell, permanent under-secretary at the Home Office. See further D. Fairn, 'Maxwell, Sir Alexander' in *Oxford Dictionary of National Biography* (online edition).

> right for the workman, for he is in clover if he failed to get a lump sum at common law. But if my Bill, as now drawn, became law, the workman would not fail in his common law action, though he might get a very small fraction of the damage he had suffered. In that event, he would not be able to claim the alternative remedy under the Workmen's Compensation Acts, though this might give him better terms.
>
> I feel it is a very serious point which will have to be examined carefully and provided for. In the circumstances, I am not disposed to ask leave to introduce my Bill today, and I think I had better not ask you to have a special meeting of the Legislation Committee on Tuesday. I will next week take the opportunity of a conference with the Home Office and, if need be, the Treasury, and if we see a way through this I might bring up my Bill before your Committee on Tuesday week. If, on the other hand, this seems to create a complication which cannot be quickly got over, I may have to drop contributory negligence out of my Bill (a great pity) and introduce a shortened measure, as soon as Parliament resumes, about frustration of contract alone ...
>
> I blame myself for not having thought it out more completely, for my old days in the County Court have made me very familiar with this corner of the law.[86]

No way through the difficulty could be found, and the provisions on contributory negligence were, therefore, dropped.[87]

It was over a year before the Departmental Committee on Alternative Remedies (chaired by Walter Monckton) considered the matter. Then, after hearing evidence from the Lord Chancellor, it indicated that the contributory negligence Bill should not apply in actions by workmen against employers.[88] Progress with the Bill could resume. Kent continued as draftsman, which unfortunately meant further battles over his subsection. Kent continued to insist on it, but by now both the Lord Chancellor and his officials were turning against it; they preferred, simply, to apply the existing rules on contribution.[89] In other words, a negligent claimant did not have to bear the risk that one of the defendants would be

[86] LCO 2/1993 Workmen's Compensation Act 1897 s. 1(4), re-enacted as Workmen's Compensation Act 1925 s. 29(2). Simon's reference to 'clover' was rather overstating it: the court was 'at liberty to deduct from such compensation all the costs which, in its judgment have been caused by the plaintiff bringing the action instead of proceeding under [the Workmen's Compensation] Act'.

[87] LCO 2/1993, 18 June 1943 (Simon's memorandum to the War Cabinet).

[88] LCO 2/3563 Law Revision Committee. Eighth Report (Contributory Negligence) Law Reform (Contributory Negligence) Bill 1945. 8 November 1944 (Napier to Kent). The Committee's report was officially published on 5 December 1944.

[89] See e.g. Simon's evidence to the Departmental Committee on Alternative Remedies, LCO 2/3563, 25 October 1944 at p. 6; Napier's letter to Kent, LCO 2/3563, 8 November 1944.

either unidentifiable or not worth suing. Kent, however, demonstrated an extraordinary stubbornness,[90] and Simon was driven to sending both Kent's version and his own (as an 'alternative') to the Attorney General with a request for the Attorney General to adjudicate.[91] Simon's version prevailed.[92]

More importantly, Simon seems to have had further thoughts about the wording of clause 1. Simon's draft of 20 December 1944 was very close to the final wording:

> Where any person suffers damage ... as the result partly of his own fault and partly of the fault of any other person or persons, a claim in respect of that damage shall not be defeated by reason of the fault of the person suffering the damage, but he or his personal representative shall be entitled to recover against any other person at fault damages in respect of such portion of the said damage as the court thinks just and equitable having regard to the extent of that other person's responsibility for the damage.[93]

Only cosmetic changes would be made to this formulation when the Bill became law. There were two important ways in which it was an improvement on the earlier draft. First, it had abandoned the Maritime Conventions Act model, under which damage to one 'or more persons' was to be apportioned between all parties at fault. That model made sense in the maritime context, where, typically, two or more ships involved in a collision would all be damaged, each would accuse the other(s) of fault, and an overall assessment of net liability in damages would be made in consolidated cross-actions.[94] In the kind of road traffic accident cases to which the contributory negligence legislation would apply, the model was less happy. It was, of course, possible that claims arising from a collision between several vehicles would benefit from the Maritime Conventions Act approach, but where the claimant was a pedestrian, who had been injured by the defendant's vehicle, to insist on taking any damage to the defendant's vehicle into account risked introducing an irrelevant, and rather tasteless, distraction into the litigation.

The second improvement was the change from 'fault' to 'responsibility' as the criterion by which the court was to apportion the damages. This

90 LCO 2/3563, 22 November 1944 (Kent to Napier).

91 LCO 2/3563, 22 December 1944 (Simon to Somervell). Simon made it clear in his letter which draft he supported.

92 LCO 2/3563, 28 December 1944 (Coldstream (?) to Kent); 2 January 1945 (Somervell to Simon).

93 LCO 2/3563, 28 December 1944.

94 Steele, 'Law Reform (Contributory Negligence) Act 1945', 170.

was particularly significant. 'Fault' was the word used in the Maritime Conventions Act 1911, and in the Brussels Convention on which it was based; but 'fault' was not defined, and that gave the Admiralty Courts a degree of flexibility in applying the test. In the draft contributory negligence bill, by contrast, 'fault' was defined, and defined narrowly; apportionment of damage according to 'fault' so defined would have excluded consideration of the causal significance of the fault. As the courts quickly recognised, it was important to be able to consider both the degree of blameworthiness of an act and its causal significance in order to do justice.[95]

By early January 1945 all but minor details had been settled, and Simon sent the Bill to Lords Wright, Goddard and Porter for their approval. Fortunately, they were all positively enthusiastic about it;[96] since all three had been members of the Law Revision Committee, their opposition during the Bill's passage through the House of Lords would have been particularly embarrassing. Simon therefore introduced the Bill, which emerged, unaltered in substance, as the Law Reform (Contributory Negligence) Act 1945. It had been a long journey.

VIII

The 1945 Act proved very successful, and remains in force today. Whilst its definition of fault has not been entirely unproblematic, the difficulties were identified and have now been resolved. Certainly the courts have made use of the flexibility in section 1. They have also marginalised the last opportunity rule, which ensures that the scope of the Act is not artificially restricted. Perhaps the main criticism of the Act was that it failed to make absolutely clear when apportionment might be available – in particular, could contributory negligence now be invoked where previously it had been unavailable, such as in intentional torts? The most recent authoritative answer has been 'no',[97] and this is most likely to be what was

[95] *Stapley* v. *Gypsum Mines Ltd* [1953] AC 663. cf. the unhappy South African experience with a contributory negligence statute requiring apportionment according to fault alone: Zimmermann, *The Law of Obligations*, 1048–9.

[96] LCO 2/3563, Goddard: 'wholehearted support' (9 January 1945, Goddard to Simon); Porter: 'I like its form' (11 January 1945, Porter to Simon); Wright: 'I admire very much the language of Sec. 1 which seems to me clear, simple, accurate and elegant' (11 January, Wright to Simon).

[97] *Standard Chartered Bank* v. *Pakistan National Shipping Corporation (Nos 2 and 4)* [2003] 1 AC 959.

intended. After all, the Act was meant to implement the report, and the report makes no mention of such a major reform.

The reform of contributory negligence, like the three Law Revision Committee projects discussed already, was a complex process. As with the three earlier projects, the academic influence is striking – with the contributory negligence project it was most obvious in the personnel of the drafting committee (whose draft was endorsed, unchanged, by the rest of the Committee): three of the four were academics. A second common theme was that, unlike modern Law Commission reports, no draft legislation was put forward by the committee. Inevitably, that created difficulties when legislation came to be drafted; and we may note that the Committee as a whole was never consulted about the solutions – only some members of it were. That brings us to perhaps the most important common theme running through the Law Revision Committee's operations, and that is the importance of inner circles. Within each of the official stages of law reform was a small group of individuals, representing a small minority of those entitled to contribute, whose ideas and influence carried weight. Furthermore, each stage of the process was not of equal importance: the parliamentary stage, which we might expect to be crucial, was, in fact, a sterile formality; key individuals made sure that it stayed that way. Being a consultant to the parliamentary draftsman, by contrast, was an apparently marginal role that, in fact, was just about the most powerful position in the process. The theory of how law reform should occur bore no relation to what actually happened.

14

Conclusion: beyond 1950

What happened in tort in the years since 1950 could easily fill another book, but it is worthwhile concluding this study of tort in the first half of the twentieth century by glancing at the most significant developments linked to the subject matter of earlier chapters.

Many of the most important changes grew out of the institutional innovations portrayed in Chapters 9–13, as the small-scale amateur approach of the Law Revision Committee was first continued (by the Law Reform Committee), and then completely eclipsed by the creation of the Law Commission in 1965.[1] Thus began an era of professionalised law reform initiatives, which one of its leading lights could claim was second only to Oliver Cromwell's in its ambition.[2] Where the Law Commission surpassed even Cromwell was in its use of consultation papers, and elaborately argued provisional Law Commission proposals became an increasingly frequent feature of the legal landscape. Some of those proposals, once implemented, had a direct effect on material discussed in the first half of this book. The common law rules on occupiers' liability, for instance, which had generated so much controversy in their application to children,[3] would be replaced by the Occupiers' Liability Acts of 1957 and 1984. Statute would also abolish common law claims for enticement and seduction, and would prevent courts from making awards for loss of consortium:[4] as a result, the legal landscape of tort principles applying to women took on a radically different appearance.[5] Similarly, the statutory removal of damages awards for loss of expectation of life relieved the courts of a task that had been peculiarly difficult in cases concerning

[1] Law Commission Act 1965. See further, J. Farrar, *Law Reform and the Law Commission* (London, Sweet & Maxwell, 1974).

[2] L. Gower, 'Looking Back' (1978) 14 *JSPTL* 155, 157. The deliberate professionalisation is nicely highlighted in Farrar, *Law Reform and the Law Commission*, 13.

[3] See Chapter 5.

[4] Law Reform (Miscellaneous Provisions) Act 1970.

[5] See Chapters 4 and 5.

children.[6] Nor were statutory reforms limited to pruning away heads of liability that no longer reflected social values. Statute could also create important new bases of claim, as did the Animals Act 1971, which effectively overturned the House of Lords' decision in *Searle* v. *Wallbank*[7] by creating a duty of care on owners of livestock towards users of the highway. Most recently, the Defamation Act 2013 has affected virtually every element of the principles of defamation, although not, we might note, the strict liability of authors.

Developments in case law have tended, by their very nature, to be less clear-cut than their statutory counterparts. The most striking change has been the centrality and pre-eminence achieved by *Donoghue* v. *Stevenson*,[8] and in particular by Lord Atkin's neighbour principle. It is difficult to imagine a sequel to this book in which the author blithely explains in Chapter 1 that *Donoghue* v. *Stevenson* has been of no great significance during the period. But neither, on the other hand, has that case transformed the law of negligence out of all recognition – the same uncertainties remain, for instance, about a public authority's liability,[9] and special rules continue to govern negligence liability for psychiatric injury.[10] Other decisions have proved surprisingly obdurate – the strict liability imposed by *Jones* v. *E Hulton & Co*,[11] for example, and the decision in *Youssoupoff* v. *Metro-Goldwyn-Mayer Pictures, Limited*[12] both seem to have outlasted the social contexts and attitudes that formed them. Employers' non-delegable duties, in contrast, which were inspired by the restrictions of the defence of common employment,[13] have found a new purpose, after the abolition of that defence, as a mechanism for imposing liability on employers beyond the traditional limits of vicarious liability for one's employees.[14] Indeed, a patchy, unpredictable and unsystematic relationship between tort and societal changes has characterised the second half of the twentieth century just as much as it did the first.

[6] See Chapter 5. Administration of Justice Act 1982, s. 1(1)(a). Note, however, that s. 1(1)(b) requires the court to include an amount in any award for pain and suffering to reflect the claimant's 'awareness that his expectation of life has been reduced'.

[7] [1947] AC 341, discussed in Chapter 7. Animals Act 1971, s. 8.

[8] [1932] AC 562. [9] See Chapter 3. [10] See Chapter 4.

[11] [1910] AC 20, discussed in Chapter 6.

[12] (1934) 50 TLR 581, discussed in Chapter 4.

[13] See Chapter 8.

[14] Eg *McDermid* v. *Nash Dredging & Reclamation Co Ltd* [1987] AC 906.

Appendix

Lipstein and Gutteridge on Defamation

At its meeting on 11 May 1939, Lord Porter told his Committee on the Law of Defamation that he had a surprise for them.

> In conjunction with Mr Wade he had arranged for a Memorandum to be prepared by the Comparative Law Department of Cambridge University upon Dominion and Foreign Law relating to Defamation; the enquiry as to Foreign Law would be carried out principally by Professor Gutteridge KC and Mr K Lipstein PhD (a former German Judge), and Mr Glanville Williams PhD would deal with Colonial and Dominion Law.[1]

Gutteridge, who had spent the previous two decades lamenting the poverty of library resources and institutions' unwillingness to develop comparative law, may have been surprised to hear that he had an entire 'Department' in Cambridge.[2] He had, at least, retained his title. Dr Lipstein and Dr Williams – two of Cambridge's earliest and most distinguished research students – had been deprived of theirs, perhaps so as not to sound too academic.[3] As Lord Porter's announcement made clear, the commissioning of these memoranda owed something to the influence of E. C. S. Wade, who was the Committee's academic lawyer and a Fellow of Gonville and Caius College, Cambridge. When, later, the Committee felt that it also needed advice on defamation in the United States, it turned to the same university, and requested a memorandum from Professor P. H. Winfield of St John's College.

[1] LCO 2/3059 Committee on the Law of Defamation. Minutes of Meetings 1939. Fifth meeting, 11 May 1939.

[2] H. Gutteridge, 'The Study of Comparative Law in France and England' (1922) 4 *Journal of Comparative Legislation and International Law* 1 84; H. Gutteridge, note (1926) 42 *LQR* 436; see also his response to R. Lee in 'Comparative Law and Comparative Lawyers' 1936 *JSPTL* 1, 6. The position had hardly improved by 1941: H. Gutteridge, 'Comparative Law as a Factor in English Legal Education' (1941) 23 *Journal of Comparative Legislation and International Law* 3rd series 130.

[3] Cf. the negative connotations made to attach to the doctorate of their Cambridge colleague 'Dr Leavis', as the literary scholar and critic F. R. Leavis was invariably described by his opponents: S. Collini, 'Introduction' in F. R. Leavis, *The Two Cultures? The Significance of CP Snow* (Cambridge, Canto, 2013) 5.

Williams was able to complete his task quickly. For Gutteridge and Lipstein, however, the process was more protracted. Lipstein's internment in 1940 cannot have helped, and their memorandum was not finally completed until at least 1942 (law journals from that year being cited in the footnotes).[4] There was then a further delay in submitting the work to the Committee, because the Committee's proceedings had been immediately suspended on the outbreak of the Second World War.[5] Once meetings resumed in 1945 and the memorandum had been safely received, there was a rather curious announcement about it:

> Professor Wade mentioned that the memorandum on Defamation in European Systems of Law which had been circulated to the Committee under the name of Professor Gutteridge, although it was read and approved by the latter, was largely the work of Dr Lipstein. Professor Gutteridge was anxious that this acknowledgement should be made.[6]

Quite how much of a misrepresentation it had been to attribute sole authorship to Gutteridge can be seen from a draft in Lipstein's distinctive hand – he wrote with a quill pen[7] – that is in the Cambridge Law Faculty archive, and transcribed in this Appendix.[8] That draft is virtually identical with the final version submitted to the Porter Committee. It is of course possible that the draft in Lipstein's hand incorporated material by Gutteridge, but the available evidence suggests that this is unlikely. For, in addition to his handwritten draft, Lipstein also retained what looks like a preliminary, incomplete draft by Gutteridge (which is also transcribed here), with a note from Gutteridge stating: 'Please criticise this freely. It may require amplification or it may overlap with what you have done already.' None of the material in this draft was included in the final draft, and the terms of Gutteridge's note suggest that primary drafting responsibility was on Lipstein. In other words, Gutteridge only had the most tenuous of claims to co-authorship, let alone sole authorship.

The four Cambridge authors approached their tasks in very different ways.[9] Winfield's brief exposition focussed on the provisions of the *Restatement of*

4 For Lipstein's internment see C. von Bar, 'Kurt Lipstein – The Scholar and the Man' in J. Beatson and R. Zimmermann (eds.) *Jurists Uprooted: German-speaking Émigré Lawyers in Twentieth-Century Britain* (Oxford University Press, 2004) 749, 753–4; for Lipstein's own description see K. Lipstein, 'Cambridge 1933–2002' in the same volume, 761, 765–6.

5 LCO 2/3065, 24 September 1939 (Lord Porter to Miss Barbara Sharp (Secretary to the Committee)).

6 LCO 2/3059 Minutes of Meetings, 10 November 1945.

7 Von Bar, 'Kurt Lipstein – The Scholar and The Man', 749.

8 Squire/SQL/EA/KL/A/1/31.

9 All three memoranda can be found in LCO 2/3060 Law of Libel Committee Memoranda.

the Law of Torts,[10] giving little indication of the controversial choices that the American Law Institute had made.[11] Glanville Williams narrowed his treatment in a different way: he limited himself to statutory modifications to defamation in British dominions. The result was a detailed and thorough survey, but it lacked a unifying analytical structure.

Lipstein and Gutteridge's memorandum was more ambitious than either Winfield's or Williams' submission. It offered a highly sophisticated, detailed exposition of defamation in civil law systems, focussing particularly on France, Germany, Italy and Switzerland, but not excluding Belgium, Brazil, China, Greece, Hungary, Japan, Malta, Mexico, Portugal and Spain. With such broad coverage it would have been easy to descend into making lists of which jurisdiction subscribed to which rule; but the authors instead interwove their extraordinary range of knowledge with an exploration of the legal rationales of the rules they were expounding, as well as indicating how underlying social structures might have shaped the law. To give one striking illustration of the latter, they tentatively attributed the prominence given to insult as an offence in continental law to housing conditions – that is, to the fact that more people lived in flats on the Continent, and were therefore forced into unwelcome contact with their neighbours. The impact of contemporary political changes was also considered – certain unfortunate alterations in the Italian law on truth, for instance, being explained by 'the political and ethical outlook of fascism'. The account of Italian law also made clear that the authors were not merely summarising the law in the books: there are several points where 'private information' was alluded to as the source for a claim about what litigants did in practice. The cumulative effect of the piece was of enormous erudition being combined with imagination and insider's knowledge to create a uniquely expert account.

Unfortunately the Porter Committee's report gives little sense of the richness of the civil law memorandum, nor do any of the Committee's recommendations appear to have been inspired by the civil law material that was brought to its attention. That is, of course, the kind of risk that anyone submitting material to a law reform body has to take. But it was particularly unfortunate that the memorandum did not have a second life: ironically, Glanville Williams' less original contribution became a law journal article,[12] whilst Lipstein and Gutteridge's work essentially disappeared. Gutteridge's standing as the greatest English comparative lawyer of the first half of the twentieth century would, in itself, justify the publication of a newly discovered manuscript dealing with a topic on which he never published. On this occasion, however,

[10] *Restatement of the Law of Torts* (St Paul, American Law Institute, 1934).

[11] G. Farnum, 'Radio Defamation and the American Law Institute' (1936) 16 *Boston University Law Review* 1.

[12] G. Williams, 'Dominion Legislation Relating to Libel and Slander' (1939) 21 *Journal of Comparative Legislation and International Law* third series 161.

even Gutteridge's thoughtful contribution was eclipsed (as he seems to have acknowledged) by Lipstein's wide-ranging, stylish and erudite analysis. This is work of such originality that it would be worth retrieving from obscurity irrespective of its author. The fact that Lipstein would go on to establish himself as one of the leading comparatists of the twentieth century, but would never publish these views on defamation anywhere else, makes the piece all the more valuable.

Editorial note

The next two items are transcriptions of two manuscripts held in the Cambridge University Law Faculty archive. Any editorial additions are shown in square brackets. One systematic presentational change has been made: footnote numbers in the original manuscripts restart at 1 on every page, but here the footnotes have been made to run consecutively. For the Lipstein manuscript a comparison has been made with the final Memorandum submitted to the Porter Committee under the joint names of Gutteridge and Lipstein.

A note attached to the front of the manuscript reads: 'KL, With many thanks for an excessively long loan CJH'. C. J. Hamson was Professor of Comparative Law at Cambridge from 1953 to 1973, having previously been Fellow of Trinity College from 1934. For further detail on his career, see 'Professor C.J. Hamson', (1974) 33 *CLJ* 1.

[DEFAMATION in European Systems of Law][1]

1. The place of defamation in continental law

On the continent, as in England, the law of defamation has a civil and a criminal side, but the criminal law of defamation is of far greater importance than in common law countries.[2] In some countries (e.g. Germany) the criminal offence of defamation also constitutes a tort. In others (e.g. France, Italy), the criminal offence of defamation differs in nature from the tort carrying the same name. Sometimes (e.g. France, Italy) the injured party may choose whether to sue the offender in an action for damages ancillary to the criminal prosecution (*partie civile*) or in an independent civil[[3]] action before a civil court. Accordingly

[Note at bottom of page:]

Cp Report from the Select Committee on the Law of Libel House of Commons, (August 6, 1879) pp 244–246; (1934) 177 L.T. Jou. 148; (1935) 180 L.T. Jo. 82, 83; (1936) 182 *ibid.* 277.

p. 2

the provisions relating to defamation cannot be found together and must be studied in their relation with various branches of the law.[4]

For the present purpose it is unnecessary to discuss procedural and jurisdictional aspects. It will be sufficient to describe the concept of defamation, and to deal with the various types of remedies under a separate head.

[1] The manuscript is untitled; this is the title of the Memorandum submitted to the Porter Committee.

[2] In Switzerland, the question was discussed at one time, whether the protection afforded by criminal law alone was sufficient, but the prevalent opinion appears to have been that it was not. See *Zürcher Kommentar* ad art. 49 O.R., note 2; art. 173–178 of the Swiss Federal Criminal Code of 21 Dec 1937.

[3] 'civil' omitted from final Memorandum.

[4] France: Loi de la Presse, of 29 July 1881 and art. 471(11) [471(2) in final Memorandum] of the *Code Pénal*, art. 1382 Code Civil. Italy: art. 493 ff *Codice Penale of 1930* (?); art. 483 Codice Civile of 1865. Is this the reference to the latest Code? [Lipstein's note.] Germany: art. 185 of the Criminal Code art. 823 Civil Code. Switzerland: art. 173–178, Federal Criminal Code of 1937. Art. 49 OR.

2. Types of defamation

The distinction between libel and slander is unknown in continental systems of law. Perhaps a similar distinction may be found in Roman law, which differentiated between *iniuria re, scriptis*

p. 3

et verbis,[5] but this distinction has been superseded by the following criteria, which are employed separately or in combination:

(1) presence or absence of the injured person (Italy);
(2) public or private defamation (France);
(3) statement of untrue facts or mere insult (France, Germany);
(4) ~~intentional or negligent allegation /malicious statement of untrue facts (Germany)~~
statement of untrue facts made maliciously or merely knowingly (Germany);
(5) attack upon personal honour or upon social reputation (France, Germany)

These criteria furnish the various categories of defamation. Apart from defamation

p. 4

committed by newspapers, the fact that the offending statement has been made in writing is irrelevant. A defamation, whether committed by word of mouth,[6] in writing (picture, letter, poster),[7] over the wireless[8] or by producing a cinematographic picture[9] is subject to the criteria discussed above, which determine whether it is of an aggravated character or not. Thus there is no room for the English concept of damage *per se*. On the other hand, since every defamatory statement, with the exception of those of a very minor and private character, are punishable with a fine or even with imprisonment, it may be suggested, with some diffidence, that in continental law practically all defamations are defamations *per se*,

p. 5

although in a different sense than in English law (of damages see below).

The various types of defamation are determined by the criteria set out above. In Germany the principal distinction is whether the defamatory statement

[5] Florian, *Ingiuria e diffamazione*, Milan (2.ed.1939), p.153.

[6] Barbier, *Code expliqué de la Presse* p.437, no.441; p.225, no.243; p.280, no.277.

[7] Florian, p.115, note 3.

[8] Barbier, Suppl. (1938), p.47 no.255 bis Trib. Corr. Bourges, 19/7/1934. D.P. 1934 1.121;

[9] Trib. Dijon. 5/5/1935. D. Hebd. 1935, p.437; App. Dijon. 8/1/1936; D.P. 1936.1.29; Gaz. Pal. 1936, 1 p.339; Barbier, Suppl. p.48 no. 257 bis; p.111, no.814; Florian, p.115 note 2.

recites facts which are untrue, or whether it is merely insulting. The former (*üble Nachrede* par. 186 of the Criminal Code) is made to third parties; the latter (*Beleidigung*, art. 185 of the Criminal Code) is directed against the defamed person, who must be present. If the untrue statement is made maliciously, with full knowledge that it is unfounded, it falls into a separate category (*Verleumdung*, art. 187). The penalties are lowest for insults, higher for simple defamations, and highest in the case of aggravated defamations.

In France[10] the same distinction is drawn as in Germany. *Diffamation* is

p. 6

une allégation ou imputation d'un fait qui porte atteinte à l'honneur de la personne ou du corps auquel le fait [11] *est impute. Injure* is *une expression outrageante; terme de mépris ou invective qui ne renferme l'imputation d'aucun fait.*[12]

This ~~distinction~~ definition of '*diffamation*' is ~~coupled with the criterion whether~~ further qualified according as the defamation took place in public or in private. *Injures* are of little importance and are treated as mere contraventions of police law.[13] A public statement is one which is made in a place which is open to everybody.[14] In Italy the use of the post does not render a statement public since the employees of the Post Office are pledged to secrecy.[15] In France a special law was passed to cover this case.[16]

p. 7

On the other hand, the Italian Criminal Code of 1930 has suppressed the distinction between statements of fact and insults[17] and has replaced it by the test whether the injured was present (*ingiuria*) or not (*diffamazione*). A statement constitutes a *diffamazione* if it attacks the *rettitudine, probità, lealtà,*[18] *dignità fisica, sociale o intellettuale dell'individuo*; an *ingiuria* is an offence against the *onore e decoro* (Codice pen) of the injured person. In the former case at least two persons must have been present;[19] in the latter case, if other persons are present in addition to the injured party the offence is one of 'aggravated *ingiuria*'. The

10 art. 29, Loi de la Presse.

11 In the final Memorandum both here, and earlier in the same sentence, 'fait' is misspelled as 'fair'.

12 The crime of *calomnie*, *viz* the malicious submission to public authorities of untrue allegations concerning third parties (art. 373 *Code pén.*) seems to lie outside the scope of this survey. See Barbier II p.38 no 594; Florian p.69; Cass. pen. 22/6/1934; Giur it. Rep. 1934, p.190; Cass.pen. 21/5/1935, Foro It. 1935.2.178.

13 Barbier, I, p.437 no. 442; p.225 no.243.

14 Barbier, I, p.230 no.250.

15 Florian, p.111.

16 Barbier, I, p.255 no.264 bis.

17 Cass Pen 13/7/31. Giur It. Rep. 1931, 133 but see App Bologna 13/7/36, Giur. It. Rep. 1937. nos. 263/3.

18 Cass Pen 8/7/32. Giur. It. Rep. 1933, 335.

19 App Catanzaro 13/2/36 13/2/36. Florian p.110 + n.1. Pret. Brienza 7/8/32. Giur. It. 1933. II. 45. Cass Pen. 11/1/32. Foro It. 1932.II. 199. App. Torino. 27/4/32. Giur It. Rep. 137.

crime of '*calunnia*' (art. 368 *Codice Penale*) recognised in Italy is identical with the *calomnie* of French law, which has been described above.[20]

p. 8

It is submitted that this new tendency to abolish the distinction between statements of facts and insults is reasonable in those countries which do not admit the plea of justification. This is so in Italy[21] and also in France,[22] with certain exceptions which will be discussed below. Consequently the *distinction*, still retained in French law, between *diffamations* and *injures* is of little importance in France, while the same distinction may be regarded as reasonable in Germany, where the plea of justification is allowed. The fact that insult as an offence in the nature of defamation has always been given more prominence on the continent than in England may be due to the character of the population or to housing conditions (flats).

p. 9

3. Innuendo

The difficulties which arise in English law under the heading of *innuendo* are hardly ever considered in continental law. To constitute a defamation, a statement must be defamatory on the face of it but no general rules have been established.[23] The question alone was discussed whether the defamed person must be named and was answered in the negative everywhere.[24] An indication is sufficient.[25] Moreover, most cases, which at a first glance may seem to fall under the heading of 'innuendo' are better described as 'indirect defamations',[26] e.g., the statement 'X is a bastard' may constitute a defamation of Y, the mother of X,[27] or the disclosure

p. 10

of certain facts of a defamatory character without naming the person who is affected thereby.[28] A reference to some cases which have been decided by French courts will bring out best the practice on the continent. In connection with the murder by means of an anaesthetic of Judge Prince, who was charged with

20 p.6.n.1. In both countries an action for defamation can be brought concurrently with a prosecution for *calomnie*. See Barbier II p.38 no.594; Florian, p.558.

21 However, in Italy, the allegation of untrue facts of a defamatory character may be treated as an aggravating circumstance. Florian, p.356, note 2.

22 art. 35, *Loi de la Presse*.

23 Barbier, I, p.399, no.404.

24 Barbier, I, p.439, no.444.

25 Barbier, Suppl. p.73, no.404.

26 Florian, p.151.

27 The intention of the offending party is irrelevant. See Cass. Pen. 16/3/34. *Giur. It. Rep.* 1934, no.190.

28 D.P. 1936 1.29; Gaz. Pal. 1936.1.339; Barbier, *Suppl* p.48 no.257 bis; p.111 no. 814.

investigation of the Stavisky scandal, a newsreel was shown in France which reconstructed the stages of Prince's activities from the hour of his arrival in Dijon [up[29]] to the arrest of the alleged culprit in a nursing home belonging to the plaintiff. A close-up picture of the nursing home was given, and the owner of the home, a medical practitioner, brought an action for defamation. The court agreed with the plaintiff's view on the ground that the combination and succession of the photographs inferred that the plaintiff had co-operated in the plot by administering the anaesthetic which led to Prince's death.

p. 11

The Court of Appeal of Riou held that the statement '*élève de l'auberge de Peirébelle*' was defamatory (*injurieux* = insult) on the ground that this Inn, situated in the Haute Loire is famous for the crimes which were committed there.[30] The French practice has been summed up as follows: 'An expression which, by itself, or according to its ordinary meaning is not defamatory, may be defamatory nevertheless in view of the meaning which is attributed to it in some locality, or having regard to allusions which it includes.'[31] Similarly, it is stated with regard to Swiss law: 'The parties must not twist the sense of a statement. The real or alleged intention of the party which has uttered it is not of paramount importance either, but the sense which the addressees (the readers) must have implied of necessity.'[32]

p. 12

The position in Italian law has been summed up as follows: 'The name of the defamed person need not be mentioned in the statement. It is sufficient that the person can be identified by direct or indirect indications of any kind. But a[[33]] statement must show unequivocally the intention of the offending person to defame and must offer means to identify the offended person with all certainty.'[34] 'Where these means are insufficient, they cannot be supplemented by the fact that those who received the defamatory statement believed that they could identify the offended person.'[35]

The problem is not discussed in Germany.[[36]] It appears that it came up once in a case of insult. The court held that it is sufficient if the defamed person recognized the defamatory character of the statement.[37] It must be remembered, however, that the offence of insult involves two persons only and cannot be committed if the plaintiff is not present. Therefore his own appreciation of the

[29] Inserted in final Memorandum.

[30] 18/4/1888. J. des Pacquets 1888.2.241. [31] Barbier.

[32] Zurcher Komm II, art 28.3.9.13. no.38.

[33] Final Memorandum substitutes 'the' for 'a'.

[34] See Cass pen. 11/11/36. [Date incorrect: should be 11/12/36.] Foro It. 1937, II.152.

[35] App. Catanzano 21/3/35 Giur. It. Rep. 1935, no.216.

[36] In the final Memorandum this sentence runs on into the next, joined by the word 'but'.

[37] Lobe, Strafgesetzbuch, art. 185, p.615.

statement is important, but this argument does not necessarily apply to other kinds of defamation.

The reason for the absence of major discussion of the difficulties which the problem involves is probably to be found in the fact that on the continent the decision of defamation cases is entrusted to the professional judge, to the exclusion of the jury.

p. 13

4. Malice

In Germany, the plaintiff must prove that the defamatory statement was made wilfully, but in practice he must only prove that the defendant realised? the defamatory character of his statement. In France '*intention de nuire*' is required coupled with 'intention de publier' but this intention is presumed when the facts disclose a clear case of defamation.[38] The same principle applies in Italy, although not without opposition.[39] However, this presumption may be rebutted by proof of good faith or by showing that the intention was to correct, answer, defend,[40] [to[41]] safeguard private interests,[42] or to make a joke,[43] even in the form of sarcastic or artistic criticism; but this form may imply an attack against the plaintiff as a private person.[44]

Although a plea of justification may not be admissible, the fact that the defamatory statement is true may show the good faith of the defendant[45] and mitigate or exclude damages or a penalty. Thus the plea of justification is introduced surreptitiously, a result which has been much deprecated in Italy.[46]

p. 14

The presumption of malice has been attacked on the ground

[38] Barbier I,[gap left in footnote]; Trib. Perugia *Giur. It. Rep.* 1935, no.216.

[39] Loschiara, note *Foro It* 1937 II, 338; Cass. pen. 30/5/34. Giur. It. Rep. 1934 no. 190. App. Bari 22/5/36. Giur. It. Rep. 1936 nos 242/3. Florian, p.216 ff, App Catania 3/4/32 [Date incorrect, should be 3/11/32]; Giur It Rep 1933 no. 154; App. Bari, 27/10/36, Giur. It. Rep. 1937, nos. 202/203; Sechi, note to Foro. It. 1931, II, 215.

[40] Torino, 3/1/36; Giur. It. Rep. 1936, no.242/3.

[41] Added in final Memorandum.

[42] App Catanzano. 10/2/37 Giur. It. Rep. 1937, no.262/3.

[43] Giur. It. Rep. 1935 no.116.

[44] Vicenza 31/3/36 Giur. It. Rep. 1936 [p.242].

[45] Barbier I p.408, no.407; p.503, no. 532; II p.4 no.556. Florian, p.208.

[46] Loreto Serigno, note *Foro It.* 1936, II. 179, Sechi, note *Foro It* 1931, II, 215; App. [should be Trib.] Torino 29/4/36, Giur. It. Rep. 1936, p.242/3; Cass. pen. 28/5/32. Giur. It. Rep. 1933, no. 154.

(1) that the difficulty of proving malice should be treated as proof of innocence;
(2) that if defamation is primarily an offence for its malicious character, this character should not be presumed.[47]

The solution of this dispute appears to be connected with a question of principle. If the law of defamation is designed to safeguard the formal honour of the individual, independent[ly[48]] of merit, the question of malice is of little importance. If the law wishes to protect deserving individuals only, proof of malice together with the plea of justification must be allotted its proper place.[49]

5. Negligent defamations

The question whether the law should take cognisance of negligent defamation

p. 15

has been discussed as a theoretical one[[50]] by an Italian writer;[51] he answers it in the negative on the ground that malice, in his view, is the most important feature of a defamation. On the other hand, negligent defamations have been recognised in France[52] and by art. 21 [of] the German Press Law 1874, so far as editors printers and newspaper vendors are concerned. Moreover, a certain type of negligent defamation constitutes a special tort in German law (art. 824 BGB). If an untrue statement has been made which is capable of endangering the plaintiff's business credit, the defendant is liable, even if the statement was made negligently regardless of whether it represents the defendant's own opinion or is based upon hearsay.[53]

p. 16

In most countries a statement which is [not[54]] of a defamatory character does not render the person who published it liable for the sole reason that it was published with malice (malice in this connection means rather more than the corresponding term in the English law of defamation). German law alone allows a remedy in this case (art. 826 BGB) in accordance with the principle[[55]] that whosoever causes damage maliciously in contravention of *boni mores* (*Gute Sitten*) is liable to pay compensation. However, a *caveat* should be entered here, for the principle is not applied frequently and creates much difficulty in

[47] Florian, p.210. [48] Added in final Memorandum.
[49] Florian, p.33. [50] Final Memorandum substitutes 'problem' for 'one'.
[51] Florian, p.203.
[52] These persons may be sued in all circumstances, but the printer can be sued if the editor cannot be found, and so on.
[53] Staudinger, *Kommentar*, art. 824, p.1807, (2c).
[54] Inserted in final Memorandum.
[55] In the final Memorandum 'principle' is erroneously altered to 'principal'.

practice for the reason that it is too general. It is in fact a unique example of a special tort of malice. But unlike the tort of negligence in English law it lies where the defendant is not bound by any legal duty towards the plaintiff.[56]

In France, Germany and Italy [alike[57]]

p. 17

malice is excluded, *prima facie*, if the defamation was the result of provocation provided it is commensurate and not excessive.[58] In Italy even a putative provocation is a sufficient defence.[59]

6. Objects of defamation

Turning to the question who can be the object of a defamation, it is unnecessary to deal with the position of heads of States, Ministers, ambassadors, public functionaries, persons vested with public authority, courts, the armed forces or of public corporations (*corps constitués*).[60] In some countries these persons and bodies are accorded increased protection against defamation[s[61]], but questions of public policy are so strongly involved as to make the value of a comparative survey doubtful. On the other hand, the position of corporations, partnerships, classes, and of the family (including husband and

p. 18

wife)[62] deserves attention.

In most countries corporations are regarded as capable of being the object of a defamation, seeing that they are distinct legal entities.[63] In German law the opposite view is held, on the ground that they are not susceptible of resenting a defamation,[64] but corporations are allowed to sue in respect of wilful or negligent defamatory statements which endanger their credit (see above, p.15).

After some discussion, the question of whether partnerships can be defamed has been decided in the affirmative [in France[65]], since partnerships are now

[56] The crime of *calomnie*, known in France and Italy, has been discussed above. It covers the field of malicious prosecution only and need not be treated here.
[57] Inserted in final Memorandum.
[58] Art. 33(2) Loi de la Presse of 29/7/81; Barbier I, p.510, no.572; App, Torino 27/4/32, *Giur. It.Rep.* 1932 no.137.
[59] Cass. Pen. 8/7/32. *Giur. It. Rep.* 1933 no.335. Cass. Pen. 26/11/34 *Giur. It. Rep.* 1935 no. 216.
[60] Barbier I, no.465; Florian p.139.
[61] Inserted in final draft.
[62] Enneccerus, II, sect. 228, I (e), p.726; Lobe art. 185, pp.612–13.
[63] Florian, p.131; Levi, *La Parte Civile* p.258. (1940) 40 Col. L.R. 1271.
[64] Barbier, I, p.504 no.534; Florian p.133; Levi, *La Parte Civile* pp.237, 241; *Zürcher Komm. IV*, 1, art. 47 OR. No.17; Riesman (1942) 42 Col. L.R. 757, n.138.
[65] Inserted in final Memorandum.

treated in French law as legal entities.[66] In Italy, where partnerships are not regarded as legal entities, the answer is in the negative in respect of both commercial and ordinary partnerships.[67] The reason ap

p. 19

pears to be that defamation is regarded as an offence against the person. Thus a partner must show that he has been defamed personally.

Great difficulties are encountered in connection with the question whether classes and groups can be the object of defamation.[68] On this question, France provides the richest source of case law.[69] The following summary may be regarded as authoritative[70], '*Où la diffamation*, par le vague intentionnel de la designation, atteint une pluralité de personnes, *chacune* d'elle *se trouvant au moins indirectement designé* et *souffrant un préjudice personnel*, a droit et qualité pour se plaindre et demander réparation. Toutefois, il convient de ne rien exagérer et quand l'imputation visant un groupe *considérable* de personnes *ne cause* en réalité à aucun *un préjudice* personnel, le délit de diffamation ne peut être

p. 20

relevé par aucune des personnes appartenant à ce groupe'. *E.g.* no complaint lies if a whole profession (the clergy, lawyers) is attacked or an entire group such as the Jews.[71] The answer is different if the defamatory statement refers e.g. to the clergy of a particular district, the solicitors in Birmingham. The rule applies in Italy,[72] in Switzerland[73] and in Germany.[74] South Africa, on the other hand, enacted a Group Libel Law in 1934.[75]

The question has been much debated whether deceased persons can be defamed.[76] It is argued[[77]] that the personal representative may sue, if the defamation took place during the life-time of the deceased person, irrespectively of whether the deceased had initiated the proceedings or not.[78] In Italy the per-

[66] Barbier, I, p.505 no. 535; Suppl. p.86.

[67] Florian, p.134. (1940) 40 Col. L.R. 1271. (1942) 42 ibid. 756.

[68] The French *Loi de la Presse*, following established practice, does not provide any remedy. See Kader in *Rabel's Z.* 4(1935) pp.565–585.

[69] Barbier, I, p.446, no.460; Mazeaud, *Responsabilité civile*, II, p.828, no.1896; no. 1898 (4) (5) (6); S. 1936.1.209; S.19361.27; S.1936.1.138; Gaz. Pal. 1937.2.137. Riesman, *Columbia Law Rev.* 42 (1942), pp.727–80.

[70] Barbier, I, p.408, no.408; p.507, no.539; Suppl. p.74.

[71] S. 1935.4.15. [72] Florian, p.131.

[73] Lobe, art. 185, pp.612/3.

[74] Zürcher Komm I, art. 28 no.38. BGE. 50.1.217 (at p.221).

[75] Ordinance no. 13 of 1934, s.4.

[76] (1940) 40 Col. L.R. 1267, 1268, n. with literature.

[77] The final Memorandum alters this to 'agreed'.

[78] Barbier, I, p.528 no.552; Florian, p.147.

sonal representative may sue even if the defamation took place after the death of the

p. 21

defamed person.[79] In France, according to the amended version of art.34 of the *Loi de la Presse*[80] a criminal prosecution may be initiated by the personal representatives, but only if it can be shown that the author of the offending statement intended to defame the heirs or the spouse.[81] In addition, an action for damages (see below) lies in France and Germany whenever it can be shown that the defendant, wilfully or negligently, has caused damage to the heirs.[82] In Germany and in Switzerland, a criminal prosecution is only admissible if an untrue fact has been alleged maliciously (*Verleumdung*). This excludes insults and defamations published wilfully, but without malice.[83] Moreover, the right of reply (see below) is generally allowed.

p. 22

[7.] Justification

In the matter of pleas of justification the Franco-Italian and the Germanic legal systems show a striking difference of attitude.[84] Either the plea of justification is admitted without restriction,[85] or it is excluded altogether,[86] or it is allowed or prohibited subject to certain exceptions.[87] The Franco-Italian system safeguards the external, formal honour and dignity of the individual, regardless of personal merit (*la vie privée doit être mûrée*); the Germanic system safeguards honour and dignity only [if[88]] founded on intrinsic merits. Consequently, the plea of justification is entirely prohibited in Italy.[89] It is excluded, in principle, in France,[90] except when the defamatory statement concerns the exercise of

[79] Florian, p.148. [80] Law of 29 Sept. 1919.

[81] Barbier, Suppl. p.88 no.546.

[82] Art. 1382 Code Civil; art. 823(1) BGB; Barbier, I, p.527 no.551; Suppl p.90 no.546.

[83] Art 189 German Crim. Code; Zürcher Komm, art. 28 no.49.

[84] Florian pp 413–416. [Section in Florian runs to 418.] Riesman, (1942) 42 Col.L.R. 1282 at p.1290. Henning, *Die Zulässigkeit des Wahrheitsbeweises bei der Ehrenkränkung in historischer und rechtsvergleichender Darstellung*, Breslau, 1939, was not available.

[85] Spain, art. 447; Portugal, art. 409; Brazil, art. 315; Argentina, art. 109; Mexico, art. 356. See also Belgium, art. 447; Denmark, art. 268; Austria.

[86] Italy: art. 596 Codice pen; Waadt [French-speaking canton of Switzerland] (1931) art. 156; Japan, art. 230; Malta, art. 240; Florian, p.413.

[87] Grounds on which the plea of justification is disallowed: interference with private life; public interest; Hungary art. 263(5); Greece, art. 20(2); China art. 360(2).

[88] Inserted in final Memorandum.

[89] Florian, p.421; art. 596 C. pen. It.

[90] Art. 35 Loi de la Presse of 29/7/81; Barbier I, p.406, no. 407; II, p.2. no. 353; p.23 no. 570.

public functions by Ministers, members of Parliament, civil servants, persons vested with public authority,[91] corporations, the armed forces and public administration.[92]

p. 23

In addition the plea of justification is admitted, if the defamation affects directors or managers of industrial enterprises which invite the public to give deposits or credits.[93] The reason underlying these provisions is clear. The law does not wish to encourage the public discussion of private feuds. On the other hand, it is interested in the maintenance of a civilized conduct of human relations. Thus a former convict with a number of previous convictions must never be called a gaolbird. But the public is interested in the efficient and proper administration of *public* affairs. Shortcomings in this sphere can often be revealed or remedied only by an appeal to the public which contains a recital of the incriminating facts. A general rule which excludes the plea of justification in these cases, would discourage revelations and would result in the survival of those defects which the statement set out to remedy.

p. 24

Italian law, which excludes the plea of justification altogether, seems to have been influenced by the political and ethical outlook of fascism and by an overestimation of the objections against the plea of justification to the effect (1) that the plea interferes with the private life of the individual, (2) that it is of no interest, unless perpetration of a crime has been alleged; and (3) that it is not in accordance with public policy.

German law, on the other hand, always allows the plea of justification, apparently on the ground that the law should not protect complaints which are without any intrinsic merit.

8. Remedies

Turning to the remedies which are available in cases of defamation, it must be noted that a great range of alternative measures can be found in the legal systems under review. The principal remedies are

p. 25

(1) Penalties imposed by criminal courts
(2) Damages awarded by criminal courts in the course of a criminal prosecution
(3) Damages awarded by civil courts in the course of an action in tort.

[91] *Ibid* art. 31. [92] *Ibid* art. 35(1).
[93] art. 31(2)(1) *Loi de la Presse*.

(4) The right of reply and the right to publish the judgement in a defamation case.
(5) An action in the nature of an injunction enjoining the defendant to refrain from publishing certain defamatory statements in the future.

It is unnecessary to consider the measures, such as fines and imprisonment, which fall under the first category. On the other hand, it may be useful to consider whether the substitution of fines for damages in libel actions would put an end to gold-digging actions in England.

(A) Damages

Since the actions for damages in categories (2) and (3) differ principally in their procedural aspects they can be discussed together.[94] German law provides a simple solution. Defamation is a criminal offence. A criminal offence is always a tort (art. 823(2) BGB) but an action

p. 26
in tort can be brought only upon proof of special damages. This rule [has[95]] caused expressions of regret on the part of German writers on the ground that the actual damage caused by a defamation cannot be ascertained in strict terms of money and that damages in defamation cases should be accorded the character of a fine designed to give the plaintiff satisfaction, not to reimburse him.[96] In this connection German writers refer to French and English law, but it should be noted that in the United States the tendency has grown in recent years not to allow more than actual damages in libel cases.[97]

Swiss law, following the German example, allows liquidated damages. In addition 'satisfaction' (comparable to a fine, or to exemplary damages) may be granted in very serious cases. But while in Germany a fine (*Busse*) is imposed

p. 27
in the course of criminal proceedings,[98] a satisfaction (*Genungtuung*), in Swiss law is awarded in the course of an action for damages.[99]

94 See Rothenberg, Journal of Comparative Legislation (1942) 3rd ser vol. 24, pp.6–14. [Igance Rothenberg, 'Damages for Libel in the United States and on the European Continent' (1942) 24 J Comp Legisl third series 6.]

95 Inserted in final Memorandum.

96 Staudinger, vol. II, p.114, *Vorbemerkung* ad. Art. 253 II.1; p.1812 ad art. 823(7a); *Kommentar der RgR* p.654, ad art. 847(2).

97 Rothenberg in *Journalism Quarterly*, 1943 [final Memorandum adds 'and J.C.L. (1942) Vol. 24 p.6'] and the literature quoted in (1942) 42 Col. L.R. 769, n.189.

98 Lobe, ad art. 188. The so-called fine is rather in the nature of special damages.

99 *Zürcher Komm* V, 1, art. 49 OR, no. 3 nos 7–17 (examples).

In France (art. 1382 C.C.) and in Italy (art. 1151 C.C.it) a defamation, which is a criminal offence in these countries, may give rise to an action in tort. But unlike in German law, the action in tort is not based upon the fact that a defamation has taken place. It is only necessary that unlawful damage has been caused wilfully or negligently.[100] However, it appears that this remedy is not popular in France[101] and hardly ever employed in Italy (according to private information). This may be due perhaps, to the fact that the plaintiff must prove [that the defendant acted wilfully or negligently and[102]] that no presumption (see above) operates in favour of the plaintiff.

p. 28

In Italy and Germany only actual damage done to property can be claimed[103] while in France damages of every kind (including dommage moral) may be taken into account.[104] The French rule is based on a series of cases starting in 1837,[105] which stated at first negatively that damages according to art. 1382 C.C. are not restricted to material damage. Leading modern textbooks state:

> 'des dommages-intérêts répareront d'une manière approximative et sans doute imparfaite, l'atteinte portée à l'affection et aux sentiments intimes du demandeur.'[106]

'Les juges arbitrent souverainement l'indemnité accordée et cette indemnité prend le caractère d'une sorte de peine civile. Parfois – la victime se contente, d'une condemnation de principe et réclame seulement 1 franc de dommages-intérêts ou la publication

p. 29

du jugement.['][107] Thus, special damages must be pleaded, but the discretion of the courts is very wide. Damages need not be in money; instead, or in addition, the court may order the publication of the judgment, the suppression of the published matter and may impose other measures.[108] Similar measures may be taken in Germany and Switzerland,[109] but in the latter country only in connection with a grant of 'satisfaction', i.e. in serious cases.

[100] Planiol et Ripert, *Traité élém.* II, nos. 818 ff, at p.287; Garraud, *Droit Criminel*, p.610; Savatier, *Responsabilité civile*, II, p.268, no.674.

[101] Barbier, II, pp.318–324, nos.876–885.

[102] Inserted in final Memorandum. [103] Levi, p.360, no.5.

[104] Mazeaud, II, no.314; Savatier, II, p.144 no. 565. It is doubtful whether a personal representative may claim 'dommage moral'. See Levi p. 366, n.5.

[105] Cass. crim. 22/9/1837, S.1838.1.331 and many other cases quoted in Colin and Capitant, II, p.175, no.187. For Belgian law see Cass. 17/3/1881, S.1882.4.9.

[106] Colin et Capitant, *Traité élém.*, II, p.309, no.868 (bis). Cp. Savatier, II, p.107, no.532.

[107] Planiol et Ripert, *Traité élém.* II, p.176. no.187.

[108] Barbier, II, p.323 no.883. Mazeaud III p.365 no.2319.

[109] *Zürcher Komm* V.1, art. 49, nos. 4–17.

As a rule, the injured party prefers to prosecute in the criminal courts to combine the prosecution with a claim for damages (reparation) and to appear in court as a 'partie civile' (parte civile). The plaintiff appears as an ancillary party in the criminal

p. 30

proceedings, in the course of which his claim is decided and enforced.

It is unnecessary to deal in this place with technical problems arising out of the existence of several concurrent remedies, such as: the relation between a claim for damages in criminal proceedings and an action based on tort;[110] the plea *electa una via*,[111] the effect of *lis pendens*, of different periods of prescription in the civil and criminal courts and of *res judicata*.[112] It must be pointed out, however, that damages claimed in criminal proceedings include special damages only, to the exclusion of *dommage moral*, for,

p. 31

although they are imposed by a criminal court they are not to be regarded as a penalty, but as a real reparation.[113] In spite of these limitations, parties prefer to lodge their claims in the course of criminal proceedings, partly on account of the speedier procedure which criminal courts apply in respect of private law claims, partly because the State itself enforces the decision and partly because the effect of prescription in private law can be evaded thereby.[114]

(B) *Astreinte*

Another remedy, which is available in the civil courts alone, deserves attention, *i.e.*, the '*astreinte*' which is known in French law (art. 1036 C.proc.civ.), and the *Unterlassungsklage* (an action in the nature of an injunction) which features in German and Swiss law. The relevant rules of German law are

p. 32

simple. If an illegal act has been committed (e.g. a defamation), even if it is not actionable or punishable because it was not committed wilfully or negligently,

[110] Barbier, II, p.301 no.856.

[111] France: action in the civil courts precludes criminal proceedings; criminal proceedings may be abandoned in favour of an action in the civil courts. See Savatier, II, p.268, no.674.

[112] France: criminal prosecution, if unsuccessful precludes a claim as *partie civile*, but not an action in tort. See Barbier, II, p.301, no.856; nos. 869–874; Suppl. p.125.
Germany: criminal prosecution, if unsuccessful does not exclude a civil action and *vice versa*. See Lobe ad art. 188, St. g B p.626 (8).

[113] See above, and Lobe, ad art. 188 StgB, p.6. [Strafgesetzbuch]

[114] Planiol et Ripert, *Traité élém*, II, p. 287 nos. 818 ff; Garraud, *Droit Criminel*, p.610; Lobe, ad art. 188 StgB, p.626 (8).

and if it is likely that the act will be repeated in the future, the person concerned may apply to the court for an order enjoining the defendant to refrain from publishing or uttering the same statement in the future. The court fixes a certain sum as a penalty, which is forfeited in case the order is disobeyed.[115]

Similar provisions apply in Switzerland, but they do not operate where [a[116]] defamation is concerned, for, according to Swiss law a defamation is solely a matter of the past,[117] while the *Unterlassungsklage* in Swiss law is designed to safeguard against future disturbances of privacy.[118] In the French-speaking cantons the *astreinte*, in the nature of an injunction, takes the place of the *Unterlassungsklage*.[119]

p. 33

Little evidence can be obtained from French case law whether the *astreinte* is used in connection with actions for defamation.[120] It would appear that it is not frequently employed for this purpose. According to private information the remedy which in Italian law corresponds to the French *astreinte* is not resorted to in defamation cases.

The question of privilege will not be discussed here, seeing that this branch of the law of defamation is strongly connected with widely differing national institutions and with considerations of public policy.[121] It may be mentioned, however, that in French and German law privileged statements may be actionable as verbal insults.

A special remedy for defamations by the Press is known on the continent. It was recognized at a very early

p. 34

stage, that the unqualified recognition and protection of a right of privacy would prevent all discussions, whether defamatory or not, of private affairs in the Press. When the first French Press Law was debated in the Chamber in 1822, the insertion of a clause protecting the right of privacy was considered and rejected.[122] A similar tendency can be observed in other countries.[123] On

115 For further details see Enneccerus, II, pp. 769, 773 sect.242; Staudinger II, *Vorbemerkung* VII E.2, p.1759; RJR. Kommentar, II, p.547. See also RJ.48, 114; 116, 153; 115, 78; 140, 393.

116 Inserted in final Memorandum.

117 *Zürcher Komm. I* nos. 76–78.

118 *Ibid.*, no.81.

119 *Ibid.*, no.81; Rossel et Mentha, *Code Civil*, I, p.100.

120 Savatier, II, p.185, no.598; Mazeaud, II, pp.519–527 (2nd?? ed) pp 660ff, nos. 2497–2507; Barbier contains no reference to the *astreinte*.

121 See Riesman, (1942) 42 Col. L.R. 1282, at p.1286 for a detailed discussion.

122 Perraud-Charmantier, *Le droit de réponse* (1930) p.56.

123 See, e.g., art. 12 of the German Copyright Act, which grants a limited right of privacy only in respect of pictures, inasmuch persons of public interest cannot claim any protection.

the other hand, the conviction spread in France that private persons should be given the opportunity to defend themselves by the same means as those which the Press was able to employ. Thus the right of reply (*droit de réponse*) found many supporters and was given statutory sanction by art 13 of the *Loi de la Presse* of 29/7/1881, amended by a law of 29/9/19.[124]

p. 35

This article, which has been copied by many continental and South-American countries forces the editor of a newspaper[125]

(1) to insert within a short time limit,
(2) at the request of the person who has been named or alluded to in the newspaper
(3) at the same place where the original statement appeared and in the same type,
(4) a reply of the same length as the original statement, with an upper limit of 200 and a lower limit of 50 lines (these limits vary in different countries; the French law of the Press of 1881, in its original wording imposed no limits, but required the plaintiff to pay, according to the usual rates for the excess, if the reply went beyond the length of the original statement).
(5) gratuitously,

Provided the plaintiff has an interest *e.g.* he has been named, and provided the reply is not contrary to law and decency, does not infringe the interests of third parties and does not offend the honour of the journalist who wrote the original statement.

p. 36

The heirs and personal representatives of a deceased person, who has been named in the Press, may exercise the right of reply, even if they are precluded from bringing an action for defamation[126] (see above, p.21).

It must be stressed, in conclusion, that the right of reply is not available if the publication takes place by means other than the Press.[127] Experience has shown that the very extensive right of reply, as known in France, is not so much a means of defence available to private individuals than a menace to the Press. French courts insist that '*le droit de réponse est général et absolu*'. Consequently, every statement which mentions a private person, even if it occurs in

[124] For the following see Riesman (1942) 42 Col.L.R. 1314, Rothenberg, *The Right of Reply in Libel Cases, Journal of the Society of Comparative Legislation* (1941), 3rd ser. vol. 23, pp.38–59. ['The Right of Reply to Libels in the Press']

[125] Barbier, I, p.131, nos. 130ff; Suppl. p.30.

[126] Barbier, *Suppl.* p.32, no. 145, p.89, nos. 549, 550.

[127] Barbier, *Suppl.*, p.29, no.118 bis.

connection with artistic or literary criticism and regardless of whether it is derogatory, non-committal or complimentary

p. 37

gives the person who has been mentioned in the article an opportunity to send to the newspaper his own version with the request to insert it in the manner indicated above. It is impossible to discuss here the immense bulk of case law which has grown out of the constant attempts of newspapers to persuade courts to interpret the rule less rigidly. All attempts came to nothing. The right of reply is still '*général et absolu*'.

In support of the attempt to restrict the operation of the rule reference was made to the doctrine of abuse of rights.[128] It has also been suggested that the right of reply should be restricted to cases where the plaintiff has been attacked, where he has a real interest[129] or where an untrue statement requires rectification. In short, a considerable

p. 38

body of opinion wishes to restrict the right of reply to *diffamations* and *injures* (the two types of defamation recognised in French law), unfair criticisms and material errors.[130] The French rule, outlined above, was adopted with some modifications by most countries in southern and western Europe as well as in the Latin-American republics, but according to private information the right of reply is rarely exercised in Italy.[131]

In Central Europe (Germany, Hungary[[132]], Czechoslovakia, Poland), on the other hand, the right of reply has been adopted in a more restricted form. Its features are similar to those appearing in the French proposals for a reform of the right of reply. According to art.11 of the German Press Law of 7 May 1874, a right of reply is admitted for the purposes of rectifying wrong statements of facts not necessarily of a defamatory nature, but the rectification must not contain any illegal contents. The reply is not limited in extent, for the reason, probably, that the limitation to the correction of untrue facts was regarded as a sufficient safeguard. If the reply exceeds the original statement in length, the writer must pay the excess according to the usual rate for advertisements.

In this form, the right of reply has fulfilled a very useful function. It has proved to be a very popular substitute for lengthy and costly actions and a

[128] Perraud-Charmantier, pp.371–381.

[129] Belgian law contains a provision to this effect. See Perraud-Charmantier, p.307.

[130] Perraud-Charmantier, p.472.

[131] It is unnecessary to deal here with the specially privileged right of rectification which French law and the systems which follow the French rule grant to public bodies. See art. 12 of the *Loi de la Presse* of 29 July 1881; Barbier, I, p.426, no.121.

[132] In the final Memorandum, 'Austria' replaces 'Hungary'.

speedy means for exposing errors and for establishing the truth. In certain American states the opportunity to make a retraction is given for the same purpose.[133]

133 Riesman, (1942) 42 Col. L.R. 1315; Rothenberg (1942) 24 *Journal of Comparative Legislation* 6.

Note

Please criticise this fully. It may require amplification or it may overlap what you have done. Harold Gutteridge

General observations

If any comparison is to be made between the law of Libel and Slander in England and the law of Defamation in the Civil Law countries due regard must be had to certain fundamental differences in the basic conceptions underlying any rules which may be the subject matter of comparison. The more important of these differences can be summarised, in brief, as follows.

(A) In the Civil Law countries defamation is primarily a crime consisting in an attack on the honour of a person. As a rule it is also a civil wrong entitling the person who has been defamed to claim compensation either as a '*partie civile*' in the criminal proceedings or as plaintiff in an action brought in the ordinary way in the civil courts. This line of approach to the question may have important consequences because if the proceedings are criminal in character there is a presumption in favour of the accused & strict proof will be demanded.

(B) In the Civil Law countries no distinction is made between the written and the spoken word.

(C) In some of these countries, e.g. France, defamatory statements in newspapers fall within the scope of special laws for the regulation of the Press.

(D) Generally speaking, the protection which the law of these countries affords to an individual who is wronged by statements tending to bring him into ridicule and contempt is somewhat wider than that given by the common law of England. It may be possible

p. 2

for a person injured in such circumstances to obtain a remedy quite apart from the law relating to defamation so that such difficulties as arose in England, for instance, in *Tolley's Case* would not be encountered. Thus under the German law of Copyright (Kunst Urheber Gesetz, Articles 22–24) a person's portrait may not, with certain exceptions, be published without his consent.[1] Under Article 12 of the German Civil Code a person

[1] These exceptions are incidents of historical interest, photographic landscapes accidentally including a portrait, photographic groups of clubs, etc. Even in such cases publication of the portrait can be restrained if it injures the lawful interests of the person portrayed.

is also entitled to object to the use of his name in a way which might reflect on his honourable reputation.[2] Further, under Article 826 of the German Civil Code a statement concerning an individual may be actionable by the individual if it offends against 'public conscience' (*Sittlichkeit* or *boni mores*).[3] In French law an unfair criticism of a literary or artistic work may be actionable as an abuse of the right of criticism (*abus de droit*). Moreover, the rules which protect an individual against any attack on his reputation are not only more extensive in the Civil Law countries but also more elastic since the truth or falsity of a statement is only material in so far as it affects the question of remedies.

p. 3

(E) The most striking difference between the English law and the law of these other countries is, perhaps, to be found in their attitude towards the question of the remedy to be afforded to the injured person. In certain systems of law there are remedies which have no counterpart in English law e.g. the *droit de réponse* given by the French *Loi sur la Presse* and the various remedies available under Swiss law. The injured party is generally speaking always entitled to an order of the Court restraining repetition of a defamatory statement & to damages for any concrete i.e. pecuniary loss which he may have sustained. But he can only claim exemplary or moral damages in exceptional circumstances. Exemplary damages cannot, in fact, be awarded

p. 4

by the German Courts in any circumstances and in other countries they are so rarely awarded & are even then so low in amount that they offer little temptation to the speculative litigant. The legal adviser in a civil law country thinks rather in terms of punishment or an injunction than in terms of monetary compensation so that there is no 'pull' in the direction of costly civil proceedings as may be the case in England. The provisions of Swiss law referred to hereafter are of interest in this connexion.

(F) In the Civil Law countries a distinction is drawn between statements made innocently and those which are made wilfully or negligently. Damages are not awarded if the statement is made innocently and in good faith.

[2] Count Zeppelin was thus able to stop the use of his name to denote a particular brand of cigars.

[3] In the *Donner Case* this was one of the grounds relied on by the German courts in restraining the exhibition of a film which depicted a domestic tragedy in the family life of the complainants.

p. 5

Note

I believe this to be correct as regards the Civil Law of Switzerland. What does the Swiss Penal Code say about criminal proceedings? Is there a partie civile in such proceedings? Perhaps Brunschweig (?) could help us are regards this.

HCG

The Law of Switzerland[4]

In Swiss Law defamatory statements concerning an individual are treated as an attack on his personality and are actionable as such under Article 28 of the Civil Code and Article 49 of the Code of Obligations. The underlying principle is difficult to explain without a lengthy exposition of the theory of personality in Swiss law but, briefly, the individual is entitled to protection in respect of his honour, family life, matrimonial relationships, physical and moral safety & well being, privacy, name, portrait and economic independence.

The most interesting feature of Swiss law in relation to defamatory statements is to be found in the rules which deal with civil remedies. The Codes as originally drafted provided for an award of damages in all cases of defamation but objection was taken to this by the Swiss newspaper proprietors who feared that a full recognition of the right to damages would expose them to speculative actions. The result was the enactment in Article 49 of the Code of Obligations of rules intended to limit the right to claim damages to cases of a serious character.[5] The successful plaintiff is always[6]

p. 6

entitled to an order of the Court restraining any repetition of the defamatory statement, but he can only claim damages in certain circumstances which are as follows.

(a) If the statement was made wilfully with knowledge of its falsity or was made negligently without proper investigation into his [its?] truth the plaintiff can also claim any pecuniary damage which he has suffered.
(b) Exemplary damages (*Réparation morale* or *Genugtuung*) can only be awarded where the statement was made wilfully or negligently & the consequences to the plaintiff are of exceptional gravity.
(c) Further the Swiss Judge is given a free hand to deal with the matter in the way he thinks is best calculated to meet the justice of the case. He may for

[4] Oser, *Das Schweizerischer Obligationenrecht* p. 282. The Law of Lichtenstein [*sic*] is to the same effect: The Code of Lichtenstein [*sic*] (Art. 39). Wyler, *Journal of the Society of Comparative Legislation*, 3rd Series, Vol. VIII p206 ['The New Civil Law of the Principality of Liechtenstein']. The Swiss Codes have with certain modifications also been adopted by Turkey.

[5] See *Law Quarterly Review* (1931) vol 47 p 203.

[6] *Ibid* p.212.

instance order the defendant to pay a sum of money to a charity, insert an apology in the press or make some other form of public atonement. He may also make a declaration affirming the honourable character of the plaintiff. The Swiss Judges appear in practice to have used the powers given to them by Article 49 of the Code of Obligations only in such cases as involve an injury of a serious character to the reputation of the plaintiff.[7]

[7] Oser, *Das Schweizerische Obligationenrecht*, p 348.

INDEX

www.ingramcontent.com/pod-product-compliance
Lightning Source LLC
LaVergne TN
LVHW011529200926
848484LV00001B/204
* 9 7 8 0 5 2 1 7 6 8 6 1 0 *